Key Thinkers on Cities

Edited by Regan Koch and Alan Latham

Key Thinkers on Cities

Los Angeles | London | New Delhi
Singapore | Washington DC | Melbourne

Los Angeles | London | New Delhi
Singapore | Washington DC | Melbourne

SAGE Publications Ltd
1 Oliver's Yard
55 City Road
London EC1Y 1SP

SAGE Publications Inc.
2455 Teller Road
Thousand Oaks, California 91320

SAGE Publications India Pvt Ltd
B 1/I 1 Mohan Cooperative Industrial Area
Mathura Road
New Delhi 110 044

SAGE Publications Asia-Pacific Pte Ltd
3 Church Street
#10-04 Samsung Hub
Singapore 049483

Editor: Robert Rojek
Editorial assistant: Matthew Oldfield
Production editor: Katherine Haw
Copyeditor: Jane Fricker
Proofreader: Rebecca Storr
Indexer: Martin Hargreaves
Marketing manager: Susheel Gokarakonda
Cover design: Wendy Scott
Typeset by: C&M Digitals (P) Ltd, Chennai, India
Printed by CPI Group (UK) Ltd, Croydon, CR0 4YY

First published 2017

Library of Congress Control Number: 2016945021

British Library Cataloguing in Publication data

A catalogue record for this book is available from the British Library

ISBN 978-1-4739-0774-4
ISBN 978-1-4739-0775-1 (pbk)

At SAGE we take sustainability seriously. Most of our products are printed in the UK using FSC papers and boards. When we print overseas we ensure sustainable papers are used as measured by the PREPS grading system. We undertake an annual audit to monitor our sustainability.

Contents

About the Editors

Regan Koch is a Lecturer in Human Geography at Queen Mary University of London. His interests are in matters of public space, urban sociality and collective culture, and the representation and imagination of urban life. Working between London and various cities across the US, Regan's research has focused on exploring novel food trends, social entrepreneurship, licensing laws and government regulations, and changing social norms related to how we live together in cities. His work has been published in *Transactions of the Institute of British Geographers*, *Urban Studies*, the *International Journal of Urban and Regional Research*, and in several edited collections.

Alan Latham teaches in the Department of Geography at University College London. His research is focused on urban sociality, corporeal mobility and public space. Writing on topics ranging from urban cycling and recreational running, cultural economies and neighbourhood change, to the overseas experiences of transnational migrants, his work explores the materialities and practices that generate distinctive forms of urban life. He has published widely in edited collections and international journals including *Transactions of the Institute of British Geographers*, *Environment and Planning D*, *Cultural Geographies* and *Urban Studies*. He is the co-author of *Key Concepts in Urban Geography*.

focus on methods / qu of what sort of problem the city is allow for levelling of small scale anthropology & high level theory — what counts as key here depends, as the editors rightly say, on what issues at stake.

Notes on Contributors

Michele Acuto, Department of Science, Technology, Engineering, and Public Policy, University College London, UK

Andrew Barnfield, Department of Health Services Research and Policy, London School of Hygiene and Tropical Medicine, UK

David Beer, Department of Sociology, University of York, UK

Raoul Beunen, Department of Social Sciences, Wageningen University, Netherlands

Ryan Centner, Department of Geography and Environment, London School of Economics and Political Science, UK

I-Chun Catherine Chang, Department of Geography, Macalester College, USA

Agustín Cocola-Gant, School of Geography, University of Lisbon, Portugal

Helen Couclelis, Department of Geography, University of California, Santa Barbara, USA

Michael DeLand, Department of Sociology, Yale University, USA

Clemens Driessen, Department of Environmental Sciences, Wageningen University, Netherlands

Martijn Duineveld, Department of Environmental Sciences, Wageningen University, Netherlands

Jürgen Essletzbichler, Department of Geography, Vienna University of Economics and Business, Austria

Michail Fragkias, Department of Economics, Boise State University, USA

Juan Pablo Galvis, Department of History and Philosophy, State University of New York at Old Westbury, USA

Angela Giglia, Department of Anthropology, Universidad Autónoma Metropolitana, Mexico City, Mexico

Joseph Heathcott, Department of Public Engagement, The New School, USA

Hanna Hilbrandt, Department of Geography, The Open University, UK

Phil Hubbard, Department of Geography, King's College London, UK

Kurt Iveson, Faculty of Science, The University of Sydney, Australia

Mark Jayne, School of Geography and Planning, Cardiff University, UK

Andrew Karvonen, Department of Urban Planning and Environment, KTH Royal Institute of Technology, Sweden

Leslie Kern, Department of Geography and Environment, Mount Allison University, Canada

Regan Koch, School of Geography, Queen Mary University of London, UK

Alan Latham, Department of Geography, University College London, UK

Melanie Lombard, Department of Urban Studies and Planning, The University of Sheffield, UK

Eugene McCann, Department of Geography, Simon Fraser University, Canada

Colin McFarlane, Department of Geography, Durham University, UK

Annie Matan, Sustainability Policy Institute, Curtin University, Australia

Louis Moreno, Department of Visual Cultures, Goldsmiths, University of London, UK

Oli Mould, Department of Geography, Royal Holloway, University of London, UK

David Pinder, Department of Environmental, Social and Spatial Change, Roskilde University, Denmark

Davide Ponzini, Department of Architecture and Planning, Politecnico di Milano, Italy

Rajyashree N. Reddy, Department of Geography and Planning, University of Toronto, Canada

Sonia Roitman, School of Geography, Planning and Environmental Management, The University of Queensland, Australia

Tom Slater, School of Geosciences, The University of Edinburgh, UK

Quentin Stevens, Department of Architecture and Design, RMIT University, Australia

Tauri Tuvikene, School of Humanities, Tallinn University, Estonia

Kristof Van Assche, Department of Planning, Governance and Development, University of Alberta, Canada

Elvin Wyly, Department of Geography, The University of British Columbia, Canada

Junjia Ye, School of People, Environment and Planning, Massey University, New Zealand

Acknowledgements

Our sincere gratitude goes to those who contributed the entries to this volume. Their effort and patience in getting each chapter finalized is greatly appreciated, and we hope they are as pleased as we are with the final results. We also want to thank Robert Rojek, Matthew Oldfield and the production staff at SAGE for their help in moving this project from commissioning to completion, and the reviewers who helped us make the difficult decisions about which thinkers to include.

Thanks also go to our colleagues and students at QMUL and UCL, who have provided ongoing inspiration and supportive environments in which to develop our own thinking about cities. We would particularly like to thank the students of Cities, Space and Power who read drafts of some of the entries. Anna Plyushteva, Jack Layton, Michael Nattrass and Sam Miles gave helpful comments on the introduction.

Regan would like to thank his family and friends for their constant support.

Alan would like to thank Rita, Thomas and Luisa for their love and patience.

*Maybe more about 'schools)
LA/Chicago etc

Introduction: How to Think About Cities

Regan Koch and Alan Latham

Thinking has its strategies and tactics too, much as other forms of action have. Merely to think about cities and get somewhere, one of the main things to know is what kind of problem cities pose, for all problems cannot be thought about in the same way.

Jane Jacobs, *The Death and Life of Great American Cities* (1961: 558)

I. Introduction

Let's think about cities. They are astonishing places. Often described as one of humanity's greatest achievements, they are a collective response to some of our most fundamental needs. Centres of innovation, cities generate tremendous wealth and opportunity. Markets and factories, skyscrapers, shopping malls and stadiums, cities are places where things get made, whether that be cars, toasters, furniture, laptops, or less tangible things like experiences, trends, contracts and code. Cities also shelter and nurture millions of people in ways that often feel close to magical. They are full of communities and people fashioning novel and striking ways of living together. They facilitate all sorts of unique freedoms, unique ways of pursuing desire and self-expression. For all that, cities can seem thrown together and accidental, a mess of incompatible and unlikely elements. They can be engines of inequality and greed; places where the fact that some people are rich is the result of others being poor. They can be dirty, smelly and polluted. They can segregate and exclude. They are often ugly and inhumane. Other aspects of city life are clearly the result of elaborate, meticulous planning. Think of the extraordinary coordination that allows millions of commuters to pulse into and out of a large city each day. Or the often taken-for-granted (until they aren't working) systems of infrastructure that keep water running, homes heated and cooled, phones and internet working. The extensive networks of care involved in educating children, caring for the sick and providing for the vulnerable, speak to the multitude of informal arrangements and formal institutions that serve and protect those in need. For all their flaws and inefficiencies, their inequalities and inequities, it is remarkable how many different things cities are and do.

This is a book about different ways of thinking about cities and urban life. Profiling the work of 40 individuals at the cutting edge of contemporary urban research, it invites readers to consider a range of theoretical traditions and methodological approaches to understanding cities. Social scientists and others have generated a number of different ways of conceptualizing and describing urban environments. Economists think about cities in ways that are different than sociologists. For anthropologists, urban environments are not the same as they are for planners or spatial scientists. Human geographers work with different tools than do artists or architects or urban designers. The 40 thinkers in this volume are representative of these diverse ways of thinking about cities, and of the trans-disciplinary field that has come to be known as urban studies. The purpose of this book is to provide a guide to this field. For the uninitiated it may serve as an entry point to the formal study of cities, and for those already immersed in urban studies it is an invitation to consider some different approaches to the kind of problem that a city is.

II. The kinds of problems that cities are

Political?
(Gender, postcolonial)

Cities and urban environments are extraordinarily diverse places. For an urban researcher, studying a city is not simply about confronting the city's problems, but also about considering the kind of problem that a city is. The answer to this question is they are not one kind of a problem, rather they are a range of problems. There are many different ways these problems might be framed. We would like to suggest six thematics through which thinking about cities and urban environments might be approached:

Economic...

One kind of problem cities are is economic. If the first industrial revolution started in rural England in the 18th century, it quickly came to be concentrated in newly emergent urban centres: Manchester, Glasgow, Liverpool, Birmingham (Briggs, 1965; Clark, 2000; Harvey, 1989). Elsewhere the story has been similar. The rise of the United States as a global economic and industrial power was largely the product of its growth as an urban society; a society built around cities like New York, Boston, Chicago, Detroit, Cleveland, Baltimore, Los Angeles. Japan's industrialization was driven through the growth of cities like Tokyo, Osaka, Yokohama, Nagoya (Allen, 1981; Berry, 1973; Glaeser, 2011; Hall, 1998; Mosk, 2001). And in the contemporary moment, the extraordinary emergence of China as an economic powerhouse is all about the urbanization of a previously rural society. Long established cities like Shanghai, Beijing and Hong Kong have seen tremendous growth, as well as the development of vast new conglomerations that scarcely existed 30 or 40 years ago: Guangzhou, Shenzhen, Harbin, Jinan, Chengdu (Brenner and Schmid, 2014; Castells, 2014; Wu, 2015; Wu and Gaubatz, 2013). This raises the question of why so much economic activity has come to be concentrated in urban areas? Why are they centres of so much wealth and power? And beyond these questions are more nuanced ones. Why is it that some cities come to dominate whole countries and regions while others do not? Why do some cities grow so quickly while others do not? And why do some cities switch from being centres of growth to places of poverty and economic distress?

Social...

The concentration of economic activity presupposes social concentration. Cities and urban environments demonstrate enormous variations in their population density; some are remarkably spread-out and ill-defined, while others concentrate enormous numbers of people in remarkably small areas (Demographica, 2016; Pacione, 2001; World Bank, 2015). Seoul's population density is around five times that of New York City. The population density of Phoenix is a thirtieth of that of Mumbai or Hong Kong, and half that of New York. Monaco compresses its entire population in two square kilometres, while Buenos Aires stretches over 2500 square kilometres. However, all cities, be they dense or sprawling, large or small, have to deal with a set of common social problems centring around how people live together in such close proximity. These range from questions like how people access the basics of life such as housing, water and nourishment, to how different ethnic groups and different social classes share the common spaces of a city. They involve questions about how children should be looked after and educated, how the elderly and vulnerable are cared for, how social order is to be maintained and policed (Gehl, 2010; Hayden, 1980; Jarvis et al., 2001; Knox and Pinch, 2010; Tonkiss, 2013; Zukin, 1995). So as well as being an economic problem, cities need also to be thought of as a social problem – as questions of social order and organization. Just as there is no single city form, nor is there any single answer to how these social questions are addressed. Different urban societies have generated an enormous variety of answers to these social questions. Some have created cities defined by patterns of systematic segregation and inequality, while others manage to create an overarching sense of egalitarianism and inclusion (Abu-Lughod, 1980; Caldeira, 2000; Espino, 2015; Hall, 2013; Lynch, 1981; McLaren and Agyeman, 2015; Massey, 2005; Robinson, 1996; Smith, 1996; Wacquant, 2008).

Institutional...

To think of cities as a collection of social and economic questions brings us to a third way of thinking about them – they are also problems of institutional order. Things like markets and exchanges, schools and hospitals, systems of electricity, water supply and sewage disposal do not just happen. They are supported and coordinated by a vast range of institutions. To start, we can think of things like law and the legal system. These institutions form the taken-for-granted backdrop through which the social and economic life of cities unfolds; it is easy to forget the role they play in structuring and organizing everyday urban life (Kim, 2015; Koch, 2015; Loukaitou-Sideris and Ehrenfeucht, 2009; Valverde, 2012). In other cases, institutions have a more obviously visible role in the life of cities. Things like planning systems and city governments are clearly intertwined with how all sorts of aspects of urban life are governed and organized (Boyer, 1994; Caldeira, 2000; Flyvbjerg, 1998; Holston, 2008; Molotch, 2014). But thinking about cities as questions of institutional organization – mediating in a whole range of ways who gets access to what – also points to the need to think about the less formal institutions that help urban life hold together (Anderson, 1999; García Canclini, 2005; McFarlane, 2011; Roy, 2003; Sennett, 2012). It is well established that cities everywhere are animated by thick networks of association. These run from relations of kinship, religion, ethnicity and occupation, through to friendship, neighbourhood and the surprising connections of shared enthusiasms like sports teams and festivals (Amin and Thrift, 2002; De Boeck and Plissart, 2004; Fischer, 1982; Simone, 2004; Wellman, 1979). What is less understood is how and why these associations sometimes serve as dividing lines in hostile relations between groups, and at other times become vital sources of solidarity and care.

Infrastructural...

This brings us to a fourth kind of problem that cities are: infrastructural problems. Cities are fundamentally about questions of sharing and distribution. And all of this is built and organized through often complex and intricate networks of physical infrastructure: things like roads and streets, electricity grids, mass transit systems, telecommunications networks, water supply and wastewater disposal systems, to name just a few possible examples (Gandy, 2014; Graham and Marvin, 2001; Hughes, 1993; Kitchin and Dodge, 2011; McShane, 1994; OMA et al., 1995). We can think of infrastructure as all those systems and networks that are necessary for the collective functioning of a society. These need not be publicly provided, but they are characterized by the fact of their collective consumption. Of course all social life in some sense involves forms of infrastructure. But cities, because of their size, because of their concentration of population, because of their heterogeneity, put extraordinary demands on the infrastructural. They have constantly required the development of socio-technological systems that allow hundreds of thousands, in some case millions, of urban dwellers to be provided with clean water, for houses and buildings to be provided with electricity and heat. In cities like Tokyo and London these systems allow several million people to travel into and from the centre of the city each day. To think of cities as an infrastructural problem, then, is to recognize that cities are not just economic or social, indeed that they are not just built environments, they are in fact socio-technological artefacts (Bijker et al., 1987; Blok and Farías, 2016; Hommels, 2005; Mitchell, 1995). And to think of cities as an infrastructural problem is simultaneously to think of cities and urban environments as sets of socio-technological problems. Cities are built as much by engineers as they are by architects or urban planners, but the fair and effective provisioning of such infrastructure raises a host of questions that go beyond technical matters.

Ecological...

Importantly, cities are not just places that are shared with other people. Urban dwellers cohabitate with a whole host of other non-human agents. Many of these go largely unnoticed: the weeds that populate a street verge; the grasses and flowers that cover an unbuilt suburban lot; the animals like mice, rats, raccoons, foxes, squirrels, sparrows, geckos and lizards, starlings, gulls, pigeons, myna birds, feral cats and dogs that find productive niches within urban environments. Indeed, there are a whole list of synanthropic species that have co-evolved to thrive in the environments that humans create. Just as a significant proportion of the human species is now 'urban', there are subsets of plants, insects and animals that too have in a range of senses 'urbanized' (Jeremijenko, 2009; Lachmund, 2013; Monbiot, 2014; Niemelä, 1999; Sullivan, 2004). The dynamics of this symbiosis are complex and go way beyond a simple sense of the natural being parasitic on the human or vice versa. Urban environments and the people within them are dependent on the physical environments within which they are built: for water, for food, for clean air. Urban dwellers are also dependent on a wide range of ecological services and infrastructures to ensure that the vast amounts of biological waste they produce do not come to act as vectors of microbial contagion (Corburn, 2013; Forman, 2014). So cities can also be understood as an ecological problem, as a set of questions about how humans are mixed together with the 'natural' processes of the physical environment, or how the human and non-human interfold. Thinking about the city as ecological involves thinking about urban environments as enormous metabolic systems of energy and matter; as sites that teem with a diversity of different forms of life; as complex organisms that are heterogeneous mixtures of the organic and inorganic, of the microscopic and the monumental (Amin and Thrift, 2002; Bennett, 2010; Davis, 1998; Gandy, 2003; Swyngedouw, 2006). And it is also to be prompted to think about how urban environments and their demands for energy and materials are an integral part of what some climate scientists have come to call the Anthropocene (Bulkeley and Betsill, 2003; Lorimer, 2015; Seto et al., 2012; Vince, 2014).

Complexity...

Finally, cities can be thought of as problems of a certain kind of complexity. This in a sense is to reiterate the points outlined in the previous five paragraphs. Understanding how cities and urban environments work requires thinking about how a range of relationships interact together simultaneously. The dynamism of cities comes in no small part from the fact that they draw together so many different elements into close proximity. They pull together people of different backgrounds, skill sets, capacities and world views. They bring together complex lattices of institutions and organizations. They draw all sorts of heterogeneous material and non-material entities into relation with each other in planned and unplanned ways. Indeed, urban mixing does not just happen through proximity, it is also about diverse connections to faraway places. This is to say that cities and their environments in a quite fundamental sense are pluralizing, diverse and heterogeneous in their character. More, is to stress that in a fundamental sense cities themselves generate much of that plurality, diversity and heterogeneity. It is not simply that cities and urban environments are with all their plurality, diversity and heterogeneity, complicated entities to understand – although of course they often are. We need to go further. It is not just that cities are complex – that they involve intricate networks of connection and interdependence. Rather cities are composed of entangled meshes of dynamic, interrelated, emergent, self-organizing systems. Or, put another way, cities are a problem of organized complexity (Batty, 2013; Jacobs, 1961; Johnson, 2001; Storper, 2013). They are made up of a host of interconnected systems where the component elements are not just related but where the effect of each component is very much greater than the simple sum of its parts (Miller and Page, 2009). Thinking seriously about cities requires taking into account the power of this complexity.

Of course not all problems encountered in cities are simply and straightforwardly 'urban' problems – problems of 'the city'. Cities and urban environments are also bound together with a range of different scales of action; the national, the regional, the international, the global, to name a few examples (Sassen, 2006; Storper, 2013). Urban economies are part of wider transactional networks. Social dynamics are not just endogenous to cities. They are entangled within broader social dynamics and often complex patterns of connection to other places, just as social and cultural institutions are. The knowledge and expertise that goes into producing the socio-technical infrastructures is almost always part of more global techno-scapes. The reach of ecological ranges are rarely conterminous with urban boundaries. And the organized complexity found within cities is itself a subsystem of a range of larger complex socio-economic systems. Indeed, one of the challenges of urban studies is disentangling these different layers of causality. And, if some thinkers within urban studies are keen to assert the privileged place of 'the urban' or 'the city', others are more circumspect, arguing only that cities and the urban are distinctive realms of action – not the most decisive.

III. Ways of thinking about cities, ways of theorizing cities

One advantage of starting with key thinkers as a way of approaching the field of urban studies is that it helps to emphasize plurality in terms of how urban problems might be addressed. Looking at the academic trajectories and research agendas that different individuals have embarked upon gives a sense of this plurality. Just as cities can be approached as a diverse array of problems, those problems can be thought about and framed through different styles of thinking. And these styles of thinking may lead towards quite different and in some cases mutually antagonistic views of how cities are organized and function. This diversity arises in part from the variety of intellectual traditions that populate the contemporary social sciences and humanities. But it is also a product of the different ways thinking itself may be understood.

It is easy to conflate thinking with theorizing. Certainly much – but by no means all – of the Western intellectual tradition emphasizes a dichotomy between mind and body, theory and practice, thought and action. We would discourage readers from flattening their thinking in this way. Thinking can be visceral, practical, imaginative, oriented to action and affecting, as much as it may be abstract, analytical and removed from emotion. Reading the entries of the thinkers collected in this volume should convey a sense of the various ways that thinking may be done in relation to the work of building theory, working with empirical evidence, and in the work of transforming urban spaces and cities. In no particular order, we would like to suggest five different ways that thinking about cities gets done within urban studies.

Thinking as local explanation and description...

Much of urban studies is interested in the distinctive elements and relationships that different urban forms draw together, the factors which make cities unique. It wants to describe how people live together in a particular place; the meanings they ascribe to their activities, the imaginaries that inform their worlds. Researchers focusing on this emplacement are aware that there are factors shared in common across different cities and spaces that will help them make sense of their research site. However, their primary interest is less in defining the exact shape of these commonalities as working at developing convincing accounts of how the relations encountered during research unfold. The work of **Elijah Anderson** is exemplary of this approach, as is that of **Dolores Hayden**. As an urban ethnographer Anderson's work seeks to describe the situated interactions through which categorizations like race and social class become manifest in American cities. Anderson is careful to place his accounts into a broader context of contemporary urban life in the US, but the persuasive force of his books is a product of the thick descriptions of the Philadelphia neighbourhoods he studies. Similarly, the force of Hayden's work as an urban historian is a product of the detail she accumulates in her description of – among other topics – the domestic worlds of suburbia, or 19th-century attempts to create gender-equal forms of housing. In a similar vein, but on a different scale, **Fulong Wu** has described the dynamics of government and market-oriented restructuring that have been at the heart of China's tremendous urban expansion. His work details the political and economic transformations which make what is happening in China distinct from previous patterns of urbanization elsewhere in the world.

Thinking as a set of tools and heuristics...

The use of description as a form of social explanation and argumentation does not preclude an interest in more generalizable kinds of theory. However, much writing within urban studies is interested in developing more formal codifications than those offered by thick description. For such work, a key part of thinking about cities involves developing explicit theoretical concepts that allow us to think with precision about the social, political, economic or ecological dynamics being studied. Here thinking about cities and urban spaces involves drawing on and developing concepts that operate as tools or heuristics that facilitate comparison across diverse cases. Practically, concepts are constructions that help us to make sense of the particular concrete, empirical puzzles that the world confronts us with. **Saskia Sassen**'s concept of the global city is a good example of this style of thinking. When it was introduced the concept of the global city described a distinctive but previously overlooked set of socio-economic relations characteristic of certain cities – indeed certain sectors within certain cities – that held a privileged position in an emergent form of economic globalization. The productiveness of the concept lies less in the question of whether she is right (whether there are indeed distinct global cities), and more in the issues and debates the concept of the global city opens up. In a somewhat different register, the writings of both **Ash Amin** and **AbdouMaliq Simone** elaborate novel theoretical concepts for thinking about urban economies, social life and infrastructure, through which we might think more carefully about how urban worlds are put together. In contrast, **Richard Sennett** eschews the production of formal theory in his writing, choosing instead through examples and description to offer his reader possible ways of thinking about important urban questions such as how strangers manage to cooperate, or how different groups live together.

Thinking as intervening...

To treat theoretical concepts as tools or heuristics is to highlight the extent thinking can be thought of as practical. The point of concepts employed in this way is not strictly speaking whether they are 'true' or not. Rather it is their usefulness in helping us accurately make sense of whatever problem the researcher finds themselves entangled with. A further way of thinking about the kind of thinking that animates urban studies is to focus on the concrete interventions undertaken in cities by urban planners, architects, politicians, artists and others. This includes a diverse range of actions from the work of crafting plans and designs, creating concrete policy interventions, to staging artistic interventions that encourage urban dwellers to think about their relationships to each other and their environment. What is most striking about this style of thinking is how it is directly entangled with the day-to-day flow of actual cities. So, for example, the artist and activist **Natalie Jeremijenko** stages imaginative interventions that encourage urbanites to interact with the non-human animals they share their city with: birds, fish, mice, plants, tadpoles. The architect **Jan Gehl** re-designs urban spaces to re-scale them to the form of the individual human body, just as **Kevin Lynch** had put his work on urban perception to use in his urban design practice. In a similar way, **Enrique Peñalosa**, the sometime mayor of Bogota, developed a series of inventive interventions that were aimed at both improving life in the city he governed and conveying a sense that the city was for everyone.

Thinking as critique...

It can be easy to overlook that intervention-oriented thinking involves not just action, but also theories of action. A fourth style of thinking however explicitly places the work of theorizing at its centre. Thinking as critique is focused on uncovering the hidden and unacknowledged biases and power asymmetries that structure contemporary cities. One style of work in this vein – which underpins much work in critical urban studies – involves describing the underlying structures or forces through which cities and urban environments are organized. Here, while theory may still be thought of as a tool or heuristic, more commonly it is understood as the objective apparatus through which the real underlying relationships within the social world are made apparent. The work of thinking about cities then comes to also be a question of theorizing the processes that structure cities. Crucially the work of theory takes on a foundational quality; without the proper theorization of the unseen processes driving urban development, researchers cannot make useful sense of the empirical phenomena that they might be interested in. The work of neo-Marxists such as **Henri Lefebvre, David Harvey** and **Neil Brenner** is exemplary of this approach. Harvey's analysis of contemporary urban life is built on the proposition that contemporary cities are fundamentally structured through the dynamics of capitalist accumulation. It follows from this that cities and the multitude of processes that structure them cannot be understood unless this reality is taken into account. Similarly, Lefebvre argues that a generalized process of urbanization has come to define the contemporary moment. As a result, as Brenner has stressed, it is essential to properly theorize 'the urban' before one can productively start making sense of contemporary urban life.

Not all forms of social critique within urban studies are premised on the need to specify underlying structures. Drawing together both the notion of thinking as description and thinking as the generation of conceptual heuristics and tools, an alternative mode of thinking as critique focuses on tracing out the way specific urban relations are assembled. The aim here is to unpack the subtle mechanisms through which patterns of inequality and unfairness are instantiated. **M. Christine Boyer's** work for example demonstrates how seemingly neutral practices of heritage conservation in fact construct limited and exclusionary narratives of collective memory in the New York cityscape. In a different vein, **Bent Flyvbjerg** has analysed how processes of urban planning in Denmark are not as transparent and democratic as they are presented to be, but rather are built upon and reproduce asymmetries of power and influence. For Boyer and Flyvbjerg, critique is a means of contributing to public debate about their cities and the ways in which planning processes might be organized differently.

Thinking as modelling...

A final style of thinking focuses on the construction of formal models. As with thinking as critique, thinking as modelling emphasizes the development of robust theoretical constructs. But it does not seek to reveal or decode an otherwise unseen reality. Rather it seeks to fashion precise analytic representations of the world. At its most basic a model is nothing more than a simplified description of relationships. In this sense each of the previous four styles of thinking involves forms of modelling. More strictly, however, thinking as modelling involves creating formalized, empirically testable, descriptions of the social world. These formal descriptions may take the form of diagrams or other visual representations. They may also be presented as mathematical formula. This style of thinking – unlike the four so far discussed – is closely related to that undertaken within the physical sciences. Given that the work of modellers relies both on the generation of robust quantitative data and the use of highly schematic assumptions about the parameters of interaction, it can produce descriptions that are simplified, highly stylized and removed from the messy complexity of actual urban worlds. However, as the sociologist Howard Becker (2005: 151) has pointed out, 'being unrealistic doesn't deprive these representations of value or usefulness'. And while writers like **Brian Berry, Michael Batty, Karen C. Seto** and **Edward L. Glaeser** are keen to stress the extent to which their models are scientific and hence produce distinct kinds of analysis compared to less quantitatively oriented urban work, one does not have to accept this claim to appreciate the usefulness of this style of thinking. Thinking with models can tell us much about the enduring morphologies of urban growth, the dynamics of scaling between and within cities, how agglomeration economies work, and much else.

Each of these five ways of thinking about cities share commonalities, not only in that they are different ways of imaging what the city is, but also what it might be. Normative or aspirational ideas about cities could be thought of as yet another way of thinking about cities. However, we think that each mode of thinking outlined above can be oriented towards imagining and enacting better urban futures. This in part accounts for a great deal of overlap between the different approaches outlined. For example, thinking as critique may begin with the work of theorizing, but it can also inspire and contribute to on-the-ground kinds of direct activism. **Henri Lefebvre's** (1996) formulations of the 'right to the city' have been the rallying call for a tremendous amount of urban political struggle and community organization. Conversely, the development of theoretical tools and heuristics often forms the basis for discussions about how more desirable alternatives might be realized. We can see this in **Ash Amin's** work, which challenges taken-for-granted assumptions that can lead to misguided kinds of urban policy making and intervention. Likewise, detailed local descriptions and speculative models can form the basis for public discussion and deliberation about how best to address the persistent and emerging problems that cities face. The larger point then is that just as the city presents itself with multiple kinds of problems, there are a variety of different ways of thinking that can be used to tackle these problems.

IV. How to use this book, and who's in it?

There are any number of textbooks and compendiums that offer an introduction to the world of cities and urban research (see Bridge and Watson, 2010; LeGates and Stout, 2011; Paddison and McCann, 2014; Parker, 2015). *Key Thinkers on Cities* (*KToC*) is not designed as a replacement. Instead, there are three ways we hope this book might be used. First, it offers an initiatory primer for anyone interested in cities but unfamiliar with urban studies as an academic field. Read together, the 40 entries in *KToC* provide a sense of the broad ranging themes, concepts and theoretical approaches that underpin a great deal of contemporary urban scholarship. Second, undergraduate and postgraduate students in urban studies and related academic disciplines will find *KToC* a useful resource for learning alongside course textbooks and assigned readings. Each entry outlines the intellectual context and basic ideas of a key figure students are likely to encounter in their studies, and will help to make connections and points of contrast between them. Third, *KToC* can be a valuable point of reference for scholars in any field that relates to cities and urban issues. The volume provides a resource for understanding the basic contours of different urban debates and research trajectories. Overall, the aim of *KToC* is to provide an engaging map of the trans-disciplinary field of urban studies. It does so by outlining the contributions of established leaders and those whose work is currently reshaping the way we think about cities and urban environments.

The 40 people featured in this book have produced some of the most influential and inspiring thinking about cities in recent decades. Some of them are very well known across different disciplines and beyond academia; others perhaps less so. The book is not a 'who's who' list or ranking exercise, nor is it an attempt to inscribe a certain canon. Rather, the entries have been selected to represent the diversity of ideas, approaches and empirical subject matter animating urban scholarship today. Indeed, one of the most exciting things about contemporary urban studies is its plurality. *KToC* highlights this plurality and invites its readers to think about cities and urban environments from a range of diverse perspectives. Some of the key thinker choices will seem obvious (how could you have a book on key thinkers without people like **Jane Jacobs**, **David Harvey** or **Saskia Sassen**?). Others might seem surprising. Some may not even appear to be obviously urban thinkers (**Natalie Jeremijenko** is an artist; **Mariana Valverde** is a legal scholar who does not just write about urban issues). We have undoubtedly overlooked some areas of urban scholarship – not least because we have chosen to concentrate on work that has at least one leg in the social sciences; and we have only included thinkers whose work is widely available in English. Nonetheless, the thinkers collected here provide a sense of the vibrancy and dynamism of contemporary urban studies.

So, how have the different thinkers been selected? The starting point was thinking in terms of core themes in urban scholarship: economics, politics and government, social and cultural life, infrastructure and technology, ecology and health, and planning and design – the six problematics outlined above. Next, we considered the principal disciplines that feed into urban studies: economics, sociology, anthropology, planning, urban design and architecture, and human geography. These were then considered in relation to diverse theoretical and methodological perspectives circulating within the field. These include comparative research (**Matthew Gandy, Jennifer Robinson, Ananya Roy**), case study (**Bent Flyvbjerg, Harvey Molotch, Mariana Valverde, Fulong Wu**) and ethnographic research (**Elijah Anderson, Teresa Caldeira, Néstor García Canclini, Loïc Wacquant, Sharon Zukin**), quantitative analysis and urban modelling (**Edward L. Glaeser, Karen C. Seto, Michael Storper**), historical approaches (**M. Christine Boyer, Dolores Hayden, Richard Sennett**), critical urbanism and political economy (**Neil Brenner, Mike Davis, Stephen Graham, Saskia Sassen, Neil Smith**), actor-network theory and assemblage theories (**Ash Amin, Jane M. Jacobs, AbdouMaliq Simone**) and various modes of urban intervention (**Jason Corburn, Jan Gehl, Natalie Jeremijenko, Rem Koolhaas, William J. Mitchell, Enrique Peñalosa**). In selecting thinkers, we sought to include a number of figures who were foundational to the initial formation of the field of urban studies in the 1960s and 1970s. This includes those such as **Janet Abu-Lughod, Jane Jacobs, Henri Lefebvre** and **Kevin Lynch** who have passed away, along with still active scholars like **Mike Batty, Brian Berry, Manuel Castells** and **David Harvey**. We have purposely omitted earlier thinkers one might expect to find in a volume on key urban thinkers – people like Walter Benjamin, Robert Park, Louis Wirth, Max Weber, Georg Simmel and Lewis Mumford. There is more than enough introductory writing on these thinkers, and we think there is as much to be learnt from the new as from the old.

Finally, as to how you might go about reading this book, there's no prescriptive formula. We suspect that few readers will work through it sequentially, cover to cover. You might start by just flipping through, looking to see how many names or key writings you are familiar with. The first entry you read might be that of one of your personal favourites, or you might want to learn about someone completely unfamiliar to you. Either way, we hope the entry will inspire you to dive deeper into some of their work, or perhaps you will follow a cross-reference onto another key thinker whose work is in some way related. Regardless of how you use this volume, we hope that you find it a helpful resource and return to it every now and again. For we think the diversity of thinkers it contains can help to promote a pluralistic urban imagination, one sensitive to the wide range of perspectives on the kinds of problems that cities present.

Welcome to the world of urban studies!   *US coming of age?*
Development of 'canon'
despite denying
this

References

Abu-Lughod, J. (1980) *Rabat: Urban Apartheid in Morocco*. Princeton, NJ: Princeton University Press.

Allen, G. (1981) *A Short Economic History of Japan*, 4th edn. London: Macmillan.

Amin, A. and Thrift, N. (2002) *Cities: Reimagining the Urban*. Cambridge: Polity Press.

Anderson, E. (1999) *Code of the Street: Decency, Violence, and the Moral Life of the Inner City*. New York: W.W. Norton.

Batty, M. (2013) *The New Science of Cities*. Cambridge, MA: MIT Press.

Becker, H. (2005) *Telling About Society*. Chicago: University of Chicago.

Bennett, J. (2010) *Lively Matter*. Durham, NC: Duke University Press.

Berry, B.J.L. (1973) *The Human Consequences of Urbanisation: Divergent Paths in the Urban Experience of the Twentieth Century*. Basingstoke: Macmillan.

Bijker, W., Hughes, T. and Pinch, T. (eds) (1987) *The Social Construction of Technological Systems: New Directions in the Sociology and History of Technology*. Cambridge, MA: MIT Press.

Blok, A. and Farías, I. (eds) (2016) *Urban Cosmopolitics: Agencements, Assemblies, Atmospheres*. London: Routledge.

Boyer, M.C. (1994) *The City of Collective Memory: Its Historical Imagery and Architectural Entertainments*. Cambridge, MA: MIT Press.

Brenner, N. and Schmid, C. (2014) 'The "urban age" in question', *International Journal of Urban and Regional Research*, 38(3): 731–755.

Bridge, G. and Watson, S. (2010) *The Blackwell City Reader*, 2nd edn. Oxford: Wiley-Blackwell.

Briggs, A. (1965) *Victorian Cities*. New York: Harper & Row.

Bulkeley, H. and Betsill, M.M. (2003) *Cities and Climate Change: Urban Sustainability and Global Environmental Governance*. New York: Routledge.

Caldeira, T.P. (2000) *City of Walls: Crime, Segregation and Citizenship in São Paulo*. Berkeley: University of California Press.

Castells, M. (2014) *Technopoles of the World: The Making of 21st Century Industrial Complexes*. London: Routledge.

Clark, P. (ed.) (2000) *The Cambridge Urban History of Britain, Vol. 2. 1540–1840*. Cambridge: Cambridge University Press.

Corburn, J. (2013) *Healthy City Planning: From Neighbourhood to National Health Equity*. London: Routledge.

Davis, M. (1998) *The Ecology of Fear: Los Angeles and the Imagination of Disaster*. New York: Vintage.

De Boeck, P. and Plissart, M.F. (2004) *Tales of the Invisible City*. Ghent and Antwerp: Ludion.

Demographica (2016) *World Urban Areas. 12th Annual Edition: 2016*. Belleville, IL: Demographica.

Espino, N.A. (2015) *Building the Inclusive City: Theory and Practice for Confronting Urban Segregation*. New York: Routledge.

Fischer, C. (1982) *To Dwell Among Friends: Personal Networks in Town and City*. Chicago: University of Chicago Press.

Flyvbjerg, B. (1998) *Rationality and Power: Democracy in Practice*. Chicago: University of Chicago Press.

Forman, R.T. (2014) *Urban Ecology: Science of Cities*. Cambridge: Cambridge University Press.

Gandy, M. (2003) *Concrete and Clay: Reworking Nature in New York City*. Cambridge, MA: MIT Press.

Gandy, M. (2014) *The Fabric of Space: Water, Modernity, and the Urban Imagination*. Cambridge, MA: MIT Press.

García Canclini, N. (ed.) (2005) *La antropología urbana en México*. Mexico City: Fondo de Cultura Económica – UAM.

Gehl, J. (2010) *Cities for People*. Washington, DC: Island Press.

Glaeser, E. (2011) *Triumph of the City*. London: Macmillan.

Graham, S. and Marvin, S. (2001) *Splintering Urbanism: Networked Infrastructures, Technological Mobilities and the Urban Condition*. London: Routledge.

Hall, P. (1998) *Cities in Civilization*. New York: Pantheon Books.

Hall, P. (2013) *Good Cities, Better Lives: How Europe Discovered the Lost Art of Urbanism*. London: Routledge.

Harvey, D. (1989) *The Urban Experience*. Oxford: Blackwell.

Hayden, D. (1980) 'What would a non-sexist city be like? Speculations on housing, urban design, and human work', *Signs*, 5(3): 170–187.

Holston, J. (2008) *Insurgent Citizenship: Disjunctions of Democracy and Modernity in Brazil*. Princeton, NJ: Princeton University Press.

Hommels, A.M. (2005) *Unbuilding Cities: Obduracy in Urban Sociotechnical Change*. Cambridge, MA: MIT Press.

Hughes, T.P. (1993) *Networks of Power: Electrification in Western Society, 1880–1930*. Baltimore: Johns Hopkins University Press.

Jacobs, J. (1961) *The Death and Life of Great American Cities*. New York: Vintage.

Jarvis, H., Pratt, A.C. and Wu, C. (2001) *The Secret Life of Cities: The Social Reproduction of Everyday Life*. Harlow: Prentice-Hall.

Jeremijenko, N. (2009) The Art of the Eco-Mind Shift. Video on TED.com, October 2009. Available at: www.ted.com/talks/natalie_jeremijenko_the_art_of_the_eco_mindshift

Johnson, S. (2001) *Emergence: The Connected Lives of Ants, Brains, Cities, and Software*. London: Penguin.

Kim, A.M. (2015) *Sidewalk City: Remapping Public Space in Ho Chi Minh City*. Chicago: University of Chicago Press.

Kitchin, R. and Dodge, M. (2011) *Code/Space: Software and Everyday Life*. Cambridge, MA: MIT Press.

Knox, P. and Pinch, S. (2010) *Urban Social Geography: An Introduction*. London and New York: Routledge.

Koch, R. (2015) 'Licensing, popular practices and public spaces: An inquiry via the geographies of street food vending', *International Journal of Urban and Regional Research*, 39(6): 1231–1250.

Lachmund, J. (2013) *Greening Berlin: The Co-Production of Science, Politics, and Urban Nature*. Cambridge, MA: MIT Press.

Lefebvre, H. (1996) 'The right to the city', in *Writings on Cities*. Ed. and trans. E. Kofman and E. Lebas. Oxford: Blackwell, pp. 63–181.

LeGates, R. and Stout, F. (2011) *The City Reader*, 5th edn. New York: Routledge.

Lorimer, J. (2015) *Wildlife in the Anthropocene: Conservation after Nature*. Minneapolis: University of Minnesota Press.

Loukaitou-Sideris, A. and Ehrenfeucht, R. (2009) *Sidewalks: Conflict and Negotiation over Public Space*. Cambridge, MA: MIT Press.

Lynch, K. (1981) *A Theory of Good City Form*. Cambridge, MA: MIT Press.

McFarlane, C. (2011) *Learning the City: Knowledge and Translocal Assemblage*. Oxford: John Wiley.

McLaren, D. and Agyeman, J. (2015) *Sharing Cities: A Case for Truly Smart and Sustainable Cities*. Cambridge, MA: MIT Press.

McShane, C. (1994) *Down the Asphalt Path: The Automobile and the American City*. New York: Columbia University Press.

Massey, D.S. (2005) *Strangers in a Strange Land: Humans in an Urbanizing World*. New York: W.W. Norton.

Miller, J.H. and Page, S.E. (2009) *Complex Adaptive Systems: An Introduction to Computational Models of Social Life*. Princeton, NJ: Princeton University Press.

Mitchell, W.J. (1995) *City of Bits: Space, Place and the Infobahn*. Cambridge, MA: MIT Press.

Molotch, H. (2014) *Against Security: How We Go Wrong at Airports, Subways, and Other Sites of Ambiguous Danger*. Princeton, NJ: Princeton University Press.

Monibot, G. (2014) *Feral: Rewilding the Land, the Sea, and Human Life*. Chicago: University of Chicago Press.

Mosk, C. (2001) *Japanese Industrial History: Technology, Urbanization, and Economic Growth*. London: M.E. Sharpe.

Niemelä, J. (1999) 'Ecology and urban planning', *Biodiversity and Conservation*, 8(1): 119–131.

OMA, Koolhaas, R. and Mau, B. (eds) (1995) *S, M, L, XL*. New York: Monacelli Press.

Pacione, M. (2001) *Urban Geography: A Global Perspective*. London: Routledge.

Paddison, R. and McCann, E. (2014) *Cities and Social Change*. London: Sage.

Parker, S. (2015) *Urban Theory and Urban Experience*, 2nd edn. New York: Routledge.

Robinson, J. (1996) *The Power of Apartheid: State, Power, and Space in South African Cities*. London: Butterworth-Heinemann.

Roy, A. (2003) *City Requiem, Calcutta: Gender and the Politics of Poverty*. Minneapolis: University of Minnesota Press.

Sassen, S. (2006) *Territory, Authority, Rights: From Medieval to Global Assemblages*. Princeton, NJ: Princeton University Press.

Sennett, R. (2012) *Together: The Rituals, Pleasures and Politics of Cooperation*. London: Penguin.

Seto, K.C., Güneralp, B. and Hutyra, L. (2012) 'Global forecasts of urban expansion to 2030 and direct impacts on biodiversity and carbon pools', *Proceedings of the National Academy of Sciences of the United States of America*, 109(40): 16083–16088.

Simone, A. (2004) *For the City Yet to Come: Changing African Life in Four Cities*. Durham, NC: Duke University Press.

Smith, N. (1996) *The New Urban Frontier: Gentrification and the Revanchist City*. New York: Routledge.

Storper, M. (2013) *Keys to the City: How Economics, Institutions, Social Interaction, and Politics Shape Development*. Princeton, NJ: Princeton University Press.

Sullivan, R. (2004) *Rats: A Year with New York's Most Unwanted Inhabitants*. London: Granta.

Swyngedouw, E. (2006) 'Circulations and metabolisms: (Hybrid) natures and (cyborg) cities', *Science as Culture*, 15(2): 105–121.

Tonkiss, F. (2013) *Cities by Design: The Social Life of Urban Form*. Cambridge: Polity.

Valverde, M. (2012) *Everyday Law on the Street: City Governance in an Age of Diversity*. Chicago: University of Chicago Press.

Vince, G. (2014) *Adventures in the Anthropocene: A Journey to the Heart of the Planet We Made*. London: Penguin.

Wacquant, L. (2008) *Urban Outcasts: A Comparative Sociology of Advanced Marginality*. Cambridge: Polity.

Wellman, B. (1979) 'The community question: The intimate networks of East Yorkers', *American Journal of Sociology*, 84(5): 1201–1231.

World Bank (2015) *East Asia's Changing Urban Landscape: Measuring a Decade of Spatial Growth*. Washington, DC: World Bank

Wu, F. (2015) *Planning for Growth: Urban and Regional Planning in China*. London: Routledge.

Wu, F. and Gaubatz, P. (2013) *The Chinese City*. London: Routledge.

Zukin, S. (1995) *The Culture of Cities*. Cambridge, MA: Blackwell.

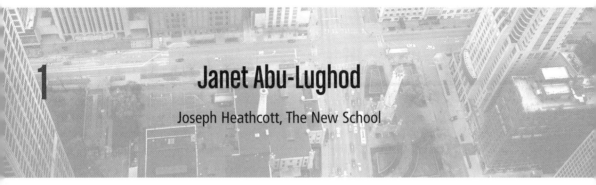

Janet Abu-Lughod

Joseph Heathcott, The New School

Key urban writings

Abu-Lughod, J. (1971a) *Cairo: 1001 Years of the City Victorious*. Princeton, NJ: Princeton University Press.

Abu-Lughod, J. (1980) *Rabat: Urban Apartheid in Morocco*. Princeton, NJ: Princeton University Press.

Abu-Lughod, J. (1989) *Before European Hegemony: The World System, A.D. 1250–1350*. New York: Oxford University Press.

Abu-Lughod, J. (1999) *New York, Chicago, Los Angeles: America's Global Cities*. Minneapolis: University of Minnesota Press.

Abu-Lughod, J. (2007) *Race, Space, and Riots in Chicago, New York, and Los Angeles*. New York: Oxford University Press.

Introduction

Janet Lippman Abu-Lughod was a leading figure in the evolution of urban studies. She made major contributions to world systems theory, social analysis, historical method, and comparative urbanism. She was also a tireless institution builder, founding and leading a series of urban programs and research centers, and cultivating a worldwide network of faculty, students, activists, and professionals committed to more just and equitable cities. As an early adopter of computer-based data processing and a gifted statistical modeler, she broke new ground in the integration of quantitative and qualitative methods in social research. Her scholarship moved deftly between the *longue durée* of empires, trade routes, and wars, and the fine-grained human relations found in a Cairene souk or Chicago neighborhood. One of her key accomplishments was to assert the importance of cities in world systems theory, preparing the ground for the development of 'global cities' scholarship.

When she died in 2013, Abu-Lughod was Professor Emerita of Sociology and Historical Studies at The New School in New York, and Professor Emerita of Sociology at Northwestern University.

Academic biography and research focus

Janet Lippman was born in 1928 in Newark, NJ. She formed her commitment to cities early in her life: in high school she read the works of Lewis Mumford, and devoted her senior project to the literature of the Harlem Renaissance. She graduated with honors from the University of Chicago in 1957 and then entered the University's experimental new urban planning program where she earned her MA in 1950. After completing her Master's, Lippman served for two years as Director of Research for the American Society of Planning Officials (ASPO), headquartered in Chicago. In 1951, she married Palestinian-born scholar and activist Ibrahim Abu-Lughod, and they moved to Princeton the next year so that he could complete his PhD in Political Science. During that time, Janet Abu-Lughod served as a research associate at the University of Pennsylvania and as a consultant for the American Council to Improve Our Neighborhoods.

In 1958, the Abu-Lughods moved their young family to Cairo. While Ibrahim directed research for UNESCO, Janet taught at the American University in Cairo and immersed herself in the language, culture, and life of the great city. She worked with the Egyptian government on an analysis of the country's census, published as the *Cairo Fact Book* (1963). She also launched what would become a decade-long project resulting in her first major book, *Cairo: 1001 Years of the City Victorious*. The family returned to the U.S. in 1960, where Abu-Lughod continued to publish work on Cairo and Islamic cities, supported by the National Science Foundation and the Radcliffe Institute. In 1963, she applied to doctoral programs in sociology. Rejected by Yale because the university would not accept a married woman with four young children, she completed her PhD at the University of Massachusetts in 1966. During that time she lectured at Smith College and regularly booked 'machine time' on computers at the MIT-Harvard Joint Center for Urban Studies to process the large data sets for the Cairo book.

In 1967, Janet and Ibrahim Abu-Lughod took positions at Northwestern University. For the next 21 years, she built a strong urban research network and gained a reputation as a provocative and original thinker. With a grant from the U.S. Department of Education, she launched the Program in Comparative Urban Studies at Northwestern, and published the groundbreaking collection *Third World Urbanization* (1977), co-edited with her graduate student Richard Hay, Jr. As early as 1969, Abu-Lughod had begun preparing for large-scale comparative research on cities in Egypt, Tunisia, and Morocco. While in Rabat she worked with government officials on a statistical analysis of the recent Moroccan census, which they completed in 1975. In 1976, she received a Guggenheim Fellowship to complete her comparative study. When data from Egypt and Tunisia failed to materialize, she focused her study on Morocco, published as *Rabat: Urban Apartheid in Morocco* in 1980. Throughout the 1980s, Abu-Lughod published research on the growth and development of Middle Eastern and North African cities, as well as the impact of Islam on urban forms and cultures. She devoted increasing attention to relations between men and women and the dynamics of family formation in cities. Her work also grew broader, taking in wide sweeps of geography and temporality, presaging the 1989 publication of her landmark book *Before European Hegemony: The World System A.D. 1250–1350*.

In 1988, Abu-Lughod left Northwestern University for an appointment as Professor of Sociology and Historical Studies at The New School in New York. There she directed the Urban Research Center, chaired the Department of Sociology, and mentored several new generations of doctoral students. She also published some of her most influential work in urban studies, shifting her research back to the U.S. after what she described as 'lengthy digressions' into the *longue durée* of world systems (Abu-Lughod, 1999: x). Her first major U.S.-based book, *From Urban Village to East Village* (1994), presents an innovative return to 'Chicago School' community research, updated with due attention to structural conditions and global contexts.

Abu-Lughod retired from The New School in 1999, though remained highly productive. That year saw the publication of her book *New York, Chicago, Los Angeles: America's Global Cities*. Funded by a grant from the American Council of Learned Societies, her research pulled the U.S. urban system squarely into the global cities debates. She followed the book with a sequel focused on urban unrest, *Race, Space, and Riots in Chicago, New York, and Los Angeles*, published in 2007. Janet Abu-Lughod passed away on 3 August 2013 in New York City at age 85.

Key ideas

At root, Abu-Lughod's work emerges out of the productive tension between normative commitments to rights and justice and the quest for a quantitative science of human society – a tension that increasingly defined social research in the 1960s and 1970s (cf. **Brian Berry, David Harvey**). Abu-Lughod approached her work first and foremost as a moral inquiry. In the introduction to *Rabat*, she explains that her purpose is not to engage in an 'antiquarian exercise in reconstructing the past,' but rather to 'explain the present and to pose a moral problem for the future' (1980: xviii). For her, the problem is twofold. First, can the postcolonial state create a new order after decades of colonial rule? Second, can scholars trained within national disciplinary frameworks contribute meaningfully to this project? As sociologist Christopher Chase-Dunn (2014) noted, this latter concern led Abu-Lughod to develop a sustained challenge to the Eurocentrism of Western social science.

Abu-Lughod's experience living in Cairo fundamentally reshaped her scholarship. Confronting the limits of the Chicago School to provide an explanatory framework for North African urbanism, she turned to the work of *Annales* historians in the 1960s, absorbing their commitment to the *longue durée*. However, she rejected the *Annales* view of climate and geography as determinative of culture and history. She agreed with her contemporaries Immanuel Wallerstein and **Manuel Castells** that cities are not simply spatial isolates, but rather emerge out of large-scale extra-territorial forces such as trade, technology, wealth accumulation, and state formation. But she argued that cities are not reducible to these forces, and that every city reveals unique characteristics grounded in particular cultural, religious, demographic, and historical factors. One of Abu-Lughod's key accomplishments, then, was to assert the importance of cities in world systems theory, preparing the ground for the development of 'global cities' scholarship (cf. **Saskia Sassen**).

Dissatisfied with the political and economic lacunae of *Annales* historiography, Abu-Lughod turned increasingly to the Marxist tradition, with its focus on forms of labor, modes of production, and structural inequalities. However, like many of her contemporaries, she acknowledged the limits of Marxism to explain the differential impacts of race, religion, gender, and other categories of experience. She also rejected the notion common among Marxists that the city is merely an epiphenomenal product of economic forces, arguing instead that cities have manifold, autonomous, often ancient patterns of development, and must be taken on those terms. In *Rabat*, she demonstrated that a Marxist interpretation alone could not account for the viciousness of racial apartheid favored by French colonial officials (1980: xvii).

In an effort to reconcile Marxist structuralism with social research methods sensitive to diverse cultural experiences, Abu-Lughod turned to world systems theory. Like many of her colleagues, she was excited by the publication in 1974 of Immanuel Wallerstein's landmark book *The Modern World System*. However, several key points of Wallerstein's thesis did not square with Abu-Lughod's detailed knowledge of Middle Eastern and North African cities, particularly his argument that the 'world system' itself was a *de novo* product of Western European intellect, might, and conquest.

In response to Wallerstein, Abu-Lughod produced what would become her most influential book, *Before European Hegemony: The World System, A.D. 1250–1350*. The book rejects the notion that the world system was created by Europe after 1500, or that trade dominance somehow comprised a new condition of world social relations. For Abu-Lughod, the 13th and 14th centuries were crucial for understanding the spatial, temporal, and cultural dimensions of world historical developments. She argues that the so-called 'rise of the West' is better understood as a process of filling the vacuum created by the 'fall of the East' after centuries of trade dominance. The establishment of mercantile networks and the ensuing conflicts around the Mediterranean basin in the 1600s represented a shift from the earlier domination of China, India, and Central Asia in trade. Her findings provoked debates in major journals and conferences, and carved out a capacious new area for research.

In the 1990s and 2000s, Abu-Lughod returned to the concerns of the Chicago School, but now within the contexts of global transformations. Her influential book *New York, Chicago, Los Angeles* rescues the cities from standard urban biography, placing their differential industrial densities, financial capacities, and social relations within political economic contexts that extend well beyond the local or even national scale. In *Race, Space, and Riots in Chicago, New York, and Los Angeles* she argues that the urban uprisings of the 1960s responded to specific and proximate episodes of injustice; however, they were rooted in processes such as racial segregation, urbanization, migration, and the dislocation of capital. In her view, these processes are not simply the products of recent disruptions, but rather unfold unevenly across 400 years of global transformations within which U.S. cities and race relations took form.

Contributions to urban studies

Over the course of her career, Janet Abu-Lughod's vision of cities as objects of study went through several stages. She made lasting contributions to urban studies in each of them. In her early work, Abu-Lughod's scholarship reflected her Chicago School training, with its emphasis on social research, statistical analysis, and close observation of neighborhoods (cf. **Elijah Anderson, Harvey Molotch**). In the 1970s and 1980s, Abu-Lughod turned increasingly to questions of colonialism, urban planning, and the postcolonial city (cf. **Jane M. Jacobs, Ananya Roy**). Her essay 'Designing a city for all' (Abu-Lughod, 1971b) provides an early articulation of a 'right to the city' position. *Rabat: Urban Apartheid in Morocco* examines the role of colonial town planners in fragmenting social relations, spatializing racial and class differences, and fostering uneven development. Her seminal article 'The Islamic city: Historic myth, Islamic essence, and contemporary relevance' (Abu-Lughod, 1987) critiques the overdetermined notion of 'Islamic' urbanism common among both Western and Eastern intellectuals. And *Before European Hegemony: The World System, A.D. 1250–1350* explicitly rejects the Eurocentric notion of the Western city as the point of departure for urban history and theory.

Throughout the 1990s Abu-Lughod continued to establish new ground in urban studies, most succinctly realized in her textbook *Changing Cities* (Abu-Lughod, 1991). Confronting the Chicago School legacy head on, she argues that 'there is no such thing as "urbanism as a way of life" which, independent of the cultural context or the particular inhabitants, leads to predictable forms of social interactions' (p. 6). And while her work prioritized economic conditions, she refused to reduce urban change to the dialectics of capital formation and class struggle. More than many of her generation, she emphasized the crucial role of religion, family formation, and the position of women in the development of cities over time (see also **Dolores Hayden**).

As with any provocative body of work, Abu-Lughod's scholarship has its detractors. André Gunder Frank and Barry Gills argue that her explication of the 'rise of the West' via the 'decline of the East' overlooks many crucial continuities that might have been better understood had she incorporated the East Indies, West Africa, and the Swahili coast into her analysis of trade circuits (Chase-Dunn, 2014: 178–179). In her rejection of a unitary 'Islamic' urbanism, some scholars suggest that she deploys a narrow definition of Islam, and underestimates the importance of Muslim planning and design codes (Haneda and Miura, 1994: 7). **Neil Brenner** (2001) shows that the broad analytic approach in her later work occasionally militates against a careful disaggregation of local conditions from global forces as causal elements in urban change. Moreover, such analyses rely on notions of the 'local' and the 'global' as possessing distinct, readily discernable contents rather than having overlapping, entwined features (cf. **Ash Amin**). Consequently, globally scaled phenomena such as capital flight, industrial dislocation, labor migration, and resource flows tend to appear more as fixed background context rather than variable constituents of urban transformation.

Nevertheless, Abu-Lughod's scholarship helped urban studies through several transitional periods, and she produced an oeuvre of work that continues to resonate today. She was an early innovator in the use of computers for large-scale data analysis of cities. Her research provided a model for generations of scholars in work across spatial and temporal scales, and has inspired much of the recent enthusiasm for comparative and postcolonial perspectives in global urban studies (cf. **Jennifer Robinson, Ananya Roy**). Above all, she came to see cities as resilient products of human creativity and struggle. In 1967, just after completing the first draft of her book *Cairo*, war erupted between Egypt and Israel. 'The future of Cairo', she wrote, 'was suddenly shrouded.' Despite the immense toll, however, she concluded that 'no creation of man is capable of retaining its underlying organization so obdurately in the face of dramatic shifts in culture and technology as the city' (Abu-Lughod, 1971a: 238–239).

Secondary sources and references

Abu-Lughod, J. (1961) 'Migrant adjustment to city life: The Egyptian case', *American Journal of Sociology*, 67(1): 22–32.

Abu-Lughod, J. (1971b) 'Designing a city for all', in L.S. Bourne (ed.) *Internal Structure of the City*. Oxford: Oxford University Press.

→Abu-Lughod, J. (1987) 'The Islamic city: Historic myth, Islamic essence, and contemporary relevance', *International Journal of Middle East Studies*, 19(2): 155–176.

Abu-Lughod, J. (1991) *Changing Cities: Urban Sociology*. New York: HarperCollins.

Abu-Lughod, J. (ed.) (1994) *From Urban Village to East Village: The Battle for New York's Lower East Side*. Oxford: Blackwell.

Abu-Lughod, J. (2000) 'Lewis Mumford's contribution to the history of cities: A critical appraisal', First Annual Lewis Mumford Lecture, University of Albany. Available at: http://mumford.albany.edu/mumford/files/1st_annual_mumford_lecture.pdf (accessed 18 June 2016).

Abu-Lughod, L. and Attiya, E.E.D. (1963) *Cairo Fact Book*. Cairo: Social Research Center, American University of Cairo.

Abu-Lughod, L. and Hay, R. Jr. (eds) (1977) *Third World Urbanization*. Chicago, IL: Maaroufa Press.

Brenner, N. (2001) 'World city theory, globalization and the comparative-historical method', *Urban Affairs Review*, 37(1): 124–147.

Chase-Dunn, C. (2014) 'In memoriam: Janet L. Abu-Lughod's contributions to world-systems research', *Journal of World Systems Research*, 20(2): 173–184.

Haneda, M. and Miura, T. (eds) (1994) *Islamic Urban Studies: Historical Review and Perspectives*. New York: Kegan Paul International.

Sarbib, J.L. (1983) 'The University of Chicago Program in Planning: A retrospective look', *Journal of Planning Education and Research*, 2(2): 77–81.

Wallerstein, I. (1974) *The Modern World System*. New York: Academic Press.

2

Ash Amin

Junjia Ye, Massey University

Key urban writings

Amin, A. (2002) 'Ethnicity and the multicultural city: Living with diversity', *Environment and Planning A*, 34(6): 959–980.

Amin, A. and Thrift, N. (2002) *Cities: Reimagining the Urban*. Cambridge: Polity.

Amin, A. (2008) 'Collective culture and urban public space', *City*, 12(1): 5–24.

Amin, A. (2012) *Land of Strangers*. Cambridge: Polity.

Amin, A. (2013) 'The urban condition: A challenge to social science', *Public Culture*, 25(2): 201–208.

Introduction

Ash Amin is a geographer best known for his challenging work on the spatialities of contemporary urban life. His extensive writings confront taken-for-granted assumptions about how social scientists should think about cities, questioning for example simplistic yet deeply held ideas about what is big or small, near and far, global and local, material and immaterial. His writings ask readers to reconsider the forms and dynamics of the powers that circulate through and within cities.

For Amin power is not just the product of human intent. It is also produced through a multitude of hybrid, more-than-human entities and networks. These include not just the built environment, but also things like infrastructure, information, code, mood even, or affect. This approach has created a series of accounts of urban life that are unsettling and inspiring in their originality. In Amin's writing urban public spaces are defined by the generative forces of materiality and infrastructure as much as they are by interpersonal relations. Globalization is not an abstract force, but rather a locally-specific process of connecting with places elsewhere. Economies are a series of cultural practices as much as they are the agglomeration of capital. And everyday realities like race and ethnicity are hybrids of biopolitics and vernacular practices rather than essential categories. Amin's scholarship presents a range of imaginative, if far from straightforward, perspectives on the metropolis as a site of conjunctures and disjunctures through which urban spatialities are perpetually reconfigured.

Amin is currently the 1931 Chair of Geography at the University of Cambridge.

Academic biography and research focus

Born in Kampala, Uganda, Amin is a British academic of Pakistani descent. He graduated from the University of Reading in 1979 with a Bachelor of Arts in Italian studies, and stayed at Reading to complete his PhD in the Department of Geography. Amin then moved to Newcastle University, where he began as Research Fellow at the Centre for Urban and Regional Development Studies, followed by becoming Lecturer and eventually Professor of Geography. In 2005 Amin moved to Durham University and was the Founding Executive Director of the Institute of Advanced Study. He took up his current position at Cambridge in 2011.

Early in his career, Amin's focus was economic geography, and in particular regional development and globalization in Europe. His work explored the emergence of new industrial complexes within the context of the extended reach of global corporate networks. In a series of edited books including *Technological Change, Industrial Restructuring and Regional Development* (with John Goddard, 1986), *Towards a New Europe? Structural Change in the European Economy* (1991), *Post-Fordism: A Reader* (1995), *Globalization, Institutions, and Regional Development in Europe* (with Nigel Thrift, 1995), Amin played a key role in shaping debates around the emergence of post-Fordist forms of industrial organization. His work examined the question of whether Europe's industrial landscape was being remade as sets of dynamic post-Fordist regional industrial clusters, or was simply reorganized by a new international, inter-regional, division of labor centering on the corporate networks of global firms. These concerns about how different forms of economic organizations are held together over space, and across administrative boundaries, led Amin to examine in detail the dynamics of the spatial development of the knowledge economy. Here his work was distinctive for insisting upon the enduring importance of tangible goods, personal networks and tacit knowledge within this economy, a position that ran counter to conventional wisdom that tended to imagine knowledge as weightless and placeless (Amin et al., 2000). Working with the economist Patrick Cohendet, Amin pulled together these key arguments in *Architectures of Knowledge* (2004).

Over time Amin's writing became more urban focused. Building on his earlier foci on regional knowledge networks, Amin started exploring how cities are entangled with a host of distant connections. In doing so, he developed novel ways of thinking about globalization and proximity. He also worked to find more supple, intellectually imaginative ways of thinking about the dynamics of ethnic, multicultural and community cohesion. Amin was convinced that the social sciences needed to invent a new repertoire of concepts to make sense of how cities functioned, given the inadequacy of established ways – whether mainstream or otherwise – of thinking about cities in the context of contemporary patterns of globalization and the rise of novel informational technologies. This thinking led to *Cities: Reimagining the Urban* (2002), co-authored with Nigel Thrift, which set out to articulate a new ontology of the city as the 'irreducible product of mixture' (2002: 3). Or put another way, urbanization should be understood as flows and interactions that constantly generate new spatial formations.

A key feature of Amin's theoretical style is his willingness to draw on insights from a plurality of social and theoretical traditions; he takes as much from American pragmatist philosophy and post-humanism as he does from critical social theory. This provides a quite different take on cities to that offered by political economy and neo-Marxist thinkers. Rather than following the conventional interest in forms of domination and oppression by certain kinds of actors and institutions, Amin's urban scholarship insists that cities must be imagined and analyzed in terms of their heterogeneity and particularity. These various and nuanced streams of his work are brought together more recently in *Land of Strangers* (2012), which is an interdisciplinary provocation to engage with the cultural complexity of the worlds we inhabit in subtle, localized ways. It looks at relations that are not reducible to interpersonal ties but which are realized through all sorts of objects, spaces and entities, human and non-human, to offer new ways of thinking about living with diversity and forging a different politics of the stranger. This is a thematic he takes up in more detail in his most recent book *The Arts of the Political: New Openings for the Left* (2013), like *Cities* (2002) co-authored with Nigel Thrift.

Key ideas

Amin's writing on cities can be read as a series of contributions to interlocking debates on subjects such as globalization, cultural identity, community and race. However, what ties his work together and lends it a distinctive style is his commitment to understanding cities in terms of their socio-material hybridity. Attending to the more-than-human, more-than-interpersonal nature of everyday life are key components of Amin's thinking. His writings imagine a progressive politics engaged through a plurality of networks, affiliations and causes, resulting in people forging new kinds of political identities. Rather than an assumed solidarity struggling against a global hegemon, Amin recognizes that it is through such multiplicitous relationships that a sense of the urban commons can be kept lively and buoyant. Broadly speaking, his writing can be summarized under three headings.

The urban social condition

Amin is interested in the nature of contemporary forms of urban togetherness (Amin, 2012, 2013). He argues that the urban needs to be analyzed through the encounter, which incorporates the importance of seemingly random or insignificant and short-lived acts, relations and presences in the making of cities, and he stresses the importance of mobility, flows and networks. The result is a social field that is temporary and hybrid, composed of strings of association of more or less coherence, durability and reach, and highly uncertain (Amin, 2007). Cities are not just clusters of neighborhoods, nor are they simply complexes of accumulation. Indeed, one of the cogent points Amin's writing makes is that cities do not compete for accumulation but rather, firms and other institutions located within cities do. In this sense, cities are not themselves economic actors but are dynamic sites facilitating economic culture (Amin and Thrift, 2007). This forms part of his approach to reimagine the urban economy. Life in the city may be highly structured and regulated, but the unexpected, serendipity, lack of control and being subjected to the suspension of order are also part of the urban condition.

Strangerhood

A key aspect of urban encounter that Amin has been interested in is everyday life between strangers. His book *Land of Strangers* (2012) engages with the cultural complexity of the worlds we inhabit in provocative ways that progress beyond concepts of everyday multiculturalism, hybridity and cosmopolitanism. This work is a response to earlier policies and narratives of multiculturalism, one that comes to terms with the thoroughly heterogeneous nature of current urban societies, which are crucibles of diverse stranger gatherings. Rather than seeking policy interventions to foster closer ties of social cohesion among strangers, Amin instead argues for a politics of the impersonal so that distance and dis-attention are respected (p. 7). For Amin, it is the collective, public acceptance of this ethos that will 'help to render the strange familiar and the familiar strange, and collective life a constant negotiation of difference' (p. 7). Through this principle, then, emerge trust, mutuality, obligation and creativity; the products rather than causes of collaborative engagement (p. 8). Such, he argues, is the nature of diversity and social life in cities populated by strangers. While Amin remains open about who the stranger might be, he does have two broad strands of who might be considered the Other. The first would be the racialized stranger, which, following 9/11, are increasingly migrants, asylum seekers and refugees (p. 9). Second are more generalized Others created through social and political processes that position many different groups as 'outsiders' (Noble, 2013: 32).

One of the most compelling points of Amin's writings on strangerhood is his description of the ways in which strangers stop being so strange to one another through public cooperation. While it is not that they necessarily become friends or enemies, strangers can, over time, become accustomed to one another's difference. These familiar strangers, as I call them in my own work, do not exist in a timeless, rhetorical vacuum but rather, are situated within various and changing degrees and modes of familiarity and strangeness from one another (Ye, 2013). This is to say that the social experience of city life is cumulative and comprised of heterogeneous forms of sociality. Amin points out that 'not all forms of situated practice bring strangers into purposeful contact with each other, capable of affective transformation through engagement' (2012: 59). Regardless, these localized practices are just as influential in the creation of public space. These shifting contours of familiarity and strangeness texturize togetherness and coexistence in everyday city life. Furthermore, these contours entail limits on human recognition in the context of swirling multiplicity, where people cannot possibly fully know or even like everyone they meet in public. At the same time, the mutual trust and obligation that strangers share create an urban commons in which everyday life is reproduced. Amin's conceptualization of the stranger is thus significant in highlighting not only the possibilities of social interactions but also the contradictions of cooperation and conflict, of hospitality and hostility.

Liveliness of urban worlds

The prominence of heterogeneity in Amin's work extends to the material as well. In his work on encounters, Amin not only refers to interpersonal human actors but also non-human entities such as infrastructure, animals, technology and viral life (2007, 2014). For Amin, 'the collective impulses of public space are the result of pre-cognitive and tacit human response to a condition of "situated multiplicity", the thrown togetherness of bodies, mass and matter, and of many uses and needs in a shared physical space' (2008: 8). His most recent work maintains that our affinities to social life are shaped not only through our interpersonal ties but also through the engagements we develop with the non-human, material world of things and spaces. Simply put, neither is there sociality without the materiality of 'stuff' nor can social life be reducible to the purely human alone (2014: 138). Rather than assuming that objects enter from the outside to shape human lives, Amin argues that the entanglements of stuff, social ties and affect generate connections between known and unknown others without straightforward civic and political connotations (2012). The materiality of human habitat forms the very basis of social identity and affiliation, creating habits of negotiating across difference.

Contributions to urban studies

Amin's contributions to wide-ranging debates about regional economies, social and cultural life, infrastructure, race and multiculturalism, governance and globalization have been tremendous. His work is often unsettling, challenging and disturbingly alien to orthodox habits of urban thinking. **David Harvey** and **Neil Smith** have criticized his work for over-extending the politics of multiplicity, resulting in disabled forms of political thought and action by the academic Left. Amin argues that critical social science, and geography in particular, needs to recognize plurality, rather than try to fit into a singular framework, Marxist or otherwise (Amin and Thrift, 2005).

Much of Amin's scholarship throughout his career speaks to the situatedness of practice as well as the porosity and the multi-sidedness of cities. Amin and Graham (1997) coined the term 'the multiplex city' as a critique of urban theories that sought to generalize without taking these elements into serious consideration. The contemporary urban, for Amin, is the co-presence of multiple spaces, times and networks of relations, tying local sites, subjects and fragments into globalizing networks of economic, social and cultural change. This rejection of generalizing claims in favor of a more nuanced embrace of cross-sectional urban complexity has formed an incisive critique of existing theories of urbanization, especially those rooted in political economy, which characteristically abstract from (stated) principles of explanatory pertinence, necessarily privileging some drivers of urban change over others amid contingent modes of realization. Recognizing these forms of situated practice further emphasizes the porosity and open-endedness of the city and city-making. In short, they urge an anti-essentialist reading of the city (Peck, 2015). Amin's wide-ranging work also contributes to a politics of urbanity mainly by focusing on politics *in* place. His work marks the need to see political activity in places as plural, open and contested (Amin et al., 2000).

Embedded throughout this work is the notion of a distinctive politics of place. Power is understood as a circulating force, enacted moment by moment, operating through local propinquities and distanciated networks, in a world of contingency and constant becoming. Some have questioned the haziness of Amin's theoretical style, arguing that it overplays the multiplicity and complexity found in cities. And as **Michael Storper** and Allen Scott (2016) have wondered, if we cannot generalize about urban processes how do we sensibly compare one city with another? Nonetheless, taken as a whole Amin's urban writings are among the most imaginative and intellectually provocative work currently being undertaken within urban studies.

Secondary sources and references

Amin, A. (ed.) (1991) *Towards a New Europe? Structural Change in the European Economy.* Cheltenham: Edward Elgar.

Amin, A. (1995) *Post-Fordism: A Reader.* Oxford: Blackwell.

Amin, A. (2001) 'Spatialities of globalization', *Environment and Planning A*, 34(1): 385–399.

Amin, A. (2007) 'Re-thinking the urban social', *City*, 11(1): 100–114.

Amin, A. (2010) 'Remainders of race', *Theory, Culture & Society*, 27(1): 1–23.

Amin, A. (2014) 'Lively infrastructure', *Theory, Culture & Society*, 31(7/8): 137–161.

Amin, A. and Cohendet, P. (2004) *Architectures of Knowledge.* Oxford: Oxford University Press on Demand.

Amin, A. and Goddard, J.B. (eds) (1986) *Technological Change, Industrial Restructuring and Regional Development.* London: Allen and Unwin.

Amin, A. and Graham, S. (1997) 'The ordinary city', *Transactions of the Institute of British Geographers*, 22(4): 411–429.

Amin, A. and Thrift, N. (1992) 'Neo-Marshallian nodes in global networks', *International Journal of Urban and Regional Research*, 16(4): 571–587.

Amin, A. and Thrift, N. (eds) (1995) *Globalization, Institutions, and Regional Development in Europe.* Oxford: Oxford University Press.

Amin, A. and Thrift, N. (2005) 'What's left? Just the future', *Antipode*, 37(2): 220–238.

Amin, A. and Thrift, N. (2007) 'Cultural-economy and cities', *Progress in Human Geography*, 31(2): 143–161.

Amin, A. and Thrift, N. (2013) *The Arts of the Political: New Openings for the Left.* Durham, NC: Duke University Press.

Amin, A., Massey, D. and Thrift, N. (2000) *Cities for the Many Not the Few.* Bristol: Policy Press.

Noble, G. (2013) 'Strange familiarities: A response to Ash Amin's *Land of Strangers*', *Identities: Global Studies in Culture and Power*, 20(1): 31–36.

Peck, J. (2015) 'Cities beyond compare?', *Regional Studies*, 49(1): 160–189.

Storper, M. and Scott, A. (2016) 'Current debates in urban theory: A critical assessment', *Urban Studies*, 53(6): 1114–1136.

Ye, J. (2013) 'Note on the familiar stranger: Thinking through ambivalence in public spaces. Part one', *NUS FASS Cities Cluster Research Blog.* Available at: http://blog.nus.edu.sg/fasrda/2013/08/23/notes-on-the-familiar-stranger-thinking-through-ambivalent-encounters-in-public-spaces-part-one/

3 Elijah Anderson

Michael DeLand, Yale University

Key urban writings

Anderson, A. (1978) *A Place on the Corner*. Chicago: University of Chicago Press.

Anderson, A. (1990) *Streetwise: Race, Class, and Change in an Urban Community*. Chicago: University of Chicago Press.

Anderson, A. (1999) *Code of the Street: Decency, Violence, and the Moral Life of the Inner City*. New York: W.W. Norton.

Anderson, A. (2011) *The Cosmopolitan Canopy: Race and Civility in Everyday Life*. New York: W.W. Norton.

Anderson, A. (2015) 'The white space', *Sociology of Race and Ethnicity*, 1(1): 10–21.

Introduction

Elijah Anderson is an urban ethnographer. His research focuses primarily on Chicago and Philadelphia, yet the implications of his work extend well beyond those particular settings. His writings have had a profound impact on understandings of how racial, ethnic, and class divisions are lived in everyday urban contexts.

For Anderson, ethnography involves the systematic study of culture. Drawing on Clifford Geertz's (1983) concept 'local knowledge' he conceptualizes culture as a set of shared understandings in a particular community. Anderson has undertaken decades of ethnographic fieldwork in which he has gained access to diverse settings in which people make sense of the world and their place within it, and deal with the practical challenges of everyday life. He has hung out with drug dealers and thieves, spent time with families in their homes, accompanied black men to their corporate office jobs, shared food and coffee in vibrant marketplaces, and drunk beers on street corners in ghetto neighborhoods. By representing these and other social settings in straightforward prose, Anderson's texts shed light on issues of urban poverty and violence, racial segregation and discrimination, group life, public space, and neighborhood change.

He is currently the William K. Lanman, Jr. Professor of Sociology at Yale University.

Academic biography and research focus

Elijah Anderson was born in the American South where his parents and grandparents worked on cotton plantations. After World War II his family followed the path of many Southern black families and moved north. His father attained stable work in an Indiana factory and Anderson spent his childhood in a racially mixed working-class community. These early life experiences shaped his intellectual interest in race and class in America.

After graduating with a BA in sociology from the Indiana University Bloomington, Anderson began his doctoral studies in sociology at the University of Chicago. There, he was influenced by department chair Morris Janowitz and urban ethnographer Gerald Suttles. While mainstream sociological thought had shifted toward macro-functionalist theories and quantitative methodologies, his teachers were dedicated to preserving interest in the old Chicago School of Sociology. Scholars in Chicago's sociology department had produced classic field studies during the 1920s and 1930s by exploring issues of urban ecology, social organization, and social interaction. Anderson's work descends from and extends this tradition. Anderson worked with Howard Becker – an iconic scholar of deviance and social interaction at Northwestern University – during the final year of his doctoral studies.

Anderson conducted fieldwork for his dissertation at Jelly's, a bar and liquor store on the city's predominantly African American south side. He befriended some of the regular patrons and documented the local rules, roles, and understandings that shaped the community at Jelly's. This fieldwork ultimately resulted in his first book, *A Place on the Corner* (1978). The book has become a classic in the field of urban ethnography for its thick descriptions of everyday life and nuanced analyses of patterns of interaction at the bar. As Anderson documents, Jelly's offered the men a place to be recognized and respected, a meaningful respite from the difficult material and emotional circumstances of a segregated black ghetto.

After a brief stint at Swarthmore College, Anderson was hired in the Sociology Department at the University of Pennsylvania. A perpetual fieldworker, Anderson quickly started getting to know the city of Philadelphia and its diverse neighborhoods and public spaces. This fieldwork provided the data for each of his next three books. Compared to *A Place on the Corner*, his second book *Streetwise* (1990) and this third book *Code of the Street* (1999) move away from the micro-group dynamics of a single setting in order to understand broader patterns of neighborhood change and inter-group violence. To speak to these larger issues he began to set his field observations more explicitly within their specific historical context in order to show how deindustrialization, the declining blue-collar job market, the crack epidemic, and gentrification were influencing social life on the ground.

Anderson's most recent book, *The Cosmopolitan Canopy* (2011), explores Philadelphia's public spaces. He shows that they can facilitate the gathering and intermingling of people who would otherwise never come into contact in their segregated residential neighborhoods. And yet, these charming spaces often hide the still-pervasive race line that can quickly be re-drawn and defended in painful reminders of black and brown people's conditional acceptance into American society.

In nearly three decades at University of Pennsylvania Anderson received valuable mentoring and developed collegial relationships with Erving Goffman, William Labov, and Renee Fox. In 2007 he accepted his current position at Yale University. He heads the Urban Ethnography Project, a research center dedicated to continuing the tradition of ethnographic fieldwork in American sociology.

Key ideas

Many of Anderson's key ideas can be traced back to his first book, *A Place on the Corner*. Through his rich and vivid depiction of the everyday life of a seemingly innocuous bar in Chicago he began speaking to issues of racial segregation, discrimination, ghettoization, poverty, and morality that he would continue to unpack in his later books. These substantive themes emerge through three distinct, though ultimately interrelated, meanings of place in *A Place on the Corner*.

Most concretely place refers to a physical, geographic, or ecological location that has subjective meaning to the people who inhabit it. In *A Place on the Corner* he shows how Jelly's bar functions as a meaningful locale in which the men can 'be somebody' away from their private family and work lives that were often fraught with various kinds of trouble. In *Streetwise* Anderson adopts a more explicitly comparative perspective by studying two places: a racially mixed gentrifying neighborhood and a racially segregated black ghetto. For residents of these areas 'street wisdom' involves shaping one's public image and projecting confidence while navigating different social milieus. These public performances are always shaped by an awareness of how one's race, gender, and class identity are understood by others in particular social settings. Anderson shows, for example, that the meaning of gentrification is not just in changing land values but in the everyday comportments of black residents who gradually begin to feel out of place in a neighborhood that was once their own. And so as urban places change, the people living in and moving through them must adopt new understandings to become 'wise' once again.

A second meaning of place refers to one's interpersonal status within a particular group or social setting. People develop a sense of themselves as others honor or undermine their claims of personhood and respectability. And so one's place in a local setting is always prone to change and negotiation. Anderson showed how the men at Jelly's created and re-created locally salient status distinctions between 'regulars', 'wineheads,' and 'hoodlums.' When the most respected regulars were not present, certain wineheads and hoodlums would make stronger bids at respectability, claiming a temporary status that would be challenged when other regulars were present. And when Anderson accompanied highly respected regulars to their blue-collar jobs he found that they organized their self-image in a way that recognized their lower occupational status. In these findings Anderson drew on a long history of interactionist research in sociology that shows that the self is fluid, situational, performed, and constantly remade.

While the sensibility for 'place' as an interpersonal status construction is present in much of Anderson's work, it plays a particularly prominent role in *Code of the Street*. Seeking to explain seemingly irrational patterns of violence among young inner-city African American men, Anderson shows that families living in communities lacking police protection, civil law, or sufficient government support have developed a code to guide their interpersonal behavior. The code emphasized the need for respectability, for toughness, and for 'nerve' or 'heart,' all of which demanded that young people show at least some proclivity for violence.

But if everybody in Philadelphia's black ghettos is aware of the 'code,' not everybody embraces it in the same way or to the same degree. Drawing on locally salient folk categories – 'decent' and 'street' – Anderson distinguishes two different orientations toward the code. Street individuals are those who fully embrace the code, living by its edicts and using it to guide their behavior. They are quick to interpret others' behavior as disrespectful and are ready to respond with violence if necessary. They are constantly 'campaigning for respect,' making bids at honor and esteem from others. 'Decent' folks, on the other hand, have a more tenuous relationship with the code and tend to embrace normative frameworks from the wider society. However, as a matter of survival in the ghetto streets even decent folks must occasionally act as if they fully embrace the code's demand for respectability. And so as with the men at Jelly's, ghetto residents code switch, reading situations in order to organize their behavior and get by. Thus, even the most 'decent' children who are fully committed to achieving academic success can get swept up in neighborhood violence as they, at times, embrace the code.

There is one final meaning of place that animates much of Anderson's writing. Influenced greatly by Herbert Blumer's (1958) essay 'Race prejudice as a sense of group position,' Anderson has long been interested in the place of African Americans vis-a-vis white Americans. In *A Place on the Corner* Anderson's depiction of the men's emotional turmoil reminds us of the harsh realities of racial segregation. In recent work Anderson has addressed the American racial hierarchy even more explicitly. *Cosmopolitan Canopy* develops the idea that some public places operate as canopies, bringing together a racially diverse array of individuals under a veneer of civility and respect. And yet, Anderson's research reveals that behind closed doors many black Americans are skeptical. In one memorable scene from the book, a successful black executive was left shaken and frustrated by a white colleague who expressed invasive curiosity and then outright surprise that a black man owned a nice house and expensive car (2011: 259–264). African Americans, Anderson showed, live with a constant awareness that their acceptance into the broader society is conditional. A moment of acute disrespect based on race – a 'nigger moment' – can strike practically anywhere and anytime, even under the pleasant shade of the canopy.

The geographic, interpersonal, and racial meanings of place are always interrelated in Anderson's writing. His most recent work continues to bring them together in novel ways. In a recent essay, for example, Anderson describes how the black ghetto, once a geographically bounded place, has become iconic. In modern America black skin is symbolically associated with the poor inner-city ghetto even when the person holds elite status and moves through elite places. And thus, many African Americans continue to feel outside the American mainstream at the same time as a gradual racial incorporation process has facilitated some upward mobility into the middle and upper classes (Anderson, 2012). This symbolic racism becomes especially salient when black Americans enter or navigate through 'white space' (Anderson, 2015). Anderson teaches us how in concrete (geographic) places, actors campaign for their (interpersonal) place, even as their (racial) place in society can undermine and frustrate their efforts.

Contributions to urban studies

Within the field of urban studies Anderson's writings uniquely reveal how large patterns of urban change practically shape and transform everyday life on the ground. He does this by providing experience-near depictions of his research subjects' lives. Rather than providing previously unknown facts about the social world, Anderson compels us to feel empathy for people living in ways conventionally understood as morally ambiguous or detestable. In contrast to many social scientific approaches, empathy is precisely the byproduct of what David Matza (1969: 8) described as the 'rigorous and disciplined humanism' of naturalistic sociology.

This approach differs dramatically from macro-theoretically inclined scholars like **Mike Davis** and **Loïc Wacquant,** who seek to explore the invisible structural forces that dominate people behind their backs. In a highly cited debate over the merits of *Code of the Street,* Wacquant (2002) criticized Anderson for thin theoretical attention to the role of the state, for reifying categories of 'decent' and 'street,' for siding with those who abide by middle-class values, and for re-describing the phenomenon of 'the street' rather than explaining its powerful hold on ghetto residents. For Wacquant, Anderson's 'conservative' and 'romantic' notions of ghetto decency are evidence of a neoliberal ideology that individualizes urban ills and lays blame on the victims themselves.

Anderson's (2002) response defended the merits of *Code* and shed light on the philosophical origins of the critique. Wacquant would have preferred to understand the 'street' orientation as stemming from a deep seated desire to disrupt and resist hegemonic power structures. But no matter how much more politically palatable that interpretation was to Wacquant, Anderson's subjects did not see their experiences in these ways. And if Anderson has a central political position, it is to paint – or in the language of ethnography, represent – an honest picture of the lives and circumstances of people as they themselves understand them.

This focus on local subjectivities also sets his work in parallel with scholars like **Teresa Caldeira** and **Sharon Zukin,** who, while paying attention to everyday experiences, analyze processes of urban change with an aim toward producing a more generalized narrative. By setting local understandings and folk categories in their historical, racial, and economic context, Anderson seeks to show how larger scale processes shape the texture of life on the ground. While many urban scholars have begun to turn their analyses to global change and development, Anderson has remained steadfast in rendering the global as mere context for in-depth explorations of local ways of life.

Anderson's accounts of urban life have infiltrated and transformed ongoing debates in the fields of public policy and planning, education, criminology, and social work. When American practitioners and educators design interventions to deal with social problems in the city they often turn to Anderson's texts to learn about the texture of the lives they hope to impact. Some have tried to use quantitative methods to test the generalizability of his theses on neighborhood life and street violence in other settings. Municipal agencies have begun to examine his description of the 'canopy' for insights into how to create, design, and facilitate integrative public spaces. And while scholars of urban inequality like William Julius Wilson and Michael B. Katz have stressed the primacy of social class, Anderson's texts have consistently pushed everyday racial injustice into the conversation.

Working within the pragmatist and interactionist tradition, Anderson constantly shows rather than tells what life is like for his research subjects. His work endures partly for its analytic insight and partly for his ability to provide vivid descriptions of social life that serve as windows into social worlds that many of his academic readers would never otherwise encounter. As one admirer notes, 'Anderson's work is good largely to the extent that he has more and better fieldnotes on street life in black American cities than anyone else, and the extent to which he shows them to us' (Katz, 2004: 86). Anderson's work will endure as scholars continue wrestling with questions about race, class, and inequality in the city and need a cool headed observer to show them around.

Secondary sources and references

Anderson, E. (2002) 'The ideologically driven critique', *American Journal of Sociology*, 107(6): 1533–1550.

Anderson, E. (2012) 'The iconic ghetto', *The Annals of the American Academy of Political and Social Science*, 642(1): 8–24.

Blumer, H. (1958) 'Race prejudice as a sense of group position', *The Pacific Sociological Review*, 1(1): 3–7.

Geertz, C. (1983) 'Local knowledge: Fact and law in comparative perspective', in *Local Knowledge: Further Essays in Interpretive Anthropology*. New York: Basic Books.

Katz, J. (2004) *Commonsense Criteria*. Arlington, VA: National Science Foundation.

Matza, D. (1969) *Becoming Deviant*. Englewood Cliffs, NJ: Prentice-Hall.

Wacquant, L. (2002) 'Scrutinizing the street: Poverty, morality, and the pitfalls of urban ethnography', *American Journal of Sociology*, 107(6): 1468–1532.

4 Michael Batty

Helen Couclelis, University of California, Santa Barbara

Key urban writings

Batty, M. (1976) *Urban Modelling: Algorithms, Calibrations, Predictions*. Cambridge: Cambridge University Press.
Batty, M. and Longley, P. (1994) *Fractal Cities: A Geometry of Form and Function*. London and San Diego, CA: Academic Press.
Batty, M. (2005) *Cities and Complexity: Understanding Cities with Cellular Automata, Agent-Based Models, and Fractals*. Cambridge, MA: MIT Press.
Batty, M. (2013a) *The New Science of Cities*. Cambridge, MA: MIT Press.

Introduction

Michael Batty is a British geographer, urban theorist, computational urban modeler, and city and regional planner. His prolific career started in the early 1970s and continues strong more than 45 years later. Batty has contributed not one or two, but at least four perspectives on cities: viewed as the objects of planning; as forms generated by rules reflecting population dynamics; as the expressions on the ground of complex socio-spatial systems; and as the physical consequences of the networks of interaction that are at the roots of urbanization. Not a quantitative scholar in the sense of specializing in data-driven analyses, Batty's broad interests have always been channeled through a consistently mathematical and computational perspective. Numerous conditions and caveats regarding the limitations of that approach, expressed in his non-technical writings, belie any impressions of narrow positivism.

Batty is the Bartlett Professor of Planning at University College London and Chair of the Centre for Advanced Spatial Analysis (CASA). He has garnered practically every honor achievable in his profession, such as membership in the most prestigious learned societies including the Royal Society, was awarded the CBE (2004) and the 'Prix International de Geographie Vautrin Lud' (2013), sometimes referred to as 'the Nobel Prize of Geography.'

Academic biography and research focus

Michael Batty was born and grew up in Liverpool, where he attended the Quarry Bank High School for Boys, the so-called 'Eton of the Labour Party,' an elite school for gifted youths from mostly non-elite backgrounds[1]. He studied Planning at the University of Manchester under George Chadwick and Brian McLoughlin, who were among the pioneers of the systems approach in urban planning and in the social sciences more generally. Batty's interest in urban models and his life-long pursuit of rational planning and a true science of cities first developed under the influence of his two mentors, and carried over to his first academic post in the Urban Systems Unit at the University of Reading. Ten years later he was hired as Professor at Cardiff University (UWIST), but was eventually lured to the USA to direct one of the three sites of the federally funded National Center for Geographic Information and Analysis (NCGIA). Equipped with the experience of running a major research enterprise, Batty returned to the UK five years later and in 1995 he started what was to become the internationally renowned Centre for Advanced Spatial Analysis (CASA) at University College London (UCL). Despite the inevitable administrative load, Batty's own research career blossomed at CASA, which from its inception has attracted some of the brightest young minds and highly distinguished senior scholars in areas broadly related to urban and regional studies and planning.

Throughout his highly productive career, Batty has remained committed to his three original interconnected interests: cities, urban planning and design, and urban modeling. These are, of course, very broad themes and within each of them Batty's research focus has shifted and evolved, as evidenced by the different thrusts of his four main books, published in 1976, 1994, 2005, and 2013. His early work was strongly influenced by his experiences as a planning student at Manchester University. Also during that time, mathematical models of urban development intended for use in planning were already being put to the test in the USA (cf. **Brian Berry**). That vision of urban models as practical planning aids towards the scientific betterment of cities captured Batty's imagination. While the term 'planning support systems' did not appear in the literature until much later, the notion was already forcefully expressed in his 1976 book, *Urban Modelling: Algorithms, Calibrations, Predictions*. The title is true to the technical emphasis of the book: 'algorithms' translate the models' mathematical equations into computer code; 'calibrations' determine the parameters that help fit the models to the data; and 'predictions' are the main products of these operations as well as the *raison d'être* of urban models.

Batty's second book, *Fractal Cities* (1994), did not appear until 18 years later, and the difference with the first one was striking. Gone was the focus on planning and the kinds of applied urban models that might support it in practice. This book marked the beginning of a new phase whereby simple mathematical structures, many of them directly inspired from physics, were used as metaphorical 'laboratories' for thought experiments about actual cities. Fractals, for example, are formalisms describing a geometry of non-integer dimensions – that is, fractional dimensions between one and two, or two and three, and so on. Fractals can reproduce natural forms with complex and irregular contours that cannot be well described by the straight lines and smooth surfaces and volumes of Euclidean geometry. In *Fractal Cities*, Batty and Longley show that many actual urban forms can be approximated by fractals, suggesting affinities between the regularities captured by that formalism and those of the growth processes of cities. Based on notions of hierarchy and self-similarity, fractals appear to provide 'a new and enriched form of [urban population] density theory' (p. 6). In the final chapters of the book, the theory is applied with good results to the density analysis of the cities of Cardiff and Seoul, and finally to regional systems of settlements such those of Norfolk and South-East England.

Cities and Complexity: Understanding Cities with Cellular Automata, Agent-Based Models, and Fractals (2005) introduces two additional formalisms already quite popular with urban modelers by that time: cellular automata, which simulate spatial growth and change processes as a function of the neighborhood (however defined) of each unit of land (cell); and agent-based models, which represent the interactions of varying numbers of 'agents' – computational abstractions of urban stakeholders making spatially explicit choices. The novelty here is the complexity science framework that unifies and relates diverse classes of models by emphasizing bottom-up rather than top-down processes, just as it highlights the limits of knowledge and the unpredictability of the future – hallmarks of complexity theory in the mathematical sense. The thought-experiment perspective is again prominent, this time with more explicit analysis of the spatial processes leading to specific kinds of outcomes. There are also many examples of real-world city forms and of human behavior patterns within actual cities (e.g., pedestrian movements) that are successfully reproduced with these methods.

Lastly, *The New Science of Cities* (2013a), Batty's most ambitious book to date, is a synthesis, an update, and a new departure. In its three parts it lays out the conceptual and mathematical foundations necessary for the rest of the book, presents six classes of models developed by himself and others, and returns to his original interest in planning and design to show how these normative disciplines can benefit from the positive models in question. New to this book is the emphasis on complex networks of interactions, viewed by many scholars as foundational to the existence and growth of cities. Here we also find a vindication of Batty's long-time interest in hierarchies, power laws, rank-size rules, fractals, and other such empirically observed mathematical regularities. The book appeared at a time of mounting interest in the phenomenon of urban scaling patterns – statistical regularities indicating robust associations between the sizes of cities in a region and the values of certain indicators such as income, number of patents, economic diversification, crime, and so on. Urban scaling analyses from around the world consistently show that the values of these and several other indicators tend to grow more than linearly (superlinearly) with growing population size. Along with Batty and his students, a number of prominent physicists are currently also publishing and lecturing on this latter topic, and are contributing to the growth of public interest in the 'new science of cities' (cf. **Karen C. Seto**).

Key ideas

Three key ideas emerge out of Batty's main books and his hundreds of other writings. First is the notion that the chaotic urban societal processes are just too difficult to grasp, and thus focusing on the tangible urban spatial structure that mirrors, enables, and constrains these may be a sound research strategy (cf. **Jane Jacobs**). This approach that seeks to reconstruct urban processes through an analysis of resulting urban forms reverses the standard scientific process-to-outcome mode of reasoning. Second is the idea that there exist certain robust, mathematically tractable regularities that underlie the intractable complexity and diversity of cities, and that these regularities can be expressed relatively simply. Third is the view of models as tentative metaphors, thought experiments, or intuition-sharpening devices, which contradicts the widely held assumption that a model is a simplification of reality. Those tempted to dismiss such 'toy models' as ivory-tower games should first explain their uncanny ability to replicate empirically verifiable properties of urban systems. Why this should be the case we still don't know. But nuggets of insight obtained through that approach can demonstrably be used to understand something new about cities in general, or to help plan a particular city.

Batty's physicalist approach to the study of cities and planning has occasionally been criticized as being too narrowly mechanistic and reductionist, and oblivious to the dramatic upheavals that urban societies have undergone in the past half-century. The rationale for choosing that approach is perhaps most explicit in the Introduction to *Fractal Cities,* where Batty writes:

> ... attention has been focused upon the institutional structure of cities, on social processes and urban conflict, on urban poverty and deprivation, on their diverse roles in the local and global economy. After a century of sustained effort at their understanding, our knowledge is still partial and fragmentary, based on a kaleidoscope of viewpoints and ideologies ... in this quest, there have been few successes in evolving our understanding from one approach to another. ... [Yet] we know instinctively that the physical form of cities is the ultimate result of a multitude of social and economic processes, constrained and shaped by the geometry of the natural and man-made world. (1994: 1)

Indeed, Batty's technical work on urban models and modeling is best understood in the context of his non-technical writings, such as the introductions to his books, his decades' worth of monthly editorials in the journal *Environment and Planning B*, and his numerous other essays discussing the philosophy of urban modeling, urban change in its relation to technological change, the limits of prediction with urban models, as well as the striking differences that can exist among actual cities. His editorials in particular are often motivated by observations from his constant professional travels to far-away cities, and reveal a keen eye for the unusual and meaningful and an advanced understanding of the social, economic, and political circumstances that may account for diverse urban fortunes. These thoughtful pieces take the reader beyond the formalisms and their limitations, to insights from angles not yet explored.

Contributions to urban studies

Batty's contributions stem as much from his own research as from his intellectual leadership within academia and beyond. As an urban scholar Batty occupies a specialized but highly influential place among the communities of urban modelers, urban designers, and planners. Even those who identify with different traditions in planning and modeling often follow his work and benefit from it.

At a time of fast expanding computational power and data availability, when millions of grant monies are spent on developing ever bigger and more technically sophisticated urban models, Batty represents the 'small is beautiful' stance. While the stated purpose of these large-scale efforts is typically conditional prediction, Batty's view of models as metaphors warns against putting too much trust in highly complex, data-hungry constructs being reliable future-forecasting devices. This is a critical point, as policy development in most domains increasingly strives to be 'evidence-based,' meaning that it is increasingly intent on deriving wisdom directly from data.

In addition to the direct contributions of his own research, Batty has mentored generations of doctoral students at CASA, many of whom are now professors at some of the most prestigious world universities. Likewise, numerous urban researchers from around the world have visited CASA for various lengths of time, fostering an agora of ideas to the benefit of senior and junior scholars alike. Another aspect of Batty's contributions is found in his outreach efforts that go well beyond his work with the journal *Environment and Planning B*. He publishes in a wide array of journals, many of them in the physical sciences, or in general-interest magazines, and maintains a popular blog, while also being in very high demand internationally as a speaker.

The niche that Batty's work occupies in urban studies and planning is not for everyone. There is little mention in there of politics or society or the economy, of social justice or inequality or poverty or difference or oppression, or of any of the other things that most of us – urban scholars or not – care about. His foray into the politically fraught topic of collective decision-making in planning and design, in the third part of *The New Science of Cities*, may be among his least satisfying efforts. It may thus be in a sense paradoxical that Batty enjoys the international respect and recognition that he does. Evidently there must be something about his ideas that speaks to scholars approaching his writings from a broad range of different perspectives. It could be the formal beauty of the simple but highly suggestive models; it could be the connections Batty is making with fields well beyond his own, in particular physics, and the visibility and innovation this imparts to urban research. Or it could be the almost metaphysical idea that relatively simple kernels of truth may connect the apparently chaotic lives of cities with their hard bodies of buildings and streets. It may indeed be Batty's notion of models as thought experiments that explains in large part the appeal of his work. At best these capture some meaningful regularity that is a tangible and measurable outcome of the intractable societal forces that drive a city's dynamics; at the very least they make you think. There are no claims of scientific authority there. The new science of cities that these models represent is always tentative and in the making. It does not take a quantitative urban scholar to reflect on the kinds of questions Batty is asking, and, as his massive citations numbers also suggest, evidently thousands have over the years.

Secondary sources and references

Batty, M. (2008a) 'Fifty years of urban modelling: Macro statics to micro dynamics', in S. Albeverio, D. Andrey, P. Giordano and A. Vancheri (eds) *The Dynamics of Complex Urban Systems: An Interdisciplinary Approach*. Heidelberg: Physica-Verlag, pp. 1–20.

Batty, M. (2008b) 'The size, scale, and shape of cities', *Science*, 319(5864): 769–771.

Batty, M. (2012) 'Building a science of cities', *Cities*, 29: 9–16.

Batty, M. (2013b) Michael Batty at TEDxLondon – City 2.0. Available at: www.youtube.com/watch?v=qOOh_oSwySw

Batty, M., Desyllas, J. and Duxbury, E. (2003) 'Safety in numbers? Modelling crowds and designing control for the Notting Hill Carnival', *Urban Studies*, 40(8): 1573–1590.

Centre for Advanced Spatial Analysis (CASA) (n.d.) The Bartlett School, University College London. Available at: www.bartlett.ucl.ac.uk/casa

Note

1. Batty is very proud of a 1957 school photograph that also includes John Lennon. See www.complexcity.info/files/2013/08/school.jpg

Brian J.L. Berry

Elvin Wyly, University of British Columbia

Key urban writings

Berry, B.J.L. (1964) 'Cities as systems within systems of cities', *Papers of the Regional Science Association*, 13: 147–163.

Berry, B.J.L. and Kasarda, J. (1977) *Contemporary Urban Ecology*. New York: Macmillan.

Berry, B.J.L. (1991) *Long-Wave Rhythms in Economic Development and Political Behavior*. Baltimore: Johns Hopkins University Press.

Berry, B.J.L. (1992) *America's Utopian Experiments: Communal Havens from Long-Wave Crises*. Hanover, NH: Dartmouth College/University Press of New England.

Berry, B.J.L. and Wheeler, J. (eds) (2005) *Urban Geography in America, 1950–2000: Paradigms and Personalities*. New York: Routledge.

Introduction

Brian J.L. Berry was an undisputed leader in bringing quantitative spatial analysis and scientific method to the field of urban scholarship. English-born but stridently an American geographer, Berry rose to prominence in the Cold War era climate when anxieties were rife about the U.S. falling behind the Soviets in scientific research. As money was flowing into universities for scholarship and mainframe digital computing, a bold new 'Quantitative Revolution' was being imagined in which social science could advance by testing and refining theoretical models with advanced statistical methods applied to vast new data sets measuring the complexity of urban-industrial society. Berry built a 'science of cities' with the potential to elevate urban studies and geography to the status, influence, and certainty of physics and the other 'hard' sciences that had developed with the philosophy of positivism in the 19th century. In contrast to the older urban studies dominated by historical approaches emphasizing the unique and contingent, Berry's positivist urbanism sought to uncover general principles of spatial organization in economic development, migration, and social change: models could be refined through testable hypotheses and replicated techniques of measurement to formulate generalizable theories and scientific laws. The youngest social scientist ever elected to the U.S. National Academy of Sciences, Berry has maintained an uncompromising commitment to scientific objectivity, empirically-tested theory, and policy-relevant research.

Berry is the Lloyd Viel Berkner Regental Professor and former Dean of the School of Economic, Political, and Policy Sciences at the University of Texas at Dallas.

Academic biography and research focus

Berry was born to working-class parents in Staffordshire, England in 1934. He excelled in school, and went on to complete a BSc in Economics (with geography as a 'special subject') at University College London in 1955. He was awarded a Fulbright Scholarship for graduate study in the U.S., and it was at that point that Berry swept into American geography as a quantitative-revolutionary force.

In his work for an MA (1956) and PhD (1958) at the University of Washington, Seattle, Berry developed a powerful fusion of economic science and spatial analysis. He synthesized economic research focused on the spatial distribution of production and exchange, and reconciled the two paths of the young field of 'regional science': logical, deductive abstract theory, versus inductive empirical measurement of observable patterns and processes. Integrating the two led him to conceptualize urbanization as a scientifically measurable process of economic competition, technological innovation, and socio-political change. Berry theorized the spatial configuration of urbanism as a fundamental feature of human society and of nature–society relations, and he backed up theory with a torrent of data and statistical analysis.

In 1958, Berry joined the faculty of the University of Chicago at the zenith of the 'Chicago School' of Sociology, which was a dominant fixture of modern, industrialized social science and urban studies. Berry's Chicago School of Geography quickly rose to prominence. In *Geography of Market Centers and Retail Distribution* (1967), his first book, he built a framework to analyze the spatial development of the flourishing postwar consumer economy; models and data could be used to measure hierarchies of different goods and services, and hierarchies in the sizes of towns and cities providing these services. Berry's book launched a vast, profitable industry of urban retail analysis. In *The Human Consequences of Urbanization* (1973) Berry applied 'regional science' to the global scale, while questioning the conventional wisdom of a universal path of modernization-urbanization. Instead, Berry analyzed how urbanization reflected and reproduced differences in culture and time, following divergent trajectories of distinctive socio-political systems in major world regions. In 'Urbanization and counterurbanization' (1976), he diagnosed the role of transportation and communications technologies in a widespread deconcentration and 'scatteration' process in the U.S., as 'a national society' was producing 'a national settlement system.' And *Contemporary Urban Ecology* (1977, with John Kasarda) refined the Chicago sociologists' pre-computer neighborhood case study methods into a wide-ranging statistical-geographic analysis of the multidimensional socio-cultural fabric inside the contemporary metropolis.

Berry was elected to the National Academy of Sciences in 1975, and in 1976 he accepted an endowed professorship in City and Regional Planning at Harvard, where he served as Director of the Laboratory for Computer Graphics and Spatial Analysis.

He moved to Carnegie Mellon to serve as Dean of the School of Urban and Public Affairs from 1981 to 1986, before joining UT-Dallas as Professor of Political Economy in 1986. Since his move to Texas, most of Berry's urban research has focused on *longue durée* dynamics of economic, demographic, and political change in urbanization.

Key ideas

Berry transformed urban studies through three key ideas. The first is a framework known as urban systems: interdependent networks of cities functionally bound together by systematic flows of goods, services, ideas, capital, labor, and political power (cf. **Janet Abu-Lughod, Saskia Sassen**). These networks exhibit persistent hierarchical structures, making it possible to predict with remarkable accuracy the number of settlements of different sizes, the diversity of their economic functions, and the size of the trade areas they serve. Predictive accuracy bolstered the scientific credibility of positivist urbanism. It also enabled the calculation of theoretically 'optimal' configurations of cities and urban services; deviations between predicted and observed, real-world patterns could be interpreted in terms of historical and geographical contingency, such as the distribution of natural resources, climatic variations and topography, and histories of colonialism, settler migration, nationalism, and war. The inherent spatiality of economic processes creates hierarchies *within* cities as well as *between* urban centers; as Berry put it in a landmark synthesis of the 'general systems theory' that shaped postwar social science, cities can be understood as 'systems within systems of cities' (cf. **Jane Jacobs**).

Berry's second key idea is long-wave rhythms of urbanization. Over more than two centuries, average annual growth rates of U.S. urban areas due to net migration trace approximately half-century-long periods of acceleration and deceleration; a nearly identical trend occurs in inflation-adjusted GNP per capita. Berry approached this tight linkage between city-building and economic fluctuations as symptomatic of deeper, long-term dynamics of social institutions in the evolving history of an urbanizing capitalism. Berry marshaled voluminous evidence documenting periodicity in prices (Kondratiev waves) and macroeconomic growth (Kuznets cycles), culminating in a multi-layered pattern of changes in the rate of change: synchronized rhythms of 25-to-30-year periods of inflationary and deflationary growth embedded within approximately 55-year cycles of crisis, recovery, prosperity, and stagnation. These long waves exceed the time horizons of nearly all political systems, corporations, investors, and individuals and families planning educational and career paths; hence, multigenerational economic rhythms become context – constituting the environment in which individuals, families, and socio-political institutions make life-shaping decisions. Unconscious adjustments to these long-term rhythms reinforce and magnify cycles, intensifying alternating periods of speculative, optimistic over-investment followed by episodes of collapse and panic. 'Like it or not,' Berry (1991: 11) suggests, 'our lives appear to be embedded in a higher order of complexity: collectively, we are a societal organism that displays self-regulating fluctuations around a path of growth, a dynamic equilibrium.'

Berry's third key idea is best described as evolutionary urban political economy. This is where Berry's biography intersects with intergenerational changes in the politics of social science in America. As a young student at Acton County Grammar School, Berry recalls the influence of headmaster G.C.T. Miles, a member of the British Communist Party's executive committee who later retired to Maoist China. 'Because it was part of the intellectual climate of the school,' Berry (2002: 19) reflected, 'we paid attention to the contest between communism and capitalism as a new socialist government struggled to nationalize England and as the Cold War deepened.' Berry also recalled that: 'There were always men outside the school, standing and occasionally asking political questions. They, too, reappeared later in my life' (2002: 19) Berry chose America, capitalism, and the frontiers of possibility he had glimpsed in an historical geography seminar in his last term at UCL: his final paper focused on Frederick Jackson Turner's (1921) evolutionary frontier model of American development. Berry's graduate work and early career success coincided with the Cold War 'Golden Age' of American Fordist capitalism – much of the funding that supported his graduate-school cohort came from government contracts for highway planning and 'civil defense,' and the Office of Naval Research – but by the time Berry was a young faculty member 'sitting in the back of Milton Friedman's courses on macroeconomics' (Berry, 1993: 439) the intersecting long waves of economy, demography, culture, and politics were setting the stage for new kinds of urban revolutions. At the same time, positivist science was under attack: it became clear that claims to objectivity and political neutrality masked a heavy reliance on state power, uncritical assembly-line thinking, and 'official' statistics that reinforced the *status quo*.

Berry fought these new insurgencies. The most spectacular battles were with **David Harvey**, a fellow Brit who wrote the 'bible' of positivist geography from Bristol but who then embraced Marxist revolutionary theory after moving to Johns Hopkins in 1969 amidst the rebellions over civil rights and the Vietnam War. When Harvey (1975: 102) called Berry the 'technocratic whiz kid' of urban geography, it was not a compliment: Robert McNamara and his team of 'whiz kids' had used systems analysis to rebuild the Ford Motor Company after the end of World War II, and then in the U.S. Defense Department they applied systems thinking to the Vietnam escalation. 'Berry is a McNamara,' Harvey (1975: 103) charged, with 'an attachment to the "liberal virtue in objectivity" in an ideological world' and a naive faith in 'technocratic "scientific" solutions' that 'contain the seeds of a larger tragedy … .'

Berry defended Science, and developed a distinctively American geography that was less revolution and more evolution. First in an article in the *South African Geographical Journal* and then several years later in his Presidential Address to the Association of American Geographers, Berry developed a theory of 'deliberate change in spatial systems' that fused his urban systems and long-wave analyses with several influential currents of general systems theory focused on evolution. The 'societal organism' can evolve, through technological innovation and better information – 'if we take full advantage of the fruits of the information age' – to become 'cybernetic' and 'power mobilizing' (Berry, 1980: 458), to dampen the catastrophic swings of long waves and to stabilize growth; 'we can be more knowing about ourselves and produce a future that is free of the collective consequences' of the 'individual excess' that is at the heart of capitalist growth (Berry, 1991: 198). Drawing on the philosopher Alfred North Whitehead's argument that the universe is a problem of constant evolution, Berry (1980: 456) conceptualized 'adaptive learning systems' premised on the idea that history, events, and expectations are bound in a process of 'anticipatory evolution' that extends 'beyond human intelligence into the entire universe – i.e., that the evolution of material substance has similar characteristics in that future events are constrained and made probable by built-in mechanisms that have emerged as a consequence of prior events and processes and that are directed towards some long-run goal.' In a remarkable prequel to today's hybrid of evolutionary economics with neoliberal deregulation and smart-city Silicon Valley disruption, Berry (1980: 456) offered the most comprehensive theory of evolutionary urbanism since the days of Robert Park's Chicago School human ecology, or Patrick Geddes' 1915 *Cities in Evolution*: '[T]he essential notion … is one of interdependent natural and cultural processes that give rise to patterns of events that include attempts to realize expectations, and that these events in turn feed back and modify the ongoing processes. In other words, the view is one of anticipatory evolution.'

For Berry (1980: 455), this meant that any academic discipline hoping to survive in America would have to conform to 'a distinctively American set of preferences that continue to shape the American scene,' specifically: 'the utilitarian belief that solutions to needs must be fashioned, for the most part, out of individual efforts in the private sector,' the commitment to 'enlarging individual opportunity, to increasing information about those opportunities, to removing barriers that have prevented some from participating in the mainstream, and to enhancing mobility, meanwhile struggling to contain excessive concentrations of power … and to buffer the fortunes of those afflicted by market fluctuations or otherwise left behind.'

Months after Berry delivered this manifesto of an American mainstream, Ronald Reagan won a landslide election achieved through a potent cocktail of right-wing anti-government cynicism and renewed political mobilization of Christian evangelicals. The U.S. federal government was now on the same path of neoliberal market acceleration as Thatcher's Britain, Pinochet's Chile, and Deng's China – but in a 'distinctively American' blend of survival-of-the-fittest economic competitions among a populace where few accept the evolutionary theories that structure the Social Darwinism that rules their lives. Since the 1980s, Berry's research has followed two paths. One continues the rigorous, precise spatial-science analysis of the evolving technologies and metropolitan spatial dynamics of post-industrializing informational capitalism in America and around the world. Another pursues a cultural political economy animated by a deepening suspicion of the kinds of new scholarly ideas, cultural trends, and idealistic hopes that represent today's version of the 19th-century utopian-city 'community havens from long-wave crisis' that Berry analyzed in a book that won the Nelson A. Rockefeller Prize in the Social Sciences (1992). Berry now looks at America, and does not like the 'long-term cultural adaptation as evolution' (1980: 457) that he sees. Berry's recent research (Elliott and Berry, 2015: 265) on 'The Obama Question' of a possible turning-point electoral transformation amidst a Kondratiev crisis warns that 'individual rights guaranteed by the Constitution' are threatened by the agile adaptation of the Democratic Party away from the old alliance between Northern ethnic city political machines and Southern racist Dixiecrat economic populists, towards today's metropolitan Obama coalition of youth, women, ethnoracial minorities, gays and lesbians, immigrants, and Native Americans.

Contributions to urban studies

Berry brought positivist science into geography and urban studies, and vice versa. The initial response was hostile: the first papers Berry submitted for publication in the late 1950s were rejected by old-guard editors as 'mathematics, not geography.' Less than a decade later, when the first edition of the Social Sciences Citation Index was compiled, Berry was the most widely-cited geographer in the world – a position maintained for the next quarter-century. Since his first publication, a co-authored chapter in a post-nuclear war survival plan for the Washington State Department of Civil Defense in 1956, Berry has published 550 reports, articles, reviews, books, chapters, and editorials. He has chaired more than 115 doctoral dissertations.

Prominence begat policy influence, as theory was put into practice. Berry's diagnosis of a latent, universal principle of socio-natural evolution – systematic hierarchies as 'a fundamental feature of the geographic organization of economic life' (1960: 12) – came to dominate theories of development and planning, and was encoded into policy by the institutions that sought Berry's expertise. He advised the White House National Goals Research staff, the World Bank, the Appalachian Regional Commission, USAID-India, the governments of Indonesia, Brazil, Sri Lanka, and many other clients. His theories remain deeply influential among investors, planners, and developers trying to keep pace with the accelerating dynamic rhythms of today's restructuring and urbanizing spatial economies. Berry led a revolution that built a science of cities, even as subsequent revolutions created a more pluralistic world of positivist and non-positivist scientific understandings of cities and urban life.

Secondary sources and references

Berry, B.J. (1960) 'The impact of expanding metropolitan communities upon the central place hierarchy, *Annals of the Association of American Geographers*, 50(2): 112–116.

Berry, B. (1967) *Geography of Market Centers and Retail Distribution*. Englewood Cliffs, NJ: Prentice-Hall.

Berry, B. (1973) *The Human Consequences of Urbanization: Divergent Paths in the Urban Experience of the Twentieth Century*. Chicago, IL: Chicago University Press.

Berry, B. (ed.) (1976) 'Urbanization and counterurbanization', *Urban Affairs Annual Reviews*, 11.

Berry, B.J.L. (1980) 'Creating future geographies', *Annals of the Association of American Geographers*, 70(4): 449–458.

Berry, B. (1993) 'Geography's quantitative revolution: Initial conditions, 1954–1960. A personal memoir', *Urban Geography*, 14(5): 434–441.

Berry, B. (2002) 'Clara voce cogito', in Peter Gould and Forrest R. Pitts (eds) *Geographical Voices: Fourteen Autobiographical Essays*. Syracuse, NY: Syracuse University Press, pp. 1–26.

Elliott, E. and Berry, B. (2015) 'Long waves in American politics, Part two: The Obama question', in L. Grinin, T. Devezas and A. Koratayev (eds) *Kondratieff Waves: Juglar, Kuznets, Kondradiev*. Volgograd: Uchitel Publishers, pp. 265–275.

Geddes, P. (1915) *Cities in Evolution*. London: Williams and Norgate.

Harvey, D. (1975) 'Review of *The Human Consequences of Urbanization*', *Annals of the Association of American Geographers*, 65(1): 99–103.

Turner, F.J. (1921) *The Frontier in American History*. New York: Holt.

6 M. Christine Boyer

Agustín Cocola-Gant, University of Lisbon

Key urban writings

Boyer, M.C. (1983) *Dreaming the Rational City: The Myth of American City Planning*. Cambridge, MA: MIT Press.

Boyer, M.C. (1985) *Manhattan Manners: Architecture and Style, 1850-1900*. New York: Rizzoli.

Boyer, M.C. (1994) *The City of Collective Memory: Its Historical Imagery and Architectural Entertainments*. Cambridge, MA: MIT Press.

Boyer, M.C. (1996) *CyberCities: Visual Perception in the Age of Electronic Communication*. New York: Princeton Architectural Press.

Introduction

M. Christine Boyer is an urban historian and theorist. Her work focuses on the history of American city planning, heritage and preservation planning and computer science. She has also made notable contributions to the understanding of the cultural and political economy of cities. Boyer's work addresses three principal concerns: the power relations that are embedded in the history of city planning; the politics of representation and the historical imagery of cities; and the relationship between the contemporary city and networks of virtual information. The first of these two topics has comprised Boyer's most significant contributions to urban studies, especially through the seminal books *Dreaming the Rational City* (1983) and *The City of Collective Memory* (1994). The historical perspective of Boyer's accounts develops a genealogical view that is crucial to understanding the role of cities and public spaces in the transition from modernity to postmodernity. Her historiography reveals how the search for profit and social control has been an inherent feature of the development of cities in capitalist societies.

Boyer is William R. Kenan Jr. Professor of Architecture and Urbanism at Princeton University.

Academic biography and research focus

M. Christine Boyer received her Master's and doctoral degrees at Massachusetts Institute of Technology where she focused on comparative urban development and the history of American city planning. Before joining Princeton University in 1991 she taught at the University of Pennsylvania and Columbia University and was Professor and Chair of the City and Regional Planning Program at the Pratt Institute, New York City.

Boyer has written extensively about American urbanism. The breadth of her research expertise is evident in the diverse subject matter of her main four monographs. Her first book was the result of an early interest in how structuralist philosophy could be employed to understand the history of city planning. Challenging the view that the evolution of city planning is a story of humanitarian progress and civic improvement, *Dreaming the Rational City* illustrates how planning has proceeded consistent with the needs of disciplinary order and capital accumulation, and so has left the structural causes of urban problems untouched. Boyer emphasises economic causation and the role that real estate developments play in capitalist societies but, more importantly, she introduces ideas extracted from the work of Michel Foucault (see Foucault, 1984) to the historical analysis of urban planning. According to Foucault, discipline is an invisible system that shapes human behaviour with the aim of reproducing the existing social structure. The imposition of social order through discipline does not require direct coercion, but it is infused across an apparatus of observation, recording and tracking that moulds daily cultural practices. Boyer applies this Foucauldian perspective to the analysis of American cities from the late 19th century to World War II, and by doing so she places city planning among an array of institutional practices contributing to social control. Through the analysis of a large body of archival materials and official discourses, Boyer offers substantial evidence that reveals the intentions of planners to impose a disciplinary order on the American city.

Boyer's second book – *Manhattan Manners* – is an account of the urban fabric of Manhattan between 1850 and 1900. Blending social history with planning and architecture, it emphasises the role of real estate interests in producing the commercial and residential areas for the elite in New York City. Boyer shows how an emerging bourgeois society used their residences and commercial buildings to display wealth and luxury, but far from such buildings being merely commissioned by individuals, Boyer documents the degree to which builders and realtors controlled the city's built form as a speculative activity.

The City of Collective Memory represents an important refinement of Boyer's political economic concerns and it made a substantial contribution to both urban history and theory. Boyer departs from the work of the French philosopher Maurice Halbwachs, who, in 1925, launched the term 'collective memory'. He rejected an individual-psychological approach to memory and suggested that memory is socially constructed according to the needs of dominant groups. Boyer illustrates how this social nature of memory is linked to places through practices of commemoration and heritage preservation. In doing so Boyer shows how the nature of memory is not only social but also spatial. From the pre-industrial city to the early 1990s, Boyer brings together sources and concepts from the arts, history, geography, planning and critical theory to show, on the one hand, how 'collective memories' have been socially reinvented over time and, on the other hand, the relationship between such memories and the restructuring of public space. Boyer also notes that the preservation of historical urban landscapes has been influenced by the pressures of the market place and commodification and this point is crucial to better grasp the changing state in the social construction of the past. While the efforts of governing elites to utilise the past have historically focused on anchoring their divergent memories in place, Boyer shows how, in the contemporary city, heritage is also used to enhance the quality of leisure and living spaces and so is a central tool in the politics of place promotion.

With the publication of *CyberCities*, Boyer's research focus shifted to computer science and networks of virtual information. Like **William J. Mitchell**, Boyer analyses how information technology changes the social and spatial order in contemporary cities. Boyer departs from the French philosopher Gilles Deleuze, who suggested that Foucault's disciplinary spaces of the modern city have given way to numerical societies of control facilitated by computer technology in which the code, not the norm, becomes the modulating device. Based on the 'cyber' terminology popularised by the novelist William Gibson, and on the time–space compressions theories of authors such as **David Harvey** or Edward Soja, in *CyberCities* Boyer argues that the virtual world will displace our local and physical space. In doing so she visualised the dangers of disassociation of humans from their place as the product of an increasing dependence on and fascination with computers and electronic technology.

Key ideas

Boyer provides a historical perspective which is crucial to understanding the contemporary city. Her methodology, however, is not intended as a conventional history that gives a linear progress of an era. Rather, Boyer draws on Foucault's genealogy as a particular type of historical inquiry aimed at identifying specific power relations in society (cf. **Bent Flyvbjerg**). Although the Foucauldian concept of power is not an obvious apparatus on the surface of society which is visible to all, it always has a spatial component, and this is where Boyer establishes the link to city planning history. Boyer's concerns are the social practices through which space has being planned and constructed from the 19th century to the 1990s, and in doing so her genealogy develops a remarkably in-depth understanding of a particular phenomenon: the role of cities and public spaces in the transition from modernity to postmodernity.

Boyer's genealogy is combined together with a Marxist diagnosis emphasising economic causation. The result is an original contribution to the understanding of the political economy of cities and the process of social construction of space. *Dreaming the Rational City* and *Manhattan Manners*, for instance, show how real estate practices are the result of the historic domination of a ruling class that sees cities as a commodity from which the highest amount of profit must be extracted. While authors such as **Henri Lefebvre** stress the importance of the production of space in the post-industrial city, Boyer illustrates historical roots consistent with the needs of advanced capitalism and shows how city planning has played a subordinate role in a development process dominated by large corporations and the real estate industry, especially by the power they have to push government levers.

Central to *The City of Collective Memory* is the historical approach through which Boyer analyses the construction of urban images. In doing so, the book represents a critique of the practices of historic preservation, urban design and postmodern architecture that were reshaping American and European cities during the 1970s and 1980s. Although authors such as **Sharon Zukin** also noted the use of historic preservation and urban design as a way to improve the symbolic capital and image of cities in the context of interurban competition for mobile capital and workers, Boyer links the contemporary politics of representation with the historical imagery of cities. She shows how images from the 19th century have been translated into contemporary views of the urban realm. The real estate interest in the restoration of former architectural and neighbourhood traces that has been so important in the production of gentrified spaces actually means 'the return of aesthetics to city planning' (Boyer, 1988: 49), the return of an instrumental use of historical fabrics that carries within its visual imaginations the influence of 19th-century procedures and representational views of city-building; and the return to architecture as a commodity and form of publicity in the promotion of the place.

Fundamental to Boyer's account of cities in the transition from modernity to postmodernity is her historical approach to collective memory and the various ways in which memory is spatially constituted. Similar to authors such as **Dolores Hayden**, Boyer shows how social memory and social space conjoin to engender much of the context for modern identities. Notwithstanding, by analysing different systems of representation from the 19th century to the 1990s, Boyer illustrates how this interest in the past and its material manifestations in space are mechanisms of political power that, in any case, shift historiographical concerns from ideology to imagery and from meaning to manipulation. Boyer's historical perspective in the social use of the past questions the originality of the postmodern interest in local traditions and vernacular landscapes and, by contrast, she shows how policies of heritage preservation rely too explicitly on models formulated in earlier periods.

The City of Collective Memory also challenges the postmodern 'negation of totalities'; the apparent war against the authority of the modernist project and the rhetorical expression of heterogeneous voices. Regarding this, Boyer reminds us of the German philosopher Walter Benjamin's claim that all history writing is a history of the triumph of bourgeois values and so the current instrumental use of the past and politics of representation is just a different stage in capitalism development. The important point for Boyer is that history and traditions have been so thoroughly invented and homogenised that any oppositional voice potentially rooted in collective memory has been eclipsed completely. And at the same time, history has been so absolutely marketed and commoditised that the new spaces it has shaped have become mere fragments – 'city tableaux' – and islands of leisure-time lifestyles. For Boyer, in this migration of history into advertising there is no space for oppositional voices outside the logic of reproduction of capital.

Central to Boyer's interpretation of the postmodern city is the role played by electronic communication in the human and urban experience. Especially important, as noted by authors such as **William J. Mitchell,** is how the virtual era changes the way we build communities. Boyer argues that the virtual world will displace the experience of our local world as telecommunications and cyberspace tend to condense the perception of time and space. Regarding this, Boyer's critique of postmodern 'pluralism', which is seen as a conquest against the authoritarian view of the modernist project, is also an essential idea of *CyberCities*. Contrary to the postmodern promise that cyberspace and the permanent connectivity will enable citizens to engender non-hierarchical and open-ended relationships to the extent of forming a 'new community', Boyer argues that the results of the virtual world are the ultimate disintegration of the connection between humans and their physical place, together with an increasingly fragmented quality of our cities and built environments. Boyer notes that the postmodern negation of totalities and the critique of the notion of unity or centre is radically anti-urban and positions itself in a state of war against the reality of the city: while the city has been the focus of modernism, it is receding and the computer is rising as the new focal point of culture and society. It is a war against the polis as the centre of Western communal life; a deconstruction of the process of city planning and the Enlightenment promise of communal consensus. For this reason, the celebration of the expansion of the virtual world, telecommunications and the consequent time–space compression can generate the illusion that we have reinstated freedom of choice and enabled the voice of alterity to rise, but as Boyer suggests, at the cost of the community and the loss of public life in the contemporary city.

Contributions to urban studies

Boyer brings to urban studies a clear indication of the need to pay closer attention to the historical roots and development of the contemporary city. Boyer's empirical work demonstrates that a number of features that are usually considered inherent to the post-industrial city – commodification of the urban space and imagery of cities, social control or the role of planning in the process of capital accumulation – have clear antecedents in earlier periods, especially since the liberal revolutions during the 18th and 19th centuries. In seeking out these historical antecedents Boyer provides a reconsideration and a critique of postmodernism, which despite being seen as a break and rupture from the modernist project, it actually represents the continuity and persistence of a power that has ruled society from the age of Enlightenment.

Boyer's interdisciplinary approach transcends the limits of historical analysis, and her work has influenced disciplines across the social sciences and humanities. Especially important has been her contribution to the relationship between memory and place: the social dimension of remembering, and the correspondingly social nature of how space is produced; the construction, therefore, of places of memory to make the connection between past and present more tangible. Regarding this, Boyer's illustration of re-edited collective memories through a system of public commemorations, monuments and heritage sites has been revered by several authors from different disciplines, especially cultural geography, sociology and cultural studies.

A key theoretical contribution Boyer's work provides is the introduction of Foucauldian thinking into the analysis of urban planning. She has also outlined post-Marxist interpretations and incorporated key ideas from critical theory, but it is her Foucauldian analysis based on the concept of power and its spatial relations that makes her theoretical research original and genuine. Boyer's theoretical contribution is especially important for the practice of planners and architects. While architects and planners ensure that people are distributed in space, the Foucauldian thinking shows how space and social conceptions are indivisibly linked. Therefore, while it is central that planners and architects control different technical skills, Boyer shows how they also ought to pay attention to the social context within which they work.

Secondary sources and references

Boyer, M.C. (1988) 'The return of aesthetics to city planning', *Society*, 25(4): 49–56.

Boyer, M.C. (1992a) 'Cities for sale: Merchandising history at South Street Seaport', in M. Sorkin (ed.) *Variations on a Theme Park: The New American City and the End of Public Space*. New York: Hill and Wang, pp. 181–204.

Boyer, M.C. (1992b) 'The imaginary real world of cybercities', *Assemblage*, 18: 114–127.

Boyer, M.C. (2007) 'Urban operations and network centric warfare', in M. Sorkin (ed.) *Indefensible Space: The Architecture of the National Insecurity State*. New York: Routledge, pp. 51–78.

Boyer, M.C. (2008) 'The many mirrors of Michel Foucault and their architectural reflections', in M. Dehaene and L. de Cauter (eds) *Heterotopia and the City: Public Space in a Postcivil Society*. London: Routledge, pp. 53–74.

Boyer, M.C. (2010) 'Societies of control and chrono-topologies', *Critical Studies*, 32: 203–222.

Foucault, M. (1984) *The Foucault Reader: An Introduction to Foucault's Thought*. London: Penguin.

7   Neil Brenner

Tauri Tuvikene, Tallinn University

Key urban writings

Brenner, N. (1999) 'Globalization as reterritorialization: The re-scaling of urban governance in the European Union', *Urban Studies*, 36(3): 431–451.

Brenner, N. and Theodore, N. (2002) 'Cities and the geographies of "actually existing neo-liberalism"', *Antipode*, 34(3): 349–379.

Brenner, N. (2004) *New State Spaces: Urban Governance and the Rescaling of Statehood*. Oxford and New York: Oxford University Press.

Brenner, N. (2009) 'What is critical urban theory?', *City*, 13(23): 198–207.

Brenner, N. (ed.) (2014a) *Implosions/Explosions: Towards a Study of Planetary Urbanization*. Berlin: Jovis.

Introduction

Neil Brenner is a leading contemporary urban scholar whose critical and conceptually rigorous work, inspired by **Henri Lefebvre** and rooted in Marxism, has widely influenced thinking on scale, neoliberalism and urban relations. His career started with publications on state rescaling and neoliberalism, brought together in the monograph *New State Spaces*. While he later returned to some of these issues, Brenner's research since then has mostly been focused on ambitious questions of urban theorizing, paying particular attention to the advancement of *critical* urban studies and the reconceptualization of what constitutes the 'urban'. The latter, entangled in the question of planetary urbanization, drives his current work as Professor of Urban Theory at the Harvard University Graduate School of Design (GSD), which he joined having for a long time been employed at the New York University as Professor of Sociology and Metropolitan Studies.

Academic biography and research focus

Brenner's approach to cities and to the key geographical concept of 'scale' began at the University of Chicago with his doctoral thesis *Global Cities, Glocal States: State*

Rescaling and the Remaking of Urban Governance in the European Union.
Interestingly, this was done in Political Science, not a particularly urban-focused
discipline. The doctoral thesis built on fieldwork in Frankfurt and Amsterdam –
cases among other European Union examples Brenner often returns to when
discussing state rescaling. Before doctoral studies, however, he spent 1995–6 at
UCLA's Department of Geography as a Master's student. This was a stage that, in his
own words, was significant for the development of his interest in, and understanding
of, socio-spatial theory, political economic geography and urban studies more generally –
particularly crucial for a person otherwise pursuing education in philosophy,
sociology and political science.

Owing to this broad social science background, Brenner's writings are characterized
by a strong theoretical and conceptual focus, with an intellectually dense and intensive
style. Brenner has contributed to urban scholarship less through careful empirical analysis and more by offering rigorous theoretical elaborations. Most of this work has been
collaborative, including co-edited books and special editions, as well as co-authored
articles with a number of academics such as Roger Keil, Bob Jessop, Christian Schmid,
Nik Theodore, Jamie Peck, Margit Mayer, David Madden, Martin Jones and Gordon
McLeod, among others. His contribution to the field should thus not only be measured
by what he has developed under his name but by the number of successful collaborations in which the inputs of different thinkers often seamlessly converge.

While various topics have coexisted in his work, Brenner's engagement in urban
studies could broadly be divided into three themes. First, his early research was oriented towards forms, institutions and actors of governance and he conceptualized the
increased importance of supra- and sub-national scales of the state, paying special
attention to the latter. He built on and contributed to the ongoing thrust in urban
research, advanced by researchers such as **Neil Smith** and Erik Swyngedouw, to understand the production and politics of scale. The second theme developed alongside his
interest in state rescaling and deals with neoliberalism and, in particular, neoliberal
forms of urban governing. The neoliberalism he outlines with Nik Theodore and Jamie
Peck is driving competitive urban strategies in the European Union, United States and
elsewhere. The third theme focuses on the conceptualization of the urban. This effort
aims to understand urbanization beyond the physical and empirical confines of cities
and explores urban relations in as *non*-urban places as the Amazon rainforest or
Antarctica. The *problematique* of the urban, which Brenner pursues under deep influence of the French Marxist philosopher and urban thinker **Henri Lefebvre,** was in
many ways present throughout his earlier work on state rescaling and neoliberalism
but has become more central and visible in the current endeavour.

Key ideas

Brenner understands urbanization as intimately connected to processes of state rescaling. As such, he forcefully argues the need to identify the emergence of new state spaces
and forms of governance, often pinpointing cities as the principal target of intervention. At the same time he problematizes the scale at which the urban has often been
positioned, as patterns and pathways of urbanization are not restricted to confined
areal units. The inadequacy of existing scalar terms to register such processes demands

a more nuanced, post-disciplinary theorization that, as Brenner proposes it, takes territory, place, space and network (TPSN) all equally into account in geographical analysis (Jessop et al., 2008). Thus, to understand Brenner's key ideas we first need to attend to his work on scale, as this analysis also underpins his take on neoliberalism and contemporary urbanization.

First, a key tenet of Brenner's thinking is an unwillingness to accept the widespread narratives that globalization and the end of the welfare state, along with the onslaught of neoliberalism, mark the erosion of the national state. Instead, Brenner insists on its continued importance and points to the ways in which state functions have morphed and become rescaled away from what has usually been perceived as national. Along with other theorists, Brenner observes – most vividly in the pages of *New State Spaces* – the shifts away from the Fordist–Keynesian welfarist and nation-state based models to new forms of governing taking place at the supra-national and sub-national scales. The neoliberal competitive state manifests new projects and strategies that are growth-oriented and competition-driven with the main state projects and strategies focused on decentralization of decision-making and financial responsibility to particular urban contexts. The role of the national state, as Brenner argues, is increasingly redefined as a mediator of uneven geographical development whereby the aim is not to build a more balanced and cohesive spatial pattern but to harness locational advantages emerging in the global system of capitalism. Cities and urban regions are thus becoming the principal actors in capitalist development. Such rescaling tendencies have rested on and led to uneven development with certain regions positioned in governmental strategies as main growth poles.

Using his political economy attuned scalar lens, Brenner has additionally challenged prevailing ideas about global or world cities. Moving away from seeing global cities as 'uniquely globalized urban nodes' located within a pre-existing world order of national states, Brenner theorizes them to be part of the 'broader, multi-scalar transformation in the geography of capitalism' (Brenner, 1998: 12) wherein the process of capitalist globalization is interlinked with shifting scalar dimensions of the state. Global cities are thus not simply manifestations of the increased importance of the global and the local at the expense of the national state. In contrast to this zero-sum understanding of scale, Brenner argues for understanding global cities as part of a broader transformation of capitalism and state power in which states act on different scales, through different institutions and following new logics.

Second, Brenner has been one of the proponents of the highly widespread academic discussion on neoliberalism. In his work, neoliberalization and rescaling are intertwined, with cities emerging as the principal nodes for neoliberal policies: on the one hand, they were subjects to budget cut-backs in post-Keynesian years, but on the other hand, cities have emerged as laboratories of neoliberal policy experiments and have become entrenched in competitive and unequal geographical arrangements. Neoliberalism, as Brenner has further maintained, morphs and adapts to the conditions it has to face. It is not just surviving – or, even less, diminishing as some have hoped after the 2007/8 financial crisis – but is gaining momentum. While Brenner acknowledges that neoliberalism is not homogeneous and unitary in its form, he is also sceptical of reverse assertions about local variation of governing forms. Instead, he claims neoliberalization to be 'variegated' (Brenner et al., 2010), meaning the interplay of general (the neoliberal system) and specific (local variation) wherein the difference is not just locally developed but a result of systemic production of difference taking place on various scales. He thus centralizes structural properties of capitalism and processes of neoliberalization, arguing them to act as 'macrospatial' background – a 'context of context' as he terms it – for the local 'regulatory projects' (2010: 202).

Third, over the last few years, Brenner has built on Lefebvre's prediction of 'complete urbanization' and argued for the need to more properly theorize what 'urban' entails. This research is now entangled in the theme of planetary urbanization, where together with Christian Schmid, Brenner has argued for the diminishing importance of the 'non-urban' (including rural and 'natural' but also suburban). A particular target for Brenner and Schmid has been the presumption that an 'urban age' has arrived only now with more than 50 per cent of Earth's population living in cities. They point out the problems of such a perspective as it tends to presume too simply the measurability of the urban/non-urban divide and draws conclusions from data that are essentially conflictual owing to the different analytical registers and definitions of what counts as 'urban' (Brenner and Schmid, 2014). The world is 'urban' for other reasons and has been for a longer time than what the 'urban age' thesis proposes. Namely, the concept of the urban is more expansive than merely the city, and the urbanization of the globe took place way before the 2000s. With such a push for the conceptual importance of the 'urban', interesting avenues for research not just in urban studies but beyond are suggested. The 'urban' emerges as a potential characteristic for whatever phenomenon is under investigation without the need to confine empirical explorations to cities as bounded entities. It does not just exist alongside topics such as family, education or culture industries, but such subject matters should all be seen as essentially urban.

Brenner has been working towards 'urban theory without an outside', with the urban conceptualized as open, variegated and multiscalar, an unevenly developed and world-wide phenomenon (Brenner, 2014a). Taking concepts from Lefebvre, Brenner claims urban processes to function as 'implosions–explosions', with implosion referring to concentration and agglomeration and explosion to the interurban connections that traverse space. Urban phenomena and processes are everywhere: transcontinental high-ways and shipping routes, supposedly natural parks for tourists to explore, even tundra and atmosphere are enmeshed in the global urban fabric. His edited collection *Implosions/Explosions: Towards a Study of Planetary Urbanization* is illustrated with photos of tar sands and other sorts of landscape modifications instead of skyscrapers or dense urban sites one would usually expect to find in such urban books. With Christian Schmid from ETH Zurich and the Urban Theory Lab at Harvard GSD, Brenner has engaged in not only conceptualizing but also visualizing in maps and graphs the new and more expansive theorizations of what counts as urban and where urban could be located. This work tackles the ways in which the theoretical and conceptual understandings of 'urban' are intertwined with how cities and urban processes are visualized.

Contributions to urban studies

While Brenner is a theorist of state, scale and neoliberalism, he is perhaps primarily a key thinker on cities, having offered many influential ideas on the ways in which urban studies should and could be revised to better grasp contemporary global conditions. One of his ongoing concerns has been the state of urban research. For Brenner, the field tends to lack clarity, methodological and theoretical focus, and is marked by epistemological narrowness. His recent theoretical engagement with planetary urbanization has hence opened up perspectives beyond cities confined to their physical form, with the 'urban', then, a concept that characterizes diverse processes in multiple locations. Such a take on the 'urban' that positions it in a more central spot in research should be supported by many in urban studies.

Yet, despite the rather abstract and open-ended urban theorization that Brenner hints at with his assertion that 'urban' should be a concept and exist beyond 'cities', he still narrows his focus down to the processes of capitalism. His approach to neoliberalism leaves little room for alternative manifestations of life. The sort of Deleuzian assemblage and Latourian actor-network theory (ANT) conceptualizations which have inspired the work of **Ash Amin, AbdouMaliq Simone, Mariana Valverde** among others to attend to minor materialities, everyday practices and urban regulations, remain out of Brenner's purview. Brenner has maintained his focus on a Marxist–Lefebvrian style of critical urbanism and defended his concentration on the critique of capitalist processes in the pages of *City* journal, where a clash between assemblage/ANT and a more Marxist take on urban processes has ensued (see Brenner et al., 2011). The same applies for the conceptualization of scale, wherein Brenner's analysis prefers scalar perspectives over flat and topological approaches – the sort of thinking about 'geography without scale' currently animating large swathes of the social sciences (see e.g. Marston et al., 2005). Among the various theory camps in urban studies, Brenner thus helps to define one wedded to a consistent focus on the critique of neoliberalism and to which analysis is predominantly inspired by the insights and concepts of Marxist scholarship.

Concurrently, Brenner's theory is largely structuralist and focused on the universal and the global. In taking such an approach he has been deeply influential and has opened new avenues of thought, although this is not necessarily because he has been first to notice something, but because he has engaged in the topic with an energy, intellectual clarity and theoretical rigour. With his mind set towards the general and abstract rather than the detailed and particular, his approach has come to friction (or potential friction) with other emerging themes in urban studies. This not only includes the already mentioned rifts with assemblage approaches to urbanism but also potential lines of encounter between the planetary urbanization framework that Brenner advocates and the comparative urbanism developed by **Jennifer Robinson** and **Ananya Roy** among others. Despite their mutual ground in seeking novel urban theory relevant for the diverse set of cities, they quite substantially diverge on the understanding of general and theoretical. While comparative urbanism tends to build theory and concepts from the diversity of experience of multiple cities and regions, Brenner's approach works more from the abstract and theoretical to local variegation. Whether the future of urban studies is for the Brennerian structuralist and critical approach or for a more rhizomatic style of research is nevertheless hard to pinpoint at this stage.

Secondary sources and references

Brenner, N. (1998) 'Global cities, glocal states: Global city formation and state territorial restructuring in contemporary Europe', *Review of International Political Economy*, 5(1): 1–37.

Brenner, N. (2014b) 'Introduction: Urban theory without an outside', in N. Brenner (ed.) *Implosions/Explosions: Towards a Study of Planetary Urbanization*. Berlin: Jovis, pp. 14–30.

Brenner, N. and Schmid, C. (2014) 'The "urban age" in question', *International Journal of Urban and Regional Research*, 38(3): 731–755.

Brenner, N., Madden, D.J. and Wachsmuth, D. (2011) 'Assemblage urbanism and the challenges of critical urban theory', *City*, 15(2): 225–240.

Brenner, N., Peck, J. and Theodore, N. (2010) 'Variegated neoliberalization: Geographies, modalities, pathways', *Global Networks*, 10(2): 182–222.

Jessop, B., Brenner, N. and Jones, M. (2008) 'Theorizing sociospatial relations', *Environment and Planning D – Society and Space*, 26(3): 389–401.

Marston, S.A., Jones, J.P. III and Woodward, K. (2005) 'Human geography without scale', *Transactions of the Institute of British Geographers*, 30(4): 416–432.

8 Teresa Caldeira

Sonia Roitman, The University of Queensland

Key urban writings

Caldeira, T.P.R. (1996) 'Fortified enclaves: The new urban segregation', *Public Culture*, 8(2): 303–328.

Caldeira, T.P.R. and Holston, J. (1999) 'Democracy and violence in Brazil', *Comparative Studies in Society and History*, 41(4): 691–729.

Caldeira, T.P.R. (2000) *City of Walls: Crime, Segregation and Citizenship in São Paulo*. Berkeley and Los Angeles: University of California Press.

Caldeira, T.P.R. (2012) 'Imprinting and moving around: New visibilities and configurations of public space in São Paulo', *Public Culture*, 14(2): 385–419.

Caldeira, T. and Holston, J. (2015) 'Participatory urban planning in Brazil', *Urban Studies*, 52(11): 2001–2017.

Introduction

Teresa Caldeira is a Brazilian anthropologist who uses ethnography to analyse cities and urban phenomena. Her work centres on three main themes: social problems and social transformations in the city (especially segregation, inequalities and crime), urban planning and cultural expressions in the urban landscape. Her research is primarily based in Brazil, in the context of its shift from a modernist planning project influenced by an authoritarian vision of the state during the military governments in the 1970s and 1980s to a more democratic and participatory model. However, she has also compared Brazil (São Paulo) and the USA (California), her home for the past 20 years.

According to Caldeira, broad socio-political processes are central to everyday dynamics in the city, which she studies through micro-social analyses. Focusing on segregation and the manifestation of social inequalities, her work highlights processes of withdrawal from the public and political realms by affluent groups. As urban elites retreat to gated communities, the space for public encounters between different social groups becomes more restricted. The city loses its role as a promoter of free social encounters, democracy and just citizenship. Caldeira also analyses the role of participatory planning instruments to foster democracy. Her recent work examines cultural expressions such as graffiti and poetry that reveal social inequalities, gender differences and power imbalances in the city. She argues that new artistic interventions in São Paulo recreate gender hierarchies and stereotypes.

Caldeira is a Professor of City and Regional Planning at the College of Environmental Design of the University of California, Berkeley.

Academic biography and research focus

Caldeira has an interdisciplinary background with a BA in Social Sciences and an MA in Political Science from the University of São Paulo, Brazil, and a PhD in Anthropology from the University of California in Berkeley. Before moving to the USA she worked at Centro Brasileiro de Análise e Planejamiento (Cebrap) and at the Department of Anthropology of the Universidade Estadual de Campinas (Unicamp), both in São Paulo. In the USA, she was first based at the University of California (Irvine) and moved to the Berkeley campus in 2007. Caldeira received a Guggenheim Fellowship in 2012.

The main theoretical influences of Caldeira come from her time at Cebrap in the 1970s and early 1980s, where she worked with a group of Brazilian centre-left sociologists, political scientists and philosophers, including Vilmar Faria, José Arthur Giannotti, Guillermo O'Donnell (Argentine), Juarez Rubens Brandão Lopes, Ruth Cardoso and Fernando Henrique Cardoso. Their research, which focused on civil society, democracy and inequality, critiqued public policies during the military governments in Brazil. Ruth Cardoso (1930–2008, née Ruth Leite) was Caldeira's main influence. She was an anthropologist who became First Lady when her sociologist husband Fernando Henrique Cardoso became President of Brazil (1995–2003). Ruth Cardoso was one of the creators of a successful social programme called 'Bolsa Família' (Family Bag). Caldeira edited a book on the work of Ruth Cardoso published in 2011.

Caldeira has also worked and published with her partner, political anthropologist James Holston. Their joint work centres on the concept of democracy in Brazil and how this is expressed in other processes such as increasing violence (Caldeira and Holston, 1999) and participatory planning processes (Caldeira and Holston, 2015).

Her work received international exposure with the book *City of Walls: Crime, Segregation and Citizenship in São Paulo* (2000). It examines spatial, social and political transformations in São Paulo as a consequence of higher social inequality and higher crime rates. She argues that the consolidation of democracy in Brazil faces challenges as a consequence of violence, discrimination and segregation that polarise society between dangerous and non-dangerous groups, rich and poor. Thus, fortified enclaves, which include gated communities, shopping malls and office complexes, appear as a 'new way of organizing social differences in urban space' (Caldeira, 2000: 4). The book is based on more than a decade of ethnographic research in São Paulo, using open-ended interviews and observations as the main research methods, but also analysing demographic data and real estate advertisements in various media. In the book Caldeira reflects on the challenges international social scientists face when trying to explain social phenomena happening in one specific geographical location and a particular culture with the frameworks of another geographical context and a different culture. She argues that her approach is an 'anthropology with an accent' (page 1). She is a Brazilian, analysing her own city of São Paulo, but her thinking has been influenced by the academic debate in the USA and could seem 'strange' or 'detached' to Brazilian researchers.

Key ideas

Caldeira's key ideas can be categorised in three main themes, even when these themes overlap and are intertwined: segregation and urban inequalities; urban planning; and cultural expressions in the city.

The first theme is the one Caldeira is most famous for and is reflected in *City of Walls*. She identifies the emergence of gated communities ('fortified enclaves' as she calls them) as a new housing concept chosen by some elite groups, who look for five basic elements: security, seclusion, social homogeneity, amenities and services. Built on class prejudices and negative references to poor and marginalised groups, gated communities are justified by discourses of fear (cf. **Loïc Wacquant**).

Gated communities contribute to segregation, which Caldeira argues has taken three forms of expression (Caldeira, 2000). The first urban form dates from the late 19th century to the 1940s. It was a period that reflected a compact city where different social groups were segregated by type of housing. The second form dates from the 1940s to the 1980s and can be understood as a centre–periphery model, where different social groups were separated by distance. Upper and middle-income residents were located in central areas of the city with good quality services and infrastructure, while lower-income residents were located in the periphery with no or very deficient provision of services and amenities. The third urban form takes place from the late 1980s, where 'different social groups are again closer to one another but are separated by walls and technologies of security, and they tend not to circulate or interact in common areas' (Caldeira, 2000: 213).

Caldeira argues that this 'new urban segregation' (Caldeira, 1996) has not been carefully analysed since most urban scholars still apply the model of centre–periphery to understand São Paulo. This new type of segregation was also identified and analysed by Sabatini and Cáceres (2004) in relation to Santiago de Chile. They referred to a reduced spatial scale of segregation when gated communities locate in low-income areas. Caldeira highlights the consequences of the multiplication of gated communities, which include privatisation of security and public spaces, enclosure of the upper classes and segregation. The modernist idea of the city as the locale to experience diversity and social difference (see also **Richard Sennett**) is lost with the emergence of fortified enclaves and the fear of 'the Other'. This is one of the main concerns Caldeira wants to share with her audience and fellow urbanists.

The second theme in Caldeira's research is urban planning, and this has been analysed in association with James Holston. Together they examine urban policies and legislation in Brazil, and the shift from a modernist urban planning approach to a new type of governance and planning. They focus on participatory urban planning as a model of urban reform and democratic intervention in Brazil. In a recent article (Caldeira and Holston, 2015) they have also examined the relationship between planning, master plans, citizens' participation and the construction of democracy in Brazil. They argue that although Brazil has progressive planning instruments like the City

Statute, there is not equal citizens' participation because participation is restricted to certain groups. The prevalent neoliberal vision of planning defines the state as an 'articulator' of public and private interests, and there is an (incorrect, according to the authors) assumption that individuals are equally free and participation is an expression of their freedom. According to Caldeira and Holston, this type of participation consolidates existing inequalities because it is non-binding and informal. Affluent and powerful groups use participatory mechanisms and the judiciary system to pursue their interests (cf. **Bent Flyvbjerg**). Their analysis centres on inequalities, power imbalances and the difficulties of achieving social justice in the city.

Social justice is considered a core principle of 'insurgent democracy'. This idea is influenced by Holston's (2008) book *Insurgent Citizenship: Disjunctions of Democracy and Modernity in Brazil*, which identifies moments in which social movements were able to make democratic gains as they fought for access to decision-making processes. Insurgence is described as 'a process of organised counter-politics that destabilises present configurations of power, defamiliarising their coherence' (Caldeira and Holston, 2015: 2013). This idea is linked to the concept of 'disjunctive democracy' developed by Caldeira and Holston (1999), which emphasises an uneven distribution of rights among citizens: while some citizenship rights might be exercised, others might be constrained. This concept also appears in her analysis of poor young men and their practices in São Paulo (Caldeira, 2012). Caldeira's conception of social justice is closely linked to Iris Marion Young's concept of social justice, referring to 'the elimination of institutionalized domination and oppression' (Young, 1990: 15). This means the elimination of disparities in the distribution of material goods and resources and also a more equal access to decision-making processes, participation and the exercise of capacities and capabilities.

The role of public space in the construction of citizenship is also considered in the analysis of urban planning. The changing nature of public space due to structural conditions including economic (dis)investment and public policies leads to strong changes in the use of and access to the city. The concept of public space is examined not only in relation to the abandonment of collective life by affluent citizens moving to gated communities, but also in relation to the use of urban places for cultural production and youth expression (Caldeira, 2014), whereby poor young men 'create a new visibility for the subaltern' (Caldeira, 2012: 389).

Caldeira's third theme is the cultural production in the city and the use and appropriation of public spaces by new modes of cultural expressions. These practices take place in peripheral public spaces, where poor groups have been segregated by the market and urban planning instruments. Caldeira examines artistic productions (rap, graffiti, *pixação*[1] *and saraus*[2]) as expressions of the contestation, anger and despair by young men living in the periphery of São Paulo (Caldeira, 2012, 2014). She points out that while these young citizens challenge class and race inequality (they are predominantly poor and black), they reproduce gender inequality because women have a very limited space in this realm. Men dominate these cultural expressions. Women would need to behave as men if they would like to be accepted, but there is also a strong sexual connotation for women and their roles in society and distrust in women (except for their own mothers). Caldeira explains that these cultural expressions are contradictory because they 'expose discrimination but refuse integration' and 'affirm rights to the city while fracturing the public' (Caldeira, 2012: 385).

Caldeira's work shows how in Latin America the periphery is associated with poverty, lack of services and inadequate infrastructure, in addition to poor housing and lack of opportunities, although this has partly changed with the construction of gated communities. Cultural interventions appear as 'symbol(s) of the periphery ... [and] the only path to freedom and to peace' (Caldeira, 2014: 416).

Contributions to urban studies

Caldeira's greatest impact has come through her work on gated communities and segregation, which has been widely recognised as pioneering. *City of Walls* is considered a classic within the literature on gated communities, for three reasons. It was the first book to analyse the consequences of the spread of gated communities, with a particular focus on segregation and crime. Second, it was the first study on gated communities in Brazil, one of the countries with the highest number of gated communities in Latin America. Finally, the book combines an analysis of the structural elements that influence the development of fortified enclaves, the examination of real estate advertisements and an ethnographic perspective based on interviews and observations. The development of gated communities manifests urban inequalities in the city: urban planning instruments that serve only the elite, while marginalising the urban poor who are forced to use cultural expressions to show their anger and discontent.

Teresa Caldeira's contribution to urban studies emphasises the interconnections of spatial, social, cultural, political and economic processes in the city, providing a solid combination of deep theoretical analysis with ethnographic data from Brazilian cities. The processes she analyses in Brazil can be identified in other cities of the Global South and beyond, thus establishing her as a vital thinker for attending to how broad sociopolitical realities shape everyday dynamics in cities around the world.

Secondary sources and references

Caldeira, T.P.R. (2011) *Ruth Cardoso. Obra reunida*. Organisation and presentation by Teresa Caldeira. São Paulo: Mameluco. Available at: www.mameluco.com.br/editora/ruth-cardoso-obra-reunida

Caldeira, T.P.R. (2014) 'Gender is still the battleground: Youth, cultural production and the remaking of public space in São Paulo', in S. Parnell and S. Oldfield (eds) *The Routledge Handbook on Cities of the Global South*. London and New York: Routledge, pp. 413–427.

Holston, J. (2008) *Insurgent Citizenship: Disjunctions of Democracy and Modernity in Brazil*. Princeton, NJ: Princeton University Press.

Sabatini, F. and Cáceres, G. (2004) 'Los barrios cerrados y la ruptura del patrón tradicional de segregación en las ciudades latinoamericanas: el caso de Santiago de Chile', in G. Cáceres and F. Sabatini (eds) *Barrios cerrados en Santiago de Chile: entre la exclusión y la integración residencial*. Santiago de Chile: Pontificia Universidad Católica de Chile – Instituto de Geografía and Lincoln Institute of Land Policy, pp. 9–43.

Young, I. (1990) *Justice and the Politics of Difference*. Princeton, NJ: Princeton University Press.

Notes

1. *Pixação* is a graphic expression, native to Brazil. It consists of writing on public space (mainly walls) to express political and social messages, especially showing resistance and discomfort. See www.dailymail.co.uk/news/arts/article-2639236/Pixacao-signature-Sao-Paulo.html (accessed 3 June 2015).
2. *Saraus* are 'weekly meetings usually in bars that congregate hundreds of people to read and listen to poetry and other literary productions' (Caldeira, 2014: 418).

9   Manuel Castells

Phil Hubbard, King's College London

Key urban writings

Castells, M. (1977) *The Urban Question: A Marxist Approach*. London: Edward Arnold.

Castells, M. (1983) *The City and the Grassroots: A Cross-Cultural Theory of Urban Social Movements*. Berkeley: University of California Press.

Castells, M. (1989) *The Informational City – Information Technology, Economic Restructuring and the Urban-Regional Process*. Oxford: Blackwell.

Castells, M. and Hall, P. (1994) *Technopoles of the World: The Making of 21st Century Industrial Complexes*. London: Routledge.

Castells, M. (1996, 1997, 1998; 2nd revised edn 2010) *The Information Age: Economy, Society and Culture* (3 vols). Oxford: Blackwell.

Introduction

Manuel Castells was a pivotal figure in the mainstreaming of a Marxist-inspired 'new' urban sociology in the 1970s. His book *The Urban Question* was a significant theoretical statement outlining the role of the city in reproducing capitalist relations through the organisation of resources, especially the forms of collective consumption – housing, education, health facilities – that are important in the reproduction of labour power. This book encouraged a generation of researchers to frame urban studies within the rich theoretical corpus of Marxism. The later, more accessible and empirically driven, *City and the Grassroots* shifted focus somewhat by offering an empirical account of the way that social groups were coalescing to fight for scarce resources, a development that took his work to wider audiences in sociology and politics while marking a move towards a post-Marxist approach to urban studies. Here, he focused on how social movements could transform the 'urban meaning' even if they could not transform society itself, and from this sought to tease out the trans-historical and cross-cultural processes of conflict between dominant classes and social movements which might produce good cities.

Subsequent to this, Castells cemented his reputation as one of the world's most influential thinkers in the social sciences by developing some of the first theoretical accounts of cyber-society. The three volumes he published on the 'Information Society' – *The Rise of the Network Society*, *The Power of Idenity* and *The End of Millennium* – proved both timely and influential in terms of theorising the relationship between time, place and space in the 'internet age'. Though the focus of his work has become broader than the city per se, Castells continues to inspire attention to the changing role of cities in an era of global capitalism, encouraging urban researchers to explore the entwining of material and virtual space.

Castells currently holds Chairs at the Open University of Catalonia, the University of Southern California, Annenberg School and the University of Cambridge.

Academic biography and research focus

Manuel Castells was born in Spain in 1942. He grew up in Barcelona where he completed his secondary education, going on to study law and economics at the University of Barcelona from 1958 to 1962. As a student activist against General Franco's fascist dictatorship he eventually had to escape to Paris, graduating from the Sorbonne's Faculty of Law and Economics in 1964. Staying in Paris, he obtained his PhD from the École des Hautes Études en Sciences Sociale in 1967. Based on a statistical analysis of high-tech industrial firms in the Paris region, his doctoral work, supervised by renowned sociologist Alain Touraine, highlighted two issues that would continue to preoccupy Castells over the next three decades – namely, the emergence of new technologies and the changing form of cities. Working in Paris at this time brought Castells into contact with leading Marxist theorists including **Henri Lefebvre**, Nicolas Poulantzas and Louis Althusser. It was thus unsurprising that Castells became caught up in the revolutionary fervour of May 1968. Expelled by the French government for his involvement, he spent time in Chile and Canada before returning to Paris in 1972 after receiving a state pardon (see Susser, 2002). In the same year he published *The Urban Question [La Question urbaine]*, a book regarded at the time as a *tour de force* and perhaps the most important text to have emerged from the neo-Marxist school of French urban sociology, albeit one very much inspired by Althusser's attempts to construct a rigorous 'scientific' theory based on the concrete concepts of Marxism rather than the Marxist humanism of Lefebvre.

In 1979, Castells moved to the University of California, Berkeley where he joined the Department of City and Regional Planning. Here, he was exposed to a more empirical tradition of sociology than was prevalent in Paris, and appeared to move away from structural Marxism (and even Marxism all together) as questions of agency moved to the foreground of his work. This was reflected in *The City and the Grassroots* (1983), a neo-Weberian comparative study of urban social movements and community, followed by a series of works on the 'informational city' (e.g. Castells, 1989; Castells and Hall, 1994). Identifying the role of cities as pivots in the global economy, this work argued that one of the key changes associated with technological innovation was the rising importance of spatial flows, and the concomitant 'loss of control' of place. Such ideas were more fully developed in his three-volume treatise on *The Information Age: Economy, Society and Culture*, comprising *The Rise of the Network Society* (1996), *The Power of Identity* (1997) and *The End of Millennium* (1998), books that were less concerned with cities per se and more preoccupied with the space of flows. Coupled with *The Internet Galaxy: Reflections on the Internet, Business, and Society* (2001), *The Information Age* raised his stock in academic, governmental and business circles where he was acclaimed a globalisation guru. Focusing on the shift from wired to wireless modes of communication shaping the 21st century, Castells extended his work on questions of agency by exploring how individual, mobile and horizontal modes of communication intersect with more traditional vertical modes of mass media. What Castells articulated was a shift from a public sphere anchored around the nation-state to a 'public sphere constituted around the media system' (Castells, 2008: 90). The implication here was that what really matters is whether you are in the network society or not, not whether you are exploiter or exploited. For some commentators, this felt like a departure from his earliest work where he had been resolutely focused on the class relations of production (see Jessop, 2003), though it continues the neo-Weberian emphasis which characterises the majority of his latter *oeuvre*.

Castells' appointment in 2002 as the Director of the Internet Interdisciplinary Institute at the Open University of Catalonia, and his simultaneous appointment as Professor of Communication and Wallis Annenberg Chair of Communication Technology and Society, at the University of Southern California, signalled his increasing focus on media and communication. Holding to the notion of 'real virtuality', Castells' post-millennial research refused to differentiate between material and symbolic sources of power, insisting that the power to shape the human mind resides in the networked power of communication (as per his 2009 book, *Communication Power*). This perspective identifies new forms of power making in the space of communication. For example, he details instances where 'power holders' have sought to infiltrate and control the horizontal networks of communication, such as the US government seeking to control the international news agenda, Rupert Murdoch's NewsCorp securing its business interests and EU powers tackling 'internet piracy' (Arsenault and Castells, 2008; Castells, 2007; Castells et al., 2006). He also continues to explore how social movements might prosper in the internet age by using communication to change people's minds (Castells, 2012).

Key ideas

While Castells' work has been highly influential for policy makers, his chief contribution to urban studies has been to enrich its theoretical foundations. Indeed, Castells' first major work, *The Urban Question: A Marxist Approach*, was heralded as a pioneering attempt to address the 'urban question' through the tenets of structural Marxism. In essence, Castells suggested that many writing about the problems and challenges facing cities in the early 1970s (e.g. race riots, poverty, criminality) were locked into an ideologically bankrupt tradition that could not possibly identify the answers to these urban problems. The tradition he was working against had its roots in 'urban ecology', and was manifest in the 'factorial ecologies' produced by many sociologists and urban geographers in the 1960s. Castells rejected this approach by drawing instead on Marxist theory that emphasised the social production of urban space. In his introduction to the volume, Castells noted his astonishment that Marxist theorists had yet to analyse cities in a 'sufficiently specific way' (Castells, 1977: 2). In the event, the book was to have remarkably little influence on those working within the Marxist tradition; its chief legacy was to inspire a generation of urban researchers to engage with theories of political economy.

First published in English in 1977, *The Urban Question* was read, alongside **David Harvey**'s (1973) *Social Justice and the City*, as a rallying call for urban researchers to utilise the conceptual armoury of structural Marxism. For all that, it was a 'notoriously cumbersome' tome (McNeill, 2014) that alienated some readers. Arguably more readable was *The City and the Grassroots*, which extended the assertion that one of the chief roles of cities in the capitalist-urban era is to provide collective consumption facilities designed to reproduce labour power. Noting the difficulties in providing equitable access to these facilities, *The City and the Grassroots* focused on the formation of protest groups and social movements seeking to improve access to such facilities. Significantly, Castells shifted his purview from exploring issues of class-consciousness to highlight the formation of 'new' social movements including those seeking the emancipation of gay and lesbian groups, based on a case study in San Francisco.

For some, this focus on agency signalled a decisive turn towards a form of neo-Weberianism (Merrifield, 2002), with **David Harvey** in particular concerned that Castells was building new theories 'from the ashes' of structural Marxism. Yet Castells' persistent interest in technology inspired a return to structural metaphors (if not structural thinking) in a series of influential works on the new informational structures of capitalism. In 1989 Castells published *The Informational City*, an analysis of the urban and regional changes brought about by information technology and economic restructuring in the US. It was prescient of the rising significance of technology in shaping the relationships between cities, becoming an important reference point in subsequent studies of 'world cities' that operate reflexively as the marshalling points of the global economy. His subsequent work on the 'informational age' developed such arguments, and though not fixated on the urban per se, provided considerable insight into the logic of the network and its implications for urban studies.

Both Castells' earlier Marxist and later neo-Weberian works have hence exercised considerable influence over the trajectory of urban thought, although it is possible to detect an important change in his conception of the city and spatial process between, for example, *The Urban Question* and *The Information Age*. In the former, Castells was scathing of those commentators who seemingly 'fetishised' the urban, bequeathing a distinct ecology that was somehow independent of capitalist structures. This included criticism of his contemporary, **Henri Lefebvre**, whom Castells alleged granted the city an autonomy and significance that it simply did not possess. Here, he bracketed Lefebvre with members of the Chicago School of urban sociology, arguing that he naively equated spatial propinquity with social emancipation 'as if there were no institutional organization outside arrangement of space' (Castells, 1977: 90). Developing this point, he argued for a structural reading of the city as a corrective to the spatial determinism evident in urban studies at this time. Yet, in doing so, Castells seemingly went to the other extreme: the city simply became a reflection of social process (Castells, 1977: 148).

Nevertheless, Castells' radical take on the urban question shook up urban studies through its insistence that the social processes resulting in the production of the city were not distinctly urban, but endemic to capitalist society. In fact, Castells was to later backtrack from this social determinism to instead suggest that 'space is not a reflection of society, it is society' (Castells, 1983: 43). Stressing that social flows are inevitably also spatial flows, Castells hence offers a different take on the social production of urban space in his work on the 'informational society' (Castells, 1989). His hypothesis is that contemporary is underpinned by a new socio-spatial logic – the 'space of flows' – that is truly global in scope. In this respect, Castells' work remains an important point of departure in the study of global and world cities, complementing other influential accounts (such as **Saskia Sassen**'s) by considering the changing place of cities in an era of 'timeless time' and 'placeless space'.

Contributions to urban studies

In much the same way that *The Urban Question* revolutionised urban studies in the 1970s, invocations of Castells' 'space of flows' idea set new agendas in the social sciences more broadly. Castells remains one of the most cited thinkers in urban studies: *The Information Age* trilogy has become an obligatory point of passage for exploring the rise of global cities, and Castells' later work on the 'new public sphere' has been significant in debates around urban social movements and public protests. In relation to the latter, urbanists such as Merrifield (2014) have drawn on Castells' work as they question whether 'the urban' can ever provide the basis for a radical transformation of society. In relation to the former, Castells' emphasis on spaces of flow has proved influential by offering a valuable corrective to sedentary, static and bounded notions of urban process.

One implication of Castells' 'space of flows' idea is that 'local' ways of life in cities are being undermined by the (network) logic of global capital accumulation: place is being annihilated by space. Elaborating, Castells (1996: 350) pointed to the proliferation of serialised a-historical and a-cultural building projects undermining the 'meaningful relationship between society and architecture', citing examples ranging from international hotels, airports and supermarkets through to the 'postmodern' office buildings that increasingly characterised the skyline of world cities (cf. **Rem Koolhaas**). Yet it has become clear that the space of places has not disappeared with the coming of network society. World cities, for instance, are not simply nodes in a network but are also distinctive 'centres of comprehension' whose pivotal role in the global economy is influenced by their distinctive social and cultural milieu. In the context of more recent comparative urban studies, and a widespread interest in relational geographies, it has been argued that some of Castells' work on globalisation appears decidedly 'one-dimensional' (Van Dijk, 1999). However, notwithstanding these critiques, Castells' research has been influential in urban studies over more than four decades. He is a thinker whose work has been foundational in shaping urban studies into a theoretically challenging, and exciting, research field.

Secondary sources and references

Arsenault, A. and Castells, M. (2008) 'Switching power: Rupert Murdoch and the global business of media politic', *International Sociology*, 23(4): 489–514.

Castells, M. (2000) 'Materials for an exploratory theory of the network society', *British Journal of Sociology*, 51(1): 1–24.

Castells, M. (2001) *The Internet Galaxy: Reflections on the Internet, Business, and Society.* Oxford: Oxford University Press.

Castells, M. (2007) 'Communication, power and counter-power in the network society', *International Journal of Communication*, 1(1): 238–266.

Castells, M. (2008) 'The new public sphere: Global civil society, communication networks, and global governance', *The Annals of the American Academy of Political and Social Science*, 616(1): 78–93.

Castells, M. (2009) *Communication Power.* Oxford: Oxford University Press.

Castells, M. (2012) *Networks of Outrage and Hope: Social Movements in the Internet Age.* Cambridge: Polity.

Castells, M., Fernandez-Ardevol, M., Qiu, J.L. and Sey, A. (2006) *Mobile Communication and Society: A Global Perspective.* Cambridge, MA: MIT Press.

Harvey, D. (1973) *Social Justice and the City.* London: Arnold.

Jessop, B. (2003) 'Informational capitalism and empire: The post-Marxist celebration of US hegemony in a new world order', *Studies in Political Economy*, 71/72: 39–58.

McNeill, D. (2014) 'Review of Andy Merrifield's *New Urban Question*', *Antipode*. Available at: https://radicalantipode.files.wordpress.com/2014/09/book-review_mcneill-on-merrifield.pdf

Mathers, A. (2014) 'Review of *Networks of Outrage and Hope*', *Sociology*, 48(6): 1063.

Merrifield, A. (2002) *Metromarxism: A Marxist Tale of the City.* New York: Routledge.

Merrifield, A. (2014) *The New Urban Question.* London: Pluto Press.

Saunders, P. (1981) *Social Theory and the Urban Question.* London: Hutchinson.

Susser, I. (2002) 'Manuel Castells: Conceptualising the city in the information age', in I. Susser (ed.) *The Castells Reader on Cities and Social Theory.* Oxford: Blackwell, pp. 1–12.

Van Dijk, J. (1999) 'The one-dimensional network society of Manuel Castells', *New Media and Society*, 1(1): 127–138.

Jason Corburn

Andrew Barnfield, London School of Hygiene and
Tropical Medicine

Key urban writings

Corburn, J. (2005) *Street Science: Community Knowledge and Environmental Health
Justice.* Cambridge, MA: MIT Press.

Corburn, J. (2009a) *Toward the Healthy City: People, Places, and the Politics of Urban
Planning.* Cambridge, MA: MIT Press.

Corburn, J. (2013) *Healthy City Planning: From Neighbourhood to National Health Equity.*
London: Routledge.

Corburn, J., Curl, S., Arredondo, G. and Malagon, J. (2014) 'Health in all urban policy: City
services through the prism of health', *Journal of Urban Health*, 91(4): 623–636.

Introduction

The city has powerful effects on health. From the provision of spaces for exercise and
the availability of fresh food, to the impacts of air pollution and communicable diseases, the layout and use of cities by residents, business and visitors are among the
many complexities that shape the life in the metropolis. Characterized by triumphs in
sanitation and urban health in Western Europe in the 19th and 20th centuries, the field
of public health postulated a new kind of relationship between the body and evolving
forms of city life and urban politics in which the associations between health and
urban reform were crucial.

Jason Corburn is an academic deeply motivated by this tradition (Corburn, 2007a).
He is a scholar who champions improved health equity in cities through engagements
with activism, professional practice and research. His work has two central aims: first,
to reunite the historical association of urban planning with social justice; and second,
to encourage the integration of health equity into all decision-making in urban governance (Corburn and Cohen, 2012). Public health in the work of Corburn concerns
physical, mental and emotional wellbeing. This covers issues such as access to safe,
clean and affordable housing; clean air and low levels of noise pollution; employment
opportunities; access to medical services, vaccinations and screening programmes; the
availability of fresh food and green spaces; and transparent governance. Health in all

policies is an ambitious reconfiguring not only of what public health is, but what urban politics looks and feels like (Corburn et al., 2014).

Corburn is Professor of City and Regional Planning at the University of California, Berkeley, where he directs the Center for Global Healthy Cities and co-directs the Centre of Global Metropolitan Studies. His current post is split between the Faculty of Environmental Design and the School of Public Health. This cross-disciplinary position is indicative of the unique scope with which Corburn works, with field sites and research projects spanning the globe including in California, Nairobi and Rio de Janeiro.

Academic biography and research focus

Corburn was born in New York City. In 1992 he left to study for a Bachelor of Arts in Politics at Brandeis University in Waltham, Massachusetts and then a Master's in City Planning (MCP) from the Massachusetts Institute of Technology (MIT) in 1996. His first position following his studies was back in New York City, working as a senior environmental planner with the Department of Environmental Protection from 1996 to 1998. He was also a mediator for the Consensus Building Institute and dealt with environmental and public health disputes. Corburn followed this by working as a community organizer in Seattle before going on to obtain a PhD in 2002 in Urban Environmental Planning from MIT. His PhD, later published as *Street Science* (2005), grew out of his research in Brooklyn from 1996 to 2002. This was followed by a postdoctoral research position in epidemiology – the statistical analysis of the distribution and determinants of health-related disease and illness across a population – at the Mailman School of Public Health at Columbia University.

Corburn's influences are varied. They include academic mentors from his studies at MIT and Harvard such as urban planning professors Lawrence Susskind and David Laws, and professor of public health Nick Freudenberg. Theoretically his influences range from urban scholar and activist **Jane Jacobs**, social epidemiologist Nancy Krieger to social theorists Bruno Latour and Pierre Bourdieu, and the American pragmatist John Dewey. In addition, Corburn is able to draw on a wealth of practical experience in the day-to-day machinations of urban planning and local government – a unique advantage for an academic in urban studies.

The focus of his research is on the relations between environmental health and social justice in cities, ideas of knowledge in science-based policy making, the role of local expertise in understanding environmental and public health problems, and techniques of promoting greater health equity in cities by reconnecting city planning and public health (Corburn, 2010). In practice this involves working with disadvantaged groups including low-income urban communities, residents of informal settlement residents and people from minority ethnic backgrounds. Such collaborations have produced integrated land-use plans and policies aimed at preventing displacement of informal settlement residents, securing land tenure and improving economic opportunities, infrastructure and environmental health. Corburn's work helps to establish partnerships between urban residents, scientists and policy makers in order to collaboratively produce strategy and planning solutions that develop the abilities of cities and the health of residents.

This approach is evidenced by Corburn's work in Greenpoint/Williamsburg, New York. He encouraged community members and professionals to work together to understand the hazards from subsistence fishing from the polluted East River, local sources of air pollution, the asthma epidemic in the Latino community and lead poisoning in children and young people. These events draw attention to the achievements and the restrictions of participatory work and highlight how residents can establish their own credibility when working in partnership with scientists. Corburn argues that this approach does not degrade science. Rather, it enhances different types of information and opens up the research, analysis and decision-making processes.

Corburn is currently working on developing a strategy for integrating health equity into all decision-making in city governance, researching metrics and indicators for urban health equity, and establishing a plan to upgrade informal settlements. His work continues to push into new ground by researching urban climate justice – in particular how climate change policies and institutions can guarantee the most susceptible urban residents gain assistance from evolving mitigation decisions.

Key ideas

In contemporary cities the rise in the prevalence of obesity and other non-communicable diseases is linked to living patterns that promote sedentariness, inactivity and unhealthy diets. Additionally, the continued reliance on motorized transportation that fosters the stationary human inside a moving vehicle leads to high levels of air pollution that cause respiratory conditions such as asthma. Further, mental health is adversely affected by the stresses of living in overcrowded conditions with unstable job prospects and uncertain living arrangements. It is attending to these sorts of issues that drives Corburn's work. His key ideas of reuniting urban planning with social justice, and integrating health equity into all decision-making in urban governance correspond with the founding tenets of his 19th-century predecessors (Corburn, 2004). However, Corburn wants to draw local residents into the evidence-gathering and decision-making process (Corburn, 2007b). This makes him an intriguing case for a book on key thinkers on cities, because while there is a lot of thinking going in Corburn's work, his key ides are about actively changing how things happen in cities, communities and everyday life.

Corburn sees health problems such as asthma, infant mortality and cardiovascular disease as indicative of the failure of urban policy and planning, rather than as individual mistakes, bad choices or endemic of city life. To understand how to make city life better for all residents Corburn calls for an examination of the relationship between economic, political and social developments that are disregarded by biomedical sciences. Corburn advocates that by bringing urban scholarship and public health into partnership with community-based organizations, foundations, international agencies and local and regional government, cases of ill health that occur in contemporary cities can be eradicated (Corburn, 2003).

The key question that drives Corburn's work is how can urban scholarship, planning and public health work with local knowledge to make cities fairer and healthier places? The first step Corburn advocates is making use of the knowledge and skills of local residents in the identification and remediation of uneven health effects, including those connected to urban processes such as deindustrialization. In *Street Science: Community Knowledge and Environmental Health Justice* (2005), Corburn has attempted to challenge the status quo in urban planning by instigating what he calls 'street science'. This term defines the drawing together of community knowledge with professionals that aim to produce solutions for local environmental health issues. Corburn envisions 'democratically robust problem solving' proposing street science as 'a practice of knowledge production that embraces the co-production framework' that 'builds on a number of existing participatory models of knowing and doing' (Corburn, 2005: 8).

What does this mean? The aim is to provide local residents with help in working with city officials to change policy to meet their needs and concerns. It involves local participation in health studies as well as increasing provisions in services and facilities. This can be seen in Corburn's work in Richmond, California which has brought about changes to local planning laws in response to air pollution from a local Chevron plant. The Richmond Health Equity Initiative instigated the health and wellbeing element in all local planning applications, and subsequently won compensation and concessions in court. Corburn acted as co-leader of the Richmond Health Equity Partnership, integrating health equity into city government decision-making processes, as well as in county health and school district planning. Based on these efforts, in 2014, Richmond became the first city in California to legislate a Health in All Policies strategy.

Corburn's second book, *Toward the Healthy City* (2009a), attempts to expand the definition of health that is currently used in planning by incorporating social welfare, public safety and economic opportunity. This new definition includes more than simply mortality or disease, developing an understanding of health as a combination of the person and the social. In order for a more comprehensive notion to be actualized in urban policy, Corburn argues that urban planners must play a participatory role in the improvement of methods of analysis and evaluation. Methods should involve drawing the social determinants of health into the regulatory practices and decision-making. The aim is to change the dialogue between health and city functions, meaning that instead of simply treating people and sending them back to the conditions that played a part in their illness, the places of habitation and other factors should be investigated and transformed.

An example of healthy city planning can be found in a method developed by Corburn called the Healthy Development Measurement Tool (HDMT). The HDMT is a product of collaborative work with the San Francisco Department of Public Health (Corburn and Bhatia, 2011) aimed at tackling issues and inequalities in urban health. The HDMT is a method for the evaluation of land-use planning and urban development that recognizes the potential impacts on citizens' and community health. The HDMT offers a range of baseline data on community health metrics for San Francisco. It also developed targets to assess the degree to which urban development projects and policy can improve health. In providing 27 measurable indicators that documented how different parts of the city were performing, the HDMT enabled a health-focused rationale to be cultivated in urban development policies.

Finally, in *Healthy City Planning* (2013) Coburn builds on his earlier work in *Street Science* to outline a framework of adaptive urban health justice. The intention is to address questions of how to improve the lives of urban dwellers that have been too often marked by inequalities and discrimination, and when city planning has a limited influence on guiding policies and programmes that address them. These harms are particularly profound for people from disadvantaged groups. Corburn suggests that because urban planning has not been attuned to health outcomes, it has contributed to exacerbating health inequalities in cities. Adaptive urban health justice is his remedy, and is based upon three distinct concepts: eco-social epidemiology, science and technology studies of the city, and adaptive ecosystem management. Together they combine thinking that is sensitive to embodiment, a relational view of urban places, and democratic process. This aim is to be sensitive to the intricacies of cities, to the movement of bodies, things and feelings – but also aware of the potential for difference, experience and participation that is evident in urban space (cf. **Harvey Molotch, Natalie Jeremijenko**).

Adaptive urban health justice is a framework underpinned by pragmatic thinking – particularly the American pragmatism of John Dewey that seeks to explain the contents of hypotheses by sketching their 'practical consequences'. Corburn seeks to use these ideas in developing new understandings of the city and its conditions, and how they can be made and remade for better urban health. This can be seen implemented in Corburn's work with the Centre for Health Promotion at the State University of Rio de Janeiro, Brazil (CEDAPS). CEDAPS has evaluated how a multidimensional approach to urban planning can promote greater health equity and improve favela health in Rio de Janeiro. Here, local community health agents implement a decentralized national government policy in city-wide health programmes, including innovative cash-transfer programmes that provide financial support for healthy food and health provisions with conditions attached. As a result, immunization, breast-feeding and under-nutrition have all improved markedly.

Contributions to urban studies

Jason Corburn isn't a theorist. He does not produce urban theory in the same way other scholars featured in *Key Thinkers on Cities* do. Rather, Corburn is attempting, through his analysis and collaborative projects, to advocate for new ways of _doing_ urban research and planning through his ideas of street science and a new decision-making framework he defines as healthy city planning. Therefore, his unique contribution to urban studies is twofold. First is his specific focus on health as an urban issue. In prioritizing health as the main outcome of inequality Corburn is prefiguring health in the debates of unequal urban societies. Second is his aspiration to encourage closer links between urban planning and public health. Here, he is attempting to bring urban planning back to its founding principles to establish health equity and social justice (cf. **Enrique Peñalosa**).

Healthy city planning is a practical engagement with urban space and the local drivers of health inequality: an attitude that moves away from removal of hazards and people towards prevention and precaution, away from overreliance on scientific rationality towards co-production of scientific knowledge, and away from moral environmentalism and physical determinism towards a more comprehensive relational view of places. Jason Corburn's work aims to bring about change in the daily lives of urban residents, particularly the most disadvantaged, by encouraging cooperation between residents, academics and politicians as a method of collaborative policy and planning solutions. It is an approach that is attentive to the many and varied stories that comprise urban space as well as the processes and experiences that are essential to urban health and life in cities.

Secondary sources and references

Corburn, J. (2003) 'Bringing local knowledge into environmental decision-making: Improving urban planning for communities at risk', *Journal of Planning Education and Research*, 22(4): 420–433.

Corburn, J. (2004) 'Confronting the challenges in reconnecting urban planning and public health', *American Journal of Public Health*, 94(4): 541–546.

Corburn, J. (2007a) 'Reconnecting with our roots: American urban planning and public health in the 21st century', *Urban Affairs Review*, 42(5): 688–713.

Corburn, J. (2007b) 'Community knowledge in environmental health science: Co-producing policy expertise', *Environmental Science and Policy*, 10(2): 150–161.

Corburn, J. (2009b) 'Cities, climate change and urban heat island mitigation: Localizing global environmental science', *Urban Studies*, 47(2): 413–427.

Corburn, J. (2010) 'Rebuilding the foundations of health: Planning for healthier and more equitable places', *Planning Theory and Practice*, 11(3): 435–441.

Corburn, J. and Bhatia, R. (2011) 'Lessons from San Francisco: Health impact assessments have advanced political conditions for improving population health', *Health Affairs*, 30(12): 2410–2418.

Corburn, J. and Cohen, A.K. (2012) 'Why we need urban health equity indicators: Integrating science, policy, and community', *PLoS Medicine*, 9(8): e1001285.

11 Mike Davis

Melanie Lombard, University of Sheffield

Key urban writings

Davis, M. (1990) *City of Quartz: Excavating the Future in Los Angeles.* London: Verso.

Davis, M. (1998) *The Ecology of Fear: Los Angeles and the Imagination of Disaster.* New York: Vintage.

Davis, M. (2000) *Magical Urbanism: Latinos Reinvent the US City.* London: Verso.

Davis, M. (2002) *Dead Cities and Other Tales.* New York: New Press.

Davis, M. (2006a) *Planet of Slums: Urban Involution and the Informal Working Class.* London: Verso.

Introduction

Mike Davis is a social commentator, urban theorist and activist. A self-proclaimed Marxist environmentalist, his work is distinguished by its unflinching critical approach to urbanization processes and a specific concern with the social and environmental effects of these processes on marginalized communities. His colourful, uncompromising and erudite writing covers an eclectic range of subjects, connected by the theme of urban injustice.

Davis's major contribution to urban studies has been as a core proponent of the so-called 'LA School', one of a group of academics who saw Los Angeles as a laboratory for urban transformation, and in this sense, his work has been instrumental in highlighting the urban iniquities of advanced capitalism, starting from the setting of LA and expanding outwards. While his staunchly Marxist approach has garnered fierce criticism from some quarters, it has not precluded a wide popular readership. His wide appeal is based on his accessible and fast-paced writing on cities, and on the broad application of his incisive analytical perspective, which he has brought to bear on urban themes ranging from boosterism to the bourgeoisie, and from urbanization to avian flu. He has published in academic but also popular journals including the *Nation* and *New Statesman*.

Davis currently holds the post of Emeritus Professor in the Department of Creative Writing at the University of California Riverside.

Academic biography and research focus

Davis's working-class background, and his employment as a meatcutter and long-distance lorry driver, are often attributed as formative experiences which shaped his writing as much as his academic biography. Born in 1946 in Fontana, California, Davis studied briefly at Reed College in Oregon in the mid-1960s; around the same time he was involved in civil rights protests and the Students for a Democratic Society movement. After a stint working in various blue-collar jobs in the western United States, he returned to academia in the 1970s to complete a BA and MA in History at the University of California, Los Angeles where he started but did not complete a PhD programme. Much of the 1980s were spent in Europe, particularly the UK, before he returned to Los Angeles in 1987. During this period, he published *Prisoners of the American Dream* (1987). This offers a Marxist interpretation to the question of why there has never been a major party representing the working class in the US. This is a theme that is reprised in the conclusion of *Magical Urbanism* (2000), a slim volume that explores the increasing presence of Latin Americans in US cities and their concomitant exclusion from both urban theory and the benefits of urban life.

Davis's enduring muse is Los Angeles, and his love–hate relationship with the city has spanned the publication of many works. His best-known, *City of Quartz* (1990), is the first book of an uncompleted trilogy that includes *Ecology of Fear*, published in 1998. *City of Quartz* (COQ) is a breathless and intricate history of the city as a microcosm of liberal capitalism, with all its triumphs and iniquities, 'sunshine and noir'. The book was a surprise bestseller and was put forward for a National Book Critics' Circle Award. Its searing account of 'The Hammer and the Rock' in Chapter 5 describes the vicious injustices of law and order's punitive response to the structural violence generated by social and racial inequality, offering a devastating critique of the penalization of poverty and minority ethnic groups in LA, which, Davis argued, could be seen as a barometer for American cities more broadly. The prescience of this account, which preceded the 1992 LA riots – a response to the beating of Rodney King by Los Angeles Police Department officers – by two years, meant that '[t]he book, and Davis himself, achieved near-prophetic status' (Stannard, 2004: 255). Following its publication, the award of a Getty Scholarship at the Getty Institute Santa Monica (1996–7) and a MacArthur Fellowship (1998) went hand-in-hand with popular acclaim.

If COQ was a blistering indictment of the social effects of urban inequality in Los Angeles, *Ecology of Fear* (EOF) is its ecological equivalent, providing a critical account of planning failures in Southern California. The book outlines the links between unrestrained urban growth in Southern California and the burgeoning environmental crisis generated by over-development, a lack of environmental protection and the ever-present threat of the region's seismic risks. Building on this premise, the essays in *Dead Cities* (2002) reprise familiar themes of the environmental damage wrought on the physical and social landscape by urban development processes driven by elite interests; but its publication also signalled an expansion of Davis's geographical and subject focus to cities such as Las Vegas and issues such as toxic waste disposal. The two strands of Davis's Marxist environmentalist stance are exemplified in *Planet of Slums* (2006a), which turns his critical lens to a global level to address the social and environmental inequities of the 'slums' that increasingly characterize urban growth around the world.

During the mid-1990s Davis held a succession of research and teaching jobs at high-profile institutions, including the post of Visiting Fellow at the Center for Comparative History and Social Theory, University of California LA in 1994; Regents Lecturer at the University of California Irving in 1996; Avenali Professor at the University of California Berkeley; and Havens Center Fellow at the University of Wisconsin in 1997. Following his MacArthur Fellowship, he taught urban theory at the Southern California Institute of Architecture and in 1999 took up a three-year appointment to teach history at the State University of New York, Stony Brook. He maintained a prolific rate of publication during the 1990s and 2000s, with an output that included the first two books of the *Islands Mysterious* trilogy of young adult fiction and several edited collections, the most recent of these being *Evil Paradises* (2008). His most recent book *Be Realistic: Demand the Impossible* (2012) presents a defence of Occupy Wall Street and sketches out future directions for the movement. He is a longstanding editor of the *New Left Review*.

Key ideas

Davis's Marxist environmentalism permeates his thinking about cities. A particular concern is the need to expose contradictions of capitalist urbanization through forensic analyses of class and power relations. Indeed, his 'trademark materialist interpretation' (Stannard, 2004) offers a method for exploring the environmental and social consequences of unconstrained urbanization, and the resulting urban crises. This is best exemplified in *COQ* and its presentation of Los Angeles as a simultaneously utopian and dystopian locus of advanced capitalism. He argues that forces of exclusion and inequality have been key to the city's formation, as the role of real estate speculation as a site of power in early 20th-century LA gave way to a city in flux – politically, socially and culturally. Emblematic of this is the ever-increasing spatial segregation that occurs as the city becomes privatized through gated enclaves and public space is increasingly diminished (cf. **Teresa Caldeira**).

A second key idea is that unbridled urbanization is further compounding environmental crisis. The second book in his uncompleted trilogy on Los Angeles, *EOF*, demonstrates how floods, fires and earthquakes are now occurring with increasing intensity, leading to potential social catastrophe. In this and other works on this theme, Davis's environmental vision seeks to lay bare the risks of urbanization in 'inhospitable' natural environments, compounded by the folly of vainglorious attempts to urbanize canyons and coastline for wealthy elites in search of 'unspoilt' landscapes, at a cost of long-term environmental damage and the privatization of the commons (see also **Matthew Gandy**, 2014). Here, once again, environmental risks are found to reflect and reproduce class divisions.

Such characteristics of modern LA – inequality, a lack of public space and consequent dearth of collective experience – along with his curiously individualizing Marxist approach, arguably shape Davis's view of contemporary cities as 'a place of breakdown' (Merrifield, 2002: 4). While 'metropolitan Marxism' – a term used by Merrifield (2002) for writers such as Marshall Berman and **David Harvey** – refers to a Marxist urbanism that highlights the city's everyday ambiguities and possibilities alongside the structural forces framing them, Davis's view is arguably less optimistic. What Merrifield

(2002: 5–6) calls the metropolitan dialectic is appreciative of the intimate relations, tensions and contradictions inherent between the positive and negative aspects of the capitalist city, between critique and affirmation. By contrast, Davis's pessimism about urban futures and the city more generally leaves him open to charges of having or engendering a nihilist perspective on cities.

Such pessimism permeates *Planet of Slums* (2006a) (*POS*), which describes how 'much of the twenty-first-century urban world squats in squalor, surrounded by pollution, excrement, and decay' (Davis, 2006a: 19). *POS* expands an argument first made in an article of the same name in *New Left Review* (2004) that drew heavily on UN-Habitat's (2003) *The Challenge of the Slums: Global Report on Human Settlements*. Davis (2006a: 200–201) sees 'slums' as 'a fully franchised solution to the problem of warehousing this century's surplus humanity' in a world where exclusion occurs at local, national and global levels. The cause of this spatial exclusion can be traced to the imposition of Structural Adjustment Programmes in the 1980s by the World Bank and the International Monetary Fund. These made life unsustainable for millions of rural poor, forcing them to move to cities – with resultant explosive urbanization. In this way, 'cities have become a dumping ground for a surplus population working in unskilled, unprotected and low-wage informal service industries and trade' (Davis, 2006a: 175).

The stark language used in *POS* successfully conveys the urgency of the issue, as part of a broader current of development debates framing urban crisis at a global scale. However, the use of the term 'slum' has been criticized as supporting a generally negative and oversimplified image of informal settlements (Gilbert, 2007: 698), thus feeding the very narratives it purports to contest. Moreover, the impressively broad scope and level of detail in Davis's account is combined with a curiously weak prescriptive approach. Attacking all solutions that have been put forward, Davis undermines the normative potential of his work. Finally, this totalizing view leaves out the perspective and politics of the poor, a striking omission given the long history of social movements in struggling for land, services and a voice in this context (Angotti, 2006). Such overwhelmingly negative depictions seem to preclude the possibility of agency in this setting, reinforcing the disempowered position of already marginalized residents.

The narrative of urban apocalypse is again revisited in *Dead Cities*, in which Davis warns of the dismal reality of racial segregation and barely contained violence which underlies the fantasy of urban America with explosive potential. Davis's wider *oeuvre* on urban apocalypse also includes writings such as his *Los Angeles Times* article (1994) warning of 'suburban nightmare'. Whether such works are truly anti-urban, as his critics suggest, or whether they are simply a radical presentation of uncomfortable truths about our urban world, as Davis has suggested in his defence, perhaps depends on the reader's political persuasion; although Davis's noir modality could also be framed within a longer tradition of baroque urban critique, expounded by Walter Benjamin among others.

Contributions to urban studies

Davis's work tends to have a divisive effect, garnering either adulation or stinging critique. The publication of his two best-selling books on Los Angeles, *COQ* and *EOF*, made his reputation as the city's 'reigning prophet of doom' (Purdum, 1999), or a genius, depending on the perspective taken. While his publications have often enjoyed popular success, his hyperbolic rhetorical tendencies have given rise to suggestions that his work is more akin to journalism than scholarship. Davis's rhetorical style is a self-proclaimed attempt to put forward 'the oppositional power of documentary realism' (1990: 87). Indeed, he is at his most florid when describing urban injustice; but although entertaining for readers, this style has also left him open to charges of sensationalism, and vulnerable to a certain amount of intellectual snobbery from fellow academics (Stannard, 2004).

Nonetheless, Davis's contribution to urban studies has been recognized in his positioning as a key proponent of the LA School. The rise to prominence of a small group of thinkers based in Southern Californian educational institutions who found in LA an urban laboratory, provided a counterpoint during the 1980s to the prevailing dominance of the Chicago School, and ultimately 'effected a shift in the way social scientists interpreted cities' (Stannard, 2004: 256). This group, which included other theorists such as Michael Dear, Allen Scott, Ed Soja and Jennifer Wolch, saw Los Angeles as a paradigmatic city from which lessons could be drawn about urban change. The collective influence of the group is matched by that of its individual members: in Davis's case, for example his account of 'Fortress L.A.' is a precursor to **Stephen Graham**'s influential work on the urban military-security complex.

However, such popular and academic acclaim has not been without confrontation. Davis has been embroiled in controversy over fact-checking several times, most notoriously having to defend himself against calls of fabrication of source material originating from 'Brady Westwater', the pseudonym of a local real estate developer in LA, following the publication of COQ. After EOF was published, Davis faced similar criticisms for apparently inflating certain figures such as the numbers of drug-related deaths in McArthur Park, as well as his alleged fabrication of an interview with a local environmentalist for a report in the LA Weekly (Purdum, 1999). Davis's response has been to suggest that his writing, as evidenced by Ecology of Fear, is a polemic in which the narrative is subservient to the political agenda (Purdum, 1999). Meanwhile, there has been some suggestion that his critics are themselves ideologically motivated, or even represent 'reprisals by the powerful sectors in LA he had upset by his exposures' (Scott, 2002: 25).

These critiques notwithstanding, Davis's major impact on the discipline of urban studies has been based on his critical approach to urban processes under advanced capitalism. Indeed, despite Davis's often dystopian perspective, his passion for the urban is evident in his writing; and his critical perspective, sharpened over many years' writing on cities in the US and beyond, still resonates strongly when applied to subjects such as Dubai (2006b). It is his 'ability to identify and articulate the connections between apparently disparate processes and events' (Stannard, 2004: 255), along with his insistence on the need for change, that characterizes his approach. His enduring contribution may be precisely the urgency with which he insists that urban revolution is needed, which has provided a certain narrative template for much of today's critical urban studies. Rather than a doomsayer, then, Mike Davis could be seen as one of urban studies' most ardent defenders.

Secondary sources and references

Angotti, T. (2006) 'Apocalyptic anti-urbanism: Mike Davis and his planet of slums', *International Journal of Urban and Regional Research*, 30(4): 961–967.

Davis, M. (1987) *Prisoners of the American Dream: Politics and Economy in the History of the U.S. Working Class.* London: Verso.

Davis, M. (1994) 'The suburban nightmare: While older suburbs experience many problems of the inner city, "edge cities" now offer a new escape', *Los Angeles Times,* 27 October.

Davis, M. (2004) 'Planet of slums: Urban involution and the informal proletariat', *New Left Review*, March–April: 5–34.

Davis, M. (2006b) 'Fear and money in Dubai', *New Left Review*, 41: 47–68.

Davis, M. (2012) *Be Realistic, Demand the Impossible.* Chicago, IL: Haymarket Books.

Davis, M. and Monk, D.B. (eds) (2008) *Evil Paradises, Dreamworlds of Neoliberalism.* New York and London: New Press.

Gandy, M. (2014) *The Fabric of Space: Water, Modernity, and the Urban Imagination*. London: MIT Press.

Gilbert, A. (2007) 'The return of the slum: Does language matter?', *International Journal of Urban and Regional Research*, 31(4): 697–713.

Merrifield, A. (2002) *Metromarxism: A Marxist Tale of the City.* London: Routledge.

Purdum, T. (1999) 'Best-selling author's gloomy future for Los Angeles meets resistance', *The New York Times*, 27 January. Available at: www.nytimes.com/1999/01/27/us/best-selling-author-s-gloomy-future-for-los-angeles-meets-resistance.html?pagewanted=all

Scott, L. (2002) 'A giant still sleeping', *London Review of Books*, 4 April: 25–27.

Stannard, K. (2004) 'That certain feeling: Mike Davis, truth and the city', *Geography*, 89(3): 254–268.

UN-Habitat (2003) *The Challenge of the Slums: Global Report on Human Settlements.* London: United Nations Human Settlements Programme/Earthscan.

12 Bent Flyvbjerg

Martijn Duineveld, Kristof Van Assche and Raoul Beunen, The Evolutionary Governance Theory Collective

Key urban writings

Flyvbjerg, B. (1998) *Rationality and Power: Democracy in Practice.* Chicago: University of Chicago Press.

Flyvbjerg, B. (2001a) *Making Social Science Matter: Why Social Inquiry Fails and How It Can Succeed Again.* Cambridge: Cambridge University Press.

Flyvbjerg, B., Bruzelius, N. and Rothengatter, W. (2003) *Megaprojects and Risk: An Anatomy of Ambition.* Cambridge: Cambridge University Press.

Flyvbjerg, B. (2006) 'Five misunderstandings about case-study research', *Qualitative Inquiry,* 12(2): 219–245.

Flyvbjerg, B., Landman, T. and Schram, S. (2012) *Real Social Science: Applied Phronesis.* Cambridge: Cambridge University Press.

Introduction

Bent Flyvbjerg came in with a bang with the English-language publication of his book *Rationality and Power.* He shook up several disciplines interested in cities, urban governance and planning. Many of these disciplines were still rooted in the modernist ideology of steering and control; ideas Flyvbjerg argued against. Flyvbjerg is a critical scholar but he is not yet another neo-Marxist obsessed with gentrification and exclusion in the 'neoliberal' city. Firmly rooted in the Foucauldian tradition, his work unmasks the hidden rationalities of power underneath the polished technical and juridical surface of city planning, politics and administration; a skill he also deploys outside academia. He is frequently featured in mainstream media, and has advised, among others, Danish, Dutch and British governmental agencies, and the Kosovo Ministry of Environment. Over the years, he has developed a perspective which links, in new ways, the organization of space, manners of talking about it, and modes of investigation. Flyvbjerg's varied work on urban planning, megaprojects, local government, case study research, power/knowledge relations and activist scholarship can help academics to bridge disciplines looking at cities, to combine reflection and practice, and to engage critically with a world of urban governance, where academic knowledge has long been discredited and manipulated at the same time.

Flyvbjerg is currently Professor of Major Programme Management at Oxford University's Said Business School. He is also the Director of the University's BT Centre for Major Programme Management.

Academic biography and research focus

Flyvbjerg's academic career started in the 1980s when he conducted research on urban planning and governance in the Danish city of Aalborg. Soon after finishing his PhD in Economic Geography from Aarhus University he received two higher doctorates from Aalborg University. In 1993 he became Professor of Planning in the Department of Development and Planning at Aalborg University, Denmark, indeed the place where his fieldwork took place. In 2009 Flyvbjerg left Denmark for the UK. He became Professor and Inaugural Chair of Major Programme Management at Oxford University, and director of an institute with the same focus.

Flyvbjerg's work has centred on three distinct yet interrelated topics. First: planning, rationality and power. This line of research started with his PhD fieldwork in the 1980s on planning and politics in Aalborg where he investigated the entwining of power and knowledge. From his research in the early 1990s two books were derived in Danish, condensed in 1998 into the book *Rationality and Power*. Theoretically this work is inspired by power theorists like Machiavelli, Nietzsche and Foucault.

The second line of his work is best summarized in his 2001 book *Making Social Science Matter: Why Social Inquiry Fails and How It Can Succeed Again*. It deals with the philosophy, methodology and legitimacy of the social sciences, inclusive of the humanities and several applied disciplines like planning. He argues in favour of an approach to social science that goes beyond mimicking the natural sciences and pleas for a social science that uses case study research to cultivate reflexivity and criticism. He suggests that an expanded and revised social science can find its own strengths to help administrations and citizens alike to question who gains, and who loses, from existing social arrangements and to discern alternative governance options.

A third line of his academic work, represented by the 2003 book *Megaprojects and Risk: An Anatomy of Ambition*, is focused on large-scale development projects. Based on many case studies and much comparative data, Flyvbjerg demonstrates that the actual costs of large projects are systematically underestimated while the benefits are overstated in order to get such projects approved. This work captured the attention of governments and those critical of them, and made him a valued advisor in many corners of the world.

Key ideas

Flyvbjerg's approach to cities is most explicit in *Rationality and Power* where he, as a modern day Machiavelli, studied how power 'really' works in the Danish town of Aalborg, in northern Jutland. His study stretched almost a decade and during that time Flyvbjerg was directly involved in the project allowing him to conduct an extraordinarily detailed study based on his participatory observations. The Aalborg project aimed at 'integrating environmental and social concerns into city politics and planning' (Flyvbjerg, 2001a: 144). The Aalborg redevelopment tried, among other things, to manage the problem of the increasing impact of cars on the old city centre. Following Foucault who considered power not as something one possesses, but as a web of relations, Flyvbjerg studied how power is exercised, to understand what 'governmental rationalities are at work when those who govern govern' (Flyvbjerg, 2001a: 131).

After 200 pages of detailed descriptions of the Aalborg project, quoting from interviews, archives and key informants, he concludes with 10 propositions. The most important one being the reversal of Francis Bacon's dictum 'knowledge is power'. Instead Flyvbjerg, much in line with Foucault, Nietzsche and Machiavelli, proclaims: power defines reality. Bureaucracies and politicians often exercise power to deliberately forget, ridicule or marginalize certain research outcomes; in some cases they stimulate or pressure researchers to limit their research to certain questions and make them avoid issues that might constrain the ambitions of bureaucrats or politicians. In Aalborg, for example, the results of a survey involving car-using consumers did not align with the ideals of the Chamber of Industry and Commerce and was therefore quickly put in the drawer. Flyvbjerg shows how the production of knowledge in a planning process is deeply political and always entangled with power: it must be understood in terms of power/knowledge configurations. In the ensuing propositions he also debunks the idea of context-independent rationality and clearly outlines the strategic and conflicting roles and forms of rationality in the exercise of power.

Foucauldian ideas have become widespread under the banner of post-structuralism, which highlights the constructed nature of knowledge, but Flyvbjerg demonstrates anew many of Foucault's insights in power/knowledge in the context of contemporary urban governance. His novelty lies in the fact that he brings these insights into real-life planning projects, where he could observe the planning process, the decisions being made, alternatives highlighted or ignored, from up close and from within, as a participant observer. He could witness that the pursuit of power itself generates its own rationality (the 'power game') and that each actor in a planning process develops its own rationality in a power/knowledge configuration; a mode of reasoning linked to an understanding of self, the world, the issue and the power game (Van Assche et al., 2014a). Governmental regimes and their embedded planning processes, linking various sorts of actors, use, exclude and produce new players and new forms of knowing. In these processes academic disciplines are more than containers of knowledge supplying rational knowledge for the sake of the planning process. They are also networks of people promoting a particular understanding of the world and a certain role for themselves in urban governance (Hillier, 2002). Knowing and the exercise of power are intricately tied and hence science and administration end up in a relation of use and abuse, in which the boundaries between science and administration are not so clear (Mansfield, 1993).

Flyvbjerg's involvement in the Aalborg project did not come to an end with the final page of the book *Rationality and Power*. For him, the book was a reference point for further activities as a policy advisor, a consultant and a media figure. For Flyvbjerg such roles are not external to the social sciences, but part of what he calls 'phronetic research' (Flyvbjerg, 2002). He argues that the social sciences should focus on context-dependent epistemologies, on practical wisdom and real-world situations. In his work on phronesis he combines Aristotle and MacIntyre's (1981) idea of phronesis (practical wisdom), as an art of judgement irreducible to scientific knowing, the phenomenological perspective of the Dreyfus brothers (Dreyfus and Dreyfus, 1986) on human learning as irreducible to the disembodied transfer of bits of information, and Foucault's conceptualization of power/knowledge. From this line of work emerges a strong argument for the legitimacy of case studies and against universalism and generalization in the social sciences. It also produces new arguments for a more prominent role of academic work, interdisciplinary and inclusive of social sciences, in the everyday business of running a city and in the visioning for its future.

Phronetic research holds the potential to affect the reality it uncovers. For Flyvbjerg it is a science that is relevant to practice. Problems should not only be problems recognized as such by academics, but also by different communities. Results are communicated not only within academia, but also in society, to the different stakeholders. Media play a central role in the dissemination of findings, and to stir up debate on alternative courses of action or renovation of an always-vulnerable democracy (Flyvbjerg, 2014). Flyvbjerg's will to affect actual planning practices is made very explicit in four main questions that, according to him, should inform phronetic research: '1. Where are we going with democracy and planning … ? 2. Who gains and who loses, by which mechanisms of power? 3. Is this development desirable? 4. What should be done?' (Flyvbjerg, 2002: 356). Clearly, these questions are both analytical and normative and will lead to answers that will be descriptive and prescriptive.

Phronetic science marks both the early stages of Flyvbjerg's academic career and his current work. Yet, it is interesting to observe that while his earlier Aalborg case is mainly a Foucauldian inspired analysis of power/knowledge configurations, his recent work on megaprojects, deconstructing risk assessment and performance of success, involves less a genealogical reconstruction of governance paths, and more the construction of counter-arguments. He develops new knowledge that undermines the dominant rationalities legitimizing megaprojects. This might suggest that Flyvbjerg learned that reflexive observation of the contingency of rationality/power at work is less effective in practice than openly criticizing decisions, courses of actions, particular uses of expertise, and proposing alternative decisions, policies, based on different forms of expertise. It is about speaking truth about power and speaking truth to power. The whole exercise can be described as phronetic science, and it can include a variety of traditional forms of expertise. Methodologically, we can also understand his approach as a combination of deep case study analysis, grounded theory, organizational ethnography and action research, with the action taking place during and after research.

Clearly the concept of phronesis carries a lot of weight and the phronetic researcher is asked to combine many roles that have traditionally been separated. Not only does she need to bridge disciplines, grasp the world of informality, reinvent scientific method, criticize the people probably employing her and the community she probably lives in, but also to propose alternatives. In some cases, this might work; in others, not. Becoming a political actor can be worthwhile and laudable, but brings its own pressures on the production and use of facts in strategizing, as Flyvbjerg himself showed. Observing and participating in a game are different things, while for the functioning of a democracy, participation and representation are different and necessary things. Bringing in a revamped phronetic scientist to shift the balance towards local participation will not necessarily lead to a better functioning democracy (Mansfield, 1993; Van Assche et al., 2014a). For Aristotle himself, phronesis was not so much a form of knowing as a quality of judgement: prudence. Judgement and leadership as a set of acquired skills involving discernment cannot be reduced to or replaced by a set of scientific rules, nor moral rules or laws. Politics and administration have been too much plagued by modernist legacies of such reductionism, and also academic work has omitted judgement and leadership from its self-image. Flyvbjerg's combination of Foucault and Aristotle makes phronesis a powerful concept to link practice and theory, urban governance and its academic observers. The concept of phronesis also makes clear that Flyvbjerg's critiques are never normative attacks from nowhere. His critiques are always focused on a particular situation in which he wants to make evident: 'Who gains and who loses; by which mechanisms of power?' (Flyvbjerg, 2001a: 356).

Contributions to urban studies

To understand the relevance of Flyvbjerg's work for urban studies, one must consider the state of European debate on planning, urban governance and public administration in the 1980s and 1990s. Political science, public administration and urban planning were generally seen as 'bureaucratic' disciplines, graduating people to be useful for the administration of social-democratic welfare states. These disciplines equipped them with applicable 'urban expertise' reduced to mostly quantitative analyses supporting and reproducing particular forms of existing urban governance. The disciplines were supposed to be useful to 'practice' and seen as a particular form of bureaucratic organization. Questioning these forms of organization was understood as less useful, and even looking closely at how things actually worked, as distinct from how they are supposed to work, was seen as critical, or, worse, theory. In line with this, many planners, political scientists and specialists in public administration often silently identified with the powers that be. Analysing these powers and reflecting upon them was easily seen as undermining the disciplines and the associated specialist roles. The appearance of Flyvbjerg and other power thinkers can thus 'be seen as a belated arrival of postmodernism in [these disciplines], a tardiness understandable in a … field often closely associated and identifying with governments steeped in high modernist ideologies of knowing, steering and remoulding society through spatial interventions' (Van Assche et al., 2014b: 2386).

   If we look at the current debates in urban studies, we can conclude that Flyvbjerg's work has contributed to a repoliticizing of the field in a theoretically, ideologically and methodologically open manner. He has shown the value of carefully scrutinizing the multiple ways in which cities are shaped, reshaped and governed. Both his empirical work as well as the method and tools that he presented those who like to use a phronetic approach, have gained impact and helped to increase the awareness for important issues like power/knowledge, case studies and the role of scientific research in urban planning and design. He has also shown that academic development requires an ongoing debate and that criticizing prevailing rationalities is a prerequisite for the further development of professions and disciplines. As testified again by a recent controversy with the authoritative American Planning Association (APA), Flyvbjerg is anything but afraid to communicate unsettling ideas. He accused the APA of moral hypocrisy and argued that the 'APA was found to actively suppress publicity of malpractice concerns and bad planning in order to sustain a boosterish image of planning' (Flyvbjerg, 2013: 157).

We can only hope Flyvbjerg will continue to be unsettling to those who prefer to conveniently disregard what planning practices and urban transformations really entail. His voice is needed, for in the corners of academia devoted to the study of urban governance modernistic ideas are still very much alive and if critical voices are heard, they are often stemming from self-referential and repetitive neo-Marxist thinkers. These mainly present critiques on everything that looks or smells neoliberal, but they tend to overlook and ignore that governing cities entails much more than just the rule of markets (cf. **Michael Storper, Mariana Valverde**). We believe it is beyond the critical void of the modernists and bureaucrats and the overly ideological thoughts of neo-Marxists, where Flyvbjerg and his work can be positioned. Following his path, and using his ideas, much work remains to be done in the quest to make cities more sustainable and democratic.

Secondary sources and references

Dreyfus, H. and Dreyfus, H. (1986) *Mind Over Machine*. New York: Free Press.

Flyvbjerg, B. (2001b) 'Beyond the limits of planning theory: Response to my critics', *International Planning Studies*, 6(3): 285–292.

Flyvbjerg, B. (2002) 'Bringing power to planning research: One researcher's praxis story', *Journal of Planning Education and Research*, 21(4): 353–366.

Flyvbjerg, B. (2013) 'How planners deal with uncomfortable knowledge: The dubious ethics of the American Planning Association', *Cities*, 32: 157–163.

Flyvbjerg, B. (2014) 'Projects, power, and politics: A conversation with Bent Flyvbjerg', *Twentyfirst*, 3: 62–75.

Flyvbjerg, B. (2015) 'More on the dark side of planning: Response to Richard Bolan', *Cities*, 42: 276–278.

Hillier, J. (2002) *Shadows of Power*. London: Routledge.

MacIntyre, A. (1981) *After Virtue*. Notre Dame, IN: University of Notre Dame Press.

Mansfield, H. (1993) *Machiavelli's Virtue*. Chicago: University of Chicago Press.

Van Assche, K., Beunen, R. and Duineveld, M. (2014a) *Evolutionary Governance Theory: An Introduction*. Heidelberg: Springer.

Van Assche, K., Duineveld, M. and Beunen, R. (2014b) 'Power and contingency in planning', *Environment and Planning A*, 46(10): 2385–2400.

Matthew Gandy

Andrew Karvonen, KTH Royal Institute of Technology

Key urban writings

Gandy, M. (2002) *Concrete and Clay: Reworking Nature in New York City*. London: MIT Press.

Gandy, M. (2004) 'Rethinking urban metabolism: Water, space and the modern city', *City*, 8(3): 363–379.

Gandy, M. (2005) 'Cyborg urbanization: Complexity and monstrosity in the contemporary city', *International Journal of Urban and Regional Research*, 29(1): 26–49.

Gandy, M. (2014) *The Fabric of Space: Water, Modernity, and the Urban Imagination*. London: MIT Press.

Introduction

Matthew Gandy is a British geographer who studies the social and cultural production of nature in cities. Drawing on ideas from the social and natural sciences as well as the humanities, he has conducted research on infrastructure networks, parks and open spaces, environmental management practices, and public health and disease in prominent cities of North America, Europe, Africa and Asia. He is best known for his contributions to the field of urban political ecology including key ideas about metropolitan nature, urban metabolism, ecological imaginaries and cyborg urbanism. This body of work challenges Marxist, neo-Marxist and post-structuralist thinking on urban nature by introducing cultural ideas from film, art and sound to forward an expansive perspective on the hybrid relations of nature, technology and humans in cities.

Gandy is Professor of Cultural and Historical Geography and Fellow of King's College at the University of Cambridge.

Academic biography and research focus

Gandy grew up in the north London borough of Islington and received a BA in Geography from the University of Cambridge in 1988 and a PhD from the London

School of Economics and Political Science in 1992. His doctoral research involved a comparative historical study of solid waste management in London and Hamburg. This work was subsequently published with an additional case of New York City as *Recycling and the Politics of Urban Waste* (1994). Here, municipal waste flows serve as a lens to examine the tensions between environmental policy making and urban economic development. He argues that market-based environmental policies for solid waste recycling that first emerged in the 1980s are incompatible with environmental protection activities due to the strong influence of the profit motive by private waste management companies as well as an impoverished conception of the relationship between urban residents and material flows.

Gandy was appointed as Lecturer at the University of Sussex in 1992 and moved to University College London's (UCL) Department of Geography in 1997. In 2005, he founded the UCL Urban Laboratory, an influential research centre on urbanization and cities that spans the social sciences, humanities and engineering disciplines, and since 2013, has served as a co-editor of the *International Journal of Urban and Regional Research*. In 2015, he returned to his alma mater, the University of Cambridge, where he was appointed as Professor of Cultural and Historical Geography and Fellow of King's College.

The notion of landscape is central to Gandy's work on urban nature. From the pastoral depictions of painters in the 16th to 18th centuries to the designs of landscape architects in the 19th and 20th centuries, landscape provides a conceptual framework to represent and position humans in the physical world. In his 2002 book, *Concrete and Clay: Reworking Nature in New York City*, Gandy adopts a landscape perspective to explore historical and contemporary conceptions of urban nature in New York City. Drawing on ideas from political economy, environmental studies, social theory, cultural criticism and the design disciplines, the book explores the larger tensions in the political, cultural and social aspects of urban nature through a series of essays on water infrastructure, parks, highways, neighbourhood politics and environmental pollution. For Gandy (2002: 5), 'The production of urban nature not only involves the transformation of capital but simultaneously intersects with the changing role of the state, emerging metropolitan cultures of nature, and wider shifts in the social and political complexion of city life.'

In addition to landscape, the dynamism of water provides additional insights on urban nature. In his 2014 research monograph, *The Fabric of Space: Water, Modernity, and the Urban Imagination*, Gandy uses hydrologic flows as a common thread to study nature in six global cities (Paris, Berlin, Lagos, Mumbai, Los Angeles and London). In each city, he focuses on a particular time period to compare and contrast the 'multiple modernities' that are embodied in the production of urban nature and their relation to lived urban experience. He argues that 'by tracing the history of water in urban space we can begin to develop a fuller understanding of changing relations between the body and urban form under the impetus of capitalist urbanisation' (2014: 29). The sewers of 19th-century Paris, the water supply system of postcolonial Mumbai and the imaginary future of a flooded London all involve dialectics of body and city, social and physical, natural and capital flows, visible and invisible.

A third emphasis of Gandy's work is the body and its relation to urban form, as evidenced in his studies of disease and public health (Gandy, 2006b; Gandy and Zumla, 2002). Building on notions of the hygienic and bacteriological city from the

19th century, he emphasizes the body–technology nexus at the heart of cultural and social interpretations of urban nature. He writes (2005: 33), 'The blurring of boundaries between the body and the city raises complexities in relation to our understanding of the human subject and the changing characteristics of human agency.' This perspective emphasizes the personal and entangled character of humans in the material world and their indelible connection to the physical fluxes of the urban condition.

Key ideas

An early idea developed by Gandy, particularly in his work on New York City, is that of metropolitan nature. Departing from contemporary notions of urban ecology as defined by proponents of environmental science and landscape design (e.g. Giradet, 1992; McHarg, 1969), Gandy (2002) argues that the natural elements of cities are an outcome of processes of urbanization and modernization. Thus, metropolitan nature involves more than the valuing of ecological services and the provision of parks and green spaces; instead, it is bound up in the technical and social networks of cities. The notion of metropolitan nature extends the field of urban political ecology (Heynen et al., 2006; Kaika, 2005; Swyngedouw, 2004) beyond critiques of capitalism by calling for a simultaneous reading of material and social changes that continuously overlap, interact and co-evolve. Nature thus emerges as an infrastructural achievement of the city and is shaped as much by cultural and political dynamics of cities as biological and ecological drivers.

The idea of metropolitan nature is closely connected to a second idea developed by Gandy, that of urban metabolism. There is a longstanding tradition among urban thinkers to describe cities as holistic systems akin to machines and human bodies, an oft-cited example being Abel Wolman's *Scientific American* article on 'The metabolism of cities' (1965). For Gandy, urban metabolism is not simply a quantitative approach to account for the flows of materials into and out of cities. Such a natural science perspective promoted by advocates of industrial ecology (Bai, 2007), ecosystem services (Daily, 1997) and ecological footprints (Wackernagel and Rees, 1998) assumes a linear and functional perspective on cities while neglecting the dynamics of material, cultural, political, economic and virtual flows. Building on the tradition of political economy inspired by Marxist and neo-Marxist scholars such as **Neil Smith** and **David Harvey**, Gandy uses urban metabolism to develop a richer understanding of urbanization and modernization as simultaneously physical and virtual, real and imagined, political and cultural, ecological and economic. Attending to the circulation of people, things and ideas allows for the interpretation of the relational, hybrid and increasingly fragmented and polarized character of the urban landscape.

Beyond metropolitan nature and urban metabolism, Gandy is interested in the historic development of collective visions of the relationship between nature and cities, what he terms ecological imaginaries. In the late 19th and early 20th centuries, influential actors forwarded ecological imaginaries based on metaphors from the biophysical and medical sciences to interpret the form and function of cities. These were later superseded by the City Beautiful and Garden City movements of urban planners and then by technological visions informed by engineers (Gandy, 2006c). Throughout this evolution of ecological imaginaries, the aim was to forward an overarching vision for the ideal synthesis between nature and culture, a vision that naturalized urban development processes while simultaneously suppressing political and cultural difference. For example, Gandy's case study of the Los Angeles River presents competing ecological imaginaries of engineers who were advocating for flood protection versus environmentalists who promoted ecological restoration (Gandy, 2006a, 2014). These visions are embedded with normative assumptions about the 'good' or 'most desirable' city and are important not only for what they include but also about what they leave out (in this case, marginalized communities with alternative imaginaries about the river). Moreover, ecological imaginaries expose explicit and implicit framings of urban nature that often reinforce the dichotomy between humans and their non-human surroundings (cf. **Natalie Jeremijenko**). However, Gandy also sees imaginaries as having an emancipatory potential to promote more complex and variegated perspectives on urban nature (such as metropolitan nature and urban metabolism described above). He writes, 'we can begin to explore the production of urban space as a synthesis between nature and culture in which long-standing ideological antinomies lose their analytical utility and political resonance' (2006c: 73).

The notions of metropolitan nature, urban metabolism and ecological imaginaries all inform Gandy's most radical idea, that of the post-human ontology of cyborg urbanism. The notion of the cyborg is often attributed to the work of sociologist Donna Haraway (1991) to challenge dualist, disembodied, masculine and teleological modes of thought. Gandy draws on Haraway and other post-human thinkers to promote a hybrid ontology that embraces the messy socio-material character of cities. Humans are not separate from the natural and technological systems that are ever present in cities; instead, they are bound together in hybrid configurations. Infrastructure networks, notably water and sewer systems, reveal this hybridity while spatializing and grounding the cyborg concept by interpreting cities as socio-technical amalgams of body, technology and space. As Gandy (2006a: 140) writes, 'networks of urban infrastructure do not simply create modern cities, they also create their own distinctive spaces or landscapes within the fabric of the city'. And building on the idea of ecological imaginaries, cyborg urbanization not only includes the physical but also the virtual: 'The cyborg metaphor allows for the simultaneity of concrete and imaginary perceptions of urban infrastructure so that the categories of the "real" and the "virtual" become interconnected facets of urban experience' (Gandy, 2005: 38). In effect, what is imagined and projected is just as important as what is real and experienced.

Contributions to urban studies

As a whole, Gandy's ideas about metropolitan nature, urban metabolism, ecological imaginaries and cyborg urbanism involve an expansive and multifaceted understanding of the role of nature in cities. He extends the existing debates on urban political ecology by going beyond the urban disciplines (geography, planning and architecture) and social sciences (political science, sociology and anthropology) to include concepts from the humanities (art history and film criticism) and the natural and medical sciences (public health and disease theory). Even for a geographer, Gandy's work is regarded as highly promiscuous in its theoretical and empirical inspirations, ranging from neo-Marxian and post-structuralist perspectives on cities to ideas from feminist studies, queer theory, postcolonial studies, art history and cultural studies. For his critics, such a nomadic form of academic scholarship results in a cacophony of ideas that never quite crystallizes into a convincing argument (see Castree and Swyngedouw, 2003; Lynch, 2004). But for others, his careful and thoughtful juxtaposition of ideas from a wide range of sources creates a multilayered and nuanced understanding of urban nature as a palimpsest of material, economic, cultural and social relations.

Beyond his theoretical and empirical contributions, Gandy's work incorporates visual materials to inform the real and imagined urban landscapes of his writings. Similar to historians, he draws on primary and secondary archival materials including paintings, drawings, photos, films, maps and plans to illustrate the contradictory character of modernization and urbanization. This emphasis on visual representation has resulted in an expanded portfolio of writings on art (Joseph Beuys, Gerhard Richter, Ulrike Mohr), landscape architecture (Giles Clement, Patrick Blanc) and cinema (Michelangelo Antonioni, Werner Herzog, Pier Paolo Pasolini). Gandy also includes his own images derived from experiential research methods, notably the peripatetic methods akin to the Parisian *flâneur* of the late 19th century, the *dérive* or drift favoured by Situationists and psychogeographers, and the walking practices of land artists such as Richard Long. In 2007, he directed and produced *Liquid City*, a 30-minute documentary to examine social inequality in Mumbai as revealed by water flows. The film exemplifies the importance of visualization in developing new ecological imaginaries about humans and their physical surroundings.

Gandy's ideas about bodies, technologies and cities provide a natural extension to the late 19th- and early 20th-century ideas on the hygienic and bacteriological city alongside sanitary reformers such as Colonel George E. Waring Jr and Edwin Chadwick, designers such as Ebenezer Howard and Patrick Geddes, and social reformers such as Jane Addams and Alice Hamilton. However, he provides a sustained critique of the scientific, rational and technocratic ideas that informed the Progressive Era of urban governance and that continue to influence contemporary urban development processes. Instead, he emphasizes the wide array of social, cultural and political currents that shape and influence the everyday, lived aspects of cities to promote an expansive and complex perspective embodied in his ideas about cyborg urbanism. This allows for a deeper understanding of how environmental justice activities in New York City are related to global circuits of capital and how the mosquitoes and the persistent threat of malaria in Lagos are symptoms of the multiple contradictions of contemporary urban development. Modernity is not a smooth, teleological process of rationality but is comprised of multiple overlapping (and at times contradictory) ruptures and frictions that make indelible connections between individuals, their immediate surroundings, technological networks, urban conglomerations, and ultimately, the world. It is through this pluralist and relational perspective on the co-evolution of social and technological systems that Gandy challenges conventional accounts of urbanization through the concurrent examination of material, political and cultural dynamics.

Secondary sources and references

Bai, X. (2007) 'Industrial ecology and the global impacts of cities', *Journal of Industrial Ecology*, 11(2): 1–6.

Castree, N. and Swyngedouw, E. (eds) (2003) 'Review symposium on Matthew Gandy's *Concrete and Clay*', *Antipode*, 35(5): 1008–1029.

Daily, G. (1997) *Nature's Services: Societal Dependence on Natural Ecosystems*. Washington, DC: Island Press.

Gandy, M. (1994) *Recycling and the Politics of Urban Waste*. London: Earthscan.

Gandy, M. (2006a) 'Riparian anomie: Reflections on the Los Angeles River', *Landscape Research*, 31(2): 135–145.

Gandy, M. (2006b) 'The bacteriological city and its discontents', *Historical Geography*, 34: 14–25.

Gandy, M. (2006c) 'Urban nature and the ecological imaginary', in N. Heynen, M. Kaika and E. Swyngedouw (eds) *In the Nature of Cities: Urban Political Ecology and the Politics of Urban Metabolism*. New York: Routledge, pp. 63–74.

Gandy, M. (2007) *Liquid City* [film]. Available at UCL Urban Lab website: www.ucl.ac.uk/urbanlab

Gandy, M. and Zumla, A. (2002) 'The resurgence of disease: Social and historical perspectives on the "new" tuberculosis', *Social Science and Medicine*, 55(3): 385–396.

Giradet, H. (1992) *The Gaia Atlas of Cities: New Directions for Sustainable Urban Living*. London: Gaia Books.

Haraway, D.J. (1991) *Simians, Cyborgs, and Women: The Reinvention of Nature*. New York: Routledge.

Heynen, N., Kaika, M. and Swyngedouw, E. (eds) (2006) *In the Nature of Cities: Urban Political Ecology and the Politics of Urban Metabolism*. New York: Routledge.

Kaika, M. (2005) *City of Flows: Modernity, Nature, and the City*. London: Routledge.

Lynch, B. (2004) 'Book review of Matthew Gandy's *Concrete and Clay: Reworking Nature in New York City*', *Society and Natural Resources*, 17(4): 373–375.

McHarg, I.L. (1969) *Design with Nature*. New York: American Museum of Natural History.

Swyngedouw, E. (2004) *Social Power and the Urbanisation of Water: Flows of Power*. Oxford: Oxford University Press.

Wackernagel, M. and Rees, W. (1998) *Our Ecological Footprint: Reducing Human Impact on the Earth*. Philadelphia: New Society Publishers.

Wolman, A. (1965) 'The metabolism of cities', *Scientific American*, 213: 179–190.

Acknowledgements: My thanks to Michael Hebbert, Regan Koch and Alan Latham for their helpful comments and suggestions.

14 Néstor García Canclini

Angela Giglia, Universidad Autónoma Metropolitana

Key urban writings

García Canclini, N. (ed.) (1998) *Cultura y comunicación en la ciudad de México*. Mexico City: Grijalbo.

García Canclini, N. (2001) *Consumers and Citizens*. Minneapolis: University of Minnesota Press.

García Canclini, N. (2005a) *Hybrid Cultures: Strategies for Entering and Leaving Modernity*. Minneapolis: University of Minnesota Press.

García Canclini, N. (ed.) (2005b) *La antropología urbana en México*. Mexico City: Fondo de Cultura Económica – UAM.

García Canclini, N. (2014) *Imagined Globalization*. Durham, NC: Duke University Press.

Introduction

Néstor García Canclini is a cultural anthropologist and key Latin American thinker across various strands of the social sciences, humanities and urban studies. The most palpable originality of his work consists in connecting domains that are often conceived as separate: popular culture, arts and media, cultural policies and development policies. Contemporary cities, and in particular the megalopolis of Mexico City, are the context in which García Canclini makes these fields interact and dialogue together.

His thinking is characterized by taking on some huge topics – cultural hybridization and its actors, urban imaginaries, cultural industries and policies, the social uses of mass media and new technologies – studied by developing original questions and a multidimensional approach in which he puts macro-social data together with in-depth studies on the practices of users and urban residents. He has produced an extensive body of work, often engaging other authors in international and interdisciplinary projects. Since his first field study on Mexican handicrafts, he has promoted and coordinated collective work groups on complex issues that one researcher could not face alone.

He has taught at the universities of Texas at Austin, Duke, Stanford, Barcelona, Buenos Aires and São Paulo. Currently, he is a Distinguished Professor at the

Autonomous Metropolitan University and Emeritus Researcher of the National System of Researchers of CONACYT Mexico. He conducts research and teaches in the PhD Program of the Anthropology Department at the Autonomous Metropolitan University.

Academic biography and research focus

Born in Argentina in 1939, he obtained a PhD in Philosophy (1978) from the University of Paris X-Nanterre with a thesis directed by Paul Ricoeur entitled *Epistemology and History: The Dialectic Between Subject and Structure in Merleau-Ponty* (UNAM, Mexico).

García Canclini arrived in Mexico City in the 1970s as a fugitive from dictatorship. In Mexico he began researching Mexican handicraft production. He made an extended fieldwork among artisans belonging to the Purépecha ethnic group, in the state of Michoacan. Through this work he developed a series of reflections about the products and producers of Mexican handicrafts and their relationship with global markets and conservation and promotion policies. His books *Popular Cultures in Capitalism* (1982) and *Hybrid Cultures: Strategies for Entering and Leaving Modernity* (2005a) show that indigenous popular cultures are absolutely not isolated, nor outdated. On the contrary, they have a complex relation of exchange and combination with cultural industries and global processes of production and circulation of goods and mass flows of information and communication. Starting from empirical and interdisciplinary studies on products and producers of handicrafts and other social actors who were named as 'subaltern' in those years, García Canclini proposed a theoretical and empirical rethinking of popular culture in Latin American society in relation to the emerging processes of the globalization of culture.

In 1982 he published the book *Popular Cultures in Capitalism*, which marked a radical change in studies of popular sectors and products in Latin America. This work also became an important influence on cultural policies in Latin America, especially after the world conference on cultural policies – Mondiacult – that took place in Mexico City a few months later (Nivón, 2012: 35–6). In the 1980s debate between preserving handcrafts by relegating them to the contemplative space of museums, or modernizing them by supporting insertion in the circuits of global consumption, García Canclini proposed that the most important point was to put the craftspeople in a position to decide on the future development of their activities.

From the 1990s, his work focused on Mexico City, where he created and coordinated the Study Program on Urban Culture (1988–2007) with the support of the Rockefeller Foundation. In this research group he brought together young scholars from around the world to work together on different aspects of cultural hybridization in the megalopolis, generating a widespread re-thinking of urban reality and urban anthropology.

In more recent years, García Canclini has investigated the networks and experiences of young creative professionals, especially visual artists, graphic designers and editors living in big cities, and in particular Mexico City and Madrid. In this research he develops a critical perspective on the concepts of 'creative economies' and 'creative class', and excavates from that particular angle the problematic of urban precariousness.

Key ideas

The first important intellectual contribution of García Canclini is his redefinition of popular culture in relation to modern society and global communication. His conceptualization of 'the hybridization process' – one of his most important and best known concepts – starts from the study of the circulation, reception and consumption of popular and artisan products in middle- and upper-class social sectors and in the international market of culture. García Canclini proposes the concept of hybridization to indicate the transformation and resignification of popular phenomena and cultural products on their way from one society to another, and from one social level or sector to another, within the same society. In this perspective culture is not seen like a static essence. Traditional, modern and postmodern attributes of culture – and their contradictions – are not fixed or static. They are defined on the basis of their position in networks and cultural fields in which they circulate and reproduce themselves, where they gain or lose value, both symbolic and material. In other words, he conceives hybridization as a constitutive piece in the contemporary production and reproduction of cultural products, eliminating the risk of essentialist and reductive visions of culture and their expressions.

A second important contribution is the redefinition of cultural processes especially in relation with urban reality. His vision of culture as an object of study is much wider in comparison with other approaches that focus primarily on the relation between the products and their uses from the point of view of certain social actors. When García Canclini studies a cultural phenomenon, he explores producers, consumers and promoters or opponents in the field of public policy at the same time. Approaching the study of urban culture, García Canclini includes cultural industries, media and culture policies as crucial actors, linked to the field of cultural consumption practices and the analysis of cultural infrastructures in the metropolis (cf. **Sharon Zukin**). Cultural phenomena in contemporary urban reality have to be studied always in relation to the market in which they can eventually move and change their meaning; and to the state for which they represent an important domain for intervention policies. These dimensions of cultural phenomena are essential to interpret the dynamics of heterogeneity and segregation in urban practices, for example taking into account the unequal distribution of museums, cinemas, galleries and other cultural sites in the metropolis. He developed a particular interest in the study of cultural consumption as a social and cultural phenomenon embedded in complex urban practices, both in public and in domestic space. He considers for example watching TV, listening to the radio, wearing a special kind of dress or eating ethnic food as practices which generate meaning, putting in connection the domestic domain and urban space.

A further key idea that García Canclini articulates is an original vision on the relationship between globalization and culture. Instead of considering globalization as a homogeneous phenomenon, able to explain everything by the normalizing power of markets and information and communications technology, García Canclini proposed a different view, linked to specific arrangements that globalization displays in Latin America. He offers an analysis of globalization as a fragmentary and uncertain process which generates differences and inequalities more than it drives homogenization and development. In his studies on globalization in the field of culture, he emphasizes its multiple interactions with local realities. He proposes the idea of 'interculturalism' (*interculturalidad*) to highlight the conflicts that characterize culture crossings in the context of globalization, to show that there are not only fusions or syncretism. The cultural field is a land dispute in which power relations are played out, and inequalities are increasingly produced in the relation between the local and the global.

Contributions to urban studies

For three decades, García Canclini linked his reflections on popular culture with the study of urban practices by promoting a series of systematic studies about urban culture, understood as a place of hybridization and interculturalism, in which multiple imaginaries articulate each other. For García Canclini these scenarios must be examined by an interdisciplinary approach that combines different analytical perspectives. Starting from his studies of Mexico City, García Canclini has renewed the field of urban anthropology in at least two ways: first, by combining quantitative and qualitative approaches; and second, by studying new aspects, almost all situated in the articulation of the local, the metropolitan, the national and the global scale.

Since the 1990s, he has promoted an unusual image of urban reality, based on his field studies on Mexico City. This city had been studied so far mainly as an example of an underdeveloped megalopolis with an impressive informal urban growth made up of poor and indigenous people coming from the countryside, and particular forms of political control of popular urban strata. In the reflections and studies promoted by García Canclini, Mexico City is a megalopolis inhabited by 'the tension between the imagined city and the city that is impossible to imagine' (2008: 79) because it has become literally incomprehensible. Therefore it is impossible to approach it only through located case studies. It has to be faced in its entireness as an object that goes beyond the spatial dimension, but without neglecting the socio-economic and socio-spatial data.

His approach to the urban reality is characterized by the formulation of new questions. Instead of asking 'How does the city grow?' like many urban sociologists might do, and 'How come the Indians move to the city and how do they establish urban space?' like many anthropologist do, García Canclini asks 'How can we imagine a city that grows without stopping?', and 'What hybridization processes result from the coexistence of such diverse and unequal inhabitants?' Like other urban thinkers, for example **Elijah Anderson** and **Richard Sennett**, García Canclini is interested in studying social difference in urban realities. In this domain, he offers an original contribution to the understanding of contemporary changes in the relationship between the private and the public sphere from his particular point of view.

Addressing the meaning of urban experience in Mexico City, he reconstructs not only the physical experience and the socio-spatial dimension of the city, but also the symbolic and imaginary experience linked to the field of mass media and communication. In order to understand urban experience, the physical city is not more important than the imagined city. The two scenarios are different but entangled. He is interested in understanding the city represented by the media and the imaginary, shared and dispersed at the same time. And he is interested in looking for the processes of production, circulation and reception of urban imaginaries in practices that link the experience of the megalopolis with its reception in television and radio messages. In this perspective, the discourse that television and radio broadcast daily on the city in news programs is a source of information as important as the concrete experience of inhabitants in the metropolitan space. While the metropolis becomes increasingly a source of uncertainty and concern, the media discourse is the field in which it is possible to renovate the illusion of a totalizing vision of the endless city. This reflection on the relationship between lived experience and mediated experience of the city gives great importance to the question of the imaginary as a horizon of meaning in the megalopolis. And it is linked to the question of the loss of vigorous spatial references in contemporary reality, expressed through the concepts of de-territorialization and relocation in the functioning of collective consciousness.

He has been a pioneer in illuminating certain aspects of the urban experience whose importance is now considered fundamental. One of these innovating aspects is the experience of mobility that he discussed in the book *La ciudad de los viajeros* in 1996. Another innovative field that he opened deals with the study of consumer experience in urban environments. In his research on cultural practices in Mexico City he pointed out the changing relationship between the private and the public space in a megalopolis of 18 million inhabitants. In this scenario, for many inhabitants the best way to spend their free time is to stay at home relaxing and watching TV. This peculiar way of conceiving the household – like a sort of bulwark against the uncertainty of the public sphere – is illuminated as an important component of urban culture.

García Canclini's megalopolis is very different from the one that urban sociologists are used to studying, and from the metropolis of anthropologists – such as Oscar Lewis or Larissa Lomnitz – who had previously worked on Mexico City. In his reflections, not only metropolitan voyages, but the consumer reception of television and radio, the visits to museums and theaters, the practices of reading and the use of technology are part of urban culture. In studying cultural consumption, he dedicates particular attention to illustrating the social inequalities in the distribution of cultural structures and equipment. His research shows not only the physical map of the city, but also the map of communication flows and circuits of cultural industries, linked with the configuration of consumption practices in metropolitan space. It is not only a material city, but a city rebuilt from cultural practices, a delocalized and imagined city. García Canclini studies the city conveyed by the news of the major radio and television media, as an imaginary set of narratives that guide the experience of the megalopolis.

Linked to this, a characteristic feature of his vision about urban reality is his proximity to the world of artistic creation, with which he has developed a permanent dialogue, carrying on an enormous number of different collaborations on specific projects, identifying and supporting the impact of art on our understanding of present society. Especially remarkable are García Canclini's analyses of the work of photographers who are recognized for their original interpretation of urban landscapes and urban life. For example, his text about Paolo Gori's photos on Mexican monuments (1992); his comment on Mexican photographer Enrique Metinides' work (2003); and recently his introduction to the work of Andy Goldstein in the book entitled *Vivir en la tierra* [*Living on the Ground*] (2012), which presents a great range of extraordinary images taken inside precarious housing – and their inhabitants – in different slums on the borders of Latin American cities. In these collaborations and in many other short texts, that are not definable as minor works, García Canclini shows at the same time his particular sensibility in the understanding of visual language and his profound competence in the interpretation of urban reality.

Secondary sources and references

García Canclini, N. (1982) *Las culturas populares en el capitalismo*. Mexico City: Grijalbo.

García Canclini, N. (1992) 'Monumentos, carteles, graffitis', in H. Escobedo and P. Gori (eds) *Monumentos mexicanos*. Mexico City: Grijalbo.

García Canclini, N. (2002) *Latino americanos buscando un lugar en este siglo*. Mexico City: Siglo XXI.

García Canclini, N. (2003) 'La gran ciudad ordenada desde los accidentes', in E. Metinides (ed.) *CONACULTA*. London: British Library.

García Canclini, N. (2004) *Diferentes desiguales y desconectados. Mapas de la interculturalidad*. Mexico City: Gedisa.

García Canclini, N. (2007) *Lectores, espectadores e internautas*. Mexico City: Gedisa.

García Canclini, N. (2008) 'Mexico City, 2010: Improvising Globalization, in A. Huyssen (ed) *Other Cities, Other Worlds: Urban Imaginaries in a Globalizing Age*. Durham, NC: Duke Univerisity Press.

García Canclini, N. (2010) *La sociedad sin relato. Antropología y estética de la inminencia*. Buenos Aires: Katz Editores.

García Canclini, N. (2012) '¿Dónde nos ponemos?', in A. Goldstein (ed.) *Vivir en la tierra*. Buenos Aires: Edhasa.

García Canclini, N. and Piedra, E. (eds) (2013) *Jóvenes creativos. Estrategias y redes culturales*. Mexico DF: Juan Pablos.

García Canclini, N., Castellanos, A. and Mantecón, A.R. (1996) *La ciudad de los viajeros. Travesías e imaginarios urbanos*. Mexico City: Grijalbo.

Nivón, E. (ed.) (2012) *Voces híbridas: reflexiones en torno a la obra de García Canclini*. Mexico City: Siglo XXI.

15 Jan Gehl

Annie Matan, Curtin University

Key urban writings

Gehl, J. (1971; 1st English edn 1987) *Life Between Buildings: Using Public Space*. New York: Van Nostrand Reinhold. [Republished: The Danish Architectural Press, 1996; and Island Press, Washington DC, 2011.]

Gehl, J. and Gemzøe, L. (2000) *New City Spaces*. Copenhagen: The Danish Architectural Press.

Gehl, J., Gemzøe, L., Kirknæs, S. and Søndergaard, B.S. (2006) *New City Life*. Copenhagen: The Danish Architectural Press.

Gehl, J. (2010) *Cities for People*. Washington, DC: Island Press.

Gehl, J. and Bundesen Svarre, B. (2013) *How to Study Public Life*. Washington, DC: Island Press.

Introduction

Jan Gehl is a Danish academic, architect and urban designer. His work focuses on public space and how people interact with the built environment, with the aim of making fairer and more convivial cities. His theories of urban design centre on maximizing the diversity of exchanges possible while bringing city users' everyday needs to the forefront of planning and design concerns. His work is a reaction to mainstream modernist-based architecture and planning that focused more on design, function and movement than on people and how they use the city. Gehl's urban design practice and theory is humanistic and responsive. His people-oriented, experiential approach has produced a remarkable suite of studies, particularly focused around a methodology that looks at the use of public spaces.

Public Spaces Public Life (PSPL) studies developed by Gehl and colleagues have been applied in some of the world's most high-profile cities including New York, London, Moscow, Copenhagen, Melbourne and Sydney. Gehl's theory centres on a 'people first, then space, then buildings' approach to designing cities and involves systematic evaluations of how public spaces are used. Gehl has been one of the most prominent professionals in calling attention to the need of cities to focus on pedestrians and public life. *Life Between Buildings* (1971), Gehl's most influential work, has been published in 23 languages. The English version is in its seventh edition. While Gehl's writing is practical in orientation, it nonetheless articulates a comprehensive and layered argument about how to make sense of the human body's relationship to urban environments.

Professor Jan Gehl is the Founding Partner of Gehl Architects, an urban design firm established in 2000 by Jan Gehl and Helle Søholt. He is a former Professor at the Royal Danish Academy of Fine Arts, School of Architecture.

Academic biography and research focus

Jan Gehl was born in Denmark in 1936. He graduated from the School of Architecture at the Royal Danish Academy of Fine Arts (RDAFA) in Copenhagen in 1960. For six years he practised as an architect. He then became a researcher with the School of Architecture at RDAFA, studying the form and use of public spaces. During this time he undertook an influential trip to Italy with his wife Ingrid Gehl (née Mundt) where he studied public life in plazas. In 1971, Gehl became a Lecturer of Urban Design and then the Head of the Department of Urban Design at RDAFA in 1976. From 2003 until his retirement from the university in 2006, he was Professor and Director of the Centre for Public Space Research at RDAFA.

Gehl began his practice, Gehl Architects, in Copenhagen, in 2000, with Helle Søholt as Founding Partner and Managing Director. He continues to work as a Senior Advisor at Gehl Architects and is responsible for many international projects. He is an honorary fellow of Royal Institute of British Architects, American Institute of Architects, Canadian Institute of Architects and the Planning Institute of Australia among others, and has been a visiting professor at over 20 universities around the world. He has received a number of honours including Cavaliere dell'Ordine Al Merito della Republica Italiana and Medaglia di Bronzo: Benemeriti della Scuola, della Cultura e dell'Arte.

Gehl considers his work to have three major phases: (1) his research and theory development (1960–1970s onwards); (2) the development and testing of his methodology in real-life projects (initially in Italy and Copenhagen: 1960s onwards); and (3) communication and expansion of his methods and ideas by working in projects worldwide (1990s onwards). The origins of Gehl's philosophy came from systematic, careful observation of how people interact with the everyday, ordinary, built environment, looking at what worked and what did not work in public space. His approach is essentially about 'making people visible' within city planning (Matan, 2011); ensuring that urban environments are configured to afford the comfortable inhabitation and movement of individual human bodies.

Of particular influence to Gehl's theoretical development has been his wife, Ingrid Gehl, and his personal hero, Ralph Erskine (1914–2005), an English/Swedish architect and Quaker. Gehl credits his wife, an environmental psychologist, with making him look at how people are influenced by urban and architectural design and question the design paradigms of the day. Meeting Erskine in the 1970s was a defining point in Gehl's work, and Erskine also became a source of ongoing support in his career. Erskine constantly emphasized that in order to be a good architect, one must love people, for architects deal with the framework of people's lives. This has been one of the guiding philosophies behind Gehl's design.

Key ideas

Gehl's research and practice started as a reaction to the lifeless cities that were being created through modernist and functionalist-based planning and design paradigms, and the subsequent preoccupation with automobiles within city design. Since the 1960s, he has constantly and consistently advocated for better alternatives. Gehl is explicitly humanist and pro-urban, emphasizing that we must design cities for people rather than purely for movement or economics, aligning his work with thinkers like **Jane Jacobs** and William Whyte. Gehl's philosophy is that if you provide attractive and welcoming public places in which people can walk around and spend time in, you will have a more attractive, sustainable and convivial city: life is attracted to life (Gehl, 2010). At the foundation of his urban theory is the need to orient urban environments towards human needs, activities and senses (cf. **Kevin Lynch**). This might seem an obvious point, yet the originality of Gehl's thinking lies in the rigour with which he has explored the relationship of urban design and planning to the concrete needs of urban dwellers.

For Gehl the overriding planning and design rule for cities should be: whatever we do in this city, everything will be done to invite people to walk as much as possible in the course of their everyday activities. The invitation is the provision of appropriate urban places, particularly in the design of the interface between the public and the private realms in both commercial and residential areas, and the provision of appropriate infrastructure and furniture that make it very easy and attractive to accomplish daily needs on foot and to spend time in the city. Gehl (1987: 47) argues that 'throughout the entire history of human habitation, streets and squares had formed focal points and gathering places, but with the advent of functionalism, streets and squares were literally declared unwanted'. Gehl has rebelled against this, focusing his philosophy entirely on the use of public spaces. His work explores both the intimate dynamics of how public spaces come to function as convivial spaces, as well as developing a grounded critique of how modernist modes of planning and architecture erase and overlook the vulnerability of urban dwellers' individual corporeality (cf. **Henri Lefebvre**).

For Gehl, the primary concern of urban planning, architecture and urban design should be the everyday activities that happen in streets. The objective should not be an 'ambitious program'; rather, it should be about 'everyday life, ordinary situations, and space in which daily life is lived' (Gehl, 1987: 53). In order to do this, Gehl stresses that design and planning need to consider human senses and physical makeup, particularly the senses of sight, smell, touch and hearing, and the movement speed, stimuli needs and the space preferences of people walking. Gehl divides everyday activities that happen in streets into three categories: 'necessary', 'optional' and 'social'. Some activities (such as going to work or school, shopping for necessities, etc.) must be done regardless of the conditions. These are necessary activities. Optional activities include recreation activities that will occur in good conditions. These include walking for leisure or sitting to have a cup of coffee. Social activities, such as talking with others or sitting on a bench watching the world pass by, are those incidental activities that occur in a high-quality environment in part because the other two activities are occurring. A high-quality urban environment enables all three types of activities to occur. Once the public space design is right, enabling all three types of activity, then the design focus can move to the buildings. Design must first focus on *people*, then *space*, then *buildings*.

Gehl divides the long-term historical uses of public space into three types: public space as *meeting* place, public space as *market* place and public space as *connection* space. The city as a meeting place refers to the city as a site for social exchanges, while market place refers to the traditional role of cities as places for the exchange of goods and services. Gehl believes that a good public realm is one that enables people to be part of society in an equal way. This is public space as connection space, facilitating a demo-cratic sense of everyday life as people interact with one another in equivalent ways.

In *New City Spaces* (2000) Gehl and co-author Lars Gemzøe categorize cities into various types: *traditional* city, *invaded* city, *abandoned* city and *reconquered* city. For them, the traditional city is 'where meeting place, marketplace and traffic continue to coexist in balance' (p. 14). These are human scale cities, that is, cities designed to the scale and speed of humans. The invaded city started appearing in the 1950s and refers to car-dependent cities where most of the public space has been given over to automo-biles. Abandoned cities are those that have become so car-dependent that public space is virtually non-existent, dominated by surface car parking, internal shopping malls, and 'where public space and public life have disappeared' (p. 14). Reconquered cities are those that were invaded or abandoned but have recognized the importance of public life and a high-quality public realm and have pursued a better balance between city life and car traffic, and between the primary uses of a city as market place, meeting place and connection space, often by putting constraints on vehicular traffic or empha-sizing pedestrian movements in their planning of activity areas (Gehl and Gemzøe, 2000; Gehl et al., 2006).

Gehl's methods, particularly his PSPL studies, have enabled experiential knowledge to come to the forefront of urban design concerns. In his practice he advocates for purposeful incremental change through the careful analysis of public life, making urban design changes and then testing the results of these changes through further observations of use. At the core of Gehl's methodology is continuous and systematic observations of how people use spaces, looking at what activities people are undertak-ing, who is using the space and how the physical layout of the public space and buildings lining it influences patterns of activity. Gehl's PSPL methodology involves both qualitative and quantitative surveys of city centres using primarily observational techniques centred on pedestrian and activity counts. These enable comparisons of cities over space and time.

Gehl has had influence on cities around the world, notably Copenhagen (Denmark), Melbourne (Australia) and New York (USA). The transformation these cities have gone through in terms of becoming more walkable and with livelier city centres has been impressive. Gehl has, however, also had influence on numerous other cities of varying sizes. Perth, Australia, was the first city in Australia to undertake a PSPL sur-vey, in 1993, which illustrated a city lacking in pedestrian amenity beyond the provision of basic infrastructure. A follow-up survey in 2009 revealed many changes within the city centre, including better conditions for pedestrians. Importantly, the survey also enabled analysis of areas where the city could be improved and provided a platform for dialogue and decision-making about the direction Perth was to take.

Contributions to urban studies

Gehl's contribution to urban studies is threefold. He has developed a distinctive humanistic theory of urban design centring on the individual urban dweller's embodied somatic engagement with the urban environment. He has produced a range of easily replicated methods to study human activity in public spaces. And, lastly, through his writing and urban design practice he has been instrumental in transforming how urban policy makers and power brokers think about public spaces in cities.

Of course, Gehl's normative vision for cities is not beyond reproach. Many within urban studies equate place-making theories with only cosmetically addressing the greater issues within cities (see **Sharon Zukin, M. Christine Boyer**), as in the words of McNeill, 'civic discourse equated with commercial pride' (2011: 170). In this interpretation, the urban interventions Gehl is involved in do little more than speed up the gentrification of older areas. Such critiques, however, miss the originality of Gehl's thinking and the normative vision he articulates for cities. This is vision that while not addressing all facets of city-making is rooted within substantive research and theorizing about how people inhabit urban environments. Gehl offers a critique of existing urban environments. He shows how the planning of these environments often repudiates and overlooks the scale of the human body. Gehl also offers a series of practical tools for their betterment. He shows how attending to the routine, mundane way people inhabit cities orients us towards thinking about practical, incremental ways of improving public spaces (cf. **Enrique Peñalosa**). Indeed, the development of his PSPL technique has helped open the everyday use of public space to representation in the planning process. Gehl's thinking is self-consciously accessible. It is also optimistic and practical in orientation.

And, this is perhaps the most important contribution of Gehl on contemporary urban thinking. His writing on cities has helped urban research remember and attend to how face-to-face, bodily encounter is at the centre of the urban experience (cf. **Richard Sennett**). As the the Danish Ministry of Culture, in nominating Gehl for the Danish National Award for Outstanding Contributions to Art and Culture, wrote: 'there is something sensitive, attentive and immediate about Jan Gehl's understanding of the importance of public space. … As a humanistic advocate for public space, [he] interprets good public space as something more than aesthetics and atmosphere – good public space is also a platform for democracy and integration' (Matan, 2011: 234).

Secondary sources and references

Gehl Architects (2004) *Places for People Melbourne 2004*. Report for the City of Melbourne. Melbourne.

Gehl, J. and Bundesen Svarre, B. (2013) *How to Study Public Life*. Washington, DC: Island Press.

Gehl, J. and Gemzøe, L. (1996) *Public Spaces and Public Life, Copenhagen 1996*. Copenhagen: The Danish Architectural Press.

Gehl, J., Kaefer, L. and Reigstad, S. (2004) 'Close encounters with buildings' (originally published as 'Naerkontakt med huse' in *Arkitekten* 9/2004). Copenhagen: Centre for Public Space Research/Realdania Research, Institute for Planning, School of Architecture, Royal Danish Academy of Fine Arts.

McNeill, D. (2011) 'Fine grain, global city: Jan Gehl, public space and commercial culture in central Sydney', *Environment and Planning A*, 16(2): 161–178.

Matan, A. (2011) *Rediscovering Urban Design Through Walkability: An Assessment of the Contribution of Jan Gehl*. PhD, Curtin University.

Matan, A. and Newman, P. (2012) 'Jan Gehl and new visions for walkable Australian cities', *World Transport Policy and Practice*, 17(4): 30–41.

16 Edward L. Glaeser

Jürgen Essletzbichler, Vienna University of Economics and Business

Key urban writings

Glaeser, E.L., Kallal, H.D., Scheinkman, J.A. and Schleifer, A. (1992) 'Growth in cities', *Journal of Political Economy*, 100(6): 1126–1152.

Cutler, D.M., Glaeser, E.L. and Vigdor, J.L. (1999) 'The rise and decline of the American ghetto', *Journal of Political Economy*, 107(3): 455–505.

Glaeser, E.L. and Gyourko, J. (2002) *The Impact of Zoning on Housing Affordability. Policies to Promote Affordable Housing.* No. w8835. Cambridge, MA: National Bureau of Economic Research (NBER).

Glaeser, E.L. (2008) *Cities, Agglomeration and Spatial Equilibrium.* Oxford and New York: Oxford University Press.

Glaeser, E.L. (2011) *Triumph of the City.* London: Macmillan.

Introduction

Edward L. Glaeser is an urban economist who is equally at home in academia and on the public policy circuit. He is credited with 'reinvigorat[ing] the field of urban economics' (Gertner, 2006: 96) and 'has been at the vanguard of an economizing current in urban studies' (Peck, 2016: 1). Theorizing urban economies as the product of interaction among utility-maximizing individuals and profit-maximizing firms, Glaeser emphasizes the proximity in physical space that cities provide. He uses these 'microfoundations' to tackle a variety of urban topics including urban growth and decline, sprawl, housing, education, inequality, poverty, segregation and crime. Glaeser has become the 'go-to' urban problem solver, advising policy makers on how to get their cities on track by unleashing the power of consumer choice and entrepreneurial drive, and eliminating government intervention that may get in the way (Peck, 2016).

Glaeser is the Fred and Eleanor Glimp Professor at the Department of Economics at Harvard University, the Director of the Taubman Center for State and Local Government and the Director of the Rappaport Institute for Greater Boston. He is also a senior fellow at the conservative think tank the Manhattan Institute.

Academic biography and research focus

Glaeser was born in Manhattan in 1967. His father was the curator of the Department of Architecture and Design at the Museum of Modern Art and his mother worked in the capital markets and finance divisions of large corporations. His father kindled his interest in cities while his mother taught him basic economic concepts such as marginal costs. Perhaps unsurprisingly, Glaeser chose urban economics as his profession, applying the tools of neoclassical microeconomics to gain an understanding of urban processes. His training started in earnest at Princeton University where he completed a BA in Economics, and then a PhD in Economics under the supervision of Jose Scheinkman at the University of Chicago – the theoretical stronghold of neoliberal economic reasoning.

While any worthy Chicago economist learns to develop abstract models of micro- or macroeconomics, Glaeser chose to plough his trade in applied urban economics. Glaeser and colleagues employ general spatial equilibrium models that result in empirically testable hypotheses; they then crunch a lot of numbers in order to show how cities and urban characteristics develop as the result of the rational decisions of firms and consumers.

Glaeser's most important early contribution to urban studies was 'Growth in cities' (Glaeser et al., 1992). Because it provides a clear demonstration of how Glaeser applies the knowledge and tools acquired at Chicago to address central urban problems, it is worth dwelling on it a bit. At Chicago, Glaeser frequently sat in on faculty seminars including, among others, economic Nobel laureates Robert Lucas and Gary Becker. Lucas was working on the importance of 'knowledge spillovers' to generate dynamic 'externalities' – people interact and exchange ideas that may generate new knowledge. As they do not pay for such new knowledge, knowledge spillovers are external to market transactions and, hence, are called externalities. It turns out there *is* such a thing as a free lunch. Because geographic proximity facilitates the exchange of ideas, these knowledge spillovers are particularly important in cities (Glaeser et al., 1992). The value added of Glaeser's contribution to these ideas is the clever empirical evaluation of competing theories on the origins of those spillovers and the role of local competition for growth. On the one hand, following in the tradition of Alfred Marshall, Kenneth Arrow and Paul Romer (MAR) are those that believe that knowledge spills over within industries, for instance from dress manufacturer to dress manufacturer. Concentrations of firms in a city thus generate growth. However, according to MAR, innovation slows down when innovators realize that they cannot appropriate entirely the return to their ideas because others imitate them, and so they reduce investment in research and development. The conclusion of MAR is that concentration is good but local competition is bad for growth. The second theoretical framework Glaeser and colleagues examine is that of Michael Porter, who argues that local competition accelerates imitation and improvement of the innovator's ideas. According to Porter, concentration is good and local competition is good. The third theory that stresses knowledge spillovers originates from **Jane Jacobs** (1969). For Jacobs, cities' dynamism is the product of their diversity. According to her, spillovers between different, rather than within same, industries generate novelty and urban growth. Glaeser and colleagues' findings supported Jacobs and Porter but not MAR.

The 1992 paper launched Glaeser's academic career, got him a job at Harvard University and resulted in a whole school of scholarship concentrated on studying the relative importance of MAR and Jacobs' externalities for urban economic growth.

The results of this paper confirm Glaeser's conviction that human capital and competition are central elements of urban economic growth, further explored in a number of papers on the relationship between human capital, skills and urban economy (Berry and Glaeser, 2005; Glaeser, 1999, 2005; Glaeser and Mare, 2001; Glaeser and Resseger, 2010; Glaeser and Saiz, 2004). Cities do well if they are able to attract skilled workers (human capital) and workers become better in what they are doing (cities speed the accumulation of human capital) if they work in cities (Glaeser and Mare, 2001). For Glaeser the goal of cities is then to attract human capital, i.e. workers with talent, skill and entrepreneurial ambition rather than trying to subsidize housing, redistribute income or create job opportunities. The question then turns to how to attract skilled and talented agents to a city. The answer for Glaeser is through good amenities, high wages and low housing costs.

Thus a second important strand of Glaeser's research concerns the relationship between urban growth and decline, housing and zoning laws. Rather than blaming the rising demand for housing for the rise in house prices, Glaeser believes that in growing metropolises it is the shortage of supply that drives up prices. In turn, supply is restricted because of zoning laws and planning restrictions. Zoning laws keep development out and density low because of political pressures by homeowners with an interest in keeping house values up. Relaxing planning regulations would increase the supply of housing and provide residence for human capital (Glaeser and Gyourko, 2002). In growing cities with strict planning restrictions such as New York, Boston and San Francisco, high house prices push out all but the very rich, changing the nature of the city and reducing diversity which is the key to future growth. On the other hand, when cities decline, house prices drop below building costs and so become a barrier to further change as low prices attract poor people or keep the poor in cities with no jobs (Glaeser et al., 2006).

The role of regulation is a third strand of Glaeser's research related to questions of segregation, poverty and inequality. Glaeser takes on board William Julius Wilson's view that social mixing – and by implication inequality at the city scale – is good because access to social networks provides positive role models and access to jobs (Glaeser et al., 2009). The key then becomes to show how the processes of segregation – conditions of reduced social mixing – occur. Taking on the segregation between blacks and whites in US cities, Cutler et al. (1999) show how collective actions were taken by whites to exclude blacks from their neighbourhoods. By the 1990s, the removal of legal barriers to enforce segregation had been replaced by 'decentralized racism, where whites pay more than blacks to live in predominantly white areas' (Cutler et al., 1999: 455). According to Glaeser and Shleifer (2005) segregation was further enforced by mayors trying to shape the electorate. In the case of Detroit, it meant pushing whites out of the city and keeping and attracting black poor residents by raising residents' income tax rates and embarking on large building projects. In *Triumph of the City*, Glaeser (2011) spells out his aversion for redistributive policies, arguing that cities should accept their fate, reduce regulation, attract human capital and shrink back to greatness.

Key ideas

Glaeser is one of the major figures of what **Michael Storper** calls the New Neoclassical Urban Economics (Storper, 2013: 15). As an economist, Glaeser's empirical research is based on formal mathematical models which are simplified abstractions of reality. Such models allow researchers to isolate relationships between a limited set of variables and, given a set of assumptions, lead to predictions that can be tested empirically. Glaeser draws on a variety of existing models in urban economics, regional science and new geographical economics and extends them in various directions (Glaeser, 2008). His economic models begin with decision-making agents, and he distinguishes three types of actors: employers/firms, builders/developers and ordinary people/consumers/ workers that choose between different locations. Aggregate urban outcomes such as growth, decline or segregation are based on microfoundations.

People maximize their utility by choosing where to live based on wages, prices (in particular housing costs) and a bundle of other location-specific amenities such as warm winters. Because wages and prices are major ingredients, urban economics also requires firms and developers to choose locations. Firms maximize profits by hiring the right amount of workers given a particular wage that depends in part on the productivity of workers. Developers maximize profits and new houses are built as long as costs do not exceed the price of existing homes. The three optimization decisions lead to three equations which are solved for three unknowns: the price of housing, wages and the number of people who live and work in a given locale. 'Individual choice over locations produces the single most important concept in urban or regional economics: the spatial equilibrium. This core insight comes from the idea that if identical people are choosing to live in two different places then those two different places must be offering equivalent bundles of advantages, like wages, prices and amenities' (Glaeser, 2008: 4).

A general spatial equilibrium links together decision makers in different places and allows for adjustment mechanisms to respond to shocks that are exogenous to the model. For instance, real wages should be equalized across locations. If real wages vary then it means that firms have to compensate for negative factors (e.g. cold winters in Anchorage) through higher real wages. If the high real wages are not offset by something bad, the market adjusts. This could be in terms of migration (to Anchorage) driving down wages, or it could simply lead to higher housing costs resulting in a reduction in real wages. Because wages might reflect compensating efforts of firms in poor amenity locations, population growth is often used as a measure of urban success by economists. One of the hallmarks of Glaeser's models is the simultaneous consideration of population, income and housing prices in a framework derived from the spatial equilibrium assumptions.

These models are then put to use to investigate empirically urban questions. The simultaneous inclusion of consumers, firms and developers allows Glaeser and Tobio (2008) to conclude that the population shift from rustbelt to sunbelt cities in the United States was the result of higher productivity gains driving income and population growth in sunbelt cities from 1950 to 1970 and lower house prices (higher real wages) after 1970 in many but not all sunbelt cities. They find little evidence that the *growth* in amenities drives those population shifts, although differences in the *levels* of amenities are considered important. In sunbelt cities with limited amenities such as

Houston or Atlanta, housing supply expands rapidly while real wages increase, while in places like coastal California, beautiful beaches and warm weather are deemed responsible for lower real wages as rising house prices outstrip wage increases. In line with other urban economists, but contrary to new geographical economists, Glaeser believes that people move first and jobs and firms follow.

Once people moved to sunbelt cities and started interacting with each other, knowledge spillovers between them emerged. This has led to externalities that attract more firms, leading to higher wages and, together with the assumption that skilled people want to live next to other skilled people, has attracted more people. The key growth generating factor is human capital. Cities such as Boston, New York and San Francisco are awash with human capital and so do well, although the low supply of affordable housing threatens to push skilled people out. Glaeser believes in supply side economics. His policy recommendation therefore is to supply affordable homes and human capital to initiate and sustain urban economic growth and more importantly, to allow declining cities to adapt to economic shocks (Glaeser and Saiz, 2004).

Contributions to urban studies

Glaeser's contribution to urban studies is threefold. First, he has reinvigorated urban economics and introduced the city as respectable object of study to economists by developing a brand of general spatial equilibrium models that simultaneously take into account the choices made by people, firms and developers. Second, based on these theoretical models he has contributed a number of carefully crafted empirical analyses of various existing research areas in urban economics. Third, and probably most importantly, he blurs the boundaries between positive and normative economics and, supported by the Manhattan Institute, has 'effectively colonized the city as a projected space of economic rationality' (Peck, 2016: 1). He has the ear of senior leaders but even more so urban emergency managers, telling them that local government has little choice to turn things around '[a]part from investing in education and maintaining core public services with moderate taxes and regulations' (Glaeser, 2011: 67). But while exerting an influence on the discipline of urban economics and public policy discourse, his influence on research in the wider urban studies community may remain limited.

Many critical urbanists have little patience with Glaeser's almost exclusive focus on supply side explanations, and his neglect of the demands of workers and the importance of institutional changes. People did not only move to the South because of weather and cheap housing, but because the Taft–Hartley Act enabled firms to bar unions, resulting in a docile and cheaper labour force. This has attracted companies and generated jobs that allow people to migrate. In Glaeser's formulations, broader industrial restructuring processes shaping the pattern of urban development are seen as inevitable, exogenous trends rather than the result of political choices in favour of finance and against manufacturing. More importantly though, the treatment of cities purely as a cog in the equilibrating machine of perfectly rational markets is difficult to accept for thinkers such as **David Harvey** and **Neil Smith**. In contrast, these scholars understand cities as myriad often irrational and diverse decisions made by individuals and the layers upon layers of built infrastructure and institutions that shape social interaction and individual behaviour in cities.

Secondary sources and references

Berry, C. and Glaeser, E.L. (2005) 'The divergence of human capital levels across metropolitan areas', *Papers in Regional Science*, 84(3): 407–444.

Gertner, J. (2006) 'Home economics', *New York Times Magazine*, 5 March: 94–99.

Glaeser, E.L. (1999) 'Learning in cities', *Journal of Urban Economics*, 46(2): 254–277.

Glaeser, E.L. (2005) 'Reinventing Boston: 1640–2003', *Journal of Economic Geography*, 5(2): 119–153.

Glaeser, E.L. and Mare, D. (2001) 'Cities and skills', *Journal of Labor Economics*, 19(2): 316–342.

Glaeser, E.L. and Resseger, M.G. (2010) 'The complementarity between cities and skills', *Journal of Regional Science,* 50(1): 221–244.

Glaeser, E.L. and Saiz, A. (2004) 'The rise of the skilled city', *Brookings-Wharton Papers on Urban Affairs*, 5: 47–105.

Glaeser, E.L. and Shleifer, A. (2005) 'The Curley effect: The economics of shaping the electorate', *Journal of Law, Economics and Organization*, 21(1): 1–19.

Glaeser, E.L. and Tobio, K. (2008) 'The rise of the sunbelt', *Southern Economics Journal*, 74(3): 610–643.

Glaeser, E.L., Gyourko, J. and Saks, R. (2006) 'Urban growth and housing supply', *Journal of Economic Geography*, 6(1): 71–89.

Glaeser, E.L., Resseger, M.G. and Tobio, K. (2009) 'Inequality in cities', *Journal of Regional Science*, 49(4): 617–646.

Jacobs, J. (1969) *The Economy of Cities*. New York: Vintage.

Peck, J. (2016) 'Economic rationality meets celebrity urbanology: Exploring Edward Glaeser's city', *International Journal of Urban and Regional Research*, 40(1): 1–30.

Storper, M. (2013) *Keys to the City*. Princeton, NJ and Oxford: Princeton University Press.

Stephen Graham

Kurt Iveson, University of Sydney

Key urban writings

Graham, S. and Marvin, S. (1996) *Telecommunications and the City: Electronic Spaces, Urban Places*. London: Routledge.

Amin, A. and Graham, S. (1997) 'The ordinary city', *Transactions of the Institute of British Geographers*, 22(4): 411–429.

Graham, S. and Marvin, S. (2001) *Splintering Urbanism: Networked Infrastructures, Technological Mobilities and the Urban Condition*. London: Routledge.

Graham, S. (2011) *Cities Under Siege: The New Military Urbanism*. London: Verso.

Graham, S. (2016) *Vertical: The City from Satellites to Bunkers*. London: Verso.

Introduction

Stephen Graham is a British geographer and planner. His key contributions to the field of urban studies have focused on the relationships between technological change, infrastructure provision and urban life. He has been especially important in pushing his readers to think critically about urban infrastructures that are often taken-for-granted, blending into the background of urban life yet fundamentally shaping the different opportunities and experiences of urban inhabitants. He is best known in urban studies for developing, along with Simon Marvin, the concept of 'splintering urbanism' to capture the impact of contemporary infrastructure provision, and for his more recent work on urban securitization and the 'new military urbanism'.

Stephen Graham is Professor of Cities and Society at the Global Urban Research Unit, based in the School of Architecture, Planning and Landscape at the University of Newcastle-upon-Tyne.

Academic biography and research focus

Graham's career has straddled the disciplines of Geography and Planning. After studying for a Bachelor's Degree in Geography at the University of Southampton, Graham pursued a Master's Degree in Planning at the University of Newcastle-upon-Tyne. He then worked as a professional planner in Sheffield for several years, before embarking on a PhD at the University of Manchester in the Programme for Policy Research in Engineering, Science and Technology; his thesis was titled *Networking Cities: A Comparison of Urban Telecommunications Initiatives in France and Britain.*

Graham took up a teaching position at the University of Newcastle while completing his PhD in the School of Architecture, Planning and Landscape. There, he was exposed to early work on the geography of the information economy conducted by Mark Hepworth. He also worked with his future collaborator Simon Marvin, who had completed a PhD at the Open University in Urban Science and Technology Studies before moving to Newcastle. Graham remained in Newcastle on completing his PhD, and was involved with Simon Marvin in establishing the Centre for Urban Technology (CUT) that brought together their interests in critical geography, urban planning and science and technology studies. Graham has stayed in the northeast of England ever since. After a five-year stint as Professor in the Department of Geography at the University of Durham from 2005 to 2010, Graham returned to the University of Newcastle. He has since moved to the University of Sheffield.

From early work focusing on telecommunications and the city, Graham and co-author Simon Marvin went on to develop a socio-technical approach to understanding urban change in their book *Splintering Urbanism: Networked Infrastructures, Technological Mobilities and the Urban Condition* (2001). This book focused on the ways in which new technologies and increasingly privatized systems of infrastructure provision were producing new geographies of urban inequality. During the 2000s, Graham's ongoing interest in socio-technical change and urban inequalities shifted to focus especially on the role of military technologies and doctrines in the making of cities, in a configuration he labelled 'the new military urbanism'. A series of influential contributions on this topic culminated in his 2011 book *Cities Under Siege: The New Military Urbanism.* Graham's body of work has been especially influential in bringing research on the provision and governance of infrastructure to the mainstream of urban studies – given their fundamental importance to the urban experience, Graham insists, the study of infrastructure and technology cannot be left to technical specialists only.

While there is no doubt that Graham belongs in a collection on *Key Thinkers on Cities*, he does not fit the classical model of a lone scholar who lingers on in the academic imaginary of what it means to be a 'key thinker'. A quick browse of Graham's publications shows that many are co-authored, and clearly one of his most important academic skills has been his ability to think and work productively with others. During his career, Graham has had especially fruitful collaborations with Simon Marvin (currently Professor at the University of Durham), his co-author on *Telecommunications and the City* (1996) and *Splintering Urbanism* (2001). Graham has also played a key role as the editor of several important collections that have launched new research agendas on different aspects of urban life – most notably, *The Cybercities Reader* (2004a), *Cities, War and Terrorism* (2004b), *Disrupted Cities* (2010) and *Infrastructural Lives* (2014, co-edited with Colin McFarlane). In reviewing his research focus and key ideas, then, it is also important to note the role that Graham's co-authors and colleagues have played in the development of his work.

Across a series of works that have focused especially on telecommunications and city, the organization and provision of urban infrastructures, and the role of military technologies and doctrines in shaping urban space, Graham's work is no less than planetary in its scope. He is interested in the urban condition, and how we think about it. So, while Graham's work is replete with empirical examples and illustrations from across a very wide range of geographical contexts (both North and South), he seeks to draw conclusions about the nature of cities and the urban more broadly. Importantly, this is not to say that the urban condition is undifferentiated in Graham's work – indeed, in much of what he has written, Graham has sought to unpack the ways in which differentiation within and between cities is produced. Here, there are some parallels with **Henri Lefebvre**, whose work on everyday life sought to keep a focus on what he called 'totality', in dialectical relationship with the particularities of everyday experiences in different historical and geographical contexts. Graham's most recent research (2016) has focused on the vertical dimensions of the urban, and their relationship to inequality and urban politics.

Key ideas

Graham's work has focused particularly on the relationship between the urban condition, technological change and infrastructure. He has sought to draw our attention to the profoundly important role of new technologies and infrastructures in urban life, and provides us with ways to think about this role that avoid technological determinism.

This interest in new technologies and infrastructures began with a specific interest in telecommunications infrastructure, which was the topic of Graham's PhD and first book (co-authored with Simon Marvin). In *Telecommunications and the City* (1996: 377), Graham and Marvin's core claim was that:

> … contemporary cities can only be understood as parallel constructions within both urban place and electronic space. Without understanding both, and the many interactions between them we will never be able to approach or understand the totality of the current transformation underway in advanced capitalist cities.

The book offered a framework for thinking about telecommunications that insists they 'arise and are applied within rather than from outside society: telecommunications-based innovation in cities is therefore socially, politically and culturally shaped rather than being purely technical' (p. 113). This framework was then applied to consider the ways in which telecommunications technologies and infrastructures were developed and applied by various actors across a range of domains of urban life – from urban economies, environments and morphologies to the social and cultural lives of cities and urban infrastructure and transportation. The emergence of new forms of social polarization in cities associated with new developments in telematics was a particular concern in this work. Graham and Marvin argued that the privilege of corporate and transnational elites was reinforced through access to new telecommunications networks and services that were used to enhance control over space and labour, while disadvantage was exacerbated through exclusion from telecommunications, telematics and information services (see 1996: 236).

It should be noted that Graham and Marvin's work on telecommunications and the city was written at a time when there was widespread discussion about the coming 'end of cities' – the notion here being that proximity would no longer matter so much for a wide range of social and economic activities that could now be conducted 'at a distance' with the assistance of new communications technologies. Here, Graham and Marvin made an important contribution to the idea that cities would remain significant alongside networked communications technologies, alongside others such as **Manuel Castells, Michael Storper** and **Saskia Sassen.**

This initial interest in telecommunications technologies and their relationship to social polarization in cities was developed into a broader analysis of urban infrastructures by Graham and Marvin in their groundbreaking book *Splintering Urbanism* (2001). This book explicitly sought to approach the contemporary urban condition by highlighting the ways in which the 'wires, ducts, tunnels, conduits, streets, highways and technical networks that interlace and infuse cities are constructed and used' (p. 8). The relative neglect of such infrastructures in urban studies is problematic, they argued, because 'configurations of infrastructure networks are inevitably imbued with biased struggles for social, economic, ecological and political power' (p. 11). In paying close attention to networked infrastructures and their provision, Graham and Marvin made the bold claim that, contrary to the ways infrastructure had tended to be treated in urban studies during the 20th century, in fact infrastructures could not be said to simply act as 'integrators of urban spaces' – binding their populations together in shared services and experiences. Rather, drawing on a holistic socio-technical enquiry into networked infrastructure provision in contemporary cities, they argued that configurations of infrastructure provision were increasingly fragmented, leading to a splintering of urban spaces and populations rather than their integration. This argument is developed through drawing on extensive empirical observations of developments from Melbourne to Mumbai and many other cities. It also draws on a wide range of disciplinary and theoretical perspectives – indeed, one of *Splintering Urbanism*'s signal contributions is its pulling together of 'relevant discussions and debates in Urban Studies, Geography, Planning, Sociology, Architecture, Urbanism, Urban History, Science, Technology and Society (STS), Engineering, Social Theory and Communications Studies into a single, integrating narrative' (p. 33). The book certainly helped to introduce writers like Dupuy, Mattelart, Latour and others to a broader urban studies audience.

Since the publication of these two books, Graham has continued to extend this work on telecommunications and urban infrastructure to think about a range of developments, not least the growing significance of software in urban infrastructure provision. An influential 2005 article introduced the notion of 'software-sorted geographies', tracing the ways in which software is deployed across a range of infrastructural networks to sort urban populations into different groups in order to allocate them differential levels of infrastructural access. A 2007 article (co-authored with Mike Crang) on 'sentient cities' similarly excavated the ways in which ubiquitous or pervasive computing technologies were being mobilized in different domains in urban life, from surveillance and control to art and politics.

Over the course of the 2000s, Graham's ongoing research into urban infrastructures came to focus on the growing influence of military doctrines, technologies and strategies in efforts to control urban spaces and populations. With the diffusion of such doctrines and technologies, Graham has argued that we are witnessing the production of a 'new military urbanism' in which cities are increasingly conceptualized as 'battlespaces'. Importantly, he suggests, this does not only apply in cities that are more obviously caught up in military combat operations, but across a wide range of urban contexts where military logics and technologies are deployed in social control efforts. Of course, this does not mean that the new military urbanism looks the same across the world. Tracing the influence of the US military in particular, Graham sees distinct configurations of military urbanism in the cities of the Global South and the 'homeland' cities of the West, where different strategies are adopted to mitigate foreign and domestic threats.

In the poor cities of the Global South, two of the key strategies being devised and practised to counter insurgent threats include de-modernization and 'persistent area dominance'. De-modernization involves the targeting of urban infrastructures that are said to give insurgents their cover in urban battlespace. 'Persistent area dominance', on the other hand, is to be achieved through the deployment of new sensing technologies and intelligence techniques which give US and allied soldiers layers of information about urban battlespaces in real-time, thereby removing any home ground advantage insurgents may have due to their knowledge of everyday urban systems and spaces. Different strategies have been conceived for cities of the 'homeland'. Because the militarization of these cities is in large part justified in the name of protecting urban infrastructures against insurgent threats, neither de-modernization nor complete indifference to civilian rights and casualties are options. 'Homeland' cities are nonetheless being reimagined and re-engineered to address supposed imperatives of national security. This has involved related but distinct forms of militarization and the diffusion of military technologies and logics, including: a radical ratcheting-up of surveillance and social control, the endless 'terror talk', highly problematic clampdowns, the 'hardening' of urban 'targets', and potentially indefinite incarcerations, sometimes within extra-legal or extra-territorial camps, for those people deemed to display the signifiers of real or 'dormant' terrorists.

While the operational procedures in occupied and homeland contexts are quite different, there is nonetheless a thread connecting security strategies across this variety of cities. Underpinning the different strategies is a desire to establish spatial dominance through networked mobilities and surveillance capabilities. In particular, and in parallel with recent scholarship by **Harvey Molotch**, Graham identifies a convergence of security and military doctrine within Western states around the task of identifying insurgents, terrorists or malign threats from the chaotic background of urban life.

Contributions to urban studies

Graham's key contribution – working alone, and with others – has been to draw attention to the ways in which urban inhabitants are separated, sorted, surveilled and targeted through the use of technologies old and new. His work has also been significant in shaping how we can think about these processes of technological change and their relationship to the urban condition. Far from a technological determinism, Graham's work has shown how different technologies become enmeshed in socio-technical configurations through their articulation with different political-economic projects and ideologies – be it the neoliberal privatization agendas that were the focus of *Splintering Urbanism* or the military ideologies of control and battlespace dominance that were the focus of *Cities Under Siege*. Graham's work has also provided a model for a more integrative urban studies, that seeks to push beyond disciplinary separations and specialisms in search of critical insights into the relationship between technology, infrastructure and the urban experience.

The picture of cities presented by Graham is far removed from writers like **Jane Jacobs** or **Edward Glaeser**'s celebration of the city. In the manner of work by folks like **Mike Davis** or **Neil Smith**, Graham seeks to shake us up with his writing, to provoke us to resist the forces that are producing splintered and militarized urbanisms. This is crucial work, especially given the glossy promises that are made for new technologies by their advocates, who frequently present smartphones and surveillance cameras and other new technologies as nothing more than useful tools to solve existing urban prob-lems. However, as you read his powerful critiques of our urban present, it is perhaps easy to despair for the future of cities. What are we to do? While instances of resistance do appear in Graham's work, they are frequently overwhelmed and they are certainly not his focus. There are those who see in some of Graham's work a problematic total-izing critique that leaves too little room for politics and contingency (see Coutard and Guy, 2007). But regardless of where one stands on this critique of Graham's work, it does not diminish the crucial contribution Graham has made to urban studies. The value of his work lies as much in the questions he has posed as in the answers that he has provided. He and his co-authors have played a crucial role in foregrounding the importance of technologies and infrastructures that were too often treated as part of the taken-for-granted background of everyday urban life and politics.

Secondary sources and references

Coutard, O. and Guy, S. (2007) 'STS and the city: Politics and practices of hope', *Science, Technology, and Human Values*, 32(6): 713–734.

Crang, M. and Graham, S. (2007) 'Sentient cities: Ambient intelligence and the politics of urban space', *Information, Communications and Society*, 10(6): 789–817.

Graham, S. (ed.) (2004a) *The Cybercities Reader*. London: Routledge.

Graham, S. (ed.) (2004b) *Cities, War and Terrorism: Towards and Urban Geopolitics*. Oxford: Blackwell.

Graham, S. (2005) 'Software-sorted geographies', *Progress in Human Geography*, 29(5): 562–580.

Graham, S. (ed.) (2010) *Disrupted Cities: When Infrastructure Fails*. New York: Routledge.

Graham, S. and McFarlane, C. (eds) (2014) *Infrastructural Lives: Urban Infrastructure in Context*. London: Routledge.

18 David Harvey

Louis Moreno, Goldsmiths, University of London

Key urban writings

Harvey, D. (1973) *Social Justice and the City*. Baltimore: Johns Hopkins University Press.
Harvey, D. (1982) *The Limits to Capital*. Oxford: Blackwell.
Harvey, D. (1989a) *The Urban Experience*. Baltimore: Johns Hopkins University Press.
Harvey, D. (1989b) *The Condition of Postmodernity*. Oxford: Blackwell.
Harvey, D. (2012) *Rebel Cities*. London: Verso.

Introduction

David Harvey's analysis of the urban dynamics of capitalism has had, over the last four decades, a profound influence both within and beyond his native discipline of geography. Though analytically complex and wide in empirical scope, at its core Harvey's project is animated by a simple objective: to develop a critical theory explaining the uneven geographical development of capitalism over time. Within this the urban emerges as a distinctive focus of investigation. In itself the focus is unremarkable, as historians had long argued that the city is a central category in understanding the historical development of world markets. Harvey, though, is distinguished by a specific emphasis on processes capable of creating and destroying urban forms of social life. In this respect, his work is both indebted to Marx's thesis that capital must be studied not as a 'thing' but a social process riven with contradictions, and defined by the proposition that the urban is the social process where these contradictions crystallize out in the production of landscapes, institutions and cultures. The scale of Harvey's intellectual ambition is only matched by the profound nature of its political intention. If for Marx changing the world requires understanding how capital works, for Harvey changing the world begins with understanding the urbanization of capital.

Harvey is Distinguished Professor of Anthropology and Geography at the Graduate Center of the City University of New York (CUNY).

Academic biography and research focus

Born in Gillingham, Kent, Harvey gained his PhD in Geography from the University of Cambridge in 1961. By the end of the 1960s, his intellectual achievements already placed him at the forefront of his field. His first book, *Explanation in Geography* (1969), offered a comprehensive account of the methodologies geographers deploy to construct knowledge of the external world. Instantly recognized as a seminal work, Harvey was placed at the vanguard of a so-called 'quantitative revolution' seeking to consolidate the analytical foundations of geographical theory. The impact of the book rewarded him with tenure at the elite US institution Johns Hopkins University in the city of Baltimore. Yet soon after landing in the States, witnessing the social fabric of American society being tested to destruction shook Harvey from his positivist slumbers. The assassination of Martin Luther King, the imperial invasion of Vietnam and the urbanization of racism raised profound questions; not only about the responsibility of intellectuals to confront power, but also the political limits of the geographical imagination. In a remarkable redeployment of his own critical method, Harvey's *Social Justice and the City* (1973) set forward a provocative test. If the discipline of geography was to become a social science, then geographers needed to be able to account for those spatial processes that constituted and exacerbated urban inequality. If they couldn't then this raised profound questions about how the construction of cities – as a set of institutional, conceptual as well as physical structures – impeded the development of urban societies.

The precision with which Harvey laid out, then dismantled, the liberal precepts of urban theory inspired a new generation of radical scholarship. Alongside **Henri Lefebvre** and **Manuel Castells**, Harvey emerged as part of a new dialectical revolution in urban theory. But where others applied Marx's ideas to spatial concerns, Harvey argued that urban questions could be only partially resolved due to the lacunary treatment of space within Marx's thought. The subsequent publication of *The Limits to Capital* (1982) was intended to close this gap, showing that the territorial obstacles capital confronts are central to its ability to extend across space and persist over time. Intended to be a historical and theoretical account of capital, uniting logic and method, however, proved a contradiction too far. *Limits* therefore appeared as a book of pure theory, with its urban dimensions developed in a pair of companion volumes: *The Urbanization of Capital* and *Consciousness and the Urban Experience* (1985).

Today *Limits to Capital* is widely recognized as a landmark of critical political economy, although on publication it was slow to find an audience. For Marxian economists the interest in space seemed obtuse, and for radical geographers Harvey's commitment to Marxian categories appeared out of step in a climate of identity politics, incipient neoliberalism and post-structural theory. But while the fortunes of Marxian theory waned more than waxed with the sea-change of financial deregulation, Harvey's mid-1980s return to Britain to take a position at Oxford University resulted in a work that tried to explain the spatial logic of late capitalism. Appearing at a moment when the momentum of Reaganism and Thatcherism was about to stall, *The Condition of Postmodernity* (1989) argued that debates about post-Fordism, post-industrialism and postmodernism manifested precisely the opposite of a move beyond capitalism. The rise of more cognitive-cultural forms of capital, for Harvey, manifested the inherently flexible and culturally mutable nature of urban accumulation. What was replacing the managerialist programme of full-employment was a fiercely entrepreneurial project of urban consumption.

Returning to Johns Hopkins in the 1990s, Harvey refined his analysis addressing the growing wave of anti-capitalist resistance to globalization and themes of body politics, ecology and utopianism (see Harvey, 1997, 2000). At the turn of the millennium, though expecting to retire, the opening of a position as Distinguished Professor of Anthropology at City University New York (CUNY) marked a remarkable intensification in Harvey's writing activity. In the wake of the Iraq war and an unimpeded expansion of global markets, Harvey (2003, 2005) wrote narrative accounts of the rise of neo-imperialism and neoliberalism. Both *The New Imperialism* and *A Brief History of Neoliberalism* consolidated his reputation as one of the few geographers able to find a wide audience as a public intellectual. And with the epochal financial crisis of 2007 and the rise of austerity policies, Harvey's *Rebel Cities* (2012) returns to urban questions. Cities encapsulate, Harvey says, the best way to diagnose the pathologies of neoliberalism and to develop anti-capitalist alternatives. The rise of Occupy and the explosive events of Istanbul, Cairo, Athens, Madrid and other cities suggest, for Harvey, the glimpse of an urban form of constitutive power: a counter-power expressing a right to collectively reshape the urban process.

Key ideas

The recapitulation of **Lefebvre**'s key concept 'the right to the city' is characteristic of Harvey's capacity to keep Marxian ideas alive to contemporary urban political concerns. A good starting point for understanding Harvey's distinctive conception of spatial dynamics is the notion of spatial fix. This simple phrase describes the way cities are shaped according to internal tensions between the use-value and exchange-value of space. The idea critiques one of the core assumptions of economic theory: that the incorporation of capital in land, labour and technology is a necessary precondition for economic growth. For Marx, however, the accumulation of capital does not arise through some natural evolution of market exchange and industrial enterprise, but through a primary circuit of productive investment dedicated to capturing increasing surpluses of value created by the labour force. What Harvey points out is that the need to invest in physical infrastructures (factories, shipping facilities, mining operations, railways, etc.) and social institutions (of public housing, education, healthcare, etc.) requires huge outlays which tie capital up for long periods. What the spatial fix invites urban researchers to consider, therefore, are the socially dynamic consequences of locking capital and labour in place over time.

In the 19th century this process was spatialized in the form of the factory, the basic unit of production able to exploit an industrial army of wage-labourers. Harvey widens the scope of analysis by asking how does fixed investment play out, not only in terms of the simple site of production but also the expanded field of social reproduction. As the development of cities absorbs more and more economic resources, capital becomes immobilized for months, sometimes years in the process of development. The spatio-temporal problems arising from fixing capital in facilities of production (such as factories) and reproduction (houses and so forth) thereby impose constraints on capital mobility, preventing it from realizing its most flexible state as money-capital in search of profit. The creation of a glut of over-accumulated capital – a superabundance of economic energy, trapped in the system, unable to realize a profit – tends towards financial crises, requiring the destruction of surplus capital; a phenomenon the economist Joseph Schumpeter (1942) famously called 'creative destruction'. What is therefore destructively creative about crisis is the way it allows capital to deterritorialize; taking flight from difficulty in one location, reterritorializing itself in another space at another moment. Globalization might be thought of as the paradigmatic form of this process today.

Since investment is always risky, the ability to mediate uncertainty is socially assigned to entrepreneurs. But despite the arrogance normally associated with the entrepreneurial character, the bearers of risk belie a state of anxiety that haunts the entire system. The object of anxiety is the fear that capital, once invested, cannot be turned into money. Hence, the almost neurotic significance that financial agents attach to perpetuating mental states of confidence in capital's ability to compound its rate of return. Clearly, confidence in growth has to depend on something more systematic than mere hope in individual ingenuity. In order to manage the complex 'turnover times' involved in capital fixed in technology, buildings and spatial infrastructure, capitalism requires a secondary circuit of investment to financially overcome the scarcity of credit and the threat of business failure. What a financial market therefore provides are securities (like stocks and bonds) based on expectations of future income subject to speculative risk. Since this kind of 'fictitious capital' (fictitious because it is a claim on revenues yet to be created) is in a form comparable to the income landowners receive in projected rent, real estate (the asset value of capital fixed in land and buildings) may also circulate in a financial market. Thus, urbanization is not only a vehicle to create physical investments that increase productivity, it is also a process able to accumulate financial claims on the income of urban inhabitants.

Moreover, because land markets and capital markets are entwined, it becomes possible to monetize and monopolize the social, physical and cultural values of cities. With the notion of 'time–space compression' Harvey argues that the financial demand for liquidity – to abolish the frictions of both distance and temporality – gives rise to a capitalist culture that is intrinsically metropolitan. Speculative property bubbles give rise to architectures (like skyscrapers) that concretize the velocity and fungibility of fictitious capital. The idea is indebted to Georg Simmel's (2004 [1900]) classic account of the urban lifestyles that crystallize out of the exchange of money. What is particularly Marxist about Harvey's interpretation, however, is his analysis of the role of the state in using cities to make people's lives dependent on market forces. For Harvey, the postwar shift from an urban capitalism based on Fordist production and Keynesian infrastructure, to neoliberal forms of flexible employment has had enormous consequences in the way urban space is developed. And what the irruption of the 2007/8 financial crisis demonstrates, is that the over-accumulation of space and debt can bear down and compress social life so heavily they tear apart its very fabric.

Contributions to urban studies

It is difficult to imagine what the critical content of urban studies might be without Harvey's contributions. At the very least, the analytical coherence of Harvey's work has provided urban studies with a theoretical whetstone, sharpening the critical edge of accounts of globalization, neoliberal urbanism and gentrification (see **Saskia Sassen,**

Neil **Brenner** and Neil **Smith**). Harvey's contribution cannot be uncoupled from what he has called his life-long 'Marx project' to reanimate the critique of political economy with a spatial content that finds a popular constituency. As such, the historian Perry Anderson says Harvey 'follows Sartre's prescription for a revitalised Marxism very closely… [fusing] the analysis of objective structures with the restitutions of subjective experience… in a single totalizing enterprise. (Harvey, 2001: 15).

For Harvey's critics, however, herein lies the problem. The Marxian project to map the totality of capitalism has led some theorists to warn of anachronism: reading off the cosmopolitics of 21st-century urbanization against a rubric of 19th-century categories. The implication is that Harvey is a structuralist, historicizing struggle in a 'capitalocentric' (Gibson-Graham, 1996), masculinist frame (Deutsche, 1998) unable to absorb alternative post-Marxist perspectives. Another criticism is that Harvey's commitment to theory has been at the expense of developing a thoroughgoing empirical account of the way capitalism creates cities in its own image (Walker, 2004). The issues are complex and continue to be debated. But one way to deal with them is to consider two prospective contributions Harvey's work is making to understand the urban future of capital accumulation and class struggle.

The first is that Harvey's critique provides a timely antidote to the so-called 'new urban agenda' which see cities as global engines of 'smart' growth. As the collapse of Lehman Brothers and the crisis of subprime mortgages showed, the relationship between economic growth and urban development is far from stable and progressive. Instead, the urbanization of neoliberalism – through the privatization of social and physical infrastructure – represents, for Harvey, a primitive form of accumulation: a form of accumulation that uses the urban process to enmesh society in a web of rent-seeking contracts. In this respect Harvey's interest in examining processes of social reproduction as an arena of value extraction links with an emerging body of literature examining the way biological, environmental, corporeal, cultural and social qualities are becoming increasingly financialized. In particular, his notion of urbanization as a process of accumulation by dispossession tallies with Saskia **Sassen**'s (2014) account of the 'expulsive' force of globalization; one which uses, for example, migration, human trafficking, unemployment and homelessness as social apparatuses that turn debt into a biopolitical claim over life.

The second might be called the 'performative' dimension of Harvey's thought. Famously, Harvey has offered a course on Marx's *Capital* nearly every year since 1971. In recent years, the course has been placed online, galvanizing a new generation looking for intellectual tools to map the limits to capital. Characteristically, then, perhaps the best introduction to Harvey's work can be found in a short video on the web.[1] Shot on the backstreets of Istanbul, sat on the doorstep of a dwelling marked for 'renewal', Harvey links the neighbourhood evictions of 21st-century Tarlabaşı to the Haussmannization of Second Empire. Just a year later, Harvey's revolutionary comparisons would come vividly to life as, just a stone's throw from Tarlabaşı, protestors against the demolition of Gezi Park made Taksim Square a new frontline of urban struggle. What the video underlines is Harvey's pedagogical talent to use the experience of everyday life as a method to connect academic research with social concerns, animating political education and activism. In the last analysis, then, perhaps Harvey's central contribution is his dialectical insistence that it is within the gift of urban citizens to free themselves from compounding their debt to capital.

Secondary sources and references

Deutsche, R. (1998) *Evictions: Art and Spatial Politics*. Cambridge, MA: MIT Press.

Gibson-Graham, J.K. (1996) *The End of Capitalism (as We Knew It): A Feminist Critique of Political Economy*. Minneapolis: University of Minnesota Press.

Harvey, D. (1969) *Explantion in Geography*. London: Edward Arnold.

Harvey, D. (1985a) *The Urbanization of Capital: Studies in the History and Theory of Capitalist Urbanization*. Baltimore: Johns Hopkins University Press.

Harvey, D. (1985b) *Consciousness and the Urban Experience: Studies in the History and Theory of Capitalist Urbanization*. Baltimore: Johns Hopkins University Press.

Harvey, D. (1997) *Justice, Nature and the Geography of Difference*. Oxford: Wiley.

Harvey, D. (2000) *Spaces of Hope*. Berkeley: University of California Press.

Harvey, D. (2001) *Spaces of Capital: Towards a Critical Geography*. Edinburgh: Edinburgh University Press.

Harvey, D. (2003) *The New Imperialism*. Oxford: Oxford University Press.

Harvey, D. (2005) *A Brief History of Neoliberalism*. Oxford: Oxford University Press.

Sassen, S. (2014) *Expulsions: Brutal and Complexity in the Global Economy*. Cambridge, MA: Harvard University Press.

Schumpeter, J. (1942) *Capitalism, Socialism and Democracy*. New York: Harper.

Simmel, G. (2004 [1900]) *The Philosophy of Money*. London: Routedge.

Walker, R. (2004) 'The spectre of Marxism: The return of the limits to capital', *Antipode*, 36(3): 434–443.

Note

1. Tarlabaşı Istanbul (2012) 'Against vested interest urbanism – An interview with David Harvey'. Available at: www.tarlabasiistanbul.com/2012/06/against-vested-interest-urbanism-an-interview-with-david-harvey/ (accessed 23 June 2015).

19 Dolores Hayden

Leslie Kern, Mount Allison University

Key urban writings

Hayden, D. (1980) 'What would a non-sexist city be like? Speculations on housing, urban design, and human work', *Signs*, 5(3): 170–187.

Hayden, D. (1982) *The Grand Domestic Revolution: A History of Feminist Designs for American Homes, Neighborhoods, and Cities.* Cambridge, MA: MIT Press.

Hayden, D. (1984; 2nd edn 2002) *Redesigning the American Dream: Gender, Housing and Family Life.* New York: W.W. Norton.

Hayden, D. (1995) *The Power of Place: Urban Landscapes as Public History.* Cambridge, MA: MIT Press.

Hayden, D. (2003) *Building Suburbia: Green Fields and Urban Growth, 1820–1900.* New York: Vintage Books.

Introduction

Dolores Hayden is a prominent urban landscape historian and feminist. Trained in the field of architecture, Hayden has presented powerful critiques of the gender and class inequalities enshrined in built forms like the skyscraper and the suburban single-family home in her early work. Bringing an explicitly feminist lens to the relationship between the built environment and society, Hayden asks us to do no less than conceptualize and realize 'a new paradigm of the home, neighbourhood, city' (1980: 171).

As an historian, Hayden conducts careful excavations of the foundations of the landscapes, forms and functions of the quintessential American environment, the suburb. She illuminates the specific historical contexts through which the American obsession with home ownership and privacy has developed, and the reasons behind the continuing gendered division of domestic labour. Hayden is also well known for her work on urban public history and collective memory. In recent years Hayden has published poetry, as well as a collection of photographs illustrating the fascinating vocabulary of suburban sprawl.

Hayden is Professor of Architecture and Professor of American Studies at the Yale School of Architecture, Yale University.

Academic biography and research focus

As an undergraduate Hayden studied architecture at Mount Holyoke College and went on to receive her Master's of Architecture from the Harvard Graduate School of Design. Hayden's architecture background facilitated her exploration of socialist housing design in *Seven American Utopias: The Architecture of Communitarian Socialism, 1790–1975* (1979). In the 1970s, Hayden began to delve into women's history as a key component for understanding the politics of housing and urban design. No doubt influenced by second wave feminism and the struggle to facilitate women's rise in the paid workforce, Hayden saw single-family homes and suburban sprawl as major obstacles for women seeking work outside the home. Her historical investigations in *The Grand Domestic Revolution* (1982) revealed, however, that there was a long history of women agitating for radical housing and community plans from the mid-19th century onward. Much of this history had been forgotten or ignored by second wave feminists. Hayden's skilled work in reconstructing this history and re-presenting the housing designs of the material feminists made her early works instant classics for feminists interested in cities, homes and planning (Wekerle, 1984).

While working at MIT (until 1979) and UCLA (in the 1980s), Hayden widened her focus to think about reconceptualizing the relationship between cities and suburbs, and confronting the social, economic and environmental consequences of sprawl. With the first edition of *Redesigning the American Dream* (1984), she brought a much-needed gender focus to the growing literature critiquing suburbia (Fishman, 1987; Jackson, 1985). Describing herself as writing from the perspective of someone who is not only a historian, but also 'an architect, wife, mother, and suburban resident' (2003: xi), Hayden combines first-hand observation of everyday life and social relations with detailed archival research. *Redesigning* exemplifies her fascination and frustration with the familiar yet deeply problematic landscape of the suburb. However, in contrast to other critics, Hayden does not seek to label the suburbs as soulless, placeless nowheres (see Kunstler, 1993), a move which is all too easily dismissive of women's work, lives and communities. A feminist perspective on place, rather, requires consideration of the everyday, banal and non-spectacular landscapes where millions of Americans live their lives.

This interest in everyday places led Hayden to launch the Power of Place project in 1984. Still grappling with the diverse, sprawling, postmodern landscape of Los Angeles, her aim was to situate women's and ethnic history in urban public spaces. *The Power of Place* (1995) is a praxis-oriented project that explores both the need for a social history of urban space, and the challenges of working to uncover, preserve and celebrate marginalized and 'minor' histories in reflexive collaboration with the affected communities.

Hayden left UCLA for Yale in 1997. Her second major text on the suburbs, *Building Suburbia* (2003), takes her readers on a tour of seven suburban forms, further teasing out the historical and spatial specificities of the American landscape, 'its promises, dreams, and fantasies' (p. 3). A historical memory of the suburbs is crucial, she argues, if we are going to tackle the problems they present and generate progressive solutions. Hayden has more recently published creative interventions that address the suburbs, such as the visual project *A Field Guide to Sprawl* (2004a), and poetry including

American Yard (2004b). These efforts illustrate her gift for combining fields of enquiry, forms of knowledge production and theory and practice.

Key ideas

Hayden's body of work is impressive in its commitment to historicize and deconstruct the very forms, systems and ways of life that have come to seem natural in the American (and increasingly global) built environment. Most distinctive, though, is Hayden's relentless effort to foreground the relationship between form and society; more specifically, the relationship between urban environments and gender inequality. She accomplishes this in part by attending to 'lost' histories of feminist organizing, socialist planning and women's and ethnic urban places. Developing a new history of ideas about home, city, gender, inequality and place, Hayden has consistently demonstrated we cannot enact feminist change without understanding, and radically reimagining, the places we create (Eichler, 1995).

Hayden argues that the suburbs represent the ultimate ideological defeat for the claims of women for equal rights to the city and paid employment, in that early feminist gains were stymied by the powerful shift to suburban life. This argument is developed in the essay 'What would a non-sexist city be like?' (1980) and the monograph *The Grand Domestic Revolution* (1982) as a way to reanimate contemporary discussions about the gendered division of labour. Refusing to understand women's subordination within and confinement to the domestic sphere in solely economic terms, Hayden uses the 19th-century work of the material feminists to explicate the spatial dimensions of gender inequality. This feminist tradition argued that housework and childcare must be socialized, and incorporated into new spatial arrangements, to facilitate women's entry into the workforce, equality with men and intellectual development. Hayden maintains that the material feminists paid attention to both the household and the public realm, to the domestic economy and the political economy, in order to overcome the split between the domestic and the public.

But what happened to the revolutionary aims and plans of these feminists? Hayden acknowledges that the material feminists sowed some of the seeds of their own defeat through their lack of acknowledgement of the differential exploitation of women across race and class. However, it was the rise to dominance of the single-family home in low-density suburbs that truly undermined their goals. As women's role became redefined as homemaker/consumer, and the built environment grew to accommodate this and only this role, the dreams, plans and radical ideas of the material feminists – everything from wages for housework, to communal kitchens, to female control of municipal services, to apartment houses for single working women – faded from view (Birch, 1985).

Hayden continued to foreground gender as she engaged in more in-depth examinations of the suburbs. By the 1980s the suburbs were under fire from a broad range of progressive thinkers, planners and environmentalists who might be grouped under the label of 'anti-sprawl' (Jackson, 1985; Perin, 1977). But in the 2002 edition of *Redesigning the American Dream*, Hayden asks: where are women in this debate? She notes that the US continues to prop up the idea of the home as a private haven through policy and ideology. The roots of this lie in the postwar period, where homes and housing policy were designed for men as workers, and women as wives. Hayden adds to this history by illustrating how the powerful intersection of patriarchy and anti-communism (the 'Red Scare') promoted a utopian ideal centred on the house/ family, rather than on the city/citizen. In *Building Suburbia*, she fine-tunes her analysis by deconstructing the suburb into seven distinctive forms that have shaped the suburban landscape in particular ways. Even as this landscape has evolved and changed, however, traditional gender roles and household composition have remained taken-for-granted.

Critically, Hayden refuses to see the suburbs as a secondary part of urban history, or a side dish to the main meal of urban studies. Rather, she reminds us that the suburbs and the city, and the social relations engendered and reproduced by them, exist in a mutually constitutive relationship. In this way, Hayden has forcefully demonstrated the importance of a feminist perspective on design and housing policy, and the need to reconnect with the suburb in research and practice.

In line with her interest in lost, minor and secondary histories, Hayden calls for a socially inclusive, collective landscape history in *The Power of Place*. Hayden here brings into conversation fields that have too often ignored one another's insights. Architecture has not dealt with social and political issues; similarly, social history often ignores space and design (Agrest et al., 1996). Both, she argues, are central for American cities. She notes the longstanding neglect of women's and ethnic history in terms of landmarks and preservation, and argues that we need to deal with politics of identity in the urban built environment through public history, preservation and design (cf. **M. Christine Boyer**). Importantly, this means that in preserving place as part of public history, we must incorporate struggle, survival, slavery, exploitation, labour history and more. This runs counter to the traditional logic of place-making, which emphasizes positive elements like national glory, or aestheticization, or consumption sites. *The Power of Place* also describes the collaborative process of the project and argues that such projects require new research processes and means of connection across difference (cf. **Néstor García Canclini**).

Contributions to urban studies

Hayden has been one of the foremost critics of American suburbia over the last 45 years. Her insistence on the equal importance of women's history to urban history has meant that any story of American housing, cities or suburbs is incomplete without an analysis of the social forces that have shaped these landscapes. Hayden's body of work has provided the necessary foundation for contemporary feminist critics of urban development, sprawl and design to tackle ongoing problems of women's exclusion from central areas of urban planning such as transportation, neighbourhood design and zoning. Without her scholarship, it is difficult to imagine how key pieces of feminist urban research on women's housing designs (Wekerle, 1988), gentrification (Bondi, 1998), architecture (Boys, 1998), condominiums (Kern, 2010) or regional planning (Jarvis, 2007) would have been generated or received.

Hayden's work contains important lessons for architects, planners, urban designers, policy makers, academics and activists. Not content to look backwards, Hayden advocates for a different urban and suburban future. One method will be to work on saving older suburbs, rather than continuing to build new ones, in order to accommodate a growing population. She offers a variety of approaches to reconstructing domestic space to account for different needs and desires, such as community services to support the private household, as well as creative approaches to public housing. Housing issues must include a consideration of paid work as well as home life. At the heart of these proposals is the contention that women's right to the city must be firmly established as a political right. Addressing national housing needs will require a major economic as well as spatial and social overhaul, and for this, a broad public consensus around the need for change must develop. And women especially will need to be involved, and organized.

Lessons for feminism also reside in Hayden's work. Contemporary feminists ignore the spatial at their peril, Hayden might suggest, as battles over domestic work that are now over a century old remain hindered by designs that privatize household and caring labour.

She also noted that the material feminists did not always understand the need for the liberation of all women, reminding us that 'only by overcoming class and race divisions can feminists ever become powerful enough to end the exploitation of women's unpaid labour' (1982: 300). In this statement lies the basis of a critique of Hayden's own work, namely, that gender is emphasized at the expense of class, sexuality and especially race as critical elements in the story of American suburbanization. While Hayden acknowledges these factors at various points (e.g. ongoing racial discrimination in mortgage lending), she does not typically foreground processes of dispossession, dislocation or displacement. It is clear that any attempts to make use of Hayden's and others' imaginative ideas will need to take on actively decolonizing, queer and anti-racist strategies for dreaming and enacting our future cities and suburbias.

Secondary sources and references

Agrest, D., Conway, P. and Weisman, L.K. (1996) *The Sex of Architecture*. New York: Harry N. Abrams.

Birch, E.L. (1985) *The Unsheltered Woman: Women and Housing in the 1980s*. New Brunswick, NJ: Center for Urban Policy Research.

Bondi, L. (1998) 'Gender, class, and urban space: Public and private space in contemporary urban landscapes', *Urban Geography*, 19(2): 160–185.

Boys, J. (1998) 'Beyond maps and metaphors? Re-thinking the relationships between architecture and gender', in R. Ainley (ed.) *New Frontiers of Space, Bodies and Gender*. London: Routledge, pp. 203–217.

Eichler, M. (ed.) (1995) *Change of Plans: Towards a Non-Sexist Sustainable City*. Toronto: Garamond Press.

Fishman, R. (1987) *Bourgeois Utopias: The Rise and Fall of Suburbia*. New York: Basic Books.

Hayden, D. (1977) 'Skyscraper seduction, skyscraper rape', *Heresies*, 1(2): 108–115.

Hayden, D. (1979) *Seven American Utopias: The Architecture of Communitarian Socialism, 1790–1975*. Cambridge, MA: MIT Press.

Hayden, D. (2004a) *A Field Guide to Sprawl*. New York: W.W. Norton.

Hayden, D. (2004b) *American Yard*. New York: David Robert Books.

Jackson, K.T. (1985) *Crabgrass Frontier: The Suburbanization of the United States*. New York: Oxford University Press.

Jarvis, H. (2007) 'Home-truths about care-less competitiveness', *International Journal of Urban and Regional Research*, 31(1): 207–214.

Kern, L. (2010) *Sex and the Revitalized City: Gender, Condominium Development, and Urban Citizenship*. Vancouver: University of British Columbia Press.

Kunstler, J.H. (1993) *The Geography of Nowhere: The Rise and Decline of America's Man-Made Landscape*. New York: Free Press.

Perin, C. (1977) *Everything in its Place: Social Order and Land Use in America*. Princeton, NJ: Princeton University Press.

Wekerle, G.R. (1984) 'A woman's place is in the city', *Antipode*, 16(3): 11–19.

Wekerle, G.R. (1988) *Women's Housing Projects in Eight Canadian Cities*. Ottawa: Canadian Mortgage and Housing Corporation.

20

Jane Jacobs

Oli Mould, Royal Holloway, University of London

Key urban writings

Jacobs, J. (1961) *The Death and Life of Great American Cities*. New York: Random House.
Jacobs, J. (1969) *The Economy of Cities*. New York: Vintage.
Jacobs, J. (1984) *Cities and the Wealth of Nations*. New York: Random House.

Introduction

Jane Jacobs (born Jane Butzner) is one of the most influential thinkers on cities in the 20th century. Her book *The Death and Life of Great American Cities* (1961) is acknowledged to be one of the most important texts in urban planning and has proven to be deeply influential to academics and practitioners alike. As a thinker, Jacobs' key contribution was to champion everyday social, cultural and economic life on the streets and sidewalks of cities, and to challenge destructive forms of planning that threatened the dynamism of urban life. She saw the diversity of city life as fundamental to economic growth and cultural wellbeing, and defended this vehemently via her writings and her books, but also through on-the-street activism throughout her life.

From the point of view of the mainstream urban thinkers and managers at the time, Jacobs was considered a perennial 'amateur' and was often denigrated and derided, seen as a fly in the ointment of large-scale change in American cities, particularly New York. But her fundamental and unique take on urban life meant that over time she was able to radically change the way the city developed, owing to her persistence in challenging city plans. Her work has gone on to influence a generation of ordinary citizens to resist 'top-down' urban planning processes, inspired by how she was able to effect radical and lasting change in the world's largest cities by simply extolling her own experience of the everyday social, political and economic life of the cities in which she lived. For that reason, even after her death in 2006, her legacy of the preservation of community life in the face of large-scale institutional urban change is cemented into urban studies, giving her the status as one of the most revered urbanists of our time.

Academic biography and research focus

Born in Scranton, Pennsylvania in 1916, Jacobs moved to New York City when she was 19 years old and began writing for various magazines. She started out at the US government's Office for War Information and the Russian-language magazine, *Amerika*. In 1952, she was hired by the *Architectural Forum* magazine and a few years later visited a Le Corbusier-inspired housing project in Philadelphia, where she first became sceptical of these large-scale urban planning schemes. Describing it as 'grim' (Goldberger, 2006), she became a vocal critic of top-down zoning processes, and began to campaign against some of the city's more established urbanists' voices. Despite her opposition towards the city's political elites, her work was encouraged and funded by the Rockefeller Foundation, and from this she was able to draft the now famous book *Death and Life of Great American Cities*. Published in 1961, the book delved into the history of urban development and argued that the social life of contemporary cities was being destroyed by large-scale modernist plans (for example she described Ebenezer Howard's Garden City movement as 'city-destroying' [Jacobs, 1961: 18]). She based much of her conceptual work on empirical observations from the street outside her apartment at 555 Hudson Street in Greenwich Village, New York City. The rich description she provided of the 'ballet of the sidewalk', performed by everyone from local restaurateurs to children, pensioners and shop workers, supported her view of these interactions as fundamental to the diversity and dynamism of urban life. She described the city as an 'organism', citing at length the mathematician Warren Weaver's (1958) essay on 'organized complexity'; an idea that prefigured contemporary conceptualisations of cities as emergent, complex adaptive systems (cf. **Michael Batty, Ash Amin**). Scientific and biological metaphors for urban life run through *The Death and Life of Great American Cities*, and are used as part of a vicious critique of the urban planning profession. Such derision was met with angry rebuttal from city officials nationwide. Despite this, the book proved popular among residents of New York and she began to increase her activism against New York's planning system and in particular the city's master planner Robert Moses.

A focal point of Jacobs' activism against Moses involved his plans to build a multi-lane expressway across lower Manhattan (in the Greenwich Village area where Jacobs lived). The road would have meant the eviction of many families and communities and the forced closure of thousands of businesses. In an age of the dominance of the motorcar, particularly in the sprawling US metropolitan regions, the plan was widely regarded as a necessary step for New York's development. However, it would also have meant the destruction of Washington Square Park and the concreting over of the neighbourhoods that Jacobs saw as so critical to the community life of New York and US cities more broadly. In response, Jacobs held rallies, chaired committees and created publications that actively resisted these plans; the first of which was successfully repelled by Jacobs' activist practices in 1958. The city attempted numerous times throughout the 1960s to build the Lower Manhattan Expressway, but each time, Jacobs was there to repel them. Her arrest in 1968 proved to be the final chapter in her 'Battle for Gotham' (Gratz, 2010) as subsequently no expressway was ever proposed.

Tired of confronting the city of New York, Jacobs and her family eventually moved to Toronto. She continued to write, and her second book, *The Economy of Cities* (1969), was similarly heralded as a fundamental text that detailed how clustering, diversity and social mixing was vital to urban economics; a theory which holds a great deal of influence in today's processes of city development. Her later work, including *Cities and the Wealth of Nations* (1984) and the less read *Systems of Survival* (1992) and *The Nature of Economies* (2000) are all grounded in a similar ethos of the complexity of economic, urban and social life, and how national governments undermine the dynamism of city life. Jacobs died in 2006 in Toronto, and since then, her work has continued to influence urban policy not just in the US, but across the world.

Key ideas

Jacobs did not research or write from within the framework of an academic (or indeed, any) institution. This does not mean however that her ideas are any less embedded into the wider urban theoretical debates. Her work is highly knowledgeable and thoroughly researched and has been used as foundational work for an array of current and widely used concepts of contemporary urbanism. There is a distinct lineage and coherence to her work, and an overall philosophy that places human ingenuity at the heart of progress and societal change, with 'big' institutional power as an impediment to it. These ideas are foregrounded with a great deal of empirical detail in *Death and Life of Great American Cities* (1961), her first and undoubtedly most important work. But her ideas then evolve more conceptually through her later work, including *The Economy of Cities* (1969) and *Cities and the Wealth of Nations* (1984). We can chart an exploration of these ideas if we focus on different scales; namely the street, the city and the nation.

Streets and sidewalks, Jacobs argued, are a city's 'most vital organs'. Yet they were being destroyed by what she called 'orthodox planning systems' such as the Garden City projects of Howard and the Radiant City theories of Le Corbusier (among others). In contrast to these ideas that she saw as dehumanising, a fundamental kernel of her thought was the importance of getting the street right. So in *Death and Life of Great American Cities*, there are numerous examples drawn from her own life and that of her friends that all show how streets function as the key arenas where urban life is conducted. She outlined a number of 'conditions' that streets require in order to maintain a vibrant atmosphere and hence have the underlying conditions for economic prosperity: a varied architecture and age of buildings (she argued for the maintenance and re-use of old buildings), a dense and varied population (age, race, class, etc.) and short blocks (what present-day urbanists have called 'walkability'). In essence, she saw the streets as the 'lifeblood' of cities, and their continued use meant that people felt safe and free to conduct their busy daily lives under the natural surveillance provided by a diversity of 'eyes on the street'. She argued famously that 'the ballet of the good city sidewalk never repeats itself from place to place, and in any one place is always replete with new improvisations' (Jacobs, 1961: 50). She saw large-scale modernist developments as destroying this street life, and hence dampening the social and economic dynamism of the city (see also **Kevin Lynch**).

The intricate ballet of the street provides a micro-level demonstration of what makes cities the crucibles of human development. They are the sites of our greatest achievements as a human race because they encourage interaction and innovation at a scale that is not achievable in other kinds of settlements. In *The Economy of Cities* (1969), Jacobs made this argument in a rather controversial and counterintuitive way. She argued that cities were not the 'end game' of settlement progression. They did not come after agricultural production and the agrarian society; they preceded agriculture. When discussing the ancient city of Çatal Höyük, she argued that:

> It was not agriculture ... for all its importance, that was the salient invention, or occurrence if you will, of the Neolithic age. Rather it was the fact of sustained, interdependent, creative city economies that made possible many new kinds of work, agriculture among them. (Jacobs, 1969: 36)

Her novel claim was that the archaeological evidence within Çatal Höyük pointed towards the fact that agricultural production was created out of a need to feed a rapidly developing population. The steady sequential growth from village to town to city was not apparent here. Evidence of arts and crafts, storage of food and innovations in work, for Jacobs, points towards the fact that the city necessitated the agricultural hinterland that grew around it. She denounced agricultural primacy as a 'dogma' (Jacobs, 1969: 35). Her ideas countered the prevailing historical and archaeological theories of the time and gave newfound importance to the role of cities within historical social science.

Given her historical analysis, she saw cities as the drivers of all kinds of economic productivity (agriculture just being one). She saw them as engines of a special kind of growth that is so rapid that they power the development of nations (whose governments she goes on to argue often hinder the 'natural' growth of cities). In *The Economy of Cites* (1969) and later *Cities and the Wealth of Nations* (1984), she details 'explosive city growth' which occurs in a select few cities (New York being one). There are historical conditions for such growth (such as a varied production and industrial base) but the main process driving it is that of 'import replacement'. Import replacement is when a city begins to produce goods that it previously imported. In Chapter 5 of *The Economy of Cities*, entitled 'Explosive city growth', she gives the example of Tokyo in the 19th century. The city imported bicycles, but as it began to be able to repair, maintain and then build its own bicycles, the city stopped importing them and began producing them instead – the import had been replaced by production, creating new jobs and labour methods that did not exist before (which she labelled as 'new work'). This freed up capital to import other goods that then also were gradually 'replaced' by production in the city. This cycle of importing goods, then producing them diversifies the city's economy, and creates explosive city growth (more than simply the linear expansion of a handful of industries). Such growth spreads to other regions and cities in a national framework; and in contrast to prevailing economic theories that saw nations as the key geographical agent, Jacobs saw cities as fuelling national development.

These ideas were very much an argument about economic development and the dynamics of agglomeration (cf. **Michael Storper**), but Jacobs was adamant that extraordinary growth was unable to flourish in cities that did not have a vibrant and dynamic street life. So with these conceptually interrelated 'scaled' topics (the street, the city, the nation), Jacobs' foundational ideology of the power of cities becomes clear. She placed the utmost importance, theoretically and empirically, on the way in which cities brought people together to create meaningful new modes of social and economic life.

Contributions to urban studies

Jacobs' work has been monumentally important to contemporary urban studies. In particular, her ideas that stem from *The Death and Life of Great American Cities* (1961) have had a huge influence in urban studies and planning. Despite the initial rebuttal from the elite planners and urbanists, throughout the subsequent decades, urban planning has fundamentally shifted towards creating the kind of cities that she championed. As modernist planning projects began to fail and produce increasing social problems for residents, planners began to take Jacobs' observations of the streets as the lifeblood of cities far more seriously. For example, her work is heavily cited as the influence behind the 'New Urbanism' movement in the United States that started in the 1980s and gained widespread popularity for its efforts to create village-like centres of mixed zoning in the suburbs, where people can walk to work and their paths criss-cross with their neighbours on a daily basis. The most vivid representation of this is the idiosyncratically labelled town of Seaside, Florida, which was the first New Urbanist town in the United States (and made famous in the 1998 film *The Truman Show*). However, such urban design has been criticised as a betrayal of Jacobs' core beliefs, which has led to aesthetically sterile urban landscapes that privilege private development over public space. In addition, her theory of 'eyes on the street' also had important influence in urban surveillance, particularly Oscar Newman's 'defensible space theory'; which again had considerable influence in the design of urban residential areas. But more, such development has led to critical accusations of over-surveillance, and the creation of gated communities.

Another of the 21st century's most popular urban policies said to have drawn inspiration from Jacobs has been that of 'creativity', made famous by urbanist Richard Florida with his book *The Rise of the Creative Class* (2002). Florida, by his own admission, is heavily influenced by Jacobs' ideas of the street and a diverse urban economy. Florida's theories, though, have led to much criticism that cities are pursuing utopian idylls at the cost of high levels of gentrification. Florida's work relentlessly employs Jacobs' legacy as an indication of how creating diverse, tolerant and 'street-level' cities leads to prosperity. Yet commentators argue that when cities employ these ideals uncritically, it results in sky-high rents and the destruction of existing communities. Other urbanists have been more cautious in adopting Jacobs' work (such as **Edward Glaeser** and **Michael Storper**) but maintain that the inherent creativity of cities comes from the interaction of people on a 'human scale', i.e. on the street. Either way, the wholesale adoption of her ideas from a planning perspective has ushered in a new form of urban development (particularly in the US) that while having street-level and community engagement as its core, can bring with it problematic issues of displacement, gentrification and social inequality.

Secondary sources and references

Florida, R. (2002) *The Rise of the Creative Class: How It's Transforming Work, Leisure, Community and Everyday Life*. New York: Basic Books.

Glaeser, E. (2011) *The Triumph of the City*. New York: Penguin Press.

Goldberger, P. (2006) 'Uncommon sense: Remembering Jane Jacobs, who wrote the 20th century's most influential book about cities', *The American Scholar*. Available at: https://theamericanscholar.org/uncommon-sense/#.VYkSAFVViko (accessed 23 June 2015).

Gratz, R. (2010) *The Battle for Gotham: New York in the Shadow of Robert Moses and Jane Jacobs*. New York: Nation Books.

Jacobs, J. (1992) *Systems of Survival: A Dialogue on the Moral Foundations of Commerce and Politics*. New York: Random House.

Jacobs, J. (2000) *The Nature of Economies*. New York: Random House.

Jacobs, J. (2004) *Dark Days Ahead*. New York: Random House.

Weaver, W. (1958) 'The encouragement of science', *Scientific American*, 199: 170–179.

21

Jane M. Jacobs

Ryan Centner, The London School of Economics and Political Science

Key urban writings

Jacobs, J.M. (1996) *Edge of Empire: Postcolonialism and the City*. London: Routledge.
Fincher, R. and Jacobs, J.M. (eds) (1998) *Cities of Difference*. New York: Guilford Press.
Jacobs, J.M. (2006) 'A geography of big things', *Cultural Geographies*, 13(1): 1–27.
Jacobs, J.M. (2012a) 'Comparing comparative urbanisms', *Urban Geography*, 33(6): 904–914.
Cairns, S. and Jacobs, J.M. (2014) *Buildings Must Die: A Perverse View of Architecture*. Cambridge, MA: MIT Press.

Introduction

Jane M. Jacobs is an Australian cultural geographer of cities, the built environment and heritage landscapes. Her work focuses on urban representations of culture and difference, especially struggles over controlling and remaking them. She has also written on the logic and politics of urban comparison. Jacobs brings together research and theorization on indigenous, immigrant and dominant groups in the city, engaging with a panoply of approaches including postcolonial, feminist, actor-network and architectural literatures. In turn, her work has moved between Australia, the United Kingdom, North Africa and Southeast Asia, reflecting a career trajectory that has spanned much of the globe. Yet at the heart of this mobile scholarship is Jacobs' abiding concern with the politics of cultural property in context. For Jacobs, cultural property encompasses all the objects and places considered formative of a particular culture – a definition that in its openness has yielded a range of sites and questions for her interventions in disputes over how culture and space intertwine in both the fixed built environment and the flux of everyday practices.

Jacobs is Professor of Urban Studies, and Director of the Division of Social Sciences, at Yale–NUS College in Singapore. She shares no relation with the Canadian-American urbanist **Jane Jacobs**, but has frequently commented on how this common name has added to her critical interest in signification, ambiguity and difference.

Academic biography and research focus

Born in 1958 in rural South Australia, Jacobs completed her BA and MA degrees in Geography at the University of Adelaide. Her MA dissertation documented the struggles and strategies of indigenous groups in Port Augusta, South Australia, seeking recognition of their land claims (Jacobs, 1983) – a document that remains a key reference for other indigenous Australian groups struggling to realize land rights. She then worked on the state-funded project 'Tourists and the National Estate' (Gale and Jacobs, 1987) to investigate indigenous art sites across Australia, highlighting the impact of tourism on culture as manifest in both physical locations and in symbols and significations. This early work shaped her lasting interest in the competing uses of emplaced culture.

Jacobs moved to England for her PhD studies in Geography at University College London. There she researched the cultural politics of redevelopment in two districts of the British capital – one primarily a corporate site of banking and finance, the other a neighbourhood largely populated by Bangladeshi immigrants. Jacobs returned to Australia in 1990 to join the Department of Geography at the University of Melbourne. Movement between studies in the UK and Australia culminated in Jacobs' most widely cited book, *Edge of Empire: Postcolonialism and the City* (Jacobs, 1996), which wove together cases across these two countries in a study of the British Empire's ongoing legacies in shaping urban cultural struggles over space and representation. Jacobs forged ahead with her collaborative, interdisciplinary work in Australia (see Gelder and Jacobs, 1998), yet always maintained a core geographical concern with land and cultural heritage. When she moved to the University of Edinburgh in 2002, Jacobs began studying practices and politics of making – as well as unmaking – the built environment, including several academic collaborations with her husband, architect Stephen Cairns, through field studies both in and beyond their professional base in Scotland.

In 2012, Jacobs accepted a position to spearhead the development of social sciences in a new joint initiative between Yale University and the National University of Singapore: Yale–NUS College. In this role, Jacobs has continued her work on the logics of urban comparison and deepened her focus on the built environment.

Key ideas

Jacobs has brought the study of imperial legacies into urban research by emphasizing how differently positioned historical claims on culture and place continue to clash in the present. While focusing on the complicated, malleable heritage of the defunct British Empire in her own work, especially in *Edge of Empire*, she has shown how a lens on empire's lingering, uneven effects can be applied more broadly to postcolonial cities elsewhere. In these contexts, such imperial legacies – among other sweeping, power-laden structures such as religions or geopolitical alignments – can take on heterogeneous valences when mobilized by various groups as they attempt to intervene in urban change. This gives a new view on development and also opens scope for different (aboriginal, ex-colonial, immigrant, etc.) actors to intervene in redevelopment processes, specifically through unsettling assertions of their right to cultural property, including claims on land, in the ostensibly settled city of post-empire. The consequence is conflicting logics of authority that yield a contested hierarchy of righteousness (cf. **Mariana Valverde**). Pivotal here is a clash of 'truths' – the very different under-standings of what is right, good, valuable, and can be taken for granted in the city.

Keeping questions of property and propriety at the core of post-imperial studies continues to be a key urban concern for Jacobs (2012c). She highlights how there is often a complicated politics of accommodation by more powerful (often but not exclu-sively more moneyed) actors towards indigenous or other marginalized interests. But these accommodating moves can obscure what the less advantaged see as 'truths' about cultural property and place, reducing them to a series of images that becomes part of a landscape made marketable and thus antithetical to the crux of many of those visions, denying any sense of property. Resistance to these manoeuvres takes the form of both protest and alternative place-making. For Jacobs, this is part of the unruliness of cities but especially of empire – despite its typical fixation with ordering and impo-sition of rules – as well as the possibilities of peripheries and the postcolonial moment. These are not always happy possibilities, to be sure, but they enable the unsettling of nostalgic notions about empire that recur in the development and branding of cities.

Engagements with disputed urban imperial legacies have prompted Jacobs to rethink approaches to cultural difference in cities across quite varied scales. She has worked to develop analytical tools going beyond frameworks that either naturalize difference and inequality in the city, or reduce them to class-defined disparities (see Fincher and Jacobs, 1998; Jacobs, 1993). Jacobs has foregrounded the feminist-geographical notion of a 'located politics of difference' – inspired by Adrienne Rich (1986), as well as Doreen Massey and Geraldine Pratt – to uncover the production of multiplicitous, intersecting social differences in the city. In *Cities of Difference*, Fincher and Jacobs (1998) spotlight how differences in cities become objects of discursive manipulation that are deeply socially charged, yet also mutable, and therefore a subject of politics. Beyond understanding difference across space, or analysing conditions within and dynamics between different areas of the city, the idea here is to grasp the politics that constitute and locate difference.

Jacobs' work on postcolonialism, difference and cities led her to question the epis-temological underpinnings of urban comparison itself. A key intervention has been the articulation of a new logic for comparing cities. She delineates a Deleuze-inspired mode of urban comparison that prizes 'the multiple'; i.e. not the 'n = 1' of single cases studied as somehow prototypes, but Deleuze's emphasis on difference as 'n − 1' (Jacobs, 2012a: 906). The principle here is to treat cases as manifestations of difference from frameworks that have attempted to create generalizable explanations through the extrapolation and overuse of a few presumably canonical cities, such as Chicago, Paris, Los Angeles or New York.

Jacobs (2012a: 906) advocates 'working with multiples (many cities, other cities, ordinary cities) not as addition (one more city case in a project of building general urban theory) but as subtraction (reading urban difference in the name of producing alternative futures)'. This is not only about comprehending multiplicity but adjudi-cating between research agendas and engaging in a politics of representation in and through comparative research on cities: '[f]or anyone or any place that has had its subjectivity constituted in relation to centers and heartlands deemed to be elsewhere, finding the appropriate conditions by which to be seen and understood is a central imperative' (2012a: 909). In this way, Jacobs recasts differences among cities as characteristics to understand as potentially unique and inherently normal in their own right, rather than as quantifiable scores on some normative (and often moralizing) hierarchy. This is not to argue against diagnostics, or efforts towards change, in regard to certain urban features. It is, however, a statement that difference need not require automatic deference to an arbitrary norm set in some distant and/or more powerful site.

Training attention on the making, siting and consequence of differences has brought Jacobs to quite literally concrete considerations of difference; that is, the located politics of difference in the making and unmaking of buildings themselves. While based in Edinburgh, Jacobs began to carry out an extensive collaborative study of the Red Road complex of state housing towers in nearby Glasgow. Upon several visits to Singapore during this same period, she began studying the state-sponsored housing towers that had become home to the majority of Singaporeans by the end of the 20th century (see Jacobs and Cairns, 2008). These disparate settings made for an excellent comparison of how a single, repeated, massive form – 'the modernist, state-sponsored, residential highrise' (Jacobs, 2006: 3) – comes to vary so much in valences across settings. In one, it is a vilified failure; in another, it is the realization of dreams of modernization. Jacobs shows how the distinctly politicized machinery of architecture, construction and regulation in each context greatly affects the physical makeup of these structures from the British Isles to Southeast Asia, as well as the experience of their residents and their popular depiction by those around them – including their treatment by powerful institutions. This is a story about how buildings literally come together out of all these elements (physical and non-physical alike), drawing partly on Bruno Latour's actor-network theory, and representing an early contribution to assemblage perspectives in urban studies (cf. Farías and Bender, 2012; McFarlane, 2011).

More than just offering an account of coming together, Jacobs is also emphatic about understanding how things come apart – literally. This was crucial for the Red Road case in Glasgow, which was partially dismantled and eventually demolished. It was also the beginning of Jacobs' most recent major focus: analysing the destruction of place, especially of urban architecture. *Buildings Must Die: A Perverse View of Architecture* (Cairns and Jacobs, 2014) provides an historical account of how architecture as a discipline thinks about buildings, and explores several major cases of buildings (or complexes) meeting their end, from Europe to Asia. This intervention is foremost an analytical and conceptual counterpoint to the 'natalist' obsession of architecture as a field; that is, architects' fixation with the process of creating and the moment of a building's birth, with no regard for its death. Cairns and Jacobs argue that architects are trained primarily as creative, with a fantasy of durability in the structures they design, hinging on the assumption that if their vision or their art is good enough, then what they create will endure forever. In tandem, they note that urban social scientists assume that the passing away of parts of cities' existing built fabric (e.g. urban renewal) is lamentable because of its social ramifications, that it is our inherent duty as analysts to defend spaces threatened by destruction; the death of a space might not be ignored in this view, but it is figured as automatically, inevitably wrong. With their book, Cairns and Jacobs create a space where it is acceptable to let built structures die and to analyze the nature of these processes of urban death. In an interdisciplinary nod, the aim here is to understand how things disassemble as a politicized process (with affinities to Jacobs' earlier work) but also how politics are mediated by – and can also themselves mediate – technical processes, in terms of the lifespan of certain materials and the effectiveness of particular construction methods. In sum, this 'perverse view' insists that we must account conceptually for how and why spatial demise occurs, but that we must equally plan for it as a practical feature of articulating 'ecological horizons' for city-making that are cognizant of obsolescence and ruin (whatever the cause), rather than defined by facile expectations of immortality.

Contributions to urban studies

Across her varied research engagements, there are two broad contributions to urban studies that define Jacobs' career. First, she has been one of the most prominent analysts of postcolonialism and the city. Her work has dealt with imperial legacies in inventive ways that exceed the more typical focus on cities within ex-colonial territories that are now autochthonously ruled. She has brought postcolonial tools into the cities of predominantly white settler societies as well as the metropole itself. This has enabled the analysis of urban indigenous struggles, plus all those enmeshed – willingly or not – in the legacies and nostalgias of empire: from powerful London bankers and developers to poor Bangladeshi immigrants in the UK. Rather than rigid comparison, Jacobs has attended to connections across sites, to the mutability of location – the edge in its manifold meanings – and this has led into her engagement with emergent theoretical debates that came along after *Edge of Empire* and which she has helped shape in their urban versions. Her work has been a beacon for an expansive urban analysis of postcolonialism, showing the way for later investigations across the British Empire and interventions in other imperial frameworks as well.

Second, Jacobs' rethinking of urban comparison has made inroads into several subfields of urban geography and sociology. By advocating research that works with 'multiples' in order to understand constitutive differences, Jacobs undermines comparative frameworks that measure status vis-a-vis an ostensibly model case.

Secondary sources and references

Anderson, K. and Jacobs, J.M. (1997) 'From urban aborigines to aboriginality and the city: One path through the history of Australian cultural geography', *Australian Geographical Studies*, 35(1): 12–22.

Farías, I. and Bender, T. (eds) (2012) *Urban Assemblages: How Actor-Network Theory Changes Urban Studies*. London: Routledge.

Gale, F. and Jacobs, J.M. (1987) *Tourists and the National Estate: Procedures to Protect Australia's Heritage*. Canberra: Australian Heritage Commission.

Gelder, K. and Jacobs, J.M. (1998) *Uncanny Australia: Sacredness and Identity in a Postcolonial Nation*. Melbourne: Melbourne University Press.

Jacobs, J.M. (1983) *Aboriginal Land Rights in Port Augusta*. MA dissertation, Department of Geography, University of Adelaide.

Jacobs, J.M. (1993) 'The city unbound: Qualitative approaches to the city', *Urban Studies*, 30(4/5): 827–848.

Jacobs, J.M. (2012b) 'Urban geographies I: Still thinking cities relationally', *Progress in Human Geography*, 36(3): 412–422.

Jacobs, J.M. (2012c) 'Property and propriety: (Re)Making the space of indigeneity in Australian cities', *Postcolonial Studies*, 15(2): 143–147.

Jacobs, J.M. and Cairns, S. (2008) 'The modern touch: Interior design and modernisation in post-independence Singapore', *Environment and Planning A*, 40(3): 572–595.

Jacobs, J.M. and Merriman, P. (2011) 'Practising architectures', *Social and Cultural Geography*, 12(3): 211–222.

Jacobs, J.M., Cairns, S. and Strebel, I. (2012) 'Doing building work: Methods at the interface of geography and architecture', *Geographical Research*, 50(2): 126–140.

McFarlane, C. (2011) 'The city as assemblage: Dwelling and urban space', *Environment and Planning D: Society and Space*, 29(4): 649–671.

Rich, A. (1986) 'Notes towards a politics of location', *Blood, Bread and Poetry: Selected Prose, 1979–1985*. London: Little Brown.

22

Natalie Jeremijenko

Clemens Driessen, Wageningen University

Key urban writings

Natalie Jeremijenko. Available at: http://nataliejeremijenko.com/portfolio
Bronx Ooz, project/design series, hosted by Bronx River Arts Center (BRAC), New York. Available at: www.environmentalhealthclinic.net/ooz/
Environmental Health Clinic. Available at: www.environmentalhealthclinic.net/
The Art of the Eco-Mind Shift. Video on TED.com. October 2009. Available at: www.ted. com/talks/natalie_jeremijenko_the_art_of_the_eco_mindshift
xDesign project archive. Available at: www.nyu.edu/projects/xdesign/

Introduction

Natalie Jeremijenko is an artist, designer, engineer and environmental scientist who has created a series of installations dealing with urban natures and human–animal relations. She is renowned for her efforts to deploy engineering – robotics, chemical detectors, information technologies – as artistic interventions to publicly engage with urban ecologies and environmental pollution. Through myriad design projects she has created material settings and devices that mediate otherwise invisible and intangible ecological and other environmental processes to human experience. Pioneering the field of digitally mediated human–animal interaction, projects function as interfaces between humans and a range of other species such as bats, ducks, fish, trees, beetles and birds.

Her experiments have generated wide media attention highlighting her take on urban natures and ecologies that imaginatively rethink and remix divisions of nature/ culture, ecology/technology, human/non-human and other dichotomies that tend to organize our experiences and guide our arguments over urban nature. In the process she has drawn attention to entanglements of the health and wellbeing of both human and non-human urban residents, and promoted ideas on everyday interventions everyone could do, while provoking thought on wider social, economic and policy issues in relation to urban natures and environmental health.

Natalie Jeremijenko is Associate Professor of Art and Art Education at New York University and affiliated with its Computer Science Department and Environmental Studies programme.

Academic biography and research focus

Natalie Jeremijenko studied biochemistry and physics at Griffith University, Brisbane, before studying neuroscience at the University of Queensland and Stanford University. She later completed a PhD in Computer Science and Electrical Engineering at the University of Queensland. Parallel to her formal scientific education she developed as an artist, creating installations for the musical festival Livid she co-founded in Brisbane (Berger, 2006).

In 1994, Jeremijenko joined Xerox's Palo Alto Research Center (PARC), which at the time was a hotbed of invention and intellectual thought at the forefront of newly emerging internet and communication technologies. Here, working on the technical preconditions and implications of internet computing went hand-in-hand with creative, critical, design and artistic efforts to explore what these developments meant for culture, sociability and experience (cf. **William J. Mitchell**). Since the early days of the world wide web and social media, Jeremijenko has thus been experimenting with new modes of human–environment relations, generating interactions with various processes in this newly emerging socio-technical world. Early works included materializing the data sent over a cable into a dancing and whirring wire ('Live Wire [Dangling String]') and monitoring suicide attempts off the Golden Gate bridge while linking these to movements on the stock exchange ('Suicide Box') (Wilson, 2002).

Working with influential figures such as the computer scientist Mark Weiser, one of the themes studied (and concepts coined) at Xerox PARC was 'ubiquitous computing': the thought that ICT would no longer consist of separate devices, but become something integrated throughout our world (Weiser, 1996). Jeremijenko then embarked on myriad projects that would make what now is called the 'internet of things' cater not just to human interests, but extend this vision to include other organisms and ecosystems, particularly urban ecosystems. She also worked on 'calm technology'; unobtrusive technologies interwoven in our mental and bodily existence, rethinking our notion of 'environment' and the separation of humans, technology and nature.

Working through a blend of counterculture and disruptive innovation – but taking it in different directions than Silicon Valley venture capitalism tends to do – Jeremijenko has been more oriented towards political activism than commercial application, being wary of potential corporate framings of her work (da Costa and Philip, 2008). In 1999, she produced through cloning a set of 20 genetically identical walnut trees, and placed them in various spots across the San Francisco Bay Area ('Onetrees'). As the trees started to grow, collectively they highlighted how the genetic makeup of organisms is not the sole determinant of their lives. The product was a field laboratory in which different environmental conditions became visualized through how the trees were doing based on a range of determinants, such as being in affluent or industrial areas.

Since leaving Xerox PARC Jeremijenko has been an artist/academic working at a range of US universities in departments of science, technology, art and communication.

In various collaborations, she has produced work to inform and promote environmental awareness and hands-on scientific literacy. 'Howstuffismade.org' is an ongoing collective project studying the environmental and social implications of the way in which products have been designed, and with Eugene Thacker she produced 'Creative Biotechnology: A User's Manual'. Her designs have been exhibited in a range of science museums and outdoor art festivals across the world.

Key ideas

Jeremijenko has produced prototype technologies that are both poetic and critical, making for an original genre to explore and communicate urban environmental concerns. Several of her projects have highlighted interconnections between urban social inequalities and environmental conditions. In her ongoing 'Feral Robots' project she has been teaching students and school children to repurpose robotic toy dogs and deploy them to detect toxic soil in urban neighbourhoods that are former industrial wastelands. At events where packs of feral robotic dogs are released, she fosters new publics to participate in environmental monitoring and the production of knowledge which can inform public debate.

A large range of devices designed by Jeremijenko aim to foster communication between humans and urban wildlife, gathered under the banner of 'OOZ' (zoo spelled backwards). 'For the Birds' was an installation that enabled wild birds to communicate with museum visitors. The animals were provided with buttons that when pressed played pre-recorded texts on the outdoor terrace:

> Tick, tick, tick. That's the sound of genetic mutations, of the avian flu becoming a deadly human flu. Do you know what slows it down? Healthy sub-populations of birds. Increasing biodiversity, generally. It is in your interest that I'm healthy, happy, well fed. Hence, you could share some of your nutritional resources instead of monopolizing them. That is, share your lunch. (Berger, 2006)

Depending on the button chosen by the birds, the visitors are informed about the relation between migrating birds and zoonotic diseases, or even urged to share some food in order to reduce biosecurity risks. The latter button was found to be used most often. Apparently museum visitors partaking in this interspecies experiment were convinced by the interlinkages between human and non-human interests, sharing their food motivated by the proposed ecological view of biosecurity.

Other installations give a voice to wildlife in less literal ways, mediating communication between human and non-human bodies. Jeremijenko's work thus explores what happens when humans and animals are brought into a more equal form of contact, and through a shared material culture engage in more interactive forms of communication. And it tests our assumptions about the motivations of animals and their relations to us. In one of her installations, the 'Beetle Wrestler' (with Chris Woebken), an elaborate interface is constructed through which a human can enter into a bodily struggle with the most powerful animal – adjusted to size – in the world: the rhinoceros beetle. By luring humans into this playful apparatus, it works to question the self-evidence of human superiority in a tangible experience in which the human does not necessarily come out on top.

Her artistic experiments have generated much media attention. Her approach to urban natures and ecologies creatively rethinks the divisions of nature/culture, ecology/technology, human/non-human and other dichotomies that tend to organize our experiences and arguments around urban nature. Installations that paradoxically use technological means to refigure the human as part of nature, as connected to ecosystems, help to imagine new forms of multispecies communities. Through her interventions, Jeremijenko extends critiques formulated by more traditional scholars such as William Cronon who urge us to rethink the commitment to nature as ideally wild and without human presence. She performs and materializes the idea that nature should not be thought of as only 'out there' in the non-urban wild (cf. **Matthew Gandy**). In doing so, her work resonates with Donna Haraway's accounts of experimenting with practices that unsettle common dualisms of social/natural and urban/wild that structure our thought and institutions, and intensify interspecies contact zones; and with Jennifer Wolch's (1996) call to reinvite animals as urban inhabitants and thereby re-enchant cities as a collective 'zoopolis'.

Jeremijenko's written work is primarily in the form of texts that accompany her project launches, performances and exhibitions – explaining and legitimating work that itself constitutes just as much the medium of experimental research and communication of her ideas. Thus she showcases how reflexive and critical thinking on cities can be done through material (blended with what earlier were called 'virtual') interventions and the construction of new interfaces, instead of having necessarily a written or spoken character. Through her 'design thinking' – or 'thingking' as she labels it – Jeremijenko offers an immersive take on urban environments that in an original way also fits with a shift from urban design as 'hardware' infrastructure to the heralding of data-driven 'smart cities' (cf. **William J. Mitchell**). An example is 'Amphibious Architecture', a grid of floating devices in the Hudson River through which fish signal their presence, health status and thus the environmental conditions of New York to interested citizens via buoys that light up when a fish swims past. Citizens in turn can send text messages that feed the fish 'energy bars' treated to cleanse PCBs (polychlorinated biphenyls) from their blood. As Jeremijenko explained in an interview:

> The idea that we eat the same stuff is a visceral demonstration that we live in the same system. Eating together is the most intimate form of kinship. By scripting a work where we share the same kind of food with fish, I'm scripting our interrelationship with them. (Berger, 2006)

Jeremijenko thus presents a new form of landscape art, one that seeks to move beyond the romantic paintings of the Hudson River School – depicting nature without traces of the human – to making intimately present natural landscapes in peril and ecologies deeply intertwined with urban lives.

In her projects, Jeremijenko inscribes an implicit (and often also explicit) moral stance towards emergent (or dwindling) urban socio-ecologies and towards institutionalized human–animal relations in urban settings such as zoos (Acampora, 2010). Bird flu gets rethought as a matter of shared vulnerabilities in global socio-natural processes and as co-produced by human behaviours and technologies – not as a strictly human biosecurity issue for which birds only appear as outside threats. Also various common spaces where animals meet or are exposed to humans – from zoos, to river water pollution, to eating – are critically engaged with. Whereby, the playful design approach makes this moralizing and politicizing into an evocative and appealing experience, as opposed to an ethics of (more direct) prescriptions, accusations and guilt.

In her work she showcases how urban design is not restricted to buildings and streets, squares and parks (cf. **Harvey Molotch**). She reveals how relations between humans and their ecological environment have been ordered in particular standard forms – and can be designed radically differently: in ways that promote ecological awareness and mutual connection. She thus refuses to consider humans as the only legitimate inhabitants of cities, nor as separable from their (often novel) urban ecologies. This requires infrastructural interventions for other species. The 'Butterfly Bridge' is a thick rope-like structure across streets planted with specific flowers that would allow butterflies safe passage. Designing a city in this vein from the perspective of other species generates different notions of infrastructure and different topologies of meaningful places (cf. **Stephen Graham, Jan Gehl**). Her key ideas are thus a contribution to both an aesthetic and the practical materializing of alternative ways of designing cities for humans, for non-human organisms and for meaningful interaction between these.

Contributions to urban studies

Jeremijenko's work can be situated within a wider movement that produces critical, participatory and activist combinations of art and technology. She thus figures in a loose collection of artists, designers and academics who are trying to harness DIY technology, hacker culture and design thinking towards environmental and other politically critical purposes (da Costa and Philip, 2008; Wilson, 2002). The large number of projects Jeremijenko has initiated provides numerous examples of how addressing social inequalities regarding environmental health can be combined with an embrace of urban nature. Her work thus opens up understandings of justice and politics to include urban wildlife and ecosystems. Making all these devices and interfaces affords a particular form of multispecies politics realized through materialized interaction – perhaps even deliberation. Whereby the most interesting of her interventions leave – and promote the granting of – agency to others than human actors, Jeremijenko makes a point of considering these as active participants in the process of design.

Jeremijenko's work can raise mixed feelings; some see it as superficially combining an idealization of nature with techno-optimism. Nature seems to emerge as an inherently benign source of good – with technology as its potential saviour – if only we have the right devices mediating human–nature interactions. However, Jeremijenko's installations and performances are not eco-modernist technological fixes, nor are they proposals for the one-dimensional harnessing of ecosystem services. Her designs do not claim to, by themselves, solve our environmental problems and associated social justice issues. These instead always require active participation, engagement, the learning of new skills as well as collective, socio-cultural transformation. The best of Jeremijenko's interventions display a deep awareness of the problems of technology associated with their wholesale generic application towards optimizing resource use.

Instead her work promotes activism and local experiments in which social and environmental concerns are intertwined and new modes of communal living are imagined and tested (cf. **Jason Corburn**).

Jeremijenko's projects may come across as a bit gimmicky. Her floating, walking and whirring eco-interfaces function at a distance from more widely accepted approaches in planning and urban ecology. They hardly fit the common formal institutions of thinking on and intervening in cities. Instead her works are often proposed as coming from alternative forms of knowledge institutions and governmental bodies, through invented organizations such as the 'Bureau of Inverse Technology' and 'Environmental Health Clinic'. Does this mean these rather transient interventions and artistic experiments, playful and evocative as they are, ultimately have limited conceptual and political clout? It is hard to ascertain the impact of this work. Evocation and inspiration are less clearly traceable in (creative) design and other interventions, as these tend not to come with reference lists acknowledging intellectual sources. But her string of artist profiles in public media, her presence as a public speaker and prominent member of a wide range of lists of the year's most 'influential thinkers/designers/innovators/etc.' are some indication that her ideas have spread in a wide variety of urban contexts. And her trail of ecological experiments and ethological interventions may have influenced wildlife behaviours and ecological relations in ways that are even harder to establish – but for that are all the more intriguing to trace and to imagine.

Secondary sources and references

Acampora, R. (2010) *Metamorphoses of the Zoo: Animal Encounter after Noah*. Lanham, MD: Lexington Books.

Berger, K. (2006) 'The artist as mad scientist', *Salon*, 22 June. Available at: www.salon.com/2006/06/22/natalie/

Clark, L. (2013) 'Natalie Jeremijenko: How kissing frogs teaches us about healthy eating and biodiversity', *Wired Magazine*, 17 October. Available at: www.wired.co.uk/news/archive/2013-10/17/natalie-jeremijenko

da Costa, B. and Philip, K. (eds) (2008) *Tactical BioPolitics: Art, Activism and Technoscience*. Cambridge, MA: MIT Press.

Jeremijenko, N. and Thacker, E. (2004) *Creating Biotechnology: A User's Manual*. Newcastle-upon-Tyne: Locust.

Raffles, H. (2014) 'Beetle wrestler. Design and violence', Museum of Modern Art, New York. Available at: http://designandviolence.moma.org/beetle-wrestler-natalie-jeremijenko-chris-woebken/

Sullivan, G. (2005) *Art Practice as Research: Inquiry in the Visual Arts*. London: Sage.

Weiner, J. (2013) 'The artist who talks with the fishes', *The New York Times Magazine*, 30 June. Available at: www.nytimes.com/2013/06/30/magazine/the-artist-who-talks-with-the-fishes.html

Weiser, M. (1996) 'Ubiquitous computing'. Available at: www.ubiq.com/hypertext/weiser/UbiHome.html

Wolch, J. (1996) 'Zoöpolis', *Capitalism Nature Socialism*, 7(2): 21–47.

Wilson, S. (2002) *Information Arts: Intersections of Art, Science and Technology*. Cambridge: MA: MIT Press.

23 Rem Koolhaas

Davide Ponzini, Politecnico di Milano

Key urban writings

Koolhaas, R. (1978; 2nd edn 1994) *Delirious New York: A Retroactive Manifesto for Manhattan.* New York: Oxford University Press. [2nd edn, New York: Monacelli Press, 1994].

OMA, Koolhaas, R. and Mau, B. (eds) (1995) *S, M, L, XL.* New York: Monacelli Press.

Koolhaas, R. (ed.) (2014) *Fundamentals: Catalogue of the 14th Biennale International Architecture Exhibition of Venice.* Venice: Marsilio.

Introduction

In nature, the most successfully surviving specimen is not necessarily the strongest or the most intelligent, but the one that is most capable of adapting to its environmental niche. Probably this could be an explanation for some intellectuals' success in cultural and public life, or influence and legacy. Explaining the profile of the architect, planner and thinker Rem Koolhaas in these bare terms would surely be reductive. Nonetheless, one can say that adaptive realism is one of Koolhaas's peculiar characteristics that allowed him to dominate the architectural and urban design debate for decades and to leverage diverse geopolitical conditions to his benefit, both as an intellectual and as a practitioner (Palermo and Ponzini, 2015; Sorkin, 2003).

Through his books, his often piercing interviews, lectures and speeches, Koolhaas has been enormously influential inside and outside academia. His work has demonstrated the failures of modernist planning as well as paradoxes of contemporary cities, while he has also worked on highly contentious projects and for the establishment in many authoritarian countries. Rem Koolhaas co-founded the Office for Metropolitan Architecture (OMA) in 1975 and, in 1998, created the twin firm Architecture Media Organization (AMO) which is dedicated to research. His professional excellence and intellectual contributions in the fields of architecture and urbanism have been acknowledged through many recognitions, including: Antonio Gaudí Prize (1992), Pritzker Architecture Prize (2000), Praemium Imperiale (2003), Royal Institute of British Architects' Royal Gold Medal (2004) and Golden Lion for Career Achievements at the Venice Biennale (2010).

Rem Koolhaas is Professor in Practice at Harvard University Graduate School of Design.

Academic biography and research focus

Remment Lucas (known as Rem) Koolhaas took a peculiar path into architecture and urbanism. He was born in 1944 in Rotterdam and was exposed early to diverse urban environments. He trained as a journalist and scriptwriter before becoming interested in architecture in 1968. He studied at the Architectural Association School of Architecture (AA) in London and then at Cornell University, where he met the architects Oswald Mathias Ungers and Colin Rowe. Then he became Visiting Fellow at the Institute for Architecture and Urban Studies (IAUS) in 1973 in New York City, under the direction of Peter Eisenman.

Since the early 1970s Koolhaas has promoted various design and research activities with the Dr. Caligaris Cabinet of Metropolitan Architecture. The same team – composed of Elia and Zoe Zenghelis, Madelon Vriesendorp and himself – founded the Office for Metropolitan Architecture (OMA). In 1974–5 he started teaching at the AA with Elia Zenghelis. This activity allowed him to promote and refine at the academic level the concepts derived from his OMA work. He taught at the AA until 1979–80.

Following a set of publications and projects on the living conditions and the transformation of the contemporary metropolis, his first book *Delirious New York: A Retroactive Manifesto for Manhattan* (1978) polemically stood against the mainstream modernist approach to urban planning. The 1350-page edited volume *S, M, L, XL* was published in 1995. The relentless flux of provocative images, essays and OMA's project descriptions conceptually follows different scales from the smallest (S) to the largest (XL) and is paralleled with an inventive vocabulary suggesting a sort of new language for contemporary architects. The design and transformation of the built environment and its relationships with economic, social and cultural spheres are presented in a wide variety of geographic contexts and genres: from New York to Lille and Yokohama, from the exhibition of the 1986 Triennale of Milan to a comic strip. Such kaleidoscopic effect fascinated critics and architectural students, even if, probably, the complexity of the message of this volume was only partially understood.

After leaving the AA Koolhaas taught at Delft University of Technology in the 1980s and at Rice University in the early 1990s. He was appointed at Harvard in 1995. His teaching and research activities focused on contemporary urban environments. His student-based long-term research initiative ('Project on the City') promoted the study of extreme urban conditions and realms (e.g. retail and consumption structures in different settings of contemporary cities; the settlements and urban life of Lagos, Nigeria). Among the publications derived from this project, one can mention the collective book *Great Leap Forward* (Chung et al., 2002) regarding the dramatic sizes, intensity and discontinuity of urban development in the Pearl River Delta region (see also **Fulong Wu**). It recognizes the paradoxes of the knowledge of urbanism: 'the urban seems less understood at the very moment of its apotheosis' (Koolhaas, 2002: 27). For this reason the book puts together students' research with the overambitious aim of setting 'the beginning of a conceptual framework to describe and interpret the contemporary urban condition (p. 28). The attempt evidently failed, but explored interesting evidence for further investigations.

In 2005, Koolhaas, together with Ole Bouman and Mark Wigley, founded *Volume Magazine*. This international initiative covered, among others, the topic of fast-track urban development in the Persian Gulf region in the special issues titled *Al Manakh* (2007) and *Al Manakh 2: Gulf Cont'd* (2010). These publications collected miscellaneous materials, facts and figures, interviews, speculations, as well as investigations on various topics providing vivid, although blurred, views regarding Dubai, Abu Dhabi, Doha and other cities experiencing extreme transformations.

One further recognition in Koolhaas's career was the appointment as Curator of the 14th Biennale International Architecture Exhibition of Venice, in 2014. Here, his *Fundamentals* initiative worked on three topics. With *Absorbing Modernity 1914–2014* Koolhaas tried to make national pavilions converge towards a common comparative reflection of how modern architecture and socio-economic processes have tended to erode and hybridize with national and local characteristics in the last hundred years. With the *Elements of Architecture* exhibition he wanted to go back to basic building components rather than reflecting on architecture. The *Monditalia* gathered exhibitions, events and performances regarding relevant transformations in the Italian context, showing the uniqueness of this country.

Key ideas

Due to his approach and to his protean cultural production, Koolhaas's ideas are not easy to distil into the traditional academic terms of urban studies and the social sciences. However, understanding his research approach and three of his most generative concepts – Manhattanism, bigness, the generic city – gives a sense of the contributions he has made to unveiling the paradoxes and idiosyncrasies of contemporary cities and urbanism.

Rem Koolhaas's research in the field of urban studies and design is deeply connected to his successful architectural practice and exceptional ability to communicate. He envisioned great opportunities for diverse forms of design-led thinking and representation, from the urban to the political and social realms. Today OMA is a large international firm with several branches in Europe, Asia and America. Completed projects include key reference buildings for contemporary architecture such as the headquarters for China Central Television (2012), Casa da Música in Porto (2005), the Seattle Central Library (2004) and the Netherlands Embassy in Berlin (2003), as well as master plans such as Euralille (1988–95). For a social science readership, it is important to stress that Koolhaas has conducted significant segments of his urban research and experimentation within these projects. In particular, the counterpart to OMA architectural practice is AMO, a research studio crisscrossing the fields of media, politics, sociology, fashion, curating and other disciplines. The cross-fertilization between teaching, research and professional activities allowed him to develop innovative concepts, test their relevance and eventually improve them. He could trespass disciplinary boundaries, adopt research, experimentation and dissemination methods that are not conventional in the academic realm and not so common in architectural practice, sometimes taking provocative, risky and scientifically unfounded positions, and yet having highly regarded and cited publications, exhibitions and projects. This approach is a peculiar interpretation of research by design that allows architects, urban designers and planners to enquire into the urban realm as a means for understanding and modifying it (cf. **Jan Gehl, Enrique Peñalosa**). In Koolhaas's approach the design realm is expanded to and nested within multiple dimensions of contemporary economy, society, media communication and culture.

The idea of Manhattanism was Koolhaas's means of coming to terms with the metropolitan conditions of urban life and was present in the manifesto of OMA in 1975. Similar conceptions circulated among other fringe and radical designers' circles in the 1970s, for example the 'instant city' by Archigram, 'No-stop city' by Archizoom, 'supersuperfice' by Superstudio. The central narrative expedient in Koolhaas's first book, *Delirious New York*, was providing the generation of Manhattan's urban form with a theory and in fact a manifesto, revealing 'strategies, theorems and breakthroughs that not only give logic and pattern to the city's past performance, but whose continuing validity is itself an argument for a second coming of Manhattanism, this time as an explicit doctrine that can transcend the island of its origins to claim its place among contemporary urbanisms' (Koolhaas, 1978: 10). In the second half of the 19th century Manhattan experienced tremendous urban and architectural technology experimentation and proliferation (electricity, high-rise towers, elevators, mass transit, etc.), making new solutions to urban congestion possible. In particular Koolhaas discussed how high-rise towers allowed the city to reduce land consumption while concentrating activities in environments of higher and higher density organized on the basis of an almost indifferent grid. In Koolhaas's view this opened the way for a less controlled and stable form of urbanism. The scale of these new buildings inevitably generated disjunction between the exterior and the interior. Their height led to the schism between the functions of individual floors. In other terms, the infrastructure of an urban grid could allow mutations of the formal and functional contents of each block. This was supposed to be the unavoidable condition of Manhattan and many contemporary metropolises. Here one can see both Koolhaas's great lucidity in understanding the influence of liberal business rationales and the lack of effective architectural and planning theories for driving the urban form.

According to the concept of 'bigness' (OMA et al., 1995), buildings and structures become aesthetically and functionally detached from the urban context, once they exceed a critical mass by virtue of their large dimensions. This is the perspective derived from the current and common practice of designing or rather engineering large and functional compounds and mega-structures, without having specific theoretical references for connecting them to the urban realm. Koolhaas has both blamed bigness for potentially killing architecture (and its need of star architects) and, at the same time, suggested that it implies the highest and most neutral expression of teamwork among different social players and technical experts of development and construction. Paradoxically, he claims bigness to be a generator of context-neutral post-architecture but could also be seen maliciously as one of its most renowned exponents.

Finally, Koolhaas argues that the rapid mutations in contemporary urban environments, their evident fragmentation, loss of clear urban centres and identity of place induce cities to become 'generic' (OMA et al., 1995). Like airports, cities tend to look and function like one another; in effect place-less. Although the 'generic city' is a puzzling category. Ironically some cities seem to be freed from the urge of identity by being generic, others become generic brands by overstressing and oversimplifying their identity. Some cities, such as the rising Asian capital cities, aspire to being generic and others try to contrast this tendency. The crisis of the public sphere and the over-standardized forms and functions of contemporary urban environments are part of this picture, which in fact seems to lead to the end of the city as conceived in European and Western countries. This concept can also be seen as a point of departure for the study of the Pearl River Delta region.

Contributions to urban studies

Rem Koolhaas has had a central role in unveiling the paradoxes of contemporary cities and urbanism and of the architect and planner's role in this context. His realistic view of ongoing transformation in radically different urban environments in the Western world as well as in Asia and Africa has shown that in an age of relentless urbanization, when humanity needs architects and planners the most, they have become less and less relevant in technical, political and intellectual terms. The absence of an effective theory and approach in tackling paramount problems and shifts in contemporary cities was on the one hand brilliantly detected, but on the other used by many for promoting new, though limitedly critical, design practices.

In Koolhaas's (1995: 969) view, urbanism cannot be founded on:

> … fantasies of order and omnipotence; it will be the staging of uncertainty; it will no longer be concerned with the arrangement of more or less permanent objects but with the irrigation of territories with potential; it will no longer aim for stable configurations but for the creation of enabling fields that accommodate processes that refuse to be crystallized into definitive form; it will no longer be about meticulous definition, the imposition of limits, but about expanding notions, denying boundaries.

Once again his adaptive approach is visible in his words: 'Redefined, urbanism will not only, or mostly, be a profession, but a way of thinking, an ideology: to accept what exists' (1995: 969–971).

For these reasons, Koolhaas found substantial attention (among others, Yaneva, 2009) and criticism as well in the fields of urban and planning studies. Hecker (2010) showed that the fly-by research strategy adopted by Koolhaas in Lagos in fact celebrated the urban conditions, without substantial attention to, or critique of, their political economy, lack of infrastructure and services, and tremendous social and economic disparities (see also **Matthew Gandy**). Although impossible to emulate, his approach and attitude was picked up by architects around the world, sometimes for instrumental reasons, sometimes taken to a ridiculous extent by wannabe followers. In this sense, his contribution could be seen as providing cultural legitimation to transnational star architects and their local partners (Sorkin, 2003), to established economic and political power in authoritarian countries (Sklair, 2013).

Mixing views of European and American cities with other contexts undergoing extreme processes of urban transformation – such as the Persian Gulf region, the Pearl

River Delta or Lagos – has helped Koolhaas explain common trends and better depict contemporary urban conditions. In this way, he has brought such views to the broad design and architectural public, which is often uninformed or uninterested in such urban, economic, social and cultural matters.

Secondary sources and references

Bouman, O., Khoubrou, M. and Koolhaas, R. (eds) (2007) *Al Manakh*. Amsterdam: Stichting Archis.

Chung, C.J., Inaba, J., Koolhaas, R. and Leong, S.T. (eds) (2001) *Harvard Design School Guide to Shopping*. Cologne: Taschen.

Chung, C.J., Inaba, J., Koolhaas, R. and Leong, S.T. (eds) (2002) *Great Leap Forward*. Cologne: Taschen.

Gargiani, R. (2008) *Rem Koolhaas/OMA: The Construction of Merveilles*. Lausanne: Epfl Press.

Hecker, T. (2010) 'The slum pastoral: Helicopter visuality and Koolhaas's Lagos', *Space and Culture*, 13(3): 256–269.

Koolhaas, R. (1995) 'Whatever happened to urbanism?', in OMA, R. Koolhaas and B. Mau (eds) *S, M, L, XL*. New York: Monacelli Press, pp. 959–971.

Koolhaas, R. (2002) 'City of exacerbated difference ©', in C.J. Chung, J. Inaba, R. Koolhaas and S.T. Leong (eds) *Great Leap Forward*. Cologne: Taschen, pp. 27–28.

Koolhaas, R., Cleinje, E. with Harvard Project on the City (2007) '2X4', in A. Adelusi-Adeluyi (ed.) *Lagos: How it Works*. Baden: Lars Müller.

Palermo, P.C. and Ponzini, D. (2015) *Place-Making and Urban Development: New Challenges for Planning and Design*. London: Routledge.

Reisz, T. (ed.) (2010) *Al Manakh 2: Gulf Cont'd*. Amsterdam: Stichting Archis.

Sklair, L. (2013) 'The role of iconic architecture in globalizing urban megaprojects', in G. del Cerro Santamaría (ed.) *Urban Megaprojects: A Worldwide View*. New York: Emerald, pp. 161–183.

Sorkin, M. (2003) 'Brand aid; or, the Lexus and the Guggenheim (further tales of the Notorious B.I.G.ness)', *Harvard Design Magazine*, 17: 4–9.

Yaneva, A. (2009) *Made by the Office for Metropolitan Architecture: An Ethnography of Design*. Rotterdam: 010 Publishers.

Films

Heidingsfelder, M. and Tesch, M. (2008) *Rem Koolhaas: A Kind of Architect*. ZDF/Arte Geie.

van der Haak, B. (2003) *Lagos/Koolhaas*. Sylvia Baan/Pieter van Huystee Film.

Henri Lefebvre

David Pinder, Roskilde University

Key urban writings

Lefebvre, H. (1991 [1974]) *The Production of Space*. Trans. D. Nicholson-Smith. Oxford: Blackwell.

Lefebvre, H. (1996) *Writings on Cities*. Ed. and trans. E. Kofman and E. Lebas. Oxford: Blackwell.

Lefebvre, H. (2003a [1970]) *The Urban Revolution*. Trans. R. Bononno. Minneapolis: University of Minnesota Press.

Lefebvre, H. (2014a) *Towards an Architecture of Enjoyment*. Trans. R. Bononno. Minneapolis: University of Minnesota Press.

Lefebvre, H. (2016 [1972]) *Marxist Thought and the City*. Trans. R. Bononno. Minneapolis: University of Minnesota Press.

Introduction

Henri Lefebvre (1900–91) was a French Marxist philosopher and sociologist whose work has had an immense if largely posthumous impact on critical urban theory, and on studies of cities and urbanization. His prolific writings – almost 70 books and hundreds of articles, translated into 30 languages – made major original contributions to many of the great themes of 20th-century social theory: modernity, capitalism, everyday life, space, alienation, the state and revolution. His influence in urban studies derives especially from a remarkable sequence of books on urban and spatial questions between 1968 and 1974. Refusing disciplinary boundaries, he never developed a system for urban thought; rather, his approach was open-ended, inventive, questing and politically committed – an evolving dialectical project that sought openings and possibilities through its heterodox engagement with Marx and other thinkers, and that continues to provoke and inspire decades on. Through confronting urban situations of his time, he articulated themes that have since been taken up and developed by many others, the most prominent concerning the social production of space, the right to the city and planetary urbanization. At the heart of his work is an insistence on the politics of urban space and on the need to take seriously in that regard everyday life, practice and the possible. He understood that, to change the world, it is crucial to transform everyday life and space. His work in this vein is finding new audiences concerned with the theory and practice of urban insurgency, and with struggling for emancipatory and democratic urban futures.

Lefebvre taught and researched at a number of institutions in France, and held professorships in sociology at Strasbourg University (1961–5) and Paris Nanterre University (1965–73).

Academic biography and research focus

Life should be understood as a project, Lefebvre believed. His own began in Hagetmau near the Pyrenees, in southwest France, in 1901. After a Catholic upbringing he studied philosophy at the Sorbonne in Paris where, with other left-wing students, he established the *Philosophies* group and journal. His involvement with avant-garde artists, writers and activists – among them dadaists and surrealists – shaped his dissident thinking and imagination. It was through the surrealist André Breton that he found the writings of Hegel and, from there, those of Marx. Always concerned with the relations between theory and practice, he joined the French Communist Party (PCF) in 1928. Despite his romanticism and anti-Stalinism, he remained a member until he was suspended in 1958, departing from its left-wing as he put it. During the 1930s Lefebvre played an important role in introducing Hegel and especially the early writings of Marx in France, working with Norbert Guterman on translations from the recently discovered *1844 Manuscripts*. Lefebvre contested dogmatic reductions of Marx to an economicism and developed instead a dialectical, pluralistic and humanistic reading of his work as a whole. Important additional influences in this project were Nietzsche and Heidegger, whom he engaged critically. His early writings and especially *Dialectical Materialism* (1968 [1939]) addressed alienation as more than economic, being an everyday experience whose discussion and critique requires attending to processes of living. This laid the grounds for his critique of everyday life, which he saw as his key contribution to Marxism and which underpinned his urban studies, elaborated most directly in the three-volume *Critique of Everyday Life* in 1947, 1961 and 1981 (2014b), and *Everyday Life in the Modern World*, in 1968 (1971a).

Lefebvre taught at universities as well as high schools. For periods he also worked in a factory, drove a taxi, broadcast on radio and fought for the French Resistance during World War II. From the 1950s he took up more established institutional positions, attaining his doctorate and then leading the sociological section of the Centre National de la Recherche Scientifique (CNRS), where he conducted empirical research on rural issues and land ownership, before holding professorships in sociology at Strasbourg and Paris Nanterre. His turn to urban questions came after witnessing the sudden construction from 1957 of a new town, Mourenx, close to his birthplace. Also influential was his association around that time with the situationists, whose critique of capitalist urbanism developed out of their experiments with psychogeography and the creation of 'situations'. Confronting the rapid urbanization and modernization of France in the 1950s and 1960s, including the class-based remaking of Paris through the displacement of hundreds of thousands of people, Lefebvre addressed how capitalism and state planning shape everyday spaces and life. But he was also concerned with how those spaces are imagined, lived, performed and struggled over. Urbanism is an ideology that is killing cities, he argued. It reduces inhabitation to habitat and eradicates the potential for encounter, play and spontaneity. How can people appropriate urban spaces and life? How can they participate in creating new spaces and ways of living without succumbing to authoritarian prescription? Along with the situationists he explored these questions in their interpretation of the Paris Commune of 1871 as a 'festival' and a 'revolutionary urbanism', through which formerly displaced workers reconquered the city. He later posed them in *Writings on Cities* (Lefebvre, 1996 [1968]), which was published on the eve of the May 1968 revolts in France that were sparked by some of his students at Nanterre, and that he heralded as another dramatic if suppressed moment of spatial contestation and change.

From the early 1970s Lefebvre travelled extensively to lecture and research, his experiences shaping his theory of urbanization and space that he unfolded through books that have only belatedly and partially been translated into English. They include *The Urban Revolution* (2003a [1970]), which grappled with the prospects of 'complete urbanization' and an emergent 'urban society' through the dissolution of the urban–rural opposition; *Vers le cybernanthrope* (1971b), which targeted the domination of urban planning by technocrats and their functional imaginaries; *Marxist Thought and the City* (2016 [1972]), which evaluated the significance and limitations of Marx and Engels for understanding the urban transformations brought about by the transition to industrial capitalism; and a recently discovered, previously unpublished manuscript *Toward an Architecture of Enjoyment* (2014a, written in 1973), which approaches architecture in terms of habitation, imagination, the body and senses. These writings culminated in his best known book *The Production of Space* (1991 [1974]), while his theorization of the state, state-space and the 'worldwide' was extended in the four volume *De l'État* (1976–8). Through his publications Lefebvre engaged in dialogues and polemics with other thinkers, among them Sartre, Foucault, Lacan, and especially Althusser whose structuralist Marxism he vigorously combated as it rose to prominence from the late 1960s. He also responded to contemporary events and places. Lefebvre believed that philosophy should not be scholastic but living, engaged and oriented to the totality. His urban thinking was developed alongside numerous 'concrete' empirical urban research projects, especially through the Institut de Sociologie Urbaine that he co-founded in 1962, and through extensive contacts and collaborations with architects, planners, urbanists and associated networks and institutions (Stanek, 2011). Publications flowed to the end of his life and even beyond, with the posthumous publication of his slim yet suggestive *Elements of Rhythmanalysis* in 1992 (2004), and the surfacing of other texts, including a collaborative planning competition entry for New Belgrade from 1986 (Bitter and Weber, 2009).

Key ideas

Lefebvre was unusual among Marxist philosophers for the seriousness with which he addressed space as well as time and history. Central to his urban studies is the maxim: '(Social) space is a (social) product' (1991 [1974]: 26). Through a Marxist analysis of production, he shifted attention from 'things in space' to 'the production of space' itself. He contended that space is more than a stage or container for it is deeply political, being generated, created and coded through social processes and thereby playing an active role. Each society – each mode of production – produces its own space, which serves 'as a tool of thought and of action'; it is 'a means of production' as well as 'a means of control, and hence of domination, of power' (p. 26). Meaningful social change therefore demands spatial change, and vice versa. Most fully advanced in *The Production of Space*, this dialectical approach understands space as physical, mental and social; it is perceived and conceived as well as lived. Lefebvre thus opened spatial analysis to a range of forces and processes, integrating but not confined to the political economic. He traced in particular the emergence of an abstract space through processes of commodification and capital accumulation as well as bureaucratization, masculine power and a logic of visualization (Gregory, 1994). This geometric, phallic and visual abstract space comes to dominate the concrete space of everyday life, which is colonized by the commodity form and the state. But the everyday is not entirely emptied out for it harbours traces of more authentic living and is also the grounds of resistance, struggle and counter-practices that hold out the potential of another (differential) space.

Lefebvre's historical and geographical account of space built on his earlier urban studies, in particular *The Urban Revolution*, which addressed a long history of urbanization through a number of fields and urban forms. He hypothesized that society had been 'completely urbanized', based on processes of 'implosion–explosion' and the generalization of urban fabric at the world scale (2003a [1970]: 16–17). While this 'urban problematic' was as yet a 'virtuality', he identified the new significance assumed by real estate speculation and a 'second circuit' of capital, paralleling that of industrial production, in shaping urban landscapes and temporarily staving off or moving around capitalist crises, a thesis later developed more deeply by **David Harvey**. Lefebvre was concerned with the consequent fragmentation and hierarchization of urban spaces, and with the marginalization, displacement, exclusion and control of their populations. Demands for the right to the city were a response, rooted in discontent. For Lefebvre this right entailed neither recovering the traditional city nor individually claiming a fairer share of what already exists. Rather it is 'like a cry and a demand' and 'can only be formulated as a transformed and renewed *right to urban life*' (1996 [1968]: 158, emphasis in original). It is a collective right to reclaim and produce spaces as an *oeuvre*, a disalienated work that is based on different needs and desires. Against the domination of exchange value and private property, it is an emancipatory project of use, participation, integration and difference in which spaces and life can become works of art.

Along with references to participation and ways of life, the right to the city was swiftly co-opted within French urban planning discourse and by others across the political spectrum. While this was not a straightforward case of recuperation, for Lefebvre had forged his perspectives in dialogue with urbanists and planners, the process often robbed the terms of radicalism. Lefebvre nevertheless continued to work with and beyond such ideas, reframing them in terms of the right to space, the right to difference and the prospects for *autogestion* (self-management) (Lefebvre, 2003a [1970], 2003b). In focusing on urban society as 'a horizon', he emphasized its dangers under a rampant neoliberal capitalism. Yet he also sought its emancipatory potential through an operation of transduction, which moves from the 'real' and given towards the possible. Central to his approach was a dialectical utopianism that attends to the possibilities embedded yet repressed within current conditions. He argued that to expand the possible it is necessary to demand what is currently defined as impossible. That is more than a theoretical exercise for it also entails artistic, architectural and urban experimentation as well as political contestation. The aim is to shatter the material and imaginative constraints that close off urban futures other than those inscribed within the image of the present.

Contributions to urban studies

Lefebvre's prolific output, iconoclastic formulations and often challenging writing style have contributed to the difficulties that many commentators have had in placing him intellectually. His impact on urban studies specifically has been internationally uneven, conditioned by vagaries of translation as well as context. Relative to a number of other languages including German, Spanish, Italian, Portuguese and Japanese, his urban and spatial works appeared late in English only after his 'rediscovery' in Anglophone urban studies and geography from the mid-1980s, the landmark publication being *The Production of Space* in 1991. His earlier reception was marked by criticism from his former student **Manuel Castells**, then influenced by Althusser. More sympathetic engagements came from **David Harvey**, who has continued to work productively with his ideas for addressing both the urbanization of capital and the urbanization of revolution. Subsequent commentaries by Edward Soja, **Neil Smith**, Mark Gottdiener, Rob Shields, Kristin Ross and Derek Gregory among others were instrumental in highlighting Lefebvre's significance for critical spatial theory. The gradual translation of selected writings since then, combined with a host of significant discussions of his work, has fuelled multidisciplinary interest and made him a key figure in a 'spatial turn' across the social sciences and humanities (see especially Elden, 2004; Merrifield, 2006; Goonewardena et al, 2008). This has in turn sparked renewed interest in these themes in France, where for a period after his death many of his publications fell out of print.

An initial strand of Lefebvrian urban studies was driven by geographers and others seeking to spatialize Marxism, and centred on his significance for analysing the production of space. Themes included the role of urban space in the reproduction of dominant social relations, and the need to expand conceptions of class struggle beyond the workplace to explore the politics of space. His writings were also found conducive within architecture, cultural studies, cultural geography and other fields for addressing everyday urban practices and experiences through attending to the body, rhythm, imagination, representation and aesthetics, while interrogating and developing his limited engagements with gender, sexuality and postcolonial critique. In the process he was often aligned with other, different theorists of everyday life such as Michel de Certeau. More recently there has been increasing appreciation of the breadth and complexities of Lefebvre's multifaceted Marxism, and the ways in which it refuses to be split into political economic and cultural dimensions through analyses that incorporate the material, ideological and symbolic. His revolutionary concerns have been re-foregrounded in the context of global urban uprisings, while there has also been interest in empirical application (Stanek et al., 2014).

Lefebvre's ideas are prominent in work on urban politics and on the right to the city, democracy and spatial justice. That extends well beyond academia with the right to the city slogan taken up by social movements as well as by urban governments and inter-national NGOs, among them UN-Habitat. Clarifying different and conflicting understandings of the term is therefore vital, as is explicating how Lefebvre's work might speak to new urban insurgencies, occupations and struggles. Interest has also returned to his prescient hypothesis on complete or 'planetary urbanization', in efforts to move beyond city-centred urban studies to develop new epistemologies of the urban (see **Neil Brenner**, 2014). There is further recognition of his concerns with time and temporality alongside space, including through developing rhythmanalysis. Much of the critical significance of his work for urban studies more generally lies in its holistic approach, its refusal to accept the inevitability of current conditions, and its insistence on opening a path 'towards a different space, towards the space of a different (social) life and of a different mode of production' (Lefebvre, 1991 [1974]: 60).

Secondary sources and references

Bitter, S. and Weber, H. (eds) (2009) *Autogestion, or Henri Lefebvre in Belgrade*. Berlin and Vancouver: Fillip and Sternberg Press.

Brenner, N. (ed.) (2014) *Implosion/Explosion: Towards a Study of Planetary Urbanization*. Berlin: Jovis.

Elden, S. (2004) *Understanding Henri Lefebvre: Theory and the Possible*. London: Continuum.

Goonewardena, K., Kipfer, S., Milgrom, R. and Schmid, C. (eds) (2008) *Space, Difference, Everyday Life: Henri Lefebvre and Radical Politics*. London and New York: Routledge.

Gregory, D. (1994) *Geographical Imaginations*. Oxford: Blackwell.

Lefebvre, H. (1968 [1939]) *Dialectical Materialism*. Trans. J. Sturrock. London: Jonathan Cape.

Lefebvre, H. (1971a [1968]) *Everyday Life in the Modern World*. Trans. S. Rabinovitch. Harmondsworth: Allen Lane.

Lefebvre, H. (1971b) *Vers le cybernanthrope: contre les technocrates*. Paris: Denoël.

Lefebvre, H. (1976–1978) *De l'État 1-4*. Paris: Union Générale d'Éditions.

Lefebvre, H. (2003b) *Key Writings*. Ed. S. Elden, E. Lebas and E. Kofman. London: Continuum.

Lefebvre, H. (2004 [1992]) *Rhythmanalysis: Space, Time, and Everyday Life*. Trans. S. Elden and G. Moore. London: Continuum.

Lefebvre, H. (2014b [1947/1958, 1961, 1981]) *Critique of Everyday Life*, Vols 1–3. Trans. J. Moore and G. Elliott. London: Verso.

Merrifield, A. (2006) *Henri Lefebvre: A Critical Introduction*. New York: Routledge.

Stanek, Ł. (2011) *Henri Lefebvre on Space: Architecture, Urban Research, and the Production of Theory*. Minneapolis: University of Minnesota Press.

Stanek, Ł., Schmid, C. and Moravánszky, Á. (eds) (2014) *Urban Revolution Now: Henri Lefebvre in Social Research and Architecture*. Farnham: Ashgate.

25   Kevin Lynch

Quentin Stevens, RMIT University

Key urban writings

Lynch, K. (1960) *The Image of the City*. Cambridge, MA: MIT Press.

Lynch, K. (1972) *What Time is This Place?* Cambridge, MA: MIT Press.

Lynch, K. (ed.) (1977) *Growing Up in Cities: Studies of the Spatial Environment of Adolescence in Crakow, Melbourne, Mexico City, Salta, Toluca and Warsaw*. Cambridge, MA: MIT Press.

Lynch, K. (1981) *A Theory of Good City Form*. Cambridge, MA: MIT Press.

Banerjee, T. and Southworth, M. (eds) (1990) *City Sense and City Design: Writings and Projects of Kevin Lynch*. Cambridge, MA: MIT Press.

Introduction

Kevin Lynch was fundamental in defining urban design as a new field of theory, research and practice distinct from the established disciplines of urban planning and architecture. He preferred calling it 'city design' or 'physical planning' to focus on the complex overall physical form of cities, as opposed to urban as merely a context for isolated large-scale architectural projects. His *Good City Form* (1981) remains the most comprehensive articulation of the field.

The broad influence and novelty of Lynch's writing stem from his detailed attention to the actual users of urban settings and their perceptions and activities, and to evaluating how well various built environments perform in meeting human needs. This was in marked contrast to designers evaluating city form primarily according to aesthetic principles and formal typologies, engineers' and social scientists' inattention to cities' visual and spatial characteristics, and psychologists' focus on laboratory-based studies. Lynch introduced empiricism, humanism and intellectual rigour to the study of city form. He argued that physical form affects the overall quality of city life, shaping opportunities for encounter, learning, creativity and social development. His thinking was grounded in practical planning experience with complex real-world projects.

Lynch was Professor of Urban Studies and Planning at the Massachusetts Institute of Technology.

Academic biography and research focus

Lynch was born in Chicago in 1918. During the Great Depression he attended one of America's first progressive high schools, inspired by the American pragmatist philosopher John Dewey, which promoted active learning and social engagement. Politically he was influenced by the social turmoil of the Depression, workers' movements and the Spanish Civil War. Dewey's pragmatism, empiricism and liberalism remained influential in Lynch's thinking. After short stints studying architecture at Yale and in Frank Lloyd Wright's atelier, studying engineering and biology, and working as a draftsman – all of which reinforced Lynch's belief in learning by doing – he was conscripted into the Army Corps of Engineers in 1941. After the war he earned a Bachelor's degree in City Planning from MIT with a thesis on *Controlling the Flow of Rebuilding and Replanning in Residential Areas*, and then worked as a planner. In 1948 Lynch joined the faculty at MIT; he remained there until 1978, never attaining any further formal qualifications.

In 1951 Lynch began studying people's visual perception of the built environment, together with an MIT colleague, painter and art theorist György Kepes. Their approach was influenced by Dewey and by the emerging field of transactional psychology, emphasizing the dynamics of interactions between people and places. A Ford Foundation grant allowed Lynch to spend 1952–3 living in Florence, a highly distinctive and memorable city form. His detailed observations and discussions of residents' perceptions and experiences of urban form in Florence and his exploration of different ways of recording these initiated a decade of research analysing people's visual interpretations of city form. With a five-year Rockefeller Foundation grant together with Kepes, Lynch analysed people's perceptions of the urban fabric of Boston, Jersey City and Los Angeles. The resulting book, *The Image of the City* (1960), remains a best-seller in city planning. Kepes' cinematic understanding of spatial experience influenced Lynch's subsequent book with former students examining the perception of urban landscapes from within an automobile, *The View from the Road* (Appleyard et al., 1964).

A second strand of Lynch's research, emerging from his work on the 1959 master plan for Boston's downtown Government Center, explored how the form and use of urban environments transform over time, and how growth and change are perceived and can be managed. This enquiry resulted in the books *What Time is This Place?* (1972) and *Wasting Away* (1990). A third area of work examined ways to describe the physical arrangement of cities, defined the scope of human needs and values impacted by built form and articulated performance criteria for evaluating how well specific urban forms served specific needs. A particular normative focus for Lynch was the potential that urban environments provide for exploration, learning and personal development (Carr and Lynch, 1968, 1981). He led a UNESCO-funded international study examining the negative impacts of economic and urban development policies on children's perception and use of their local urban environments, reported in *Growing up in Cities* (1977). These conceptual and normative interests framed his most substantial book, *A Theory of Good City Form* (1981).

Key ideas

Two core concepts frame Lynch's original contribution to city planning and design. First, a city's physical form, and particularly its public realm, is important to the general quality of urban experience and social life, and is not chiefly a matter for expert aesthetic judgement. Second, it is essential to observe, ask and work with residents to understand and meet their needs in relation to city form. Lynch's research responded to the increasing speed and scale of postwar urban development and to increasingly non-visual, social-science-driven planning approaches. Similar issues were explored by contemporaries **Jane Jacobs** and Christopher Alexander, and later by **Jan Gehl**. Lynch's work is unique in its scope, and in his ability to synthesize a deep reading of the history and theory of city development with innovative fieldwork into ordinary people's use and perception of environments to develop general schemas applicable to diverse contemporary situations. His ideas are well illustrated with city plans, photographs and distinctive small marginal sketches of urban forms, processes and relationships.

Lynch's early, most seminal work, *The Image of the City* (1960), focused relatively narrowly on how people visually recognize and remember urban environments in order to navigate through them. Lynch's empirical methodology of asking random passing pedestrians to describe and sketch walking routes through the city became highly influential. He was the first to apply such cognitive mapping methods in urban settings rather than laboratory experiments. *The Image of the City* significantly stimulated field research into human–environment relationships generally, and influenced the nascent discipline of environmental psychology. The book introduced the concepts of 'wayfinding', 'legibility' and 'imageability' to urban planning. The study's well-known conclusion was that people form reasonably invariant abstract mental schemas composed of five general formal elements: paths, edges, districts, nodes and landmarks. Lynch's five elements were grounded in the visual aesthetic tradition of European urbanism, but his research sought to explore empirically their links to users' perceptions and movements and to particular land uses and activity patterns.

Another influential analytical concept emerging out of this project was urban 'grain', first used to describe Boston's elongated street block pattern, and subsequently to analyse land use mix (Lynch, 1954), but ultimately more broadly characterized as 'The extent to which ... typical [urban] elements and densities are differentiated and separated in space[, which] can be defined as coarse or fine ... and sharp or blurred in terms of the manner of separation' (Lynch and Rodwin, 1958: 205). This emerged before **Jane Jacobs** (1961) independently asserted the importance of mixed uses, short city blocks and mixed building stock for urban vitality. The grain size of urban land uses, building types and city blocks has become a standard measure for analysing their performance.

Lynch's attention to people's perceptions of urban form developed in a new direction in connection with his interests in the history of city forms, processes of urban development and future urban visions. In *What Time is This Place?*, he emphasized that built environments continually change and argued that providing visible, legible evidence of the passage of time in urban form is a crucial dimension of human wellbeing, key to self-identity and helping people understand, manage and even celebrate environmental and social change. Few previous scholars had seen historical cityscapes in such present, dynamic terms, or considered positive aspects of ongoing urban transformation. Lynch's humanistic orientation is evident in his consideration of ways people might psychologically and spatially adapt or contribute to urban change. Though broadly philosophical and imaginative, the book also drew upon questionnaire responses, an appendix suggests other relevant social-science data-gathering methods, and Lynch also included policy proposals. Lynch's critique of planning's emphasis on growth and its inattention to environmental degradation significantly pre-dates more recent research into urban decline, shrinkage and abandonment. Later, in *Wasting Away*, Lynch drew attention to the massive, varied flows of resources and wastes through cities, the wastage and re-use of space and materials in urban form itself, the important functions of wild, marginal urban spaces and the necessity of planning for urban dumps and burial grounds.

Lynch's most mature work, *A Theory of Good City Form*, is an unrivalled attempt at an overarching theory to guide the design and normative critique of city form (cf. **Jan Gehl**). Reflecting his concern for ordinary citizens and their views, Lynch aimed to provide a basis for people to debate what made their city's form good and how to manage it. He framed five broad performance dimensions for evaluating different urban forms in relation to human activity: vitality, access, and three relatively 'neglected values' central to his own work: behavioural fit and adaptability, sensory quality and user control (Lynch, 1981: 56). He also discussed how the relative performance levels and the social distribution of each quality within a given settlement form can be evaluated against two counterbalancing 'metacriteria', efficiency and justice (the latter informed by his progressive upbringing). Lynch's theory is grounded in an extensive review of past and current urban formal models, theories and policies that guided city development, and the (often unacknowledged) values underpinning them. Particularly lucid is his critique of the three main normative metaphors for understanding cities' structure: as models of cosmic order, as efficient machines and as biological organisms.

Lynch's work is rich in ideas. He writes with great clarity, logic and depth about exceeding complex settings, processes and relationships. His writing is always evocative of concrete possibilities for urban form, activity and management. He found utopias and negative 'cacatopias' particularly stimulating for exploring ideals.

Contributions to urban studies

Lynch gave thinking about urban form a new conceptual, empirical and normative grounding. He emphasized human experience and the affordances of the built environment over the prevailingly narrow focus on aesthetics and symbolism. Lynch spanned the environmental design disciplines to social science and humanities thinking on cities and to cognitive psychology. His proposition that built form decisions significantly condition the quality of urban life has been influential in architecture, planning and landscape design practice, and in the emerging field of environmental psychology. So have numerous performance dimensions of built form that Lynch defined, including its sensory quality, memorability, fit to activity patterns, and user control and adaptability. Lynch pioneered the use of empirical fieldwork involving the general public to evaluate existing and proposed urban forms, demonstrating a range of analytical techniques such as behavioural observation, interviews, photo-elicitation and map-making (Lynch, 1960, 1977). Lynch's ideas were less influential in urban studies more broadly, but *The Image of the City* and *What Time is This Place?* remain important touchstones for work in human geography, urban sociology and ethnography examining the built environment, particularly research in tourism, heritage and the phenomenology of place. Through his UNESCO project (Lynch, 1977), Lynch's distinctive normative, humanistic focus on the environment's role in the development of human capacities encouraged significant interdisciplinary work on young people's open space needs.

Lynch's five elements and his concept of imageability rank among the best-known ideas about urban form among designers. But Lynch never prescribed that city layouts should emphasize these elements, or that visual clarity is an important end in itself. He felt his own methods and findings were 'preliminary' and 'speculative' (Lynch, 1960: 5), and he later critically reviewed *The Image of the City*'s main shortcomings (Lynch, 1984). First, his empirical methodology and data were limited. As with most urban design research, there has been little wider critique and testing of Lynch's ideas. Second, city perceptions vary considerably with class, age, gender and culture. Third, as Lynch's later work highlighted (Lynch, 1972), the city image evolves with the continuous development of the city fabric, its activity patterns and the individuals who experience it, ideally providing unfolding complexity. Fourth, people's experiences of a city's formal structure are inevitably strongly conditioned by the meanings they assign to places. Finally, Lynch felt his work lacked impact on planning policy and design, because aesthetics and wider perceptions of form remained treated as 'special, idiosyncratic and not subject to rational debate' (Lynch, 1984: 160). Urban design policy has subsequently given increasing attention to enhancing pedestrian wayfinding, skyline controls, local character studies, visual preference surveys and form-making codes. Nevertheless, despite Lynch's ambitions in *Good City Form*, 'sense' has not become a general, important, explicit performance criterion for urban design alongside vitality, fit, access and control. One unacknowledged limitation of *The Image of the City* and of Lynch's later thinking on sense in urban form (Lynch, 1981) was his continued focus on visual issues, despite later arguments he made about the importance of the senses generally. The recently expanding research into other sensory qualities of urban spaces, their touch, sound and smell, while also informed by other thinkers, has indirectly been inspired by Lynch's pioneering study of people's perception of cities.

Lynch's own emphasis on research methodology, on observing and asking ordinary inhabitants, and being rigorous and self-critical, has had limited influence on urban design thinking and practice. Lynch read widely across the social sciences, humanities and engineering. He posed unanswered questions rather than just expounding treatises, and carefully collected and analysed empirical field data from real cityscapes and actual users to test and develop his hypotheses. Most of Lynch's books contain epilogues and appendices where he reviews existing theories, values and formal patterns, and outlines his own research methodology, discussing limitations and modifications of particular methods and evaluative criteria. Perhaps Lynch's greatest contribution to urban design thinking has been to inspire others to proceed carefully, look carefully, and ask questions.

Secondary sources and references

Appleyard, D., Lynch, K. and Myer, J.R. (1964) *The View from the Road*. Cambridge, MA: MIT Press.

Carr, S. and Lynch, K. (1968) 'Where learning happens', *Daedalus*, 97(4): 1277–1291.

Carr, S. and Lynch, K. (1981) 'Open space: Freedom and control', in L. Taylor (ed.) *Urban Open Spaces*. New York: Rizzoli.

Jacobs, J. (1961) *The Death and Life of Great American Cities*. New York: Vintage.

Lynch, K. (1954) 'The form of cities', *Scientific American*, 190(4): 54–63.

Lynch, K. (1984) 'Reconsidering The Image of the City', in L. Rodwin and R. Hollister (eds) *Cities of the Mind*. New York: Plenum.

Lynch, K. (1990) *Wasting Away*. San Francisco: Sierra Club Books.

Lynch, K. and Hack, G. (1962; 2nd edn 1971; 3rd edn 1984) *Site Planning*. Cambridge, MA: MIT Press.

Lynch, K. and Rodwin, L. (1958) 'A theory of urban form', *Journal of the American Planning Association*, 24(4): 201–214.

26 William J. Mitchell

David Beer, University of York

Key urban writings

Mitchell, W.J. (1995) *City of Bits: Space, Place and the Infobahn*. Cambridge, MA: MIT Press.

Mitchell, W.J. (1999) *E-topia: 'Urban Life, Jim – But Not As We Know It'*. Cambridge, MA: MIT Press.

Mitchell, W.J. (2003) *ME++: The Cyborg Self and the Networked City*. Cambridge, MA: MIT Press.

Mitchell, W.J. (2005) *Placing Words: Symbols, Space and the City*. Cambridge, MA: MIT Press.

Introduction

William J. Mitchell was an architect and social critic who explored the relations between digital and networked media forms and the urban experience. Working at the MIT Media Lab, he was particularly influential in developing ideas around 'smart cities', intelligent environments and the connectivity of the body with digitized spaces. Mitchell's books, which are often poetic in their flourishes and evocative in their tone, mix together architecture, human and cultural geography, urban sociology, media studies and even software studies.

At times Mitchell was as much concerned with anticipating the future as he was in observing the here-and-now. He was certainly not a thinker who was constrained by any overbearing sense of disciplinary belonging or of academic convention. Indeed, Mitchell was a key thinker on cities who was writing for a wide audience. It was Mitchell's approach, as well as his foresight, that made him one of the key thinkers on the technological mediated city and the interweaving of information and concrete space.

Mitchell was the Dean of the MIT Department of Architecture and Planning from 1992 to 2003, and then Professor of Architecture and Media Arts until his death in 2010.

Academic biography and research focus

The social transformation that defined Mitchell's work as an urban theorist was the emergence of the internet. Mitchell was one of the first to respond intellectually, and he was certainly one of the first to think about what the internet meant for notions of space, place, the body and the city. As the internet took hold, Mitchell wrote an 'informal trilogy' (Mitchell, 2003: 250) of books that have had wide-reaching implications for both the study of media and the study of urban space. Beginning with *City of Bits* in 1995, which was really the time when the internet began to move into wider use, the trilogy then continued with *E-topia: 'Urban Life, Jim – But Not As We Know It'* in 1999 and finished with *ME++: The Cyborg Self and the Networked City* in 2003. Although, there was also a kind of appendix to this trilogy involving a number of short pieces gathered together in 2005's *Placing Words*. At the beginning of this trilogy the focus was upon the new types of space that open up as a result of the internet or cyberpsace (as it was often referred to at the time). As the trilogy progressed he began to mesh information technology and concrete spaces. These later books were written as mobile devices, connectivity and mobility became social realities. The specifics of his ideas will be explored in what follows, but it is worth noting first how Mitchell's intellectual biography was woven into a particular set of socio-technological changes to which he was responding.

William J. Mitchell was born in Australia in 1944. He arrived at MIT as the Dean of School of Architecture and Planning in 1992 after previous positions at Harvard, UCLA and a brief early period as a lecturer at the University of Cambridge. So by the time this informal trilogy of books was underway Mitchell was already turning 50 and was in a role of significant administrative responsibility. Yet he was not set in his intellectual trajectory. His books show his willingness to adapt his craft and ideas to what he no doubt saw as a rapidly changing social environment. But this was not a sudden change of direction. He published *The Reconfigured Eye: Visual Truth in the Post-Photographic Era* in 1992 and *The Logic of Architecture: Design, Computation and Cognition* in 1990. In addition to this he had been interested in computer-aided architecture since the late 1970s (see Grimes, 2010), publishing books that explored what computer technologies meant for architectural design. Notable instances here are his 1977 book *Computer-Aided Architectural Design* and his 1987 book *The Art of Computer Graphics Programming: A Structured Introduction for Architects and Designers*. Yet, despite this interest in the computational, he never lost sight of the materiality of spaces, with the above books being followed shortly in 1988 by a co-authored volume on *The Poetics of Gardens* (Moore et al., 1988).

What happened in the mid-1990s was that his existing interest in the transformative capacities of computer technologies morphed as the computers he was interested in moved out of the design studio and into the spaces of everyday life. So this interest in the technological reconfiguration of various aspects of social and cultural life spreads through his intellectual life – beginning with the way that computers shaped design practice and then evolving into an interest in how computing reconfigures urban space. It would seem that Mitchell was still interested in such issues when he died of cancer in 2010 at the age of 65. When interviewed by Pau Alsina in 2005 it was clear that Mitchell was continuing to map out further work in this area. His last book, *Placing Words*, a collection of his short articles, illustrated his ongoing interests in understanding the technological transformation of everyday spaces. The introduction to that book shows how central these questions continued to be in his work.

Key ideas

Mitchell's scholarship can perhaps best be understood as an attempt to explore the technological transformation of the relations between bodies, objects and spaces (cf. **M. Christine Boyer**). He was interested in how digital and networked technologies remade these relations, and often noted just how deep these disruptions might be. His work was also concerned with the future. As such, he was eager to plot out trajectories and to imagine where these technological disruptions might take us in the future. Despite in some instances being dated, Mitchell's work has a good deal to say about a topic that many scholars still fail to take seriously: the mediatization of our lives, of material objects and of everyday spaces. Mitchell's approach was to show how embedded these media already were in bodily practices and senses of space. Mitchell dwelt extensively on the idea that places and objects were getting 'smarter' and that there was an emergent agency or thinking power within the environments that we populate. This interest in 'smart places' really begins to take hold in *E-topia* (1999), yet it is a characteristic of all of his work. Mitchell wanted to explore what it meant to have objects, devices and even places that could think or that could, in some way, be considered to be 'smart'. His interest was in uncovering and realizing the implications of 'embedded intelligence' (Mitchell, 1999: 45).

From the first book in his trilogy, *City of Bits* (1995), Mitchell identified the dual processes of miniaturization and dematerialization as being crucial. Indeed, these dual processes permeate his later works. Put simply, he was interested in what happened as media technologies shrank in size. The result is that they become more mobile and so the possibilities for embedding devices into bodily routines or even implanting them into objects and bodies increase. Alongside this he was interested in what the rise of new virtual forms meant for material spaces. His observation was that we were moving into a period of dematerialization in which larger parts of our lives would be lived and experienced virtually. This was something of a prophetic observation in 1995 – a time before music downloading, social media, streaming and the like. As he put it in *E-topia*, 'virtuality now vies with materiality' (p. 147).

For Mitchell, the dual processes of miniaturization and dematerialization opened up a vast range of questions concerning the future of bodies and spaces. He began to draw upon cyborg imagery in *City of Bits* (1995), but this, as the title would suggest, reached something of a climax with the vastly influential book *ME++: The Cyborg Self and the Networked City* (2003). A number of other writers were already using the cyborg as a concept for understanding how bodies were being transformed by technologies, these included the feminist writers Donna Haraway and Katherine N. Hayles. The cyborg, or cybernetic organism, was borrowed from science fiction and adapted to provide an understanding of the way that human bodies interfaced with the increasingly informational environment. For these writers, our bodies extend out into the spaces we occupy and connect into networks and objects. The result is that the boundaries of the body become contested or open. Mitchell's particular take on the cyborg enabled him to think about how bodies extend into increasingly technologized and mediatized urban spaces. We are not 'skin bounded' but, Mitchell (1995: 167) argued, we are moving into an 'era of electronically extended bodies'.

What is particularly interesting in Mitchell's work is that the implications of the cyborg moved beyond an understanding of the body. Mitchell instead used the metaphor to understand the changing city space as well. What we find is that Mitchell begins to use intriguing combinations of biological and technological metaphors to emphasize the intermingling of the organic and the inorganic. This encourages the reader to see and imagine city spaces in new ways. It provokes us to think about how technologies do not just turn bodies into machines, but that they also turn cities into smart living things. Mitchell frequently uses organic phrases and terminology to describe inorganic and material spaces. For instance, he writes of 'buildings with nervous systems' (Mitchell, 1999: 59). This type of terminology is common in his work, but it is difficult to fully elaborate. Instead, let me provide you with a key passage from ME++ (2003: 19) that illustrates the point and also gives a flavour of Mitchell's engaging writing style:

> Now the city/body metaphors have turned concrete and literal. Embedded within a vast structure of nested boundaries and ramifying networks, my muscular and skeletal, physiological, and nervous systems have been artificially augmented and expanded. My reach extends indefinitely and interacts with the similarly extended reaches of others to produce a global system of transfer, actuation, sensing, and control. My biological body meshes with the city; the city itself has become not only the domain of my networked cognitive system, but also – and crucially – the spatial and material embodiment of that system.

In this key passage the organic and inorganic both extend and blur into one another. The body becomes increasingly inorganic and the city becomes more organic. The body networks into the city space and the boundaries between the two become complex in both a material and conceptual sense. The city develops cognitive properties: it can think, and the nervous and sensory systems of its population blend together with the nervous and sensory systems of urban infrastructures. This may seem fantastical, but it forces the reader to think about the nature of the relations between bodies and spaces and to ask questions about the changing nature of these relations.

Having said all of this, Mitchell does not package his ideas in nice structured theories about the world. Rather, his work buzzes with ideas. His writing drives us along through spaces of materiality and imagination. Mitchell pulls us towards ideas and then cuts us loose to think through the implications. Mitchell does not really deal in theories, as such, but in sensitizing descriptions. Indeed, I would suggest that Mitchell's mode of presentation and communication – his writing style – is a 'key idea' in itself. The writing is absorbing, revealing and exciting to read. Occasionally the reader finds her or himself wondering if Mitchell is caught up in hyperbole or if his accounts end up being reduced to a kind of technological determinism (where technological change is simply seen to drive and define social and cultural change). But, given his ambitious and unbendable interest in revealing the social world, we should forgive the moments in which things perhaps do not work out quite as hoped or where the predictions about the future now seem to have dated. Projecting ideas outwards in order to imagine the future of the cities or lifeworlds yet-to-come is not easy. Mitchell's aim is provocation. He is experimenting with ideas in front of the reader's eyes. I would suggest that the mode of writing and delivery is the first thing we should note in his work and it is something that others should replicate. Mitchell's first priority was to be engaging and to draw the reader into the world he was simultaneously observing and imagining.

Contributions to urban studies

As this would suggest, it is in understanding the technological transformation of urban space that Mitchell's work has been most influential. Alongside this, Mitchell was one of the first thinkers to apply the cyborg concept to urban or city spaces. This remains a key breakthrough because it brings both the body and technological transformation into dialogue with the material environment. Understanding the human implications of the rise of 'smart' cities also had a transformative effect on how cities are understood. No longer are they passive backdrops to everyday life, Mitchell encourages us to see them as thinking places that are active and lively. Can a building or city have a nervous system? This is the type of question he poses to us. Mitchell was left in no doubt that city spaces and experiences are irreversibly transformed by networked devices and the internet. He leaves his reader in no doubt of this, and thus a further key contrition has been to provoke urban studies into addressing these changes.

From the late 1990s Mitchell was already writing about 'augmented reality'. This has been a theme that has been central to work on ubiquitous computing, media geographies and work on mobile devices of different types. In his later work, *Placing Words* (2005), the terminology shifted a little to a more nuanced notion of an 'urban information overlay'. By then Mitchell was viewing all spaces as being defined and configured by a type of blanket of information. This information overlay defines how space is experienced and lived. If we pause here, we might imagine how Google Maps (including Street View) shapes our experiences of places, how various apps guide us through spaces or recommend activities and consumer practices we might engage in; how GPS systems show us around while we listen to music, play games or enjoy whatever feature of our phones that might currently have attracted our attention. It is in such practices that we begin to see Mitchell's information overlay becoming a reality and in which we might see ourselves as cyborgs in the networked city.

Secondary sources and references

Beer, D. (2007) 'Thoughtful territories: Imaging the thinking power of things and spaces', *City*, 11(2): 229–238.

Gane, N. (2006) 'When we have never been human, what is to be done? An interview with Donna Haraway', *Theory, Culture and Society*, 23(7–8): 135–158.

Grimes, W. (2010) 'William J. Mitchell, Architect and Urban Visonary, Dies at 65', *The New York Times*, 16 June. Available at: http://www.nytimes.com/2010/06/16/us/16mitchell.html?_r=0

Haraway, D. (1991) *Simians, Cyborgs, and Women: The Reinvention of Nature*. London: Free Association Books.

Hayles, N.K. (1999) *How We Became Posthuman: Virtual Bodies in Cybernetics, Literature and Informatics*. Chicago: University of Chicago Press.

Hayles, N.K. (2006) 'Unfinished work: From cyborg to cognisphere', *Theory, Culture and Society*, 23(7–8): 159–166.

Hayles, N.K. (2009) 'RFID: Human agency and meaning information-intensive environments', *Theory, Culture and Society*, 26(2–3): 47–72.

Mitchell, W.J. (1977) *Computer-Aided Architectural Design*. New York: Mason Charter.

Mitchell, W.J. (1987) *The Art of Computer Graphics Programming: A Structured Introduction for Architects and Designers*. New York: Van Nostrand Reinhold Company.

Mitchell, W.J. (1990) *The Logic of Architecture: Design, Computation and Cognition*. Cambridge, MA: MIT Press.

Mitchell, W.J. (1992) *The Reconfigured Eye: Visual Truth in the Post-Photographic Era*. Cambridge, MA: MIT Press.

Mitchell, W.J. and Alsina, P. (2005) 'Interview: William J. Mitchell', *ArtNodes*, January. Available at: www.uoc.edu/artnodes/espai/eng/art/mitchell1204.html

Moore, C.W., Mitchell, W.J. and Turnbull, W. (1988) *The Poetics of Gardens*. Cambridge, MA: MIT Press.

27

Harvey Molotch

Eugene McCann, Simon Fraser University

Key urban writings

Molotch, H. (1976) 'The city as a growth machine: Toward a political economy of place', *American Journal of Sociology*, 82(2): 309–332.

Logan, J.R. and Molotch, H.L. (1987; 20th anniversary edn 2007) *Urban Fortunes: The Political Economy of Place*. Berkeley and Los Angeles: University of California Press.

Molotch, H. (1993) 'The political economy of growth machines', *Journal of Urban Affairs*, 15(1): 29–53.

Molotch, H. (2005) *Where Stuff Comes From: How Toasters, Toilets, Cars, Computers and Many Other Things Come to Be as They Are*. New York: Routledge.

Molotch, H. (2012) *Against Security: How We Go Wrong at Airports, Subways, and Other Sites of Ambiguous Danger*. Princeton, NJ: Princeton University Press.

Introduction

In urban studies, Harvey Molotch's name is synonymous with the influential concept of the growth machine. As elaborated in his 1976 *American Journal of Sociology* paper and his classic co-authored book with John Logan, *Urban Fortunes* (1987), the growth machine is a coalition of local business, political, and allied elites who promote and benefit from economic development and population expansion in a city. Indeed, for Molotch (1976: 310), growth, in the American context, is the 'very essence' of most places. The influence of this thesis is indicated by its continued key role in critical studies of urban development, the debates it has provoked, and, not least, the fact that *Urban Fortunes* was republished in a 20th anniversary edition in 2007.

Yet Molotch's interests and influence range more widely than urban growth. They largely revolve around the nexus of power, persuasion, and place. He has engaged and extended social constructivist approaches to key social issues by deploying largely qualitative methods, including discourse analysis, interviews, and ethnographic observation. He writes in an engaging, often witty style that draws insight from a broad range of theoretical literatures and empirical examples.

Molotch is Professor of Sociology, Metropolitan Studies, and Social and Cultural Analysis at New York University and was Chair and Professor of Sociology at the University of California, Santa Barbara.

Academic biography and research focus

Molotch grew up in Baltimore, the son of a family of car and home appliance dealers. He studied philosophy as an undergraduate at the University of Michigan, then received an MA and, in 1968, a PhD in Sociology from the University of Chicago. His doctoral dissertation was published as *Managed Integration: Dilemmas of Doing Good in the City* (1972). It is a study of Chicago's South Shore neighborhood at a time of significant change in the racial composition of its resident population. As white residents left the neighborhood and African Americans became its majority population, South Shore was notable for organized local attempts to manage the changes and create a stable, racially integrated neighborhood. The strategy sought to make the neighborhood attractive to both white and black residents, thus promoting integration. For Molotch, this ultimately unsuccessful effort revealed that, *pace* the Chicago School of urban ecologists' argument that people competed with each other for urban space, key interests in particular urban places also compete to attract residents and land uses to their locations. His first publication, submitted while still conducting his doctoral research, lays out this conceptualization of the city as a collection of land-based interests (Molotch, 1967). Thus, as we will see below, the seeds of the growth machine thesis are embedded in his earliest work.

Molotch's upbringing in postwar Baltimore and his time in Chicago brought him into close contact with the dynamics and tensions of urban change; his move to the University of California, Santa Barbara in 1967 might have seemed to offer a more placid environment. California was certainly at the cutting edge of cultural change, but elite Santa Barbara, with its 'ideal climate, gentle beauty and sophisticated "culture"' (Molotch, 1970: 131) was perhaps less *avant-garde* than elsewhere in the state. Yet, any feeling of calm was soon shattered when, in January 1969, an oil platform blow-out spilled 80,000–100,000 barrels of crude onto Santa Barbara's beaches. As Molotch (1970: 131) insightfully put it in an influential paper, '[m]ore than oil leaked from … [the platform] – a bit of truth about power in America spilled out along with it.' He proceeded to unpack the power dynamics of the spill, noting that its impact on an elite enclave made a difference to the ensuing reaction. The response was also profoundly conditioned by national political and economic elites, who controlled the regulatory system, and by the media who framed the issue in specific ways (see also Molotch and Lester, 1974). For him, the study of this local disaster provided insight into much wider questions of how places are shaped and represented by powerful interests, operating across a range of sites, and illuminated the limits of local elites' abilities to influence decisions made at other scales, another theme that re-emerges in his later discussion of the growth machine.

If Chicago and Santa Barbara are important waypoints in Molotch's academic biography, his encounter with John Logan in 1976 was another profound marker. The pairing was an arranged marriage of sorts. Having published Molotch's growth machine paper in the same 1976 issue as Logan's study of suburban development, the editors of the *American Journal of Sociology* asked each to comment on the other's work. The ensuing debate contained elements of a deepened and expanded growth machine concept and led, 11 years later, to their co-authored *Urban Fortunes*.

Key ideas

While much of Molotch's work has analyzed the nexus of power, persuasion, and place, this focus is particularly apparent in the growth machine thesis. A growth machine is a loose coalition of local business, political, and allied elites whose interests converge around their dependence on drawing income, profit, and, in some cases, political power from their control and development of local land. Thus, for Logan and Molotch (1987), they are 'place entrepreneurs,' intent on creating the preconditions for growth and attracting investment to their locality. Core members of the growth machine include developers, construction companies, property financiers, and the real estate industry. All are tied to their place. Small landlords, for instance, have limited means to buy and rent out more land in other cities, while local developers benefit greatly from the strong ties they have nurtured in their local land market but have little ability to become similarly embedded elsewhere. Therefore, their interests lie in promoting growth locally as they hope this will push up demand for land, land prices, and rents.

Logan and Molotch argue that local politicians, media companies, power utilities, arts and entertainment organizations, sports teams, organized labor, and universities, among others, are also fundamentally interested in increasing the size of their local markets because their ability to gain revenue elsewhere is limited. Central to this confluence of interests between local economic and political elites – epitomizing what *Urban Fortunes* calls the 'political economy of place' – is the growth machine's tension-filled relationship with non-elite urban residents. Logan and Molotch argue that the majority of urban residents' interests are not primarily tied to maximizing profit from land. Yet they are profoundly affected by development decisions. Thus, a key focus of growth machine activities is to persuade the majority of the local population that growth is not only good for local elites' interests, but that growth is good for all, even in the face of evidence and political activism that argues otherwise. This struggle makes cities what they are.

Molotch's (1976: 313) original argument invoked notions of elites, ideology, the redistribution of resources, and locality to make the intentionally provocative, 'extreme statement' that efforts to affect the distribution of growth are 'the essence of local government as a dynamic political force.' By 1987, an expanded conceptual framework underpinned *Urban Fortunes*. Key concepts included: place and its social production as a rubric under which to emphasize the role of conflict among groups of activists in shaping cities; use and exchange values as a framework to organize analysis of the interests frequently squaring off in growth-related conflicts; capital and rentiers to differentiate corporate, less place-dependent economic interests on the one hand, and place-dependent interests that draw income from various forms of rent on the other; serendipitous and active entrepreneurs and structural speculators as three different types of place entrepreneurs, where structural speculators are the most involved in influencing public policy making for their own ends; the myth of 'value-free' development as a way to highlight the ideological arguments made by pro-growth advocates about the universal benefits of development; and systemic power, indicating the deep intertwining of political and business elites' interests in contemporary cities. Through a rich set of American examples, Logan and Molotch (1987: 98) argue that, in most cases, local growth is 'a transfer of wealth and life chances from the general public to the rentier groups and their associates. ... [To] question the wisdom of growth for any specific locality is to threaten a benefit transfer and the interests of those who gain from it.' Yet, the later chapters of the book, inspired in part by Molotch's experience in Santa Barbara, search out signs – particularly in the environmental movement – of effective strategies for engaging in an appropriately critical stance.

In the last 15 years, Molotch has continued to develop important ideas for the analysis of power, persuasion, and place. These have intersected with a growing focus in urban studies on materialities (e.g., Rantisi and Leslie, 2010). His ideas address two related themes. First, he has developed a sociological and geographical study of the design and provenance of the mundane things that are 'lashed up,' or assembled with our daily lives (Molotch, 2005: 2). In this work, represented by his book *Where Stuff Comes From* (2005), and influenced by Latour's (1987) actor-network theory, he argues that objects, from cars and home appliances (Baltimore again ...), to furniture, medical appliances, engines, buildings, and toilets (a longstanding interest of his: Molotch, 1988; Molotch and Norén, 2010), reveal much about how contemporary society operates and is experienced (cf. **Mariana Valverde**). For Molotch (2005: 20), drawing on his ethnographic research on the largely urban-based design professionals who craft much of the material world, a '[b]etter understanding of the stuff system, including its "deep" mechanisms of change and stability, can [help] ... improve goods – both socially and ecologically – and comprehend more about the society that produces them' (cf. **Natalie Jeremijenko**).

Most recently, in the wake of September 11, 2001 – a day on which he watched the Twin Towers collapse from his New York apartment – Molotch has developed a second set of ideas, concerning disasters (Santa Barbara again ...), fears, anxieties, threats, and the securitization of cities. In *Against Security* (2012), he argues that the new urban security 'normal' also involves the lashing up of objects and infrastructures with daily life. He documents the way urban infrastructures like subway systems, airports, streetscapes, and skylines are being designed, governed, and built in the thrall of 'security.' Certainly, these sorts of assemblages reveal a lot about the society that is producing them and these hegemonic socio-material and socio-spatial systems of power are thoroughly urbanized, both in terms of where they are designed and where they are consumed, implemented, and experienced. Again, Molotch's analyses are timely, emerging at a juncture when urban residents and scholars are grappling with the increasingly evident militarization of cities (e.g. **Stephen Graham**, 2012).

Contributions to urban studies

Molotch, then, has a history of making opportune, insightful contributions to urban scholarship. His most established contribution is the growth machine concept, which emerged at a useful time. The 1970s and 1980s were an era of great ferment in urban studies. The ecological, liberal, neoclassical, and positivist perspectives of the Chicago School and its successors were being challenged by alternative perspectives inspired by

Marxian, Weberian, and emergent postmodernist approaches. In various ways, these new critical and radical perspectives were concerned with the location and operation of power and with both explaining and changing inequalities in contemporary society. An elite theory of power that critiques mainstream pluralist understandings of urban politics, growth machine theory brought a number of helpful concepts to the center of debate.

Molotch's work with Logan undoubtedly continues to have great influence on how urban studies scholars conceptualize urban politics (e.g., Bedore, 2014; Jonas and Wilson, 1999). Yet, it has also been a topic of criticism and debate over the years. Reviewers at the time of its publication critiqued what they saw as *Urban Fortunes'* tendency to give too much conceptual weight to individual activities, even as parts of coalitions, instead of the historical structural forces that position people in opposition to each other or in particular relationships to capital and the land. Place, for many, especially geographers, appeared undertheorized in the book, as did scale, while questions were raised about the international applicability of a theory developed entirely in the U.S. context. The growth machine category itself was critiqued as encompassing too many disparate actors and many felt it failed to adequately conceptualize the power of the state. Moreover, the reliance on dualisms in the theory of growth machines (use/exchange value, local rentiers/capitalists) was questioned.

These questions emphasize the growth machine's worth as a concept: it has focused attention on how best to analyze important structures and inequalities in cities and, even through disagreements, has helped strengthen contemporary critical urban studies as a result. Logan and Molotch have responded to many of the critiques and Molotch especially has addressed questions of international applicability, for example, through research on other contexts and by continuing to defend an agency-centered approach to the study of urban development (Molotch, 1993). Of course, cities and their political economies continue to change. Concerns over the environment, while even more politically potent (Warner and Molotch, 2000), have also increasingly been incorporated into development regimes via terms like sustainable development, while once locally-bound real estate interests and institutions, like universities and sports teams, have found ways, in a deregulated world, to 'jump scale' and tap sources of income beyond their original locality. These and other changes bear ongoing investigation and they encourage continued critical engagement with the growth machine thesis.

Yet Molotch's contributions to urban studies extend beyond the growth machine thesis. His recent work on consumer products, infrastructures, and the lived realities of urban security intersect productively with scholarship on materialities, actor networks, and security/militarization. As he has done in his previous work, Molotch resists and critically unpacks hegemonic notions of how cities work. Then, through engaging narratives, he presents alternative visions of how they might work, and be lived, better. These insights suggest that his influence will continue to inflect urban scholarship for years to come.

Secondary sources and references

Bedore, M. (2014) 'The convening power of food as growth machine politics: A study of food policymaking and partnership formation in Baltimore', *Urban Studies*, 51(14): 2979–2995.

Graham, S. (2012) 'When life itself is war: On the urbanization of military and security doctrine', *International Journal of Urban and Regional Research*, 36(1): 136–155.

Jonas, A.E. and Wilson, D. (eds) (1999) *The Urban Growth Machine: Critical Perspectives, Two Decades Later*. Albany: State University of New York Press.

Latour, B. (1987) *Science in Action: How to Follow Scientists and Engineers through Society*. Cambridge, MA: Harvard University Press.

Molotch, H. (1967) 'Toward a more human Human Ecology: An urban research strategy,' *Land Economics*, 43(3): 336–341.

Molotch, H. (1970) 'Oil in Santa Barbara and power in America', *Sociological Inquiry*, 40(Winter): 131–144.

Molotch, H. (1972) *Managed Integration: Dilemmas of Doing Good in the City*. Berkeley and Los Angeles: University of California Press.

Molotch, H. (1988) 'The rest room and equal opportunity', *Sociological Forum*, 3(1): 128–132.

Molotch, H. and Lester, M. (1974) 'News as purposive behavior: On the strategic use of routine events, accidents, and scandals', *American Sociological Review*, 39(1): 101–112.

Molotch, H. and Norén, L. (eds) (2010) *Toilet: Public Restrooms and the Politics of Sharing*. New York: New York University Press.

Rantisi, N.M. and Leslie, D. (2010) 'Materiality and creative production: The case of the Mile End neighborhood in Montréal', *Environment and Planning A*, 42(12): 2824–2841.

Warner, K. and Molotch, H. (2000) *Building Rules: How Local Controls Shape Community Environments and Economies*. Boulder, CO: Westview Press.

Acknowledgements: I am grateful to Harvey Molotch, Tom Baker, Regan Koch, and Alan Latham for their helpful comments.

28

Enrique Peñalosa

Juan Pablo Galvis, State University of New York
at Old Westbury

Key urban writings

Peñalosa, E. (2003) 'Parks for livable cities: Lessons from a radical mayor', *Places*, 15(3): 30–33.

Peñalosa, E. (2004a) 'Social and environmental sustainability in cities', *Proceedings of the International Mayors Forum on Sustainable Urban Energy Development, Kunming, China*, pp. 19–31.

Peñalosa, E. (2008) 'Politics, power cities: Private interest and public good', in R. Burdett and D. Sudjic (eds) *The Endless City*. London: Phaidon Press, pp. 307–319.

Introduction

Enrique Peñalosa is a Colombian politician and world renowned expert on urban planning and transportation policy. The mayor of Bogota, Colombia between 1998 and 2001, he became an influential voice in global urban forums and, like many other famous former mayors, speaks extensively on the international urban lecture circuit. As board president of the Institute for Transportation and Development Policy (ITDP), he also advises city governments worldwide, mainly on transportation planning issues. It is through his consultancy and lecturing activities, rather than traditional academic work that Peñalosa has disseminated his ideas. Yet his ideas are particularly relevant for urban scholars given his experience as mayor of a large city in the Global South at a time when such cities have become home to most of the world's urban population. He thus complements recent trends in urban thought that seek to expand urban theory and practice beyond the Euro-American experience. As a thinker, Peñalosa is positioned to provide insights on the common problems of Northern and Southern cities. As a consultant and practitioner, he is one of the most influential agents of the Global North–South circulation of urban policy. It is no surprise, then, that he was recently chosen in a poll among urban scholars and practitioners as the 9th most influential urban thinker. He was re-elected as mayor of Bogota in 2015.

Refocusing urban design around the principle of equality, particularly in the Global South, is one of Peñalosa's key ideas. To place equality first and foremost, he proposes a strong, activist city government that puts collective interests over individual ones, and opposes the idea of unfettered market forces driving urban development. In particular, Peñalosa points to public transport (particularly Bus Rapid Transit [BRT] systems) and bicycle-friendly infrastructure as equality-inspired solutions to urban transportation problems. Quality pedestrian public spaces (such as parks, plazas, and waterfronts) also feature prominently in his discourse as means to foster equality and not just give cities charm and character. Testament to his worldwide influence among practitioners, these kinds of solutions are now being implemented worldwide. In addition, his emphasis on these solutions as political strategies for fostering equality has attracted the attention of many urban scholars.

Academic biography and research focus

The son of a prominent Colombian politician and diplomat by the same name, Enrique Peñalosa was born in 1953 in Washington, DC. He grew up at a time of profound transformations in Colombian society as it rapidly urbanized and witnessed the problems generated by processes like urban land speculation and elite concentration of services and amenities. Influenced by his father's liberal political agenda, Peñalosa's insistence on equality as a principle and the need for strong city governments to foster it dates back to this experience. Peñalosa studied Economics and History at Duke University and earned Master's degrees in Management and Public Administration from the Institute International d'Administration Publique, University of Paris II, France. These studies signaled Peñalosa's intentions to return to Colombia and follow his father into politics. During the 1980s, he began to build the résumé of public service that would eventually propel his political career. During this time, he also published his only two books, advocating for 'third way' politics toward the end of the Cold War: *Capitalismo: ¿La mejor opción? [Capitalism: The Best Option?]* (1989) and *Democracia y capitalismo: desafíos del próximo siglo [Democracy and Capitalism: Challenges for the Coming Century]* (1984). In 1990, Peñalosa was elected to the Colombian House of Representatives for Bogota and, after two unsuccessful bids for the city's mayoral office, he was elected in 1997, but became the Mayor of Bogota on 1 January, 1998.

His very successful tenure as mayor transformed Peñalosa from a relatively minor local political figure into a national celebrity and a very influential international thinker on urban issues. This success can be accredited to his vision for a more 'livable' city, which he implemented in Bogota with impressive efficiency. The capital of a country beleaguered by internal conflict and narco-terrorism, 1990s Bogota was seen as an unviable city by its own inhabitants, let alone international observers. By the time he became mayor, a series of administrative and financial reforms had been put in place which promised to take the city out of its political dysfunction. Peñalosa took advantage of this context to embark on an extensive program of public works. The city's first Bus Rapid Transit line was built, introducing Bogotanos to mass transit for the first time. His administration also built miles of bike lanes and revamped sidewalks and parks all over the city. More importantly, the city invested heavily in 'neighborhood demarginalization' plans in some of its poorer areas. These plans included improvements in public spaces, schools, libraries, and public utilities. He spoke of public access to collective goods and against the reign of the private car in ways citizens of Bogota were not used to hearing. But more than just a physical makeover, all these developments combined to give Bogotanos new pride in their city and unheard of optimism about its future. At the end of his tenure in 2001 – Colombian law does not provide for the re-election of mayors while in office – Peñalosa was among the most popular Colombian politicians.

Peñalosa's international reputation is even more enduring than his local popularity. He is credited for Bogota's story of improbable transformation, which is very appealing for international audiences. He is also acclaimed internationally as a standard-bearer for the causes of urban equality and for public transport and green urban development, policies which formed the core of his agenda as mayor. Indeed, Peñalosa's examples represented a breath of fresh air for many progressive urban thinkers and practitioners mired in the aggressive and privatizing policies of the 1990s. If the right-wing mayor of New York City Rudolph Giuliani had established a strong presence in urban policy debates by the early 2000s, Peñalosa was internationally embraced as a necessary mayoral counterpoint.

Key ideas

In no small way, despite being out of office for more than a decade, Peñalosa still thinks like a mayor. His ideas and prescriptions for the cities of the future are often anchored in concrete governance possibilities from transportation to affordable housing. All these policy prescriptions focus on one guiding principle: how urban planning can be harnessed to produce more egalitarian urban societies (cf. **Jason Corburn**). Among the many urban thinkers that advocate for urban equality, Peñalosa stands out for his experience implementing some of these ideas on the ground. His lectures and advice to cities are often couched in ways that connect the complicated elements of city planning to the overall principle of furthering urban equality. Added to this is Peñalosa's experience leading a large Global South city. Indeed, his ideas have become even more powerful because he articulates them explicitly in terms of rethinking the goals and methods of urban design for the cities of the Global South. 'In developing countries, where most cities are still to be built,' Peñalosa writes in his foreword to the Spanish edition of **Jan Gehl**'s *Life Between Buildings*, 'it is possible to use Gehl's analyses to propose new radical models for the city'[1] (Peñalosa, 2004b).

In proposing these 'new radical models for the city' Peñalosa is inspired by the writings of scholars like **Jane Jacobs** and William H. Whyte, who conceptualize the social and political aspects of physical public spaces. Perhaps most influential in Peñalosa's thinking is the work of **Jan Gehl**. Among the most radical of Peñalosa's proposals, and the one that generated the most resistance when he was mayor, is his stance against the reign of the private automobile in the design and running of the city. Connecting his ideas about equality in public space to those about equality in transportation, Peñalosa advocates for restricting the circulation of private cars by whatever means necessary. He argues for eliminating parking spaces in favor of wider sidewalks, allowing traffic jams to function as a self-regulating mechanism against car use, and even a ban on private car use during rush hours. In the Global South, where car ownership rates are ostensibly smaller than in the North, Peñalosa positions the private car as the ultimate expression of the inequities that plague these cities. Wealthier citizens influence policies that favor infrastructure for private cars over public transport. Poor cities spend scarce resources building infrastructure for the cars of the rich, while public transport systems and basic pedestrian and bicycle infrastructure are overlooked.

Stressing the political decisions over the technical considerations involved in preferring public over private transport is one of Peñalosa's key contributions. His case for public transport is particularly powerful because it is articulated in terms of the larger social goal of furthering urban equality, rather than the narrow technical one of alleviating congestion. Transit-oriented growth should be pursued, in other words, not because it is the most efficient, environmentally friendly kind of growth, but because it is the most egalitarian. Another example of Peñalosa's emphasis on the politics of urban equality is his ideas about bike lanes. More than just a quaint urban feature or an environmentally friendly transportation system, Peñalosa sees bike lanes as a space where people can meet one another as equals. In his view, by eliminating the barriers of car ownership, bikes allow all people to enjoy the city regardless of their social status. Urban amenities such as public transportation systems and open public spaces are not just utilitarian means to achieve mobility or recreation. One of Peñalosa's key ideas is that they are mainly means to reduce the obscene levels of social inequality that plague cities of the Global South.

This key insight also implies that it is in the enjoyment of urban amenities that social equality is actually realized. At his most inspiring, Peñalosa speaks of grand public spaces where all people, not just the rich, meet and make social difference secondary. In short, in public transit, bike paths, and wonderful parks alike, everyone is middle class. Celebrated internationally by progressive urban thinkers for his emphasis on equality, Peñalosa has twice lost the race for Bogota mayor to candidates to his left. This is partly due to the fact that he envisions a middle-class city for everyone without giving much thought to the material conditions that allow for everyone actually enjoying it. A key example is that of street vendors, which Peñalosa sees as private citizens that take advantage of a public asset reducing its equalizing potential. Ironically, by making a living in the street, they are depriving the city as a whole of the grand public spaces that would make it more equal. This contradiction is key because it is in the Global South city where such uses of public space are more common.

Contributions to urban studies

The focus on cities of the Global South is one of Peñalosa's most important contributions to urban studies, both as a thinker and a consultant. This is not to say that his ideas apply only to these cities. Rather, his relevance stems from the fact that he draws inspiration from the particular problems of Global South cities to make bold propositions about city building anywhere (cf. **Rem Koolhaas**). This is particularly timely not only because the Global South will contribute most of the new urban population – and spaces – over the following decades, but also because of the increasing levels of inequality present in Northern cities. In this way, Peñalosa can be placed as part of a trend in urban studies to challenge Northern-centered urban theory and practice. Scholars such as **Ananya Roy** and **Jennifer Robinson**, among others, have led urban studies in theorizing the so-called North/South divide and developing ways to compare across it. Peñalosa, in turn, has been influential in considering the consequences for large cities of the Global South of uncritically adopting Northern models. In addition, he speaks widely about his experience as a mayor, reflecting on how the lessons from Bogota can be applied in other cities rich and poor. In a very concrete way, Peñalosa is himself an agent of comparison and policy circulation across the North and South. As a globe-trotting consultant, he embodies the multiple connections between diverse cities, engaging practitioners and scholars alike.

Urban transportation is the issue where Peñalosa's influence is perhaps most felt. Encouraging practitioners and scholars to see through the prism of equality, he urges them to weigh transportation options against the effect they can have in providing more access to more people to enjoy the city's amenities. In his interventions, Peñalosa articulates a critique of the wholesale adoption of the American, car-centered urban model and the consequences this will have for the cities yet to be built in the Global South. In doing so, he has influenced thinkers and urban managers to propose different models and look for ways to amend the mistakes of the past. After all, transportation inequalities are often one of the main reasons the poor are prevented from enjoying, rather than merely surviving the city. This is the point where Peñalosa's contributions as a thinker transcend the purely academic. Thinking as a mayor, articulating his ideas in terms of concrete governance possibilities, he has the ability to greatly influence the translation of his ideas into public policy in many places.

Riding one of the BRT systems that continue to spring up worldwide, millions of urban dwellers intimately feel Peñalosa's impact on our thinking about urban transportation. The BRT, a mass transit system built over infrastructure previously reserved for the private car, is exemplary of Peñalosa's particular approach to urban issues. The symbolic impact of carving out road space for public transport, where the private car used to be king, serves for him as a statement of priorities for all citizens rich and poor. This kind of reasoning sets Peñalosa apart as more than a transportation expert and successful urban practitioner. His insistence on highlighting equality as a guiding principle and subordinating the technical to the social aspects of city-making explain his popularity as an urban thinker. Moreover, his influence is greatly amplified by his record as a mayor and his credibility as someone who can put these principles into practice.

Secondary sources and references

Beccassino, A. and Peñalosa, E. (2000) *Peñalosa y una ciudad 2600 metros más cerca de las estrellas*. Bogotá: Grijalbo.

Peñalosa, E. (1984) *Democracia y capitalismo: desafíos del próximo siglo*. Bogotá: Fundación Hacia el Desarrollo.

Peñalosa, E. (1989) *Capitalismo: ¿La mejor opción?* Bogotá: Fundación Hacia el Desarrollo.

Peñalosa, E. (2000) *La Bogotá del tercer milenio: Historia de una revolución urbana.* Bogotá: Alcaldía Mayor.

Peñalosa (2004b) 'Foreword', in J. Gehl, *La humanización del espacio urbano. La vida social entre los edificios.* Barcelona: Reverté.

Note

1.   Translation by the author.

29

Jennifer Robinson

Rajyashree N. Reddy, University of Toronto

Key urban writings

Robinson, J. (1996) *The Power of Apartheid: State, Power, and Space in South African Cities.* London: Butterworth-Heinemann.

Robinson, J. (2002) 'Global and world cities: A view from off the map', *International Journal of Urban and Regional Research*, 26(3): 531–554.

Robinson, J. (2005) 'Urban geography: World cities, or a world of cities', *Progress in Human Geography*, 29(6): 757–765.

Robinson, J. (2006) *Ordinary Cities: Between Modernity and Development.* London: Routledge.

Robinson, J. (2011a) 'Cities in a world of cities: The comparative gesture', *International Journal of Urban and Regional Research*, 35(1): 1–23.

Introduction

Jennifer Robinson is an urban geographer who has made pioneering contributions to postcolonial and comparative urban studies. Her early research focused upon the spatiality and politics of segregation in South Africa, during and post-apartheid. She then turned to focus more broadly on urban theory, highlighting the ways urban scholarship has been dominated by ideas and frameworks drawn from a small hand-ful of iconic Western cities. Her seminal book *Ordinary Cities: Between Modernity and Development* (2006) provides a timely corrective to the Western bias of urban theory, outlining a compelling case for studying all cities within a world of cities through a postcolonial framework. Robinson's postcolonial approach offers a potent critique of the 'developmentalist' views of cities in the Global South; questions the privileged association of a few Western cities with modernity; stresses the necessity of conceptualizing all cities as 'ordinary'; and articulates a methodological commitment to comparative urbanism in order to internationalize urban theory. This work has made her a leading figure in the field of contemporary urban debates and scholarship.

Jennifer Robinson is a Professor of Geography at University College London.

Academic biography and research focus

Born and brought up in South Africa, Jennifer Robinson's scholarship remains empirically grounded in South African cities. She completed Bachelor (1984) and Master's (1987) degrees at the University of Natal (now University of KwaZulu-Natal), Durban, and then moved to the UK to complete doctoral studies in Geography from the University of Cambridge. Following the PhD, Robinson returned to South Africa to take up an academic position at her alma mater. There Robinson completed her first book, *The Power of Apartheid: State, Power, and Space in South African Cities* (1996), which offered a careful analysis of the apartheid state's territorial, segregationist residential location strategy and demonstrated the significance of racial organization of urban space to the constitution and exercise of state power, and made vital contributions toward deepening South African urban historiography.

In 1995, Robinson left her post at the University of Natal and returned to the UK. She first took up an academic position at the London School of Economics and then moved to the Open University, where she published her groundbreaking second book, *Ordinary Cities*. In the preface, Robinson describes how in relocating from Durban to London she was particularly struck by entrenched theorizations of modernity and development in urban studies that resulted in Durban and other South African cities being understood in pejorative developmentalist terms. These biases not only negated the dynamism and modernity of these cities and relegated them to the bottom of 'global' or 'world city' rankings, they also led to an impoverished field of urban theory. *Ordinary Cities* and subsequent scholarship by Robinson has thus been animated by (1) the imperative to critique dominant 'architecture of knowledge about cities' (2006: xi) that views cities like Durban as primarily poor and in need of development; and (2) the imperative to reconceptualize all cities non-hierarchically as 'ordinary' cities in a world of cities. In this endeavor, postcolonial theory has become an important resource for Robinson, who has in turn helped to draw postcolonial perspectives into more mainstream urban studies.

Postcolonial theory is an interdisciplinary body of scholarship that studies the complex historical relationship between the colonizer (typically, the West) and the colonized (e.g., the East and South) and the cultural legacy of colonialism in the present. Within the rich and varied body of postcolonial scholarship, the problematique of knowledge production is a recurrent theme, as knowledge-making is acknowledged as key to colonial structures of domination and exploitation. Postcolonial theory hence has a constitutive interest in understanding the discursive strategies deployed by the West to produce knowledge of elsewhere, as Western theories and epistemic categories remain the privileged starting point for contemporary representations of the East/ Global South. Undermining Western-centrism and decolonizing knowledge is thus one of the foremost aims of postcolonial critique. Drawing upon postcolonial approaches, Robinson underscores the Western-centrism of the canon of urban theory, and in particular the relatively narrow canon of theory and schools of thought that serve as essential reading and reference for urban scholars.

Taking up a Chair in Geography at University College London in 2009, Robinson's research became focused on developing a more internationalized urban studies. Moving beyond a critique of the canon of urban theory, her work has become devoted to building cosmopolitan theoretical and comparative analytic approaches, drawing on the experience of a broad range of cities around the world and generating theory from places normally excluded from the theoretical imaginaries of urban studies.

Key ideas

Robinson is a central figure in the development of a more postcolonial urban imagination. She has been instrumental in developing the idea that urban knowledge production and representation must become more provincial, and she has promoted a more properly internationalized field of urban theory. With postcolonial theorist Dipesh Chakrabarty (2000) as her point of departure, Robinson has highlighted the parochial, Western origins of the established urban canon and underscored the epistemic violence of deploying urban theory of Euro-American provenance to understand the diverse urbanisms of cities of the Global South.

Specifically, Robinson makes three key interventions. First, she exposes the parochial origins of theories of urban modernity that disavow the manifest modernity of Global South cities. Second, she underlines the dangers of promulgating 'global cities' as a model of urbanization based upon limited evidence from a few exemplary cities, even as Global South cities continue to be understood through the negative prism of developmentalism. Third, she promotes comparative urbanism as a promising method that will facilitate cosmopolitan theory generation by bringing into view cities that were off the conventional maps of urban theory. Each of these ideas warrants further discussion.

Robinson (2006: 4) defines urban modernity as the 'cultural experience of city life' and the associated 'valorization and celebration of innovation and novelty.' She has outlined how, within the field of urban studies, cities such as Berlin, Paris, London, New York, and Chicago are viewed as quintessentially modern while cities in Africa and elsewhere in the Global South are viewed as lagging behind and transitioning into modernity by copying the original innovations of Western cities. Robinson (2006) shows that the ascription of an originary modernity to, and the privileged designation of, a narrow subset of cities as archetypically modern is the legacy of Western theory broadly. The Chicago School in particular postulated – based upon evidence from the limited, provincial case of Chicago – a theory of urban modernity that asserted the incommensurability of folk and primitive traditions (that remain a dominant facet of non-Western cities) with a modern urban way of life. In contradistinction to the Chicago School, mid-20th-century comparative studies conducted by urban anthropologists in Copperbelt cities of Africa found no incongruity in urban ways of life in these cities being unequivocally modern while also embracing primitive traditions. By excavating this largely forgotten body of comparative studies of Copperbelt cities, and also drawing upon Walter Benjamin's dialectical reading of modernity and primitive traditions, Robinson dislocates ideas about originary modernity.

As part of the effort to dislocate originary modernity, Robinson develops examples like the history of New York's skyscrapers, which have long stood as the epitome of American urban modernity and which New York has confidently claimed as its own autonomous innovation. In her work, Robinson shows them to be the product of local innovation but also of imitation and appropriation of architectural styles from elsewhere. By making evident the always, already innovative and imitative dimensions of New York's signature skyscrapers, Robinson dispels anxieties regarding the imitative nature of the modernity of Global South cities. Robinson further develops the important idea of multiple origins of modernity in Southern cities by providing myriad examples that show that workers' lives in many African cities were not only simply one of drudgery but marked by excitement and wonder of cities that translated into the innovate paintings and music they produced. Overall, by rendering Western cities' claim to originary modernity dubious, and asserting the contemporaneous modernity of intensely innovative and creative Global South cities, Robinson pushes urban studies to embrace them as an essential locus of enunciation for the theorization of urban modernity.

Robinson's insistence upon locating enunciations of urban modernity within cities of the Global South is particularly important because developmentalism remains the dominant optic through which these cities continue to be understood in urban studies. Developmentalist tropes classify cities in the Global South as backward, economically stagnant places that are plagued by problems (lack of water, electricity, roads) which require development assistance to modernize and develop. By the logic of synecdoche, the poorest parts of the Global South city that development focuses upon have come to stand for the whole city, rendering their experiences as incommensurable with cities elsewhere. For Robinson (2002: 531) such a developmentalist view of the Global South represents a 'persistent dualism,' whereby the West develops theory while the Global South instantiates theory by serving as sites of data. She argues that 'global/world city' approaches to urban studies reproduce the 'theory/development' dualism and reinforce the developmentalist view of Global South cities.

Understanding urbanization through 'global' or 'world cities' approaches is an attempt to explicate the role of cities and their interrelations in constituting new forms of globalization. **Saskia Sassen**'s (1991) important contributions popularized the idea that a new kind of city – the 'global city'– that offers 'advanced producer services' in sectors such as banking, finance, accounting, insurance and law are the 'strategic sites' for the coordination and management of the territorially dispersed production of the global economy. Since Sassen's intervention global/world city approaches have become paradigmatic in urban studies, with scholars narrowly focusing upon sectors like banking and finance that have global reach to rank cities into hierarchies based upon the power and connectivity of the transnational banking and finance networks (cf. **Michael Storper**).

Foregrounding 'all sorts of links and connections' that Global South cities have to the world economy, Robinson (2006) argues that the narrow economism of global city categories results in the myriad global links of Global South cities being disregarded. The consequence of such omission is that global/world city frameworks determine the global significance of cities by the severely restricted criteria of transnational banking and finance networks. When judged by these criteria, Global South cities – with their infrastructural woes and lack of sectors like banking and finance that produce 'advanced producer services' – have either been completely left out or ranked at the bottom of global/world city hierarchies and deemed to be 'structurally irrelevant' to the global economy. Insisting upon the 'globalness' of all cities, Robinson emphatically declares that it is not the Global South city that is irrelevant rather it is the 'global/world city' framework that is insufficient, as it is not capable of assessing the global connections made within a world of cities.

Nonetheless, the idea that global cities represent the pinnacle 'command and control' (Sassen, 1991) centers of the world economy is one that has widespread appeal among city planners and policy makers, many of whom have launched risky speculative strategies to foster service sectors with 'global city' functions at the cost of supporting and sustaining the unique diversity of city economies that provide employment and opportunities to millions (including the poorest) in Global South cities. Because of such detrimental effects, Robinson (2002: 549) concludes that the global/world city framework is 'at best irrelevant and at worst harmful to poor cities around the world.'

Robinson elaborates the idea of the 'ordinary city' as a corrective to the 'regulative fiction' of 'global cities' that is enticing city planners and builders to embark upon exclusionary global/world city-making projects. She defines ordinary cities as 'diverse, creative, modern and distinctive, with the possibility to imagine (within the not inconsiderable constraints of contestations and uneven power relations) their own futures and distinctive forms of city-ness' (2002: 546). For Robinson recognizing *all* cities – those at the top (New York) and the bottom (Durban) of global/world city rankings – as ordinary cities in a world of cities is vital as this allows the diverse economic sectors that constitute all cities the opportunities to innovate, grow and generate employment, thereby making it possible for all cities to imagine progressive city futures.

A key argument that runs through Robinson's work is that urban theory must become more international in order to remain relevant for understanding the world of 21st-century cities. Robinson's current research is focused upon this task, with the firm conviction that a diverse range of ordinary cities, but particularly cities that have traditionally been left off the map of urban theory, are essential sites and resources in the endeavor. For, Robinson (2011a, 2011b) comparative methods that bring into view a number of cities hold great potential for internationalizing theory. Therefore, in her current research, she has focused on revitalizing comparative methods, which Robinson argues had become less prominent as developmentalism became ascendant and bifurcated the world of cities into 'developed' and 'developing' cities, and discouraged comparativism across the divide. The result was an impoverished field of comparative studies that limited comparison to 'most similar cities.' Robinson thus begins the task of revitalizing the comparative method by encouraging comparative studies between 'most different cities' across the Global North–South divide such as comparing cities in the United States with cities in Nigeria and making the unit of comparison not the city as such but some abstract urban flows and circulations that connect these cities. Robinson herself has focused upon the circulations of neoliberalism and argued that understanding the spatiality of neoliberal policy circulations can bring into view new causalities that open up the theory itself to interrogation based upon the evidence from a wider world of cities (see Parnell and Robinson, 2012).

Contributions to urban studies

Robinson's main contribution to urban studies has been to promote the untethering of urban theory from Northern and Western global cities. She has advocated the value of thinking the urban, and imagining urban modernity and city futures, from places conventionally off the map of the established urban canon. Her pioneering use of postcolonial theory to reinvigorate and internationalize urban studies is particularly valuable, as the locus of urbanization has shifted from the Global North to the

Global South. In this context, the type of internationalized urban theory that Robinson has sought to produce is, to use Cindi Katz's (1996) term, a 'minor theory' that is flexible and revisable and with the explicit understanding that it may not have universal applicability. Robinson's efforts have been complemented by the work of urban theorists such as **Ananya Roy**, who has called for 'new geographies' of urban theory to be generated. Together with Roy, Robinson's groundbreaking contributions have catalyzed comparative urban research, and a growing number of writers are exploring how Southern urbanism contributes to urban theory.

However, as scholars engage closely with Robinson's ideas, she has nonetheless been criticized for producing empirically thin explications of high theory rather than the minor theory her work aspires to, and for overstating the novelty of comparative urbanism, given that comparative thinking has long been a focus of urban scholarship (cf. **Abu-Lughod**). Yet Robinson's call to internationalize urban theory remains urgent as influential theorists such as Alan Scott and **Michael Storper** dismiss postcolonial critiques of urban theory as producing 'new particularisms,' while **Neil Brenner** and his collaborators are suggesting that the totalizing framework of 'planetary urbanism' should become the new epistemology of the urban.

Secondary sources and references

Brenner, N. and Schmid, C. (2015) 'Towards a new epistemology of the urban?', *City*, 19(2–3): 151–182.

Chakrabarty, D. (2000) *Provincializing Europe: Postcolonial Thought and Historical Difference.* Princeton, NJ: Princeton University Press.

Katz, C. (1996) 'Towards minor theory', *Environment and Planning D: Society and Space*, 14(4): 487–499.

Parnell, S. and Robinson, J. (2012) '(Re)theorizing cities from the Global South: Looking beyond neoliberalism', *Urban Geography*, 33(4): 593–617.

Robinson, J. (2004) 'In the tracks of comparative urbanism: Difference, urban modernity and the primitive', *Urban Geography*, 25(8): 709–723.

Robinson, J. (2011b) 'Comparisons: Colonial or cosmopolitan?', *Singapore Journal of Tropical Geography*, 32(2): 125–140.

Roy, A. (2009) 'The 21st-century metropolis: New geographies of theory', *Regional Studies*, 43(6): 819–830.

Sassen, S. (1991) *The Global City: New York, London, Tokyo.* Princeton, NJ: Princeton University Press.

Scott, A.J. and Storper, M. (2015) 'The nature of cities: The scope and limits of urban theory', *International Journal of Urban and Regional Research*, 39(1): 1–15.

30

Ananya Roy

Hanna Hilbrandt, The Open University

Key urban writings

Roy, A. (2003a) *City Requiem, Calcutta: Gender and the Politics of Poverty.* Minneapolis and London: University of Minnesota Press.

Roy, A. (2005) 'Urban informality: Toward an epistemology of planning', *Journal of the American Planning Association*, 71(2): 147–158.

Roy, A. (2009a) 'The 21st-century metropolis: New geographies of theory', *Regional Studies*, 43(6): 819–830.

Roy, A. (2011a) 'Slumdog cities: Rethinking subaltern urbanism', *International Journal of Urban and Regional Research*, 35(2): 223–238.

Roy, A. and Ong, A. (eds) (2011) *Worlding Cities: Asian Experiments and the Art of Being Global.* Malden, MA: Blackwell.

Introduction

Ananya Roy is a specialist in urban studies and international development, with a particular focus on planning and poverty politics. Geographically, Roy's enquiries centre on India but her work operates on a global scale, incorporating cities as diverse as Beirut, Shenzhen and Cairo. Her urban research connects transnational relations of dependence – between the core and periphery of the state, between global aspirations and their local contestations, between the subaltern urbanism of the poor and the confinements brought on by global circuits of capitalism. In bridging these foci, Roy has advanced a multiscalar approach that combines anthropological perspectives on everyday urbanisms with a macro-account of the power structures within which they are embedded.

Ananya Roy is currently Professor of Urban Planning and Social Welfare, holds the Meyer and Renee Luskin Chair in Inequality and Democracy and directs the Institute on Inequality and Democracy at UCLA Luskin School of Public Affairs.

Academic biography and research focus

Raised in Kolkata, India, Roy pursued her university education in the United States. With a Bachelor's degree in Comparative Urban Studies from Mills College, she moved to UC Berkeley's Department of City and Regional Planning where she completed her Master's and then PhD in 1999. Immediately following, she started teaching in the Department and was tenured in 2006. In 2015 she took up her current position at UCLA.

While institutionally located in the US, Roy's research has predominantly focused on India. Her first monograph, *City Requiem, Calcutta: Gender and the Politics of Poverty* (2003a), is based on doctoral research in her native city, the renamed capital of West Bengal. The book explores 'the politics of an unmapped city' (2003a: 137) where – in the absence of master planning – land distribution and development is managed and negotiated in informal ways. The themes first introduced in *City Requiem* have guided much of Roy's work that has followed. For instance, *Urban Informality: Transnational Perspectives from the Middle East, Latin America, and South Asia* (2004), co-edited with Nezar AlSayyad, connects accounts of informality to state interventions and questions the ethics of urban development. In doing so, it lays the foundations for a series of critical interventions through which Roy has crucially influenced debates on these themes (2005, 2009b, 2011a). A second concern that Roy explores in *City Requiem* lies at the nexus of gender and poverty. Roy's work in Kolkata points to the 'double gendering' of urban life (2003a: 86), a term she introduces to point out that women not only carry the burden of wage-earning, but are also forced to secure household livelihoods through norms of domesticity that maintain gender hierarchies and privilege masculine patronage. Roy traces these themes through a feminist approach that deconstructs problematic categories and essentialisms, which she has further developed in many subsequent contributions. For instance, *Poverty Capital* (2010) – a critical account of international development industries – explores, among numerous other concerns, how micro-credit reifies unequal relations of gender and of poverty (2010: 226). *Poverty Capital* also explores a third theme that is already embedded in *City Requiem*, namely the global connectivity of the power relations that shape urban development. As Roy shows throughout the book, the poverty of Kolkata's periphery is dependent on family norms, political patronage and the uncertainty of access to land. But the vantage point of this perspective is not merely 'the borderland': Roy's frame of interrogation holds an account of 'the underdogs' or the poor in tension with wider scales of analysis, including the state, hegemonic economies and global non-state bodies such as international donors or the UN. This understanding of global relations is most explicitly developed in her latest book, *Worlding Cities: Asian Experiments and the Art of Being Global* (2011), which she co-edited with Aihwa Ong.

Throughout her scholarly engagement, Roy speaks to power. While some of her concerns – particularly her engagement in poverty politics – address practitioners or politicians, all of her work is guided by an attempt to foster a transformative scholarly praxis. Roy seeks to disrupt teleological notions of development, unsettle the inherited geographies of urban studies, and rethink the injustices of dominant planning regimes. Committed to scrutinizing her own positionality, her approach also offers frequent reflections on the complicity of academia in the making of urban development (2003a, 2003b). This tendency is most explicit in *Poverty Capital* (2010), where she introduces the 'double agent', a figure she creates to capture the entanglements of scholars and practitioners who may contest neoliberal development while they remain entwined in its production. In a university protest in 2010, Roy rehearsed this role. Deeply invested in university politics, she lent her voice to a fight against the restructuring of public education through rising tuition fees, privatization and austerity politics. One might be critical of this stance or wonder, as her colleague Michael Watts (2012: 540) does, whether the double agent is not 'a power-narcotic in the operations of hegemony'. But Roy remains hopeful. For her, this figure is a call to arms, an attempt to revive the political and translate (neoliberal) complicity into friction and contestation.

Key ideas

Roy's work frames urban development within the intricate relations of global power structures and their resulting inequalities. This attention to interdependence has offered much to existing debates around the themes of informality, the making of subject positions and the connectivity of global rule.

First, Roy has changed predominant understandings of how urban informality operates. Typically, scholars and policy makers link the idea of informality to urban housing, infrastructure or economies existing outside of official protocols, plans or laws. Yet for Roy, informality hardly constitutes a realm outside of institutional reach. Rather, it describes a city-building habitus that works through the deregulation of the state's very own apparatus. Following the publication of *Urban Informality* (2004), Roy (2009a, 2009b, 2009c, 2011a) has contributed numerous pivotal pieces that develop her approach. Rather than stressing the distinctiveness of informal dwelling or planning, Roy relates informality to the power relations that govern the politics of land and points to the ambiguities of state politics and to the flexibility of regulatory regimes. Thereby, she aims to show that the enactment of regulations is hardly neutral. Rather, as she notes, the formal–informal distinction appears to work as a strategic denomination and a powerful mechanism of control. For Roy, states use regulations as tools through which to carve out room for manoeuvre and control the possibilities through which the informal may or may not unfold. Thereby, as she notes, institutions employ 'extra-legal' contracts that allow them to flexibly breach, ignore or alter regulatory frames. Accordingly, the 'formal' planning of the state results, as she argues, from the constant illegitimate resetting of its supposedly fixed statutes (2009c). In her view, informality itself is managed in decentralized, privatized and strategic ways through social and political agency. For Roy informality constitutes an 'idiom of urbanization' (2009b: 76), 'a system of norms that governs the process of urban transformation itself' (2005: 148).

Second, Roy speaks to debates about the making of governable subjects in the production of urban development. A key idea in her thinking is that the everyday governance of space through social and political institutions works to construct representations of people and their position in the city. As systems of meaning produce subject positions – such as the domesticated women in Roy's account of Kolkata's urban fringe (2003a) – they also bear on policy and planning (2009d; AlSayyad and

Roy, 2006). In short, '[r]egimes of enunciation', are, as she writes, 'regimes of place and power' (Roy, 2006: 9). To clarify this idea, it is useful to emphasize that Roy draws strongly on postcolonial scholarship, a strand of critical theory that developed after the independence of formerly colonized countries and seeks to deconstruct perceptions, power relations and attitudes that are founded in colonial thinking. Based on this intellectual tradition, Roy attends not only to how powerful narratives marginalize urban subjects, she also demonstrates the social agency of the poor. However, Roy restrains from reading their struggles as processes of subversion (2009b: 84). For her, the politics of urban development resist simple classifications of subjection and resistance. Rather, as she notes, governance works to produce urban orders that constitute the subaltern simultaneously as disobedient and desiring, self-exploitative and disciplined (2009a: 827; 2009d: 168). Roy develops this position throughout her work. In her exploration of Kolkata, 'domestications' (2003a: 103) not only narrate gender, by which she means that her representation in discourse constructs a certain idea of the role of the women (2003a: 222), these imaginations also undergird the politics of poverty, as they ensure the compliance of poor households in scrupulous systems of governing. The idea that the formation of subject positions enables the workings of regimes of rule also animates *Poverty Capital*'s (2010) exploration of micro-finance, a central tool of development. Therein she links the ethicalization of millennial capitalism – the industry's attempt to not only democratize capital by helping the poor to gain access to loans, but also to guide this process through codes of ethics – to the construction of the modern global citizen who donates micro-credit.

Third, Roy's (2010, 2012a, 2012b) work demonstrates the interdependence of global rule. She advocates for an analytical approach that explores the global horizon of urbanization through the connectivity of processes across place (cf. **García Canclini**). This approach is based on the idea that context – despite local particularity, historical difference and the versatility and ambiguity of urban development trajectories – hardly constitutes a bounded locality, but needs to be positioned in relation to global regimes of rule. Roy demonstrates this idea by documenting interrelated processes that bind the local to wider geographies of power. For instance, *Poverty Capital* (2010) illustrates how circuits of money and expertise shape local poverty politics. Unlike *City Requiem*, *Poverty Capital* is no longer about the urban poor or the receivers of international loans, but about the managers of development and finance. In following the travels of all concerned with the production and mediation of poverty, including technical experts, scholars and first-world volunteers who mediate millennial development beyond the state, Roy is able to demonstrate a global mode of governing that builds on the interdependency of capital and authoritative knowledge. *Worlding Cities* (Roy and Ong, 2011) similarly points to forms of connectivity through the global aspirations of the rising megacities of Asia. In this account, Roy explores connectivity through the travelling of urban representations and the inter-referencing of global imaginaries that are intertwined in the production of global order.

Contributions to urban studies

Roy's theories and methods have contributed much to the burgeoning postcolonial turn towards a more global urban studies. In line with thinkers such as **Jennifer**

Robinson and **AbdouMaliq Simone**, her research is animated by the contention that the Euro-American academy has tended to produce theories that emanate from only a few cities in the Global North, and points to a geography of theoretical blind spots – places from which theories are rarely produced. However, Roy's central concern is not only the argument that much of urban theory has envisioned a pathway of moderniza-tion that sees the cities of the Global South as a 'planet of slums' (cf. **Mike Davis**), that is, at best, catching up with the 'West'. Instead, Roy has contributed a toolbox through which urban studies has begun to overcome such thinking and decentre urban theory. These techniques allow for transnational enquiry, or, as she puts it, for 'studying what goes on over here in terms of what goes on over there' (Roy, 2003b: 465). For instance, in *Worlding Cities* Roy and Aihwa Ong offer the notion of 'worlding' as an instrument through which to forge new lines of global enquiry and deconstruct denominations of core and periphery. Building on postcolonial theory, its focus on subaltern agency and the traces left by the 'colonial wound', 'worlding' points to the relationality of global metropolitanism. But in distinction to postcolonial accounts, 'worlding' seeks to high-light developments, formations and resistances that oppose or remain untouched by postcolonial development patterns (2011: 308).

Scholars have taken up this heuristic to respond to Roy's claim that the concep-tual apparatus used in urban studies is inadequate for capturing contemporary geographies of urbanization and the power relations through which they emerge. Roy's call for a transnational enquiry has not only inspired urban scholars to sketch new imaginaries of geography, but also to reinvent existing categories of knowl-edge. Alongside the expansion of her concepts into new empirical terrains, researchers have adopted her relational and connective thinking to expand concep-tual repertoires and redraw the geographies of knowledge, particularly across North–South divides.

These and other insights pave a promising route. The field of urban studies con-tinues to have much to learn from her research in order to meet what Roy (2003b: 466) calls 'the challenges of a globally configured world'. Roy's work provides a hopeful inspiration to tackle the openings and closures inherent in a global produc-tion of spaces. In the face of increasing inequality and domination, this engagement is vital.

Secondary sources and references

AlSayyad, N. and Roy, A. (2006) 'Medieval modernity: On citizenship and urbanism in a global era', *Space and Polity*, 10(1): 1–20.

Roy, A. (2001) 'A "public" muse: On planning convictions and feminist contentions', *Journal of Planning Education and Research*, 21(2): 109–126.

Roy, A. (2003b) 'Paradigms of propertied citizenship: Transnational techniques of analysis', *Urban Affairs Review*, 38(4): 463–491.

Roy, A. (2006) 'Praxis in the time of empire', *Planning Theory*, 5(1): 7–29.

Roy, A. (2009b) 'Why India cannot plan its cities: Informality, insurgence and the idiom of urban-ization', *Planning Theory*, 8(1): 76–87.

Roy, A. (2009c) 'Strangely familiar: Planning and the worlds of insurgence and informality', *Planning Theory*, 8(1): 7–11.

Roy, A. (2009d) 'Civic governmentality: The politics of inclusion in Beirut and Mumbai', *Antipode*, 41(1): 159–179.

Roy, A. (2010) *Poverty Capital: Microfinance and the Making of Development*. New York: Routledge.

Roy, A. (2011b) 'Urbanisms, worlding practices and the theory of planning', *Planning Theory*, 10(1): 6–15.

Roy, A. (2012a) 'Ethical subjects: Market rule in an age of poverty', *Public Culture*, 24(1): 105–108.

Roy, A. (2012b) 'Subjects of risk: Technologies of gender in the making of millennial modernity', *Public Culture*, 24(166): 131–155.

Roy, A. and AlSayyad, N. (eds) (2004) *Urban Informality: Transnational Perspectives from the Middle East, Latin America, and South Asia*. Lanham, MD: Lexington Books.

Watts, M. (2012) 'Modular development, diminutive capitalists and the financialization of capitalism', *Antipode*, 44(2): 535–541.

31   Saskia Sassen

Michele Acuto, University College London

Key urban writings

Sassen, S. (1991; 2nd edn 2001) *The Global City: New York, London, Tokyo*. Princeton, NJ: Princeton University Press.

Sassen, S. (1994; 4th edn 2012) *Cities in a World Economy*. Thousand Oaks, CA: Pine Forge Press and Sage.

Sassen, S. (1996) 'Whose city is it? Globalization and the formation of new claims', *Public Culture*, 8(2): 205–223.

Sassen, S. (2011) 'The global street: Making the political', *Globalizations*, 8(5): 573–579.

Introduction

Saskia Sassen is best known in urban studies for her work on the encounter of the global and the urban, famously captured by the concept of the 'global city' (1991). Yet Sassen's work is of far broader remit. Certainly her scholarship is deeply entrenched in the relation between the city (in an economic and social sense) and the processes of globalization as a defining juncture of our time. However, Sassen's core contribution to urban studies, and social theory more in general, is a studious pursuit of creative disruption in theorizing. From migration, to sovereignty and the political economy of globalization, Sassen has for the past few decades been busy acting, by her own admission, as an 'ignorant carpenter' pulling apart and reconstructing major categories and key theoretical concepts in 'a time of unstable meanings' (Ong and Sassen, 2014: 19). Sassen's popularity extends well beyond academia. The global city concept rapidly proliferated among urban practitioners throughout the 1990s and 2000s. Nonetheless, Sassen's bibliography is now counting in the hundreds and with translations in over 15 languages, and is a constellation of musings on the dynamics of globalization, transnational flows and urban transformations. Connecting these themes, Sassen's work is ultimately a call for empirical engagement 'on the ground' as continuous conceptual (r)evolution and self-examination; a feature that is a key lesson for present generations of urban theorists far beyond the limits of the global city.

Saskia Sassen is Lynd Professor of Sociology and co-Chair of the Committee on Global Thought at Columbia University, and Centennial Visiting Professor of Political Economy at the London School of Economics.

Academic biography and research focus

Sassen's scholarship surpasses a limited focus on the urban, possibly best fitting the broader category of 'social theorist'. Her globetrotting background is a key contributor to her scholarly focus on globalization, international flows and cities. Polyglot, Sassen was mostly raised in Buenos Aires, Argentina, by Dutch parents. She was originally educated in the mid-1960s in politics and philosophy at the universities of Buenos Aires, Rome (Italy) and Poitiers (France). Her doctoral alma mater is the University of Notre Dame, Indiana (United States), where she graduated in 1974 with a thesis focused on how non-dominant ethnic populations like African Americans and Chicanos where being integrated (or not) as a component of the United States' political economy.

Sassen continued her academic career with posts as postdoctoral fellow at Harvard and then New York University. Her scholarly recognition blossomed in those years thanks to a prolific production record that extended her concern with migration and labour issues – eventually becoming a fully-fledged *Sociology of Globalization* (Sassen, 2007) encompassing issues of citizenship, global financial markets and (de)territorializaton. In these years Sassen's preoccupation was with the processes of growth at the core in advanced market economies where she developed an interest in the 'peripheralization' of labour relations.

At Harvard, Sassen worked with international theorists Joseph Nye, Raymond Vernon and Samuel Huntington as part of a larger project on transnationalism. Here Sassen's urban engagement became more and more explicit (Sassen, 1988). The city emerged as a key strategic site for the kind of global flows and restructuring at the heart of Sassen's concern. Not surprisingly, and after flirting with Los Angeles (in a visiting professorship at UCLA), it is New York that takes the lion's share of Sassen's fieldwork and enquiry (Sassen-Koob, 1986). In the Big Apple, and successively with work in Tokyo and London, Sassen lays the groundwork for her seminal work on globalization and cities. During this period Sassen also moved to the University of Chicago, where she was appointed as Ralph Lewis Professor of Sociology and where she first published her landmark book *The Global City* (1991).

If *The Global City* represents perhaps the most visible legacy of Sassen's urban thinking, a series of other publications in the first decade of the 2000s are equally important for urban studies but tend to be overshadowed by the catchy nature of the global city construct. In 1994, for instance, Sassen published the first edition (now in its fourth) of *Cities in a World Economy*, which took the theorization of global cities one scale 'up' into a global economy viewpoint, further expanding on how these locales have emerged as new social formations within flows of money, information and people.

At the turn of the millennium, while revising *The Global City* for a second edition (2001), Sassen moved to Columbia University as Lynd Professor of Sociology and co-Chair of the Committee on Global Thought. At the same time she began a visiting professorship at the London School of Economics. In these years Sassen turned her attention even more explicitly to charting a political sociology of globalization. This developed especially in relation to sovereignty and the state, another master category Sassen seeks to disentangle, resulting in the now popular *Territory, Authority, Rights* (Sassen, 2006). Sassen's focus on the new organizing logics of 'de-nationalization' continues with an eye at the restructuring of the global economy articulated in her recent *Expulsions* (Sassen, 2014a), which considers more specifically the processes by which people, enterprises and even places are being expelled from the core socio-economic order of our time. Yet the city has not disappeared from Sassen's work. Rather, thanks to Sassen's engagement in a number of popular urban initiatives and policy fora, it remains a central context for Sassen's theorization of transnational processes and a key frontier for the formation of a new global order.

Key ideas

If in the case of her husband **Richard Sennett** some might argue that his 'urban writing is animated by a single basic idea', with Sassen we are essentially confronted by a kaleidoscope of social-political-economic observations in continuing evolution. By her own admission Sassen is a 'bit of nomad' in social theory, pitching temporary theoretical tents across geography, urban studies, international theory or sociology. The city is nearly always there amid socio-economic, political and technological considerations, with occasional excursions into conflict and feminist writing; but at closer inspection it is nearly impossible to brand Sassen with one urban concept. The global city is for Sassen a strategic platform for broader political-economic considerations.

Sassen conceived her take on this theme in the 1990s to define those strategic sites of production of global control capacities that constitute the hinges of our society. For her, global cities are emerging as core articulators 'not only for global capital, but also for the transnationalization of labour and the formation of trans-local communities and identities' (2005: 28). In contrast with understandings of power as dislocated and decentralized through networks, Sassen illustrated how control over transnational processes is concentrated by those who take advantage of command-and-control functions embedded in specific central places, and how these processes recast the socio-political texture of the contemporary metropolis. This results in a complex of arguments based not only on the concept of the 'global' (always adjective, never a reified noun for Sassen) but also on the socio-economic and spatial redefinition of the city.

Critically, for Sassen, globalizing cities are perhaps the most vulnerable to class divergences and social polarizations because their economic structure is progressively becoming dominated by financial, business and producer services, along with increasing demand for low-skilled jobs readily available through immigration. *The Global City* is a statement on the relevance of place in a context of fast cross-border transnational flows, but also a further refinement of Sassen's concerns for the peripheralization of labour relations in these cores of the world economy. This is a consideration that, along with the 'dual city' (Mollenkopf and Castells, 1991) and 'splintering urbanism' (Graham and Marvin, 2001), sets out much of the contemporary thinking on inequality 'at the core' of contemporary global cities. However, Sassen's global city scholarship has very often been prey to simplification. The global city has partly become a focus of rankings and economic internationalization concerns, while its core argument is in fact, as Sassen puts it, about our capacity to detect the global 'as it is filtered through the specifics of a place, its institutional orders, and its socio-spatial fragmentations' (2006: x). Rather than a simple statement on global financial centres, Sassen's global city is a complex of assumptions about how particular urban spaces represent a 'nexus for new politico-economic alignments' (2007: 122).

A key theme in Sassen discussion of these reconfigurations is the concept of 'assemblage' (Ong and Sassen, 2014). As Sassen uses it, thinking of city, state or sovereignty as assemblages is as an empirical orientation with which to unpick the dynamics of how the modern world order emerged. Especially in her more recent work since 2006, Sassen relies on this logic to chart how global assemblages are being constructed from the very components that comprised the modern world, as those components are reoriented to different projects beyond the nation-state (2006), and across the redefinition of contemporary political-economic orders (2014a). The global city, as much as 'territoriality', are then for Sassen constructs to be disentangled rather than categories to be theorized systematically and replicated scrupulously. By Sassen's own admission, her own enquiry has 'never [been] about the city *qua* city: it's an analytic construct – a light to shine on the global' (Sassen, 2014b: 468). The city becomes a medium, albeit a critical one, for a broader transnational exploration. Sassen's concern then is to develop conceptual architectures that allow us to detect what we might think of as counter-geographies of globalization, and what we might consider as transnational processes, without losing sight of their embodiment in place (Acuto, 2013; Sassen, 2014a).

Today, while captured by the fame of the global city and absorbed in a complex rethinking of the sovereign state as it is transformed by new political-economic dynamics, Sassen's focus has in fact returned to the terrain of the city. Inspired by the uprisings of the Middle East and North African region, Sassen's has become an alternate, more grounded, take on the global city – that of the 'global street' (Sassen, 2011). The street of the global city, or the global street, is for Sassen a space where new forms of the social and the political can be recast and the transnational turbulence of our time expressed. Powerlessness, she argues unpacking the geopolitics of the street, has become a complex (urban) condition beyond categories of empowerment. Where Sassen's work is headed is now towards what she calls 'systemic edges' (2014a), those points where political-economic conditions take on formats so extreme that they cannot be easily captured by the standard measures of governments and experts and become invisible, ungraspable, 'subterranean' to the dominant order – a consideration ripe for urban engagement.

This shift exemplifies an important concern for any urban researcher seeking to connect embedded enquiry with its broader global relevance. As Sassen remarks, the key methodological standpoint for *The Global City* was to begin with the global political economy processes, rather than with the urban, and ask herself: 'do these flows and markets ever *hit the ground*, so to speak, and if so where do they hit?' (Sassen, 2014b: 468, emphasis added). The global street and the systemic edge, while still in embryonic form in comparison to the two decades of development of the idea of the global city, are an apt successor to the preoccupations of the 1990s: they push the social theorist to remain wary of the turbulence of global transformations and transnational orders, but lose no sight of the entrenchment of these processes in the everyday materiality of urban life. In this sense, the city has remained throughout Sassen's career as a strategic site for new politics and a fundamental territory where the political-economic bases of our time, as with sovereignty and citizenship, are recast, contested and transnationalized, but also grounded and expressed physically between walls and asphalt.

Contributions to urban studies

Undisputedly, Sassen has popularized urban research beyond the confines of the academe. A regular guest speaker and media commentator, Sassen's popularity in urban studies has flourished in the past decade. Her popularity, and propensity for eagerly providing commentary on pressing international issues should not detract from richer theoretical underpinnings. Two of Sassen's foci are of particular importance to the newer generations of urban theorists: the conceptual wariness of master categories and the complex transnational embeddedness of the global city.

In the shadow of C. Wright Mills, much of Sassen's scholarship is characterized by a continuous problematization of 'master categories' (Sassen, 2008) like the state or the city. As such Sassen's writing is at the same time unsettling, hard to fully grasp and highly intertwined with a wide array of complex global questions, but yet provocative and in constant change. Not surprisingly her urban thoughts have appeared in varying editions of her key texts, from *The Global City* to *Cities in a World Economy*, but also in numerous iterations of journal articles, commentaries and op-eds. At the heart of this ever-mobile gaze is Sassen's attempt to generate new questions for research to unveil what might be excluded by dominant narratives.

Sassen's concern on this front is that of embedding urban processes and the governance of cities in a world economy. Within this large-scale consideration, Sassen points at the centrality of place, an *urban* place in particular. In this sense, Sassen has been one of the forebears of what we might consider the second generation of global city scholars, after the original enquiries of Peter Hall (1966) and Peter Taylor (1982), into a political-economy of the city as central place of globalization. This remains an important consideration, and precursor to the 'ordinary' and 'planetary urbanization' moves made respectively by **Jennifer Robinson** and **Neil Brenner**. Sassen then pushes us beyond case study-based urbanism without rejecting the case itself, for the contemporary urban thinking needs not be overwhelmed by the complexity of global transformations but also not to turn a myopic eye to the global while seeking comfort in the closeness of the specific case study (cf. **Janet Abu-Lughod**). A critical contribution of this scholarship is then that of setting the urban, and the city in particular, in a global context. The lesson here is therefore one of setting the urban in context, not too far away from the 'planetary' and scalar orientation of Brenner or the world system concerns of Taylor, but also well wary of the micro-social interactions at the heart of cities, as in **Mariana Valverde** and **AbdouMaliq Simone**.

Ultimately, then, Sassen's most insightful contributions for urban theory, as with the polarized nature of the global city, runs the risk to be vastly overlooked. For Sassen the investigation of the urban and the city in particular is about the intersection of globalized, denationalized, processes and territorializing, place-based, realities. It is this concern for what is quite literally 'hitting the ground' in cities (and beyond) that holds the greatest potential to inspire an outward-looking urban scholarship wary of the place of the city in its wider socio-economic dynamics.

Secondary sources and references

Acuto, M. (2013) *Global Cities, Governance and Diplomacy: The Urban Link*. Abingdon: Routledge.

Brenner, N. and Keil, R. (eds) (2006) *The Global Cities Reader*. Abingdon: Routledge.

Graham, S. and Marvin, S. (2001) *Splintering Urbanism*. Abingdon: Routledge.

Hall, P.G. (1966*) The World Cities*. London: Weidenfeld and Nicolson.

Mollenkopf, J.H. and Castells, M. (eds) (1991) *Dual City: Restructuring New York*. New York: Russell Sage Foundation.

Ong, A. and Sassen, S. (2014) 'The carpenter and the bricoleur', in M. Acuto and S. Curtis (eds) *Reassembling International Theory: Assemblage Thinking and International Relations*. Basingstoke: Palgrave Macmillan.

Sassen, S. (1988) *The Mobility of Capital and Labor*. New York: Oxford University Press.

Sassen, S. (2005) 'The global city: Introducing a concept', *Brown Journal of World Affairs*, 11(2): 27–43.

Sassen, S. (2006) *Territory, Authority, Rights: From Medieval to Global Assemblages*. Princeton, NJ: Princeton University Press.

Sassen, S. (2007) *A Sociology of Globalization*. New York: W.W. Norton.

Sassen, S. (2008) 'Unsettling master categories: Notes on studying the global in C.W. Mills' footsteps', *International Journal of Politics, Culture, and Society*, 20(1): 69–83.

Sassen, S. (2014a) *Expulsions: Brutality and Complexity in the Global Economy*. Cambridge, MA: Harvard University Press.

Sassen, S. (2014b) 'Saskia Sassen interview with M. Steger and P. James', *Globalizations*, 11(4): 461–472.

Sassen-Koob, S. (1986) 'New York City: Economic restructuring and immigration', *Development and Change*, 17(1): 85–119.

Taylor, P.J. (1982) 'A materialist framework for political geography', *Transactions of the Institute of British Geographers*, 7(1): 15–34.

32   Richard Sennett

Alan Latham, University College London

Key urban writings

Sennett, R. (1970a) *The Uses of Disorder: Personal Identity and City Life*. New York: Alfred
A. Knopf.

Sennett, R. (1977) *The Fall of Public Man*. New York: Alfred A. Knopf.

Sennett, R. (1990) *The Conscience of the Eye: The Design and Social Life of Cities*. London:
Faber and Faber.

Sennett, R. (1994) *Flesh and Stone: The Body and the City in Western Civilization*. London:
Faber and Faber.

Sennett, R. (2008) *The Craftsman*. New Haven, CT: Yale University Press.

Introduction

Richard Sennett is an American historian, sociologist and novelist. His work has two
principal themes: the relationship between public and private identity in cities, and the
dynamics of work and identity formation within contemporary North American and
European economies. It is the first of these themes that is most central to Sennett's
contribution to contemporary urban thought. His writing is committed to the idea that
the design and architecture of cities, along with the rituals of their use, play a central
role in the formation of a society's social and political culture. In a series of books
spanning four decades Sennett has explored the failure of contemporary urban environments to generate spaces where different people can mix and interact as fellow
citizens. Rather than fostering connection and complexity, contemporary cities are
largely characterized by the desire to create simplified, socially homogeneous, coherent
places. Sennett's work aims to uncover the historical origins of this will to homogeneity.
In seeking out these historical antecedents Sennett also provides a reconsideration and
reanimation of older ways of thinking about and dwelling within cities, bringing them
into dialogue with contemporary urban thought. Sennett's writing is characterized by
a mix of historical case study, philosophical reflection, ethnographic detail and the
autobiographic that is as distinctive as it is non-replicable.

Sennett is Professor of History and Sociology at New York University and Professor of Sociology at the London School of Economics. He is married to the sociologist Saskia Sassen.

Academic biography and research focus

Born in 1943 to left-wing political activist parents, Sennett spent the early years of his life in Chicago's notorious Cabrini Green public housing estate; an estate that was to become a byword in America for urban poverty and blight. A talented cellist, Sennett originally intended a career as a professional musician. An injury to his wrist in his early twenties forced him to refocus his talents onto intellectual life. A Bachelor's degree from the University of Chicago was followed in 1969 by a PhD from Harvard University under the supervision of the sociologist David Riesman. At Chicago and Harvard, Sennett was mentored by a number of prominent faculty who had a lasting influence on his thought. Notably, the philosopher Hannah Arendt prompted Sennett to think about the relationship between work, politics and self-identity, and the psychoanalyst Erik Erikson offered a conceptual frame for Sennett to think through how selves evolve.

Sennett's first book, *Families Against the City: Middle Class Homes of Industrial Chicago, 1872–90* (1970b), explored the attitudes of middle-class Chicago residents to the wider social changes occurring in their city during the 19th century.[1] The book argued that the middle classes were withdrawing from public urban life in favour of the warmth and emotional intimacy of private domestic life. This historical argument was to be central to the themes developed in the two subsequent books that launched Sennett as a public intellectual: *The Uses of Disorder: Personal Identity and City Life* (1970a) and *The Fall of Public Man* (1977). Both books are inspiring, at times infuriatingly intuitive, mediations on the dangers of an excessive focus on the individual self in social and political life. And both – along with a book co-written with Jonathan Cobb, *The Hidden Injuries of Class* (1972), that Sennett sandwiched between them – were animated by a critique of the New Left thinking that had swept through America's social activist circles in the 1960s. Where New Left thought was explicitly anti-authoritarian, sceptical of discipline and tradition, committed to community activism, and celebrated the search for self-discovery, Sennett's writing highlighted the importance of ritual, artifice, discipline and justifiable authority to the development of progressive politics. This critique reached its apotheosis in *Authority* (1980), an exploration of the need for legitimate authority in social and political life.

Authority had been intended as the first volume in a series of 'four related essays on the emotional bonds of modern society' (Sennett, 1980: 3). The other three were to be on solitude, fraternity and ritual. Just after announcing this project Sennett was to abandon it to write a series of novels: *The Frog Who Croaked* (1982), *An Evening of Brahms* (1984) and *Palais Royale* (1986). In the mid-1970s Sennett had, with the novelist Edmund White, co-founded The New York Institute for the Humanities. Bringing together artists, novelists, poets, historians and philosophers, the Institute was a bold attempt to reinvent the humanities as a vital, pluralistic, future-facing enterprise in energetic dialogue with the public life of the city that housed it. As such, Sennett's turn to fiction was less an abandonment of his previous intellectual concerns and more an attempt to readdress the issues raised in *The Uses of Disorder*, *The Fall of Public Man* and *Authority* through a different medium. Indeed, while not producing the quartet of books on emotional bonds promised in the introduction to *Authority*, the two non-fiction books that followed his foray as a novelist loosely followed the publication plan he had set out earlier. *The Conscience of the Eye* (1990) picked up key themes developed in *Fall* but focused more intensely on the role contemporary architecture and urban design had come to play in generating a sense of corporeal disengagement and solitude in urban environments. *Flesh and Stone* (1994) in contrast reached back as far as ancient Athens to explore the different rituals, beliefs and architectures through which Western civilization has organized the experience of bodily sensations in urban life.

The past two decades have seen Sennett's attention shift to the changing experience of work and identity formation within the contemporary North American and European economies. Reaching back to concerns first explored in *The Hidden Injuries of Class*, in a trilogy of books – *The Corrosion of Character* (1998), *Respect in a World of Inequality* (2003) and *The Culture of the New Capitalism* (2005) – Sennett has explored what it means to forge (or fail to forge) a career in an economy where job security is increasingly precarious. Most recently, Sennett has embarked on a further trilogy focused around the theme of man as Maker, as *Homo Faber*. *The Craftsman* (2008) examines the nature of skill and craftsmanship, *Together: The Rituals, Pleasures and Politics of Cooperation* (2012) explores the idea of cooperation. The final volume, provisionally titled *Open City*, will focus on the arts of city building. In between writing the *Homo Faber* trilogy Sennett has also found time to publish a short reflection on the foreigner in urban life. Appropriately enough this is entitled *The Foreigner* (2011).

Key ideas

Sennett's urban writing is animated by a single basic idea: that the city is the central place where social difference is encountered. As such, cities are the primary places where people are confronted with how to deal with the vast diversity of beliefs, abilities, wealth and personal histories that exist across contemporary societies. For Sennett this confrontation presents a political and ethical question. Politically this difference prods us to ask, in what ways should society recognize and acknowledge that difference? Ethically the presence of social difference forces us to question how we should respond to the presence of this otherness. How should we react to the experience of others, their suffering as well as their successes?

For Sennett, developing the appropriate relationship between public and private identities is key to addressing these questions, in everyday as a well as political life. In part this centres on individuals' ability to balance the distances and anonymity of public life with the intimacies of the private. This of course raises the questions what does it mean to 'be in public' or 'act in public' and what relationship does that have with the private? Building on Erik Erikson's (1950) theory of self-formation, *The Uses of Disorder* developed a largely psychological account of the self's capacity to act with autonomy, equating public-ness with self-autonomy, and arguing that the tightly planned landscapes of American cities thwarted this development. *The Fall of Public Man* (1977) historicized this psychological account. Rather than seeing the formation of self as historically invariable, it offered a genealogy of the modern inwardly oriented American self.

Central to this account was the overturning of the public culture of the 18th-century *ancien régime*. In Sennett's telling, the emergent bourgeoisie in cities such as London and Paris dealt with the challenges of the anonymity, disorder and opacity of early-modern urban life through the creation of a vital public domain; a domain independent of royal and aristocratic patronage. Echoing Jürgen Habermas's (1989 [1962]) history of the public sphere, *Fall* describes how urban dwellers fashioned a series of rituals and behaviours that allowed them to interact reliably with the strangers with whom they were surrounded. These rituals and the institutions that came to support them such as the theatre, coffee house and street generated a 'public geography' that literally realized the city as public (Sennett, 1977: 19). The 19th and 20th centuries saw an erosion of these arts of public interaction as ideas of the boundaries between the self and one's private life shifted. This is partly the result of an increasing valorization of individual personality. But Sennett also relates this erosion to the rise of styles of mass spectatorship that replace the boisterous crowds of the *ancien régime* with more passive audiences, and a gradual turn inwards away from the ambiguities of public life towards the solace of the domestic. These were trends intimately intertwined with the emergence of a market-based industrial consumer society. And by the mid-20th century they were to lead to the emergence of a narcissistic society obsessed with personal intimacy that no longer recognized the boundaries between public and private life. This is the fall of public man of the title. And it is a fall simultaneously of the potentialities of urban life; a fall which generates cities full of 'dead public space' (Sennett, 1977: 12) and devoid of a properly publicly oriented political culture.

The idea developed in *Fall* is that a certain kind of ritualized impersonality is necessary for public life to unfold and that this unfolding requires specific spaces where this encounter might happen. This idea weaves through all Sennett's subsequent writing. We have already seen what that meant politically. Books like *The Conscience of the Eye*, *Flesh and Stone* and *Respect* pay much more attention to what it means ethically. *Conscience* and *Flesh* both focus on the way architectural forms and urban design work together with the bodies that inhabit them – whether that be individual bodies or those of a crowd – to engage the body's senses. Both also develop the argument put forward in *Fall* that contemporary public space has become in some sense 'dead', that it no longer engages the body in ways earlier urban environments did. Urban space has come to be defined by a 'tactile sterility', a 'sensory deprivation' that generates a sense of neutrality, a sense of indifference (Sennett, 1994: 15). And both books trace out a history of this numbness. Part of the originality of Sennett's argument is simply that the body has a history, and following on from the work of first Max Weber and then Michel Foucault that this history is not part of straightforward story of a power or authority imposed from above. But what is also original in Sennett's writing is the importance of thinking about the limits of design, of narrative, of coherence, of community, indeed of encounter; that very thing that Sennett craves for most in the contemporary city.

The arguments that Sennett has developed do not lend themselves to simple solutions. They present as much a series of warnings and in-depth mediations about the complexities and ambiguities of social and political life in cities as they do any simple set of policy prescriptions. In his more recent books, however, he has moved towards unfolding his arguments through a closer attention to both the contemporary and the ethnographic. *Respect* finds Sennett using his childhood in the social housing of Cabrini Green public housing estate in Chicago to think about how mutuality can be negotiated across divisions of class and talent. While *The Craftsman* and *Together* – drawing on the dialogically oriented ethnographic approach used in his study of contemporary American office workers *The Corrosion of Character* – set up extended dialogues around the contemporary meanings of craft and cooperation with the aim of suggesting novel ways of reinventing a progressive politics. Again, rather than offering solutions, these books work to provide the reader with a set of tools for thinking through what craftsmanship or cooperation might involve in the contemporary world.

Contributions to urban studies

Sennett is a peripatetic thinker. His writing does not aim to produce recognizable theory. Instead, Sennett's writing worries away again and again at a range of intercon-nected concerns – public-ness, identity, the body, arousal and indifference, ritual, community and so forth – each time approaching them from a slightly different van-tage. The point of this approach is not to seek resolutions or stable definitions. Rather it is to work at generating productive ways of thinking through and with the dilem-mas and paradoxes thrown up by these concerns. Sennett himself describes his writing as 'a report on the act of thinking' (in Benn, 2001). This is a style of theory that owes a great deal to the American philosophical tradition of pragmatism. A tradition that is sceptical of overly abstract theories and ideas, seeking instead to 'engage with ordi-nary, plural, constructive human activities' (Sennett, 2008: 287). This has put him slightly to the side of critical urban studies. Nonetheless, this framing of the problem of the city as a site of public interaction has been enormously influential. His argu-ments have informed the work of a wide range of urban planners and designers working to reanimate the public life of cities across Europe and North America. And while urban theorists such as **Ash Amin** and **AbdouMaliq Simone** have been seeking to reframe notions of urban public-ness through focusing more explicitly on the diverse materialities of cities, these theories do not so much supersede Sennett's argu-ments as extend and complement them.

Secondary sources and references

Benn, M. (2001) 'Inner-city scholar', *The Guardian*, 3 February.

Erikson, E. (1950) *Childhood and Society*. New York: W.W. Norton.

Habermas, J. (1989 [1962]) *The Structural Transformation of the Public Sphere: An Inquiry into a Category of Bourgeois Society*. Cambridge, MA: MIT Press.

Sennett, R. (1969) *Classic Essays on the Culture of Cities*. New York: Prentice Hall.

Sennett, R. (1970b) *Families Against the City: Middle Class Homes of Industrial Chicago, 1872–90*. Cambridge, MA: University of Harvard Press.

Sennett, R. (1980) *Authority*. New York: Alfred A. Knopf.

Sennett, R. (1998) *The Corrosion of Character: The Personal Consequences of Work in the New Capitalism*. New York: Alfred A. Knopf.

Sennett, R. (2003) *Respect in a World of Inequality*. New York: Alfred A. Knopf.

Sennett, R. (2005) *The Culture of the New Capitalism*. New Haven, CT: Yale University Press.

Sennett, R. (2011) *The Foreigner: Two Essays on Exile*. London: Notting Hill Editions.

Sennett, R. (2012) *Together: The Rituals, Pleasures and Politics of Cooperation*. New Haven, CT: Yale University Press.

Sennett, R. and Cobb, J. (1972) *The Hidden Injuries of Class*. New York: Alfred A. Knopf.

Thernstrom, S. and Sennett, R. (1969) *Nineteenth-century Cities: Essays in the New Urban History*. Princeton, NJ: Yale University Press.

Turner, J. (2012) 'Superficially pally', *London Review of Books*, 34(6): 29–31.

Note

1.   Sennett also co-edited two essay collections, *The Nineteenth Century City* (1969) and *Classic Essays on the Culture of Cities* (1969).

Karen C. Seto

Michail Fragkias, Boise State University

Key urban writings

Seto, K.C. and Kaufmann, R.K. (2003) 'Modeling the drivers of urban land use change in the Pearl River Delta, China: Integrating remote sensing with socioeconomic data', *Land Economics*, 79(1): 106–121.

Seto, K.C. and Fragkias, M. (2005) 'Quantifying spatiotemporal patterns of urban land-use change in four cities of China with time series landscape metrics', *Landscape Ecology*, 20(7): 871–888.

Seto, K.C., Sánchez-Rodríguez, R. and Fragkias, M. (2010) 'The new geography of contemporary urbanization and the environment', *Annual Review of Environment and Resources*, 35: 167–194.

Seto, K.C., Güneralp, B. and Hutyra, L. (2012a) 'Global forecasts of urban expansion to 2030 and direct impacts on biodiversity and carbon pools', *Proceedings of the National Academy of Sciences of the United States of America*, 109(40): 16083–16088.

Seto, K.C., Reenberg, A., Boone, C.G., Fragkias, M., Haase, D., Langanke, T., Marcotullio, P., Munroe, D.K., Olah, B. and Simon, D. (2012b) 'Urban land teleconnections and sustainability', *Proceedings of the National Academy of Sciences of the United States of America*, 109(20): 7687–7692.

Introduction

Karen Seto's research has advanced the understanding of how urbanization contributes to global environmental change. Her work is notable for the use of Earth observation data and remote sensing techniques to understand and document urbanization, especially urban land use and its spatial structure. This has involved measuring and monitoring urban land use and change, understanding the drivers behind urban expansion, and developing forecasts of urban growth patterns. Bridging the social and natural sciences, her work also assesses the environmental consequences of urbanization by developing new conceptual frameworks for urban teleconnections – zones of influence beyond the immediate urban surroundings – and developing novel remote sensing methods to characterize urbanization.

Seto is Professor of Geography and Urbanization Science at the Yale School of Forestry and Environmental Studies at Yale University. She was one of two Coordinating Lead Authors for the new urban chapter of the Fifth Assessment Report of the Intergovernmental Panel on Climate Change (IPCC AR5), and she served as a Coordinating Lead Author and on the Editorial Team for the United Nations Convention on Biological Diversity (CBD), *Cities and Biodiversity Outlook*.

Academic biography and research focus

Seto was born in Hong Kong but her family immigrated to the US when she was five. After earning a Bachelor's degree from the University of California at Santa Barbara, she spent one year traveling primarily through Central America by bus and on foot. The experience made a lasting impression on her, consolidating an interest in the relationships between humans and their environments, one that she had developed traveling internationally as a child. Seto's MA and PhD were from Boston University, where she studied under two prominent scholars: Curtis Woodcock, a remote sensing scientist and a long-time member of the NASA Landsat Science Team, and Robert Kaufmann, an ecological economist and energy expert. Her doctoral research combined satellite remote sensing data, fieldwork, and time series econometrics models to analyze urban land-use change. The result was a groundbreaking study of the drivers of urban expansion in China. Seto documented the loss of agricultural land due to urban land-use change. This revealed the magnitude and rate of urban expansion in China (cf. **Fulong Wu**). She demonstrated that the official estimates of agricultural land loss in China did not match those measured through satellite data (Seto et al., 2000). This work opened up the use of satellite data and especially integration with socio-economic data to study patterns of urban land use and urbanization.

Seto then expanded her geographic focus beyond south China to include Vietnam, India, and ultimately the whole of China. By undertaking multiple place-based case studies, she has been able to identify common themes and key differences in urban expansion across the world. Her research shows that despite differences in institutions, governance, and histories, the spatial patterns of urban land-use change are remarkably similar across many countries around the world.

Her work has come to be defined by three broad themes. First is a concern with developing rigorous techniques for measuring and monitoring how urbanization is changing the Earth's surface. Imaging of Earth done by NASA's Landsat satellites over the past four decades has transformed how urban change is studied. Seto's research has developed new algorithms to quantify urban expansion at local and global scales. Her collaborators and students have drawn on innovative methods ranging from time series econometrics (Kaufmann and Seto, 2001) and geostatistics (Boucher et al., 2006) to artificial neural networks (Seto and Liu, 2003; Liu et al., 2004), and logit models (Seto and Kaufmann, 2003).

Second, Seto's work has focused on characterizing different trajectories of land-use change. Her work in this area is heavily influenced by her training in time series and spatial data analysis. The description of landscape mosaics and patterns has a long tradition in ecological studies where habitat fragmentation, landscape heterogeneity, and the distribution of landscape disturbance are important for understanding ecological processes. Seto has integrated approaches from landscape ecology with satellite-based analyses to characterize changes in urban form and structure (Schneider et al., 2005; Seto and Fragkias, 2005).

Third, Seto has begun to undertake studies of worldwide urban expansion, connecting expansion to global environmental change. This research demonstrates that urban areas around the world are generally becoming less dense, with urban land cover expanding at rates faster than urban population growth. It also shows that economic growth is a dominant driver of urban land expansion in China, whereas population growth is more important in driving urban expansion in India (Seto et al., 2011). She has used these findings to further forecast urban land-use change and its impacts on biodiversity and terrestrial carbon stocks (Seto et al., 2012a). This research has been important in terms of the geographic scope and scale of the analysis, as well as the complexity of the models undertaken. Her recent studies complement and add to United Nations projections of global urban population change which do not provide intra-country variations of urban population distributions, the location of urban areas, or changes in urban land cover. Her studies provide a major advance in understanding how future urbanization will affect Earth system functioning. In recent years, Seto's work has focused increasingly on the links between urbanization and food systems.

Key ideas

One of the key contributions of Seto's work has been the use of remote sensing for urban studies. The conversion of Earth's land surface to urban uses is one of the most powerful, visible, and permanent anthropogenic changes on the planet, affecting the biosphere, atmosphere, oceans, and human wellbeing. Although urban areas take up between 1 and 3 per cent of the Earth's surface, urban form and structure at local and regional scales are major determinants of urban energy use and carbon emissions. The expansion of urban areas also affects habitat loss and fragmentation, biodiversity and urban climate. Historically, studies of urban land use relied on data such as maps, census or tax data, ground surveys, or aerial photography. Satellite remote sensing has revolutionized the process of monitoring and measuring urban land use, its spatial structure and dynamics. Earth observation data allow scholars to undertake multiple case studies across different spatial scales and political regimes in order to compare urban development patterns.

Urban expansion is most commonly described as a change in the absolute area of urban space, or in terms of the rate at which non-urban land is converted to urban uses. However, aggregate growth rates give limited information about the spatial patterns of urbanization or the underlying processes that shape urban areas. Seto combines time series satellite data with methods from landscape ecology to quantify and describe urban land-use patterns beyond total extent and cumulative growth rates. These methods have been used to quantify the spatial structure and form of urban areas: including compactness and fragmentation, grain size and urban pattern, urban form complexity, the spatial arrangement of land use and its mix, and the degree of linearity. These characterizations provide empirical and comparable measures of urban form beyond descriptive notions. The time series nature of her studies further contributes to understandings of urban morphology. What is novel about Seto's work in this regard is its use of raw, unprocessed satellite data. Because Seto develops custom remote sensing algorithms, she is able to extract multiple types of urban information from a single satellite image.

Planetary-scale changes in the Earth system – through the modification of oceans, land, atmosphere, and biotic systems – are referred to as global environmental change or global change. Since its inception in the early 1980s, this field of research has been dominated by biophysical studies of the climate system. Urbanization was considered a relatively unimportant component of global change, in part because urban areas make up a small portion of the global land area. The exclusion of urbanization from global change research was compounded by traditional views of urban environmental impacts as a local issue. Historically, studies of urban air and water pollution, waste management, air quality, and sanitation have focused on environmental hazards inside or around the city. A central theme of Seto's research is that urbanization affects the global environment. Aggregated globally, urbanization affects the functioning of the Earth system through modification of land cover, biogeochemistry, and biodiversity. Seto's research places urbanization as a central component of global change and not just a local or regional environmental issue (cf. **Matthew Gandy, Natalie Jeremijenko**).

Seto's work on global environmental change has extended beyond research and scholarship. She has been a proponent of bringing an urbanization focus to international science and policy debates. In 2004, she co-founded and subsequently chaired the Urbanization and Global Environmental Change (UGEC) project. This was an international science program incorporating a global network of scholars and practitioners with a key focus on bringing attention to the vulnerability and adaptive capacity of urban areas to climate change. Seto was also instrumental in advocating for and developing a new urban chapter in the Intergovernmental Panel on Climate Change Fifth Assessment Report. In prior IPCC assessment reports, the mitigation potential of cities was examined through individual sectors such as buildings, transport, and energy systems. The Fifth Assessment Report was the first time a chapter was dedicated to the mitigation potential of urban areas and spatial planning.

Framing urbanization as a global environmental issue has required new analytical frameworks and methods for urban scholarship. A core idea is that of urban land teleconnections, a conceptual framework that links urbanization with distant processes and places (Seto et al., 2012b). The key idea here is that urbanization needs to be analyzed for its social and environmental tradeoffs in faraway places. Thus it is a framework for exploring the consequences of urbanization at great distances from points of origin that would otherwise go unrecognized. The urban land teleconnections idea has driven new interpretations of the nature of urban sustainability over the past few years.

Seto has also argued for an 'urbanization science' (Solecki et al., 2013; cf. **Michael Batty, Edward Glaeser**). This science would focus on crucial features of urbanization processes: 'origins, development, organization, emergent properties and connections to other social and biophysical processes' (pp. 13–14). This is a framework that centrally positions urbanization in the study of natural–human systems, whether examining single urban places or systems of cities, and which follows from a belief that urbanization science needs to be grounded in empirical evidence. This approach complements similar work on 'the science of the city' by thinkers like **Michael Batty** (2008) and Luis

Bettencourt (2013), nonetheless it differs in several aspects. First, the framework examines how cities develop and what distinctive features emerge in terms of how they are linked to wider planetary processes. Thus, urbanization science captures fundamental components of global urban processes. Second, urbanization science aims to understand the interrelationships among various components of the urban system, including the natural ecosystems, human activities, and the built environment. In other words, how do the living and non-living systems and components within urban areas interact? Third, urbanization science seeks to understand and predict urbanization, including how and why urban systems change from a cross-scale perspective – from the smallest local change to global dimensions.

Contributions to urban studies

Seto has modernized the study of urbanization by applying new geographic data and tools to understand the global impacts of local urban processes. Her seminal urban remote sensing studies have illustrated the power of 'big data' and 'millions of pixels' to elucidate urban processes on the ground. Her research has brought urbanization to the attention of global change communities.

Seto calls herself an urban scientist, and utilizes systematic, comparative, and empirical approaches in her study of urbanization. Her writings emphasize that the subject of her research is the process of urbanization, using the term as a verb. Whereas traditionally urban studies has focused on the city, its environs, and activity within it, Seto's work has focused on the linkages between urbanization and other systems such as the biota, land, and atmosphere. She has promoted the importance of natural science perspectives and paradigms in the study of urbanization, providing new urban-centric frameworks for sustainability science. As such, her work has placed urbanization as an important component of other areas of inquiry such as biodiversity loss and climate change.

Finally, Seto is an expert in urbanization in China and India and has undertaken parallel studies in both countries – an area that has been neglected in the field of urban studies. Trained as an interdisciplinary scientist, she is interested in repeatable observations and testable hypotheses across different world regions. During her career, she has been able to contrast trends and explain processes at local and national levels in China and India and her work has motivated further research into comparative case studies.

Secondary sources and references[1]

Batty, M. (2008) 'The size, scale, and shape of cities', *Science*, 319: 769–771.

Bettencourt, L.M.A. (2013) 'The origins of scaling in cities', *Science*, 340(6139): 1438–1441.

Boucher, A., Seto, K.C. and Journél, A.G. (2006) 'A novel method for mapping land cover changes: Incorporating time and space with geostatistics', *IEEE Transactions on Geoscience and Remote Sensing*, 44(11): 3427–3435.

Kaufmann, R.K. and Seto, K.C. (2001) 'Change detection, accuracy, and bias in a sequential analysis of Landsat imagery in the Pearl River Delta, China: econometric techniques', *Agriculture, Ecosystems & Environment*, 85(1): 95–105.

Liu, W.G., Seto, K.C., Wu, E.Y., Gopal, S. and Woodcock, C.E. (2004) 'ART-MMAP: A neural network approach to sub-pixel classification', *IEEE Transactions on Geoscience and Remote Sensing*, 42(9): 1976–1983.

Schneider, A., Seto, K.C. and Webster, D. (2005) 'Urban growth in Chengdu, western China: Application of remote sensing to assess planning and policy outcomes', *Environment and Planning B*, 32(3): 323–345.

Seto, K. and Liu, W. (2003) 'Comparing ARTMAP neural network with Maximum-Likelihood classifier for detecting urban change', *Photogrammetric Engineering and Remote Sensing*, 69(9): 981–990.

Seto, K.C., Fragkias, M., Güneralp, B. and Reilly, M.K. (2011) 'A meta-analysis of global urban land expansion', *PLOS ONE*, 6(8): e23777.

Seto, K.C., Kaufmann, R.K. and Woodcock, C.E. (2000) 'Landsat reveals China's farmland reserves, but they're vanishing fast', *Nature*, 406(6792): 121.

Solecki, W.D., Seto, K.C. and Marcotullio, P. (2013) 'It's time for an urbanization science', *Environment*, 55(1): 12–17.

Zhang, Q. and Seto, K.C. (2011) 'Mapping urbanization dynamics at regional and global scales using multi-temporal DMSP/OLS nighttime light data', *Remote Sensing of Environment*, 115(9): 2320–2329.

Zhang, Q. and Seto, K.C. (2013) 'Can night-time light data identify typologies of urbanization? A global assessment of successes and failures', *Remote Sensing*, 5(7): 3476–3494.

Note

1. Seto follows the authoring convention in the natural sciences, where the senior author, if not listed first, is listed last.

34 AbdouMaliq Simone

Colin McFarlane, Durham University

Key urban writings

Simone, A. (2004a) *For the City Yet to Come: Changing African Life in Four Cities*. Durham, NC: Duke University Press.

Abouhani, A. and Simone, A. (eds) (2005) *Urban Africa: Changing Contours of Survival in the City*. Dakar: Council for the Development of Social Science Research in Africa/ London: Zed Books.

Simone, A. (2010a) *City Life from Jakarta to Dakar: Movements at the Crossroads*. London: Routledge.

Simone, A. (2014a) *Jakarta, Drawing the City Near*. Minneapolis: University of Minnesota Press.

Introduction

AbdouMaliq Simone's work has played a pioneering role in urban studies because of his unique focus on the making of urban life. Focused on cities of the Global South, his work explores how everyday forms of experience and opportunity emerge from the intersections of various social and economic networks and practices. Where most accounts of urban life in the Global South focus on formal processes of planning and civil society organizations, the vital contribution of Simone's work has been his elaboration on the often poorly understood role of networks and practices that are linked to but exceed those domains. This includes forms of collaboration, conflict, networking and practice through which people get by, adapt and pursue new opportunities. Through a committed ethnographic engagement with cities in Africa and Asia, Simone has carefully examined the multiple relations that constitute a range of ordinary urban spaces, including markets, informal associations, neighbourhood networks and the political life of migration. In the process, he has developed new conceptual trajectories that locate the making of urbanity not in predefined institutions but in the multiple streams of everyday life.

Simone is currently Research Professor at the Max Planck Institute for the Study of Religious and Ethnic Diversity, Germany. He is also a Visiting Professor in Sociology at Goldsmiths College (University of London) and at the African Centre for Cities (University of Cape Town), and is an associate of the Rujak Centre for Urban Studies in Jakarta.

Academic biography and research focus

Simone's research asks fundamental questions of urbanism and provides genuinely unique approaches and responses. These questions include: how might we understand how life is made for the majority of urbanites? What sorts of practices, networks and imaginaries do urbanites put to work and for what sorts of reasons? What does that mean for how we conceptualize cities and urbanism? On the face of it, his approach to these urban questions may seem familiar, in that he is concerned with close analysis of everyday life. But his combination of close ethnographic analysis, thick description of urban complexity and an impressive level of conceptual generation and experimentation presents a profound challenge to how we research, conceive and write urbanism.

In contrast to the mainstream idea that cities in the Global South are 'dysfunctional' or 'failing', Simone's work presented compelling, ethnographically immersive accounts of how life is actually made. In doing so, he has demonstrated the need to rethink or invent new concepts appropriate to life and politics as we find it.

For example, his wide-ranging book *For the City Yet to Come* (2004a) tackles the idea that African cities 'don't work' by showing how they are produced through makeshift relations that allow for services, goods, community provisions and economic opportunities to emerge. This theme was developed the following year in his co-edited collection, *Urban Africa* (2005), which demonstrated how in precarious circumstances ordinary people are able to carve out informal relations between one another and formal institutions that allow for life to continue. *City Life from Jakarta to Dakar* (2010a) was written more directly for undergraduate students, but again draws extensively on research fieldwork to show how urban life and politics are constituted through the different ways in which ordinary residents anticipate and intersect with one another. The shift in Simone's work beyond African urbanism continues forward into his (2014) book *Jakarta, Drawing the City Near*, which investigates how an urban majority – neither the poorest nor quite the middle class – copes with urban change in a city with an increasingly exclusive political economy. Here, residents work together through markets, mosques and community institutions but keep also their distance, use some social and economic networks while withdrawing from others and differently attempt to find ways of adapting the uncertainties and heterogeneities of life in the city.

This work has provided unique illustrations of how mundane possibilities emerge in people's lives, both through their own labours and networks, and through changing circumstances outwith their control (such as the changing political economies of the city, or new policy pronouncements that affect the operation of markets). The focus, consistently, is with the city that residents inherit – in often challenging and uncertain conditions – and attempt to remake. This has led to crucial contributions and challenges to how we make sense of the city and the theoretical lexicon we use to understand urban life.

Simone's work is influenced by a rich range of debates, including but not limited to those around African development and infrastructure as well as wider critical debate on urban life and politics, postcolonial accounts of urban culture and politics, Deleuzian thought and intellectual strands of 'new materialism'. These theoretical influences are immersed in and woven through rich ethnographic material in Simone's work, and levered into policy and practice. For example, in Jakarta and Phnom Penh, Simone has helped train a new generation of young urban researchers, focusing on the impact of urban redevelopment on the lives, places and livelihoods of low-income residents. He has also worked closely with the Urban Poor Consortium, an Indonesian-based NGO (see Simone, 2010b).

Key ideas

Urban research in the Global South typically understands urbanism – social, economic and political – from the perspective of policy, governance and formal institutions and processes. Yet Simone has shown that those categories and processes often have a relatively small role to play in the lives that the majority of urban residents pursue most of the time. This constitutes a significant shift: urban scholars tend to begin their analysis from a position where the key actors in urban life are broadly known in advance (states, formal economic actors, civil society organizations, etc.). In Simone's accounts the central forms of organizing urban life emerge through often loose networks and ways of doing that cut across different residents. These networks – or 'platforms' of urban life, as Simone sometimes calls them – may dissipate and reform over time, and both appear to and are used by people in quite different ways. The platforms emerge then as 'bundles' of relations between people, ways of thinking and doing, and different actors in the city (Simone, 2010a: 157). These bundles are made of shifting and multiple preferences, tradeoffs, speculations about the present and the future, tensions and collaborations of different sorts.

Governance and citizenship conditions, of course, matter to cities and feature across Simone's urban analyses. But oftentimes, 'securing the possibility of being able to make urban life' is located in attempting to channel 'the density of heterogeneous public transactions' that life in heterogeneous, busy places offers (Simone and Fauzan, 2012: 146). By 'channelling' – my term rather than Simone's – I mean attempting to cope with or optimize a host of changing circumstances, from rumours on commodities, to threats of demolition or new regulations, to opportunities for new ways to make a little extra money or improve housing and infrastructure or develop new networks, and so on.

The city that Simone conjures is always in motion, exceeding logics of control, and offering up different kinds of resources through which residents may be able to use each other to get by. For example, Simone (2008: 13) has argued that African cities are 'the result of a productive deployment of sensibilities, practices, effort, and collective formations that are made possible by the very uncertainties incumbent within cities deeply punctuated by fragmented infrastructures'. Cities here emerge through 'incessantly mutating practices' (2008: 13) of routine, disruption, breakdown, improvisation coping and uncertainty – 'making do', perhaps, but not in terms of becoming resigned to the city's inequities, but in terms of the active making of urban life and possibilities through social and material infrastructure (Simone, 2008).

Given the different levels of uncertainty that accompany the adjustments and anticipations that urban residents, traders and activists make, processes of *speculation* are often important. Speculation is key to how people learn to 'read the signs' of how urban conditions are changing. As Simone (2010a, 2014b) has shown in relation to ordinary neighbourhoods and markets in different parts of the urban Global South, speculation is a defining practice and form of infrastructure-making in everyday life (where infrastructure is both material and social). Simone (2014a) identifies how the devices associated with global capital – speculative finance, global products, production mechanisms and so on – are appropriated by urban actors as a means to substantiate practices of creating space and opportunities.

What we get from Simone is a distinct theorization of the city and of urban life, as well as a powerful illustration of the revelatory potential of immersive ethnographic research. Here, the city is located in maintenance of social and economic infrastructures, as well as in the making of new practices, habits and things and the attempt to deal with new sets of conditions as they arise. Moments of improvisation can emerge which entail putting together new combinations of people–knowledge– materials in the negotiation of everyday urban life – a kind of 'urban piracy' that appropriates and recasts the inherited city in contingent ways (Simone, 2006). The relation of time and possibility runs through Simone's analysis of urban spaces, for example in what he calls the 'materialization of anticipation', a sense of knowing how and when to make a 'next move' as an 'incremental accretion' of capacity and possibility (2014b). The focus Simone brings to the heterogeneity and intensity of urban life positions urbanism not just as a trajectory of expansion but as a multiplicity of interactions that enable or disable, enhance, alienate, exploit or inspire different forms of urban life.

Simone has developed a new conceptual vocabulary for understanding the heterogeneous nature of urbanism in motion, focusing on (to use some of his terms) the 'endurance', 'speculation', 'improvisation', 'intensity', 'resilience', 'incrementalism' and 'infrastructural collaboration' of 'urban majorities' living in the 'near South'. Where other forms of urban writing aim to resolve complexity and simplify urban life for their readers, Simone has deployed concepts such as heterogeneity and multiplicity as navigational tools. His aim is to illuminate rather than reduce the diverse spatial and temporal trajectories that make and unmake urban life, and he does so without losing sight of the key processes that structure urban production and change.

Contributions to urban studies

Simone has made foundational contributions not just to how cities in Africa or the Global South are written about, but to how cities are understood more generally. His focus on the informal forms of organization of urban life has made his work an indispensable resource for urban theory and research in general. In the efforts to develop a global urbanism that transgresses the Global North–South divide, Simone's work has provided a vital motivation as it has entered into wider debates on urban theory and research methodology (around the potential of ethnography for instance).

Not everyone is convinced by Simone's effort to locate the making of urban life and politics in the networks and practices of everyday social and economic transactions. For example, in a commentary on Simone's 2009 *Urban Geography* lecture, Cindi Katz (2010) asks whether mediating institutions such as the religious organization, civil society groups, unions or neighbourhood alliances might play more of a role in urban life than Simone suggests. Katz suggests that in practice the relations between such institutions and everyday networks are more interwoven, whether through support or conflict or some other relation. Katz also questions Simone's characterization of politics emerging from people anticipating new possibilities, arguing that such practices have more to do with resilience or with what James Scott (1985) called 'weapons of the weak' than political forms such as resistance.

What Simone opens up, however, is the possibility that reimagining and rebuilding the urban commons can begin with a detailed understanding of the ordinary ways in which residents and others become involved with and attempt to make the best from the intersections of everyday social and economic activities in the city. Even though many of these efforts – to construct infrastructure, improvise services, improve wellbeing or find jobs – often do not succeed, or play out as political successes, they represent a certain 'faith in the city', or at least in a particular notion of the city, through which we might locate the referent points for a better urbanism (Simone, 2014a: n.p). Or as Simone (2010a: 333) has put it: 'If we are not willing to find a way to live and discover within the worlds these residents have made, however insalubrious, violent, and banal they might often be, do we not undermine the very basis on which we would work to make cities more liveable for all?'

Secondary sources and references

Katz, C. (2010) 'Making change in the space of injury time', *Urban Geography*, 31(3): 315–320.

Scott, J. (1985) *Weapons of the Weak: Everyday Forms of Peasant Resistance*. New Haven, CT: Yale University Press.

Simone, A. (2004b) 'People as infrastructure: Intersecting fragments in Johannesburg', *Public Culture*, 16(3): 407–429.

Simone, A. (2006) 'Pirate towns: Reworking social and symbolic infrastructures in Johannesburg and Douala', *Urban Studies*, 43(2): 357–370.

Simone, A. (2008) 'Emergency democracy and the "governing composite"', *Social Text*, 26(295): 13–33.

Simone, A. (2010b) '2009 *Urban Geography* plenary – On intersections, anticipations, and provisional publics: Remaking district life in Jakarta', *Urban Geography*, 31(3): 285–308.

Simone, A. (2011) 'The surfacing of urban life', *City*, 15(3–4): 355–364.

Simone, A. (2013) 'Cities of uncertainty: Jakarta, the urban majority, and inventive political technologies', *Theory, Culture and Society*, 30(7–8): 243–263.

Simone, A. (2014b) 'Cities, neoliberalism and the urban commons', *Theory, Culture and Society*, website commentary, June 2014. Available at: http://theoryculturesociety.org/abdoumaliq-simone-on-cities-neoliberalism-and-the-commons/ (accessed 1 July 2015).

Simone, A. and Fauzan, A.U. (2012) 'Making security work for the majority: Reflections on two districts in Jakarta', *City and Society*, 24(2): 129–149.

35

Neil Smith

Tom Slater, University of Edinburgh

Key urban writings

Smith, N. (1979a) 'Toward a theory of gentrification: A back to the city movement by capital, not people', *Journal of the American Planning Association*, 45(4): 538–548.

Smith, N. (1982) 'Gentrification and uneven development', *Economic Geography*, 58(2): 139–155.

Smith, N. and Williams, P. (eds) (1986) *Gentrification of the City*. London: Routledge.

Smith, N. (1996) *The New Urban Frontier: Gentrification and the Revanchist City*. New York: Routledge.

Smith, N. (2002) 'New globalism, new urbanism: Gentrification as global urban strategy', *Antipode*, 34(3): 427–450.

Introduction

Neil Smith (1954–2012) was a Scottish geographer and activist intellectual, whose prolific, passionate and politically engaged writings played a significant role in shaping the present-day landscape of urban studies, human geography and indeed the entire spectrum of the social sciences. While best known for his contributions to the study of cities and particularly the process of gentrification, his work extended to a thorough dissection of the political and economic processes of uneven development – where a robust formulation of the production of geographical scale became central to much urban scholarship – and also the study of geography's history and philosophy. Based on a critical and detailed engagement with Marxist and socialist thought, Smith had a life-long commitment to the pursuit of social justice and was an active participant in many social movements, particularly around housing issues in New York City, where he was based for much of his career.

Following Smith's first tenured appointment at Columbia University, he moved to Rutgers University in 1986. In 2000 he was appointed Distinguished Professor at the Graduate Center of the City University of New York where he founded and led the Center for Place, Culture and Politics, which remains a hotbed of radical intellectual thought and critical dialogue with activists from far and wide. He died in September 2012, aged just 58.

Academic biography and research focus

Smith was born in Leith, Scotland, but spent nearly all his childhood in Dalkeith, a working-class town southeast of Edinburgh. As a teenager he became fascinated by the sharp contrasts and divisions in the glaciated and volcanic landscapes of the Lothians. Armed with a natural flair for mathematics, he enrolled at St. Andrews University on track to become a glacial geomorphologist. However, on a student exchange programme in Philadelphia he observed the contrasts and divisions within Philadelphia's Center City and began to realize that social forces carved up urban landscapes with the same awesome power and precision as the physical forces that carved the backyard of his youth. Politics, class struggle and flows of capital etched their way onto buildings and streets, and for Smith this became even more compelling to study than the physical forces that scratch and sculpt glacial environments.

Back at St. Andrews, in his final year of undergraduate study, Smith was particularly moved by the teachings of Joe Doherty, who proved instrumental in opening his eyes to the radical potential of urban geographical enquiry. Doherty supervised Smith's undergraduate dissertation (1977) that tracked those above-mentioned social forces via an investigation of the process of gentrification in the Philadelphia neighbourhood of Society Hill. Having first noticed gentrification earlier in 1972, on Rose Street in Edinburgh, when a trendy new bar called *The Galloping Major* distinguished itself from neighbouring pubs by serving 'quite appetizing lunches adorned with salad' (Smith, 1996: xviii), Smith retained an interest in the process throughout his career, producing over 45 original articles and two books on the topic.

After graduating from St. Andrews, Smith moved to Baltimore in 1978 to pursue docoral studies under **David Harvey** at Johns Hopkins University. Harvey's *Social Justice and the City* (1973) and its deep engagement with Marxist thought was galvanizing a generation, reorienting urban studies away from positivist spatial science towards more normative concerns about what societies might look like if profit-seeking as a direct and socially accepted goal were to be replaced by a 'genuinely humanizing urbanism' (p. 314). Smith's writings are best understood in the context of these revolutionary changes in geographical and urban thought, of which he was both student and teacher. His PhD thesis (1982) became his masterwork: *Uneven Development: Nature, Capital and the Production of Space* (1984). The influence of this book goes far beyond urban studies; Smith's argument that 'nature' is not just transformed under but produced by the logic of capitalist accumulation was an insight foundational for the entire field of political ecology. Two other books are worth noting for scholars of cities: *The New Urban Frontier: Gentrification and the Revanchist City* (1996), which continues to be mined by scholars for its penetrating insights on capitalist state power and its effects on cities; and *The Endgame of Globalization* (2005), a spirited critique of the violence of American-led, capitalist globalization in the years leading up to the 2008 financial crisis.

Key ideas

Smith's earliest writings on cities are hard-hitting Marxist critiques of the highly influential neoclassical economic land-use models of the Chicago School. Smith was sceptical of those models because of the consumer sovereignty paradigm undergirding them, which held that the rational choices of individual consumers of land and housing determined the morphology of cities. Middle-class consumer demand for space apparently explained suburbanization, a process seen by many neoclassical scholars to be the future of all urban places. But the empirical reality of Society Hill – gentrification – seemed to call that paradigm into question. Smith could not accept that consumers were suddenly demanding *en masse* the opposite to what had been predicted, and choosing to gentrify central city areas instead. In Society Hill he unearthed data showing that a majority of middle-class people had never left for Philadelphia's suburbs because space was being produced for them via state-sponsored private sector development. This created handsome profits for developers at the expense of working-class people who were displaced from central city space. His undergraduate dissertation was modified and published in *Antipode* in 1979, and that same year it was refined further in the *Journal of the American Planning Association* (*JAPA*) where the pivotal theory of the rent gap was first articulated.

A starting point for Smith's rent gap theory is that as disinvestment in a particular district intensifies, it creates lucrative profit opportunities for developers, investors, homebuyers and local government. To understand the much-lauded American 'urban renaissance' of the 1970s, the argument and title of the *JAPA* essay went, it was much more important to track the movement of capital rather than the movement of people (the latter movement was the exclusive focus of the 'back to the city' rhetoric and scholarship of the time). In 1920s Chicago, Homer Hoyt had identified a 'valley in the land-value curve between the Loop and outer residential areas ... [which] indicates the location of these sections where the buildings are mostly forty years old and where the residents rank lowest in rent-paying ability' (Hoyt, 1933: 356–358). For Smith (1979a: 543), this 'capital depreciation in the inner city' means that there is likely to be an increasing divergence between capitalized ground rent (the actual quantity of ground rent that is appropriated by the landowner, given the present land use) and potential ground rent (the maximum that could be appropriated under the land's 'highest and best use', as economists often put it). So, Hoyt's land value valley, radically analysed and reconceptualized, 'can now be understood in large part as the rent gap' (Smith, 1979a: 543).

For Smith, abandoned urban buildings are not the outcome of any naturally occurring neighbourhood 'decay' – they are actively produced by clearing out existing residents via all manner of tactics and legal instruments such as landlord harassment, massive rent increases, redlining, arson, the withdrawal of public services and eminent domain. Closing the rent gap requires separating people obtaining use values from the present land use in order to capitalize the land to the perceived highest and best use. The role of the state in regard to these actors is far from laissez-faire, but rather one of direct facilitator, for example via public mortgage financing and the development of public–private institutions to direct that financing. The rent gap theory highlights specific social – that is to say, class – interests, where the quest for profit and economic growth takes precedence over the need for shelter. The rent gap must also be understood within Smith's larger body of work on uneven development, where he added a geographical, spatial dimension to something that had fascinated Marx – the powerful contradictions of capital investment and accumulation. For Smith, capital investment is always animated by a geographical tension: between the need to equalize conditions and seek out new markets in new places, versus the need for differentiation (and particularly a division of labour that is matched to various places' comparative advantage). The result is what Smith (1982) called a locational 'see-saw' of investment and disinvestment over time and across space. The rent gap theory of gentrification helps us to view that see-saw in motion.

The political activation of that see-saw was the subject of Smith's 1996 book, *The New Urban Frontier: Gentrification and the Revanchist City*. Revanchists (from the French word *revanche*, meaning revenge) were a group of bourgeois nationalist reactionaries opposed to the liberalism of the Second Republic and the socialist uprising of the Paris Commune. The revanchists were determined to reinstate the bourgeois order with a strategy that fused militarism and moralism with claims about restoring public order on the streets. They hunted down enemies with a noxious blend of hatred and viciousness, intent on exacting revenge upon all those who had 'stolen' their vision of French society from them. In the late 1980s, Smith was disturbed by the developments in New York City that had emerged to fill the vacuum left by the disintegration of 1960s/1970s liberal urban policy. He coined the concept of the revanchist city to capture a seismic political shift: whereas the liberal era of the post-1960s period was characterized by redistributive policy, affirmative action and anti-poverty legislation, the era of neoliberal revanchism was characterized by a discourse of revenge against minorities, the working class, feminists, environmental activists and recent immigrants: the 'public enemies' of the bourgeois political elite and their supporters. Under the Rudolph Giuliani mayoral administration, New York City in the 1990s became an arena for concerted attacks on affirmative action and immigration policy, street violence against homeless people and aggressive policing techniques. Just as the bourgeois order was perceived as under threat by the revanchists of 1890s Paris, in 1990s New York a particular, exclusionary vision of 'civil society' was being reinstated with a vengeance – an attempt to banish those not part of that vision from the city altogether. Smith argued that gentrification was the leading edge of a state strategy of revenge – an attempt to retake the city from the working class.

Smith's later work on gentrification was concerned with how the process was changing from its 1960s and 1970s localized urban anomaly to a thoroughly generalized urban strategy affecting cities all over the world, and he wrote several essays to that effect inspired by **Henri Lefebvre**'s (1970) *The Urban Revolution* [*La Révolution urbaine*] (see Smith, 2002). He also analysed the dawn of a 'revanchist planet' (Smith, 2009), a new class struggle fuelled by a 'dead but dominant' neoliberal ideology. Given the 2008 financial crisis and waves of foreclosures and evictions, the emergence of austerity measures and their cumulative effects on cities, and the 2011 Arab Spring and Occupy uprisings, he was thinking and writing even more deeply about urban revolution in the years and months before his death.

Contributions to urban studies

Smith's writings on gentrification have thoroughly shaped the theoretical and empirical discourse of debates on gentrification and urban displacement. As well as spawning a series of riveting empirical tests (e.g. Clark, 1987; López-Morales, 2011), the rent gap theory led to some heated exchanges between urban scholars who saw gentrification as the product of the post-industrial expansion of middle-class professionals with a preference for central city living (Hamnett, 1991; Ley, 1986), and scholars who felt that Smith's focus on gentrification 'from above' was inattentive to human agency and the views of gentrification at ground level (Rose, 1984). But for Smith, the rent gap is fundamentally about class struggle, about the structural violence visited upon so many working-class people in contexts that are usually described as regenerating or revitalizing. Smith's writings teach us that, contrary to journalistic portraits of white 'hipsters' versus working-class minorities, the class struggle in gentrification is between those at risk of displacement and the agents of capital who produce and exploit rent gaps. For this reason, the rent gap theory has proved especially useful to urban social movements dedicated to elevating housing to the level of a human right and securing community control over land (Rameau, 2012). To understand struggles under capitalism, Smith argued, we have to understand the way capitalism produces the very spaces and scales that make its existence possible. Long cycles of accumulation demand that capital has to devalue land in order to reinvent investment opportunity. The violence and human consequences of varying cycles of building and destroying, of creating and tearing apart, make the rent gap of lasting purchase and relevance – analytically and politically – in grasping the basic function of rent: to underpin investment and reinvestment opportunity, which in turn underpin uneven development under capitalism.

Smith's thesis on the revanchist city, while criticized by some as inapplicable to the lives of homeless people in countries with stronger welfare states and for neglecting the mediating role of third sector organizations (Cloke et al., 2010), offered a challenge for scholars to expose and critique the vengeful tactics used by developers, owners and agents of capital and policy elites as they stalk potential ground rent. A focus on revenge can also shed light upon the ways in which profitable returns are justified among those actors and to the wider public, and raise legitimate and serious concerns about the fate of those urban dwellers not seen to be putting urban land to its 'highest and best use'. Furthermore, it points to the darkly troubling downsides of reinvestment in the name of 'economic growth' and 'job creation'; and carves the path for the reinstatement of the use values (actual or potential) of the land, streets, buildings and homes that constitute an urban community. Neil Smith never gave up hope that another, post-capitalist world is possible; that radical and revolutionary change can happen if the political will is there to be mobilized.

Secondary sources and references

Clark, E. (1987) *The Rent Gap and Urban Change: Case Studies in Malmö 1860–1985*. Lund: Lund University Press.

Cloke, P., May, J. and Johnsen, S. (2010) *Swept Up Lives? Re-Envisioning the Homeless City*. Oxford: Wiley-Blackwell.

Hamnett, C. (1991) 'The blind men and the elephant: The explanation of gentrification', *Transactions of the Institute of British Geographers*, 16(2): 173–189.

Harvey, D. (1973) *Social Justice and the City*. Baltimore: Johns Hopkins University Press.

Hoyt, H. (1933) *One Hundred Years of Land Values in Chicago*. Chicago: University of Chicago Press.

Lefebvre, H. (2003 [1970]) *The Urban Revolution*. Trans. R. Bonnonno. Minneapolis: University of Minnesota Press.

Ley, D. (1986) 'Alternative explanations for inner-city gentrification: A Canadian assessment', *Annals of the Association of American Geographers*, 76(4): 521–535.

López-Morales, E. (2011) 'Gentrification by ground rent dispossession: The shadows cast by large scale urban renewal in Santiago de Chile', *International Journal of Urban and Regional Research*, 35(2): 330–357.

Rameau, M. (2012) 'Neil Smith: A critical geographer,' *Environment and Planning D: Society and Space*, 30(6): 947–962.

Rose, D. (1984) 'Rethinking gentrification: Beyond the uneven development of Marxist urban theory', *Environment and Planning D: Society and Space*, 2(1): 47–74.

Smith, N. (1979b) 'Gentrification and capital: Practice and ideology in Society Hill', *Antipode*, 11(3): 24–35.

Smith, N. (1984) *Uneven Development: Nature, Capital and the Production of Space*. Athens, GA: University of Georgia Press.

Smith, N. (2005) *The Endgame of Globalization*. New York: Routledge.

Smith, N. (2009) 'Revanchist planet', *Urban Reinventors*, 3: 1–17. Available at: www.urbanreinventors.net/3/smith1/smith1-urbanreinventors.pdf

36

Michael Storper

Alan Latham, University College London

Key urban writings

Storper, M. and Walker, R. (1989a) *The Capitalist Imperative: Territory, Technology and Industrial Growth.* Oxford: Blackwell.
Storper, M. (1997) *The Regional World: Territorial Development in a Global Economy.* New York: Guilford Press.
Storper, M. and Manville, M. (2006) 'Behavior, preferences and cities: Urban theory and urban resurgence', *Urban Studies,* 43(8): 1247–1274.
Storper, M. (2013) *Keys to the City: How Economics, Institutions, Social Interactions and Politics Shape the Development of City-Regions.* Princeton, NJ: Princeton University.
Storper, M., Kemeny, T., Makarem, N. and Osman, T. (2015) *The Rise and Fall of Urban Economies: Lessons from San Francisco and Los Angeles.* Stanford, CA: Stanford University Press.

Introduction

Michael Storper is an economic and urban geographer. His writing focuses on the contemporary dynamics of technological change, globalization and economic development with a particular emphasis on how these unfold in city regions. His work explores why economic activity concentrates in urban areas, and why some cities grow and develop faster and over longer periods than others. Stressing the importance of a range of place-based agglomeration economies, Storper has developed a sophisticated theory of urban economic development that emphasizes the importance of cities as centres of economic production and technological innovation. His work maps out the spatial dynamics of contemporary economic globalization, examining why some economic activities have become globally dispersed while others are concentrated in a small number of large wealthy, metropolitan centres. Highlighting the continued importance of face-to-face interaction to many high-value forms of economic activity, his research stresses the evolutionary, path-dependent nature of technological innovation and change. In explicating the centrality of cities and regions to economic development Storper is part of a heterodox school of economic thinkers working to reconfigure mainstream economic theory to give more emphasis on the importance of embedded institutions, cultural traditions and conventions; an emphasis that simultaneously demonstrates the importance of place and historical context to the dynamics of economic growth.

Storper holds professorships at the Luskin School of Public Affairs, UCLA; Institut d'Études Politiques de Paris; and the London School of Economics.

Academic biography and research focus

Michael Storper gained a BA in Sociology and History (1975), followed by an MA (1979) and PhD (1982) in Geography from the University of California, Berkeley. Working under the supervision of Richard Walker (at the time a protégé of **David Harvey**) his early work was rooted in the late 1970s and early 1980s flourishing of neo-Marxist urban geography and sociology. Breaking with orthodox Marxist thinking, writers like Harvey, Walker and the sociologist **Manuel Castells** argued that the process of urbanization was central to the organizing dynamics of contemporary capitalist societies and indeed to the periodic crises that beset them. Taking up these claims Storper's early work elaborated and clarified the mechanisms through which capitalism developed within and through particular territories. His first two books, *Production, Work, Territory: The Geographical Anatomy of Industrial Capitalism* (1986, co-edited with Allen Scott) and *The Capitalist Imperative: Territory, Technology and Industrial Growth* (1989a, co-authored with Walker), set out an ambitious theoretical agenda for understanding the dynamics of economic growth as not simply a socio-economic phenomenon but also a territorial one. As such, Storper's work can be understood as part of a wider trend within the social sciences to re-spatialize social theory (cf. Soja, 1989).

Storper's first academic position was at the University of California Los Angeles School of Urban Planning. Here he came into contact with a community of scholars including Allen J. Scott, Edward Soja, Michael Dear and Jon Friedman, who like him were interested in mapping the changing dynamics of contemporary urban economies. Collectively known as the Los Angeles School – although Storper himself preferred the moniker Californian School – these writers argued that in all sorts of ways Los Angeles could be understood as paradigmatic of late 20th-century urbanism. More specifically, they argued that contemporary Los Angeles was characterized by a series of historically innovative changes in its dominant forms of economic activity. Generally, this was a movement away from vertically integrated, mass production industrial systems towards ones defined by an emphasis on flexible specialization and disintegrated production networks that incorporated both distinctive patterns of spatial agglomeration and intensive links with the global economy. Storper's own work on the LA motion picture industry – with Susan Christopherson – was an exemplary case study of just this dynamic (Christopherson and Storper, 1986; Storper and Christopherson, 1987). The focus of Storper's work, however, was not to assert the pre-eminence of Los Angeles and the wider Southern Californian metropolitan region. Rather, the aim was to develop a robust conceptual architecture through which to make sense of the novel emerging forms of industrial organization that were coming to dominate the global economy.

As such, Storper's next books, *Industrialization, Economic Development, and the Regional Question in the Third World: From Import Substitution to Flexible Production*

(1990), *Les Mondes de production* (1993, co-authored with Robert Salais and published in English in revised form as *Worlds of Production: The Action Frameworks of the Economy* [1997]), and *The Regional World: Territorial Development in a Global Economy* (1997), were defined more by questions of how firms and regions developed than with cities or urban agglomeration per se. Nonetheless, cities and city regions had an important place in Storper's evolving theoretical account of economic development. Collectively these books knitted together and refined a conceptual framework that explicated the relationship between the microeconomic organization of firms, inter-firm networks of trade and specialization, the untraded spillover effects of agglomeration and the formation of both industrial and territorial clusters. Empirically, this work drew on American examples such as Los Angeles and San Francisco and on research Storper had carried out in Brazil, France and Germany. This work demonstrated a remarkable theoretical dexterity. While *The Capitalist Imperative* retained a basic fidelity to neo-Marxist precepts, *Worlds of Production* and *The Regional World* were located on a rather different intellectual terrain; knitting together an intricate combination of economic sociology, institutional economics and economic geography that went beyond bland claims about the innately uneven geographical development of capitalism.

While much of Storper's work has a regional emphasis, in his most recent work such as *Keys to the City* and *The Rise and Fall of Urban Economies: Lessons from San Francisco and Los Angeles* (co-authored with Thomas Kemeny, Naji Makarem and Taner Osman) it is quite clear economic growth and development – or the lack thereof – are to a very great extent matters of urban growth and urban development.

Key ideas

The overriding aim of Storper's approach to studying urban economies is to develop a conceptually robust framework for understanding economic activity, industrial organization, technological innovation and metropolitan regional development. He produces general theories that describe and explain specific empirical phenomena through the articulation of careful case studies. Conceptually his accounts focus on what Storper has labelled the 'holy trinity' of economic development – organizations, technologies and territories (Storper, 1995, 1997). His central intuition is that economic activity does not just create a particular geography of industrial development and growth, but that territory (or geography) is deeply implicated in the dynamics of economic growth and technological and organizational innovation itself.

The first part of Storper's trinity is organization. Conventional economic theory starts with the idea of the firm as a stable and clearly defined entity. Closer examination of actual firms and the industries of which they are a part by writers such as Coase (1937) and Williamson (1985), however, reveals enormous variety in the size, scope and structure of firms within and across industries. This transactional economics shows that the ways that firms and industries are organized is in fact a dynamic process. Drawing on and developing the work of Allen Scott (1998, 2008) Storper emphasizes it is also a spatially variable process. Certain patterns of industrial organization tend to encourage firms to cluster together while others lead to dispersal. A key factor in structuring these organizational dynamics is technology, the second part of Storper's trinity. The level of technological complexity and maturity within an industry shapes its geographical reach. The clustering of novel, technologically innovative, industries happens because much of the knowledge that goes into production is non-tradeable; it is not yet standardized and codified and so firms need to be close together to ensure the free flow of information and expertise between them. As industries mature there is a tendency for parts of the production process to become standardized and relocatable to other cheaper locations. Thus, some industries create complex and spatially distributed production systems. Examples include both the American automobile industry and high-end consumer electronics generally, both of which have supply chains that stretch around the world. The final part of the trinity is territory. The emergence of an industry and its production system is always closely intertwined with a web of place-bound formal and informal institutions. These are things like legal systems, work practices, educational institutions and so on. All these elements feed into the development of a range of conventions for doing things in a particular place, conventions which are sustained by the everyday relational webs within a territory.

With its interweaving of organizations, technology and territory, Storper's account of economic development helps in understanding how industries are both localized and stretched across great distances. Putting things another way we might say that urban economies are oriented both locally and globally. This in itself would not be a distinctive insight. Many scholars have argued that from the 1970s the global economy had come to be defined by a new international division of labour (NIDL) (see Dicken, 1986; Harvey, 1989). Storper's argument however moves beyond the NIDL thesis that advanced parts of the production process are located in wealthy developed cities and regions while standardized labour-intensive parts locate to poorer cities of the less-developed world. In Storper's view this is too simplistic; territorial economic development is path dependent. An industry or a production process may have many different ways of being organized. The specific organizational, technological and territorial trajectory along which an industry develops owes a great deal to where and when it emerged. The organizational and locational dynamics of the automobile industry in metropolitan regions like Stuttgart and Munich are quite different to those of Detroit, for example. Some industries such as high-end financial services come to be dominated by a small number of globally prominent clusters like London, New York and Hong Kong. Other industries, however, demonstrate a much more variegated geography – fashion and design being two examples. And, in fact, different parts of an industry may have distinctively different locational dynamics. The supply chains of high-end fashion tend to be much more localized than those of mass market clothing production.

If a great deal of Storper's urban geography focuses on regional production systems and industrial networks, then the cities and the interactions that take place within them are nonetheless central to his theories. They are places where many key technological and organizational innovations happen. The kind of technological spillover effects that define highly innovative urban agglomerations like Silicon Valley are the product not just of high densities of skilled people living near each other, but also of informal conventions of working together and thinking through problems. Urban environments have a particular 'buzz' (Storper and Venables, 2004) and this is in no small part because they bring people face-to-face. For all the talk of modern communication technology transforming how businesses interact, face-to-face conversation remains an extraordinarily efficient means of solving problems, motivating people and facilitating learning. Cities are where this face-to-face interaction happens. As a result they produce locally distinct sensibilities and ways of working, cultures which are sustained and reproduced by organizational and institutional structures and spillovers. Storper's work highlights this through illustrations such as the peculiar dynamics of the restaurant industry, where French cities are remarkably better at producing high-quality, reasonably priced restaurants than their North American counterparts. Or in a more carefully worked through example, his research into the Los Angeles film industry traces out the distinct informal organizational networks that sustain Hollywood as the still unrivalled centre of global film production. Places like Bollywood (Mumbai), Nollywood (Lagos) and Wellington are also dynamic centres of film production but each has its own distinctive industry flavour.

Contributions to urban studies

Storper's writing offers some of the most sustained and intellectually rigorous frameworks for making sense of the intricacies of contemporary urban economic systems. Starting from and then moving beyond the neo-Marxist insight that economic development varies enormously between cities and regions, Storper's work demonstrates the microeconomic and institutional bases of this variation. In doing so he provides a sophisticated account of relationships between technological innovation and variations in urban economic development. Contrasting with thinkers like **David Harvey** and **Neil Brenner**, who also focus on the dynamics of capitalist urbanization, Storper focuses on the fine-grained relational dynamics of urban economies. Not only does this provide insights into why some economies thrive while others fail, it also helps to raise questions about the kinds of concrete interventions that facilitate economic development by enhancing productivity, efficiency and equity.

Storper's work is also distinctive for its willingness to bring the insights of economic geography into conversation with conventional neoclassical economics. His emphasis on cities as centres of production provides an explicit critique of the arguments of economists like **Edward Glaeser** and Richard Florida, who suggest that the so-called return to the city that characterizes many metropolitan regions in North America and Europe has been driven by the rediscovery and creative reinvention of urban lifestyles. Storper emphasizes that urban amenities are an outcome not a cause of successful local economies (Storper, 2013). Or, put another way, the creativity of cities is driven by their economies. This perhaps is the central claim of Storper: that different cities, for all their variation, can be understood through the use of a range of general principles. This puts him in strong contrast with current approaches to urban studies that seek to understand cities through their particularities and are thus averse to general theories (cf. **Ananya Roy, Jane M. Jacobs**). For Storper understanding the shape and scope of the agglomeration economies that underpin processes of urbanization allows us to say a great deal about particular urban places (Scott and Storper, 2015). Stressing cities as sites of difference is all well and good. But without the appropriate generalizable urban theory there is not much than can be learnt from that difference.

Secondary sources and references

Christopherson, S. and Storper, M. (1986) 'The city as studio; the world as back lot: The impact of vertical disintegration on the location of the motion picture industry', *Environment and Planning D: Society and Space*, 4(3): 305–320.

Coase, R.H. (1937) 'The nature of the firm', *Economica*, 4(16): 386–405.

Dicken, P. (1986) *Global Shift*. London: Sage.

Harvey, D. (1989) *The Urban Experience*. Oxford: Blackwell.

Kemeny, T. and Storper, M. (2012) 'The sources of urban development: Wages, housing and amenity gaps across American cities', *Journal of Regional Science*, 52(1): 85–108.

Rabari, C. and Storper, M. (2015) 'The digital skin of cities: Urban theory and research in the age of the sensored and metered city, ubiquitous computing and big data', *Cambridge Journal of Regions Economy and Society*, 8(1): 27–42.

Salais, R. and Storper, M. (1997) *Worlds of Production: The Action Frameworks of the Economy*. Cambridge, MA: Harvard University Press.

Scott, A.J. (1998) *Metropolis*. Berkeley: University of California Press.

Scott, A.J. (2008) *Social Economy of the Metropolis: Cognitive-Cultural Capitalism and the Global Resurgence of Cities*. Oxford: Oxford University Press.

Scott, A.J. and Storper, M. (1986) *Production, Work, Territory: The Geographical Anatomy of Industrial Capitalism*. London: Allen and Unwin.

Scott, A.J. and Storper, M. (2015) 'The nature of cities: The scope and limits of urban theory', *International Journal of Urban and Regional Research*, 39(1): 1–15.

Soja, E. (1989) *Postmodern Geographies*. London: Verso.

Storper, M. (1988) 'Big structures, small events, and large processes in economic geography', *Environment and Planning A*, 20(2): 165–185.

Storper, M. (1989b) 'The transition to flexible specialization: The division of labour, external economies, and the crossing of industrial divides', *Cambridge Journal of Economics*, 13(2): 273–305.

Storper, M. (1990) *Industrialization, Economic Development, and the Regional Question in the Third World: From Import Substitution to Flexible Production*. London: Pion Books.

Storper, M. (1992) 'The limits to globalization: Technology districts and international trade', *Economic Geography*, 68(1): 60–93.

Storper, M. (1993) 'Regional "worlds" of production: Learning and innovation in the technology districts of France, Italy and the USA', *Regional Studies*, 27(5): 433–455.

Storper, M. (1995) 'The resurgence of regional economies, ten years later: The region as a nexus of untraded interdependencies', *European Urban and Regional Studies*, 2(3): 191–221.

Storper, M. (2001) 'The poverty of radical theory today: From the false promises of Marxism to the mirage of the cultural turn', *International Journal of Urban and Regional Research*, 25(1): 155–179.

Storper, M. (2010) 'Why does a city grow? Specialization, human capital, or institutions?', *Urban Studies*, 47(10): 2027–2050.

Storper, M. (2011) 'From retro to avant garde: A reply to Paul Krugman's "New Economic Geography at Middle Age"', *Regional Studies*, 45(1): 9–15.

Storper, M. and Christopherson, S. (1987) 'Flexible specialization and regional industrial agglomerations', *Annals of the Association of American Geographers*, 77(1): 104–117.

Storper, M. and Scott, A.J. (1995) 'The wealth of regions: Market forces and policy imperatives in local and global context', *Futures*, 27(5): 505–526.

Storper, M. and Scott, A.J. (2009) 'Rethinking human capital, creativity and urban growth', *Journal of Economic Geography*, 9(2): 147–167.

Storper, M. and Venables, A. (2004) 'Buzz: Face-to-face contact and the urban economy', *Journal of Economic Geography*, 4(4): 351–370.

Williamson, O.E. (1985) *The Economic Institutions of Capitalism*. New York: Basic Books.

37

Mariana Valverde

Regan Koch, Queen Mary University of London

Key urban writings

Valverde, M. (2003a) *Law's Dream of a Common Knowledge*. Princeton, NJ: University of Princeton Press.

Valverde, M. (2008) 'The ethic of diversity: Local law and the negotiation of urban norms', *Law and Social Inquiry*, 33(4): 895–924.

Valverde, M. (2009) 'Laws of the street', *City and Society*, 21(2): 163–181.

Valverde, M. (2011) 'Seeing like a city: The dialectic of modern and premodern ways of seeing in urban governance', *Law and Society Review*, 45(20): 277–312.

Valverde, M. (2012) *Everyday Law on the Street: City Governance and the Challenges of Diversity*. Chicago: University of Chicago Press.

Introduction

Mariana Valverde is a central figure in the field of socio-legal studies. Her work focuses on governance and different forms of knowledge–power in governmental regulation and legal processes. Early in her career Valverde made significant contributions to socialist feminism and gay rights activism, and later wrote important historical sociologies of moral reform and the management of alcohol. More recently her attention has turned to cities and urban life.

In her book *Everyday Law on the Street*, Valverde demonstrates the unexpected ways that urban governance shapes life in the 'world's most diverse city' of Toronto. Other projects have examined the socio-legal technologies used to regulate urban spaces historically and in the present, drawing on the ideas of philosopher-historian Michael Foucault and insights from actor-network theory. In doing so Valverde has provided a rich understanding of the flexible, fragile and often contradictory workings of urban government and the ongoing attempt to maintain order. She has also challenged urban scholars to think in more open and systematic ways about the unpredictable combinations of entities that shape urban life and the resources that empirical research can bring to light.

Valverde is a Professor and former Director of the Centre for Criminology and
Sociolegal Studies at the University of Toronto.

Academic biography and research focus

Born in Rome and brought up in Barcelona, Valverde's adult life has been based in
Toronto. Her unique approach to urban scholarship owes much to her distinct intellectual trajectory. Valverde's Master's and Doctoral degrees were in Social and Political
Thought at York University (1982). Yet by the time her dissertation was completed she
had become immersed in feminist and gay liberation activism. Her first monograph,
Sex, Power and Pleasure (1985) was a key contribution to the 'sex debates' of the
1980s. She then decided to retrain as a social historian, not taking her first academic
post until 1988 in the Women's Studies Department at Trent University. A year later
she moved to the Sociology Department at York where she published *The Age of
Light, Soap, and Water: Moral Reform in English Canada, 1885–1925* (1991) – a
powerful explication of how gender, class and race were organized in the making of
modern Canada.

Valverde's next move was to the University of Toronto and its then-named Centre
for Criminology. Once more, her intellectual focus shifted – for while crime had never
been on her radar, the field was expanding to consider broad processes giving rise to
social order and disorder. Drawing on the work of Nietzsche and Foucault, Valverde
developed a genealogical approach to exploring how different aspects of social life
become problematized as matters of governmental concern. Examining how various
rationalities and techniques are configured in the management of such problems (what
Foucault termed 'governmentality'), her work has made evident the distributed, heterogeneous and unsystematizable nature of power. *Diseases of the Will* (1998), for
example, considers how alcohol has been identified as a serious problem for governmental authorities, health officials and for many drinkers, yet has never been
successfully medicalized or prohibited in Western societies. Alcohol's dangers and
pleasures are instead managed through peculiar constellations of religious morality,
licensing law, clinical psychology and self-help therapy. The governance of problematic
activities and spaces is also the subject of *Law's Dream of a Common Knowledge*
(2003a). Uniquely, the focus is on low-status legal tools and knowledge formats used
by municipal officials charged with maintaining public order in relation to sex, drugs
and the lifestyle activities of suspect communities. In 2007, Valverde became Director
of the Centre for Criminology, to which the suffix 'and Sociolegal Studies' was added.
This came on the heels of both *Law and Order: Signs, Meanings, Myths* (2006a),
a social semiotic analysis of crime in popular media, and *The Force of Law* (2006b),
which examines the violence integral to supposedly civilized legal systems.

Cities have more recently become a central focus for Valverde. Her foray into the
field has been ambitious. *Everyday Law on the Street* (2012) was the result of four
years of ethnographic study into the daily routines of law enforcement officials, licensing tribunals and public hearings on planning issues in Toronto. What it highlights are
the basic governance architectures used to manage wide-ranging conflicts around
issues of nuisance, land use, employment conditions and urban development projects.
Importantly, it also traces out various ways in which 'law in action' can have effects

that diverge widely from the intentions and rationales underpinning 'law in the books'. Her current research is focused on two distinct projects. First is a historical, comparative enquiry into how cities define and separate 'good' neighbourhoods and neighbours from 'bad' ones, focusing on the 'century of the suburb' in North America and Britain from 1870 to 1970. Second is a contemporary analysis of 'urban planning by contract' in the building of urban infrastructure and social amenities, uniquely focusing on universities, sports bodies and other non-profits for which the term public–private is misleading. Her most recent book, *Chronotopes of Law: Jurisdiction, Scale and Governance* (2015), offers a series of theoretical meditations on how such fine-grained attention to law alters how scholars might understand questions of jurisdiction and spatio-temporal scale.

Key ideas

Students of cities looking for ontological precision about the nature of 'the urban' will not find it in Valverde's work. Nor does she offer an explication of structural forces or utopian visions that might shape cities yet to come. Valverde's grounding in Nietzschean-Foucauldian philosophy has led her to eschew Big Theory in favour of grounded analysis (cf. **Bent Flyvbjerg**). Rather than ask grand questions of 'why' or 'what it all means', her proclivity is for questions of 'how' the work of governance is done. This does not mean that Valverde shies away from matters of theory or method that can be used to animate urban studies in a variety of ways.

To start, Valverde's work outlines a number of intellectual moves that should *not* be made when thinking about cities. We should not begin with linear paradigms of social processes supposed to either succeed or fail. Neoliberalization, modernization, globalization and so on all exist in some form but Valverde reminds us that as processes their movements are never internally consistent or self-identical. Relatedly, we should not think of governance projects as fitting within distinct historical eras – e.g. the age of surveillance, discipline, risk and so forth – but rather as hybrid formations of new and existing techniques being used to address emergent and reoccurring problems. In distinction with thinkers like **Mike Davis** and **Loïc Wacquant**, Valverde also insists that scholars should avoid reifying 'the state' or 'the field of bureaucracy' in making sense of governmental power. Thinking of such entities as the *products* of governance and not the other way around puts the analytic focus on the specificity of different socio-legal configurations that need to be examined in terms of their effects.

A sense of Valverde's socio-legal perspective is demonstrated in her analysis of a single street corner in Toronto (2009, 2012), an intersection near her university where the force of law is not immediately evident. In contrast to the organic vision of street life posited by **Jane Jacobs**, Valverde demonstrates how law and regulation are everywhere. The streets, sidewalks and buildings at the intersection are governed primarily by the municipal corporation – a medieval form of government that Valverde details as being more or less coercive as state law. But there are cross-jurisdictional powers and other forms of governance that intersect in peculiar ways. On the street, for example, a municipal permit system stipulates what kinds of vehicles can be driven, while state licensing laws govern who can drive and under what conditions. Drivers can be stopped and are legally required to show identification even without probable cause that a law has been broken. This rather illiberal form of police power contrasts with civil-state protections afforded to pedestrians on the sidewalk, but providing local governments with a primary (and rarely questioned) means of scrutinizing their citizens. Sidewalk activities other than walking frequently require a permit or licence, as Valverde points out, and permanent objects are subject to an array of design standards, technical specifications and bylaws. At the intersection she analyses, decorative gates and ornamental concrete have been recently added through neoliberal policy mechanisms that enable public–private partnerships to upgrade the local public realm. While helping to beautify the area, they also represent a departure from more egalitarian forms of municipal amenity provision. Finally, the buildings along the intersection are subject to a century-old legal architecture of strict land-use zoning. The tremendous variation in building heights, styles and uses, however, can be explained by the ubiquity of 'legal nonconforming uses' granted by planning officials such to the extent that exceptions to codified rules are the norm. While far from being a fully rational system, the pragmatic reality is that without such flexibility, zoning ordinances would be subject to continuous and potentially ruinous court challenges. The arrangement also provides regular opportunities for local councillors to build political capital by negotiating compromises.

This snapshot of the kind of analysis Valverde's work offers leads us to some of the key ideas she brings to urban studies. More than providing a mere inventory of different kinds of law on the books, her scholarship highlights aspects of municipal governance that tend to be overlooked when thinking about urban inequality. For example, while there is substantial evidence that many forms of urban governance disproportionately impact upon those already disadvantaged, Valverde reminds us that rules are rarely written so that they apply to particular individuals or groups. Rather, the law tends to be structured in objective terms around the management of objects, activities and spaces, and is justified as a necessary intervention on behalf of a greater good. Rights-based campaigns for justice often fail to find traction within municipal jurisdictions because they do not work through the law on its own terms (cf. Blomley, 2011). Further, because the powers of municipal government are primarily about policing, those responsible for the on-the-ground law enforcement have an integral need for discretion when making judgements – a need that has been consistently upheld by state courts. What Valverde has articulated in this regard is a dialectical process of urban governance that perpetually hinges between modern, objective knowledge formats based on quantifiable standards and more pre-modern forms of interpretation that are embodied and subjective. This flexible regulatory gaze – what she terms 'seeing like a city' (2011), in contrast to James Scott's 'seeing like a state' (1998) – is what makes local governance and law enforcement a continuous work of improvisation that has to be studied in terms of its specificity. Moreover, attention to this work of improvisation highlights limitations within some of the established ways urban theorists (cf. **Neil Brenner** and **Neil Smith**) think about geographical scale. Valverde's point, developed in *Chronotopes of Law*, is that we need more complex and pluralistic ways of thinking about temporal-spatial scaling than these afford.

A key argument running through Valverde's work is that increasingly diverse societies demand new governance structures if conflicts are to be managed in socially just ways. Her detailed empirical studies in Toronto demonstrate how existing regulatory architectures often work against the ideals of diversity that city leaders and citizens often proudly claim to embrace. Ethnic-minority taxicab drivers and street food vendors are systematically disadvantaged by culturally narrow rules and ethnocentric bureaucratic norms (2008, 2011). Zoning regulations privilege the idealized nuclear family model by shielding certain homes from noises, smells and social problems that other urban inhabitants must endure (2003a, 2005). Planning processes organized to mediate public concerns for new buildings become forums for much larger issues such as immigration and terrorism, which they are inappropriately designed to address (2011). Archaic laws and unjust governance mechanisms persist, Valverde argues, because their operations are rarely questioned and because few venues exist for collectively reflecting on how they might be improved. These issues are hardly unique to Toronto. Valverde (2003a, 2003b, 2011) has outlined remarkable historical and geographical continuities in terms of legal tools and regulatory mechanisms used by governments. The tendency among urban researchers to focus on specific developments and high-profile campaigns tends to exaggerate differences between cities, with the effect of obscuring similarities in underlying legal and regulatory architectures. This is a key insight, given the leverage they can provide in the making of more democratic and socially just cities.

Contributions to urban studies

Valverde brings to urban studies clear demonstrations of the need to pay close attention to the particular socio-legal configurations through which our cities are governed. Her patient enquiries into the historical development and contemporary operations of different legal processes and mechanisms highlight the valuable, and often quite surprising, insights that can be gained from such work. Importantly, Valverde also provides an imaginative range of conceptual resources and methods that urban scholars can put to work in making sense of why urban life takes the shape that it does in different contexts.

The research frameworks she has outlined (sometimes in collaboration with Nicholas Rose and Pat O'Malley) help to clarify and build upon Foucault's ideas, setting forth new agendas for enquiring into the rationalities and techniques of governance. Comparative and case study focused urban research has much to gain from these insights, particularly in terms of developing projects that do not artificially isolate single modes of governance and which are sensitive to the particularities of the scale and jurisdiction of law (2009). In a different vein, Valverde's writings on social semiotics provide a clearly articulated set of techniques through which urban scholars can analyse discourses of order and disorder that underlie contemporary fears about city living, and which give credence to the need for intrusive forms of security and policing.

Valverde's empirical studies also demonstrate how ideas from actor-network theory (Bruno Latour's work in particular) can animate urban studies in creative ways. Conceiving of legal processes as networks in which objects, activities and spaces are assembled facilitates attention to the interactions among widely different elements, illuminating how they can give rise to conflict or produce certain kinds of order (cf. **Jane M. Jacobs**). Such methods can reveal how objects as varied as courtroom bibles, hotdogs and weeds growing in a neighbour's lawn can all become protagonists in complex legal dramas (2005, 2008, 2015). Valverde also demonstrates how those who make their living from activities, spaces and objects deemed disruptive or risky to public order frequently become enrolled as deputy enforcement agents of the state. When one's job legally requires a licence or permit, the state extends sovereign power and surveillance at a distance, shaping human conduct in ways that are rarely subject to critical scrutiny. Through insights such as these, Valverde invites others to consider the operations of a whole range of mundane legal mechanisms and regulatory techniques – ordinances, bylaws, licences, permits, land-use requirements, zoning laws – which are often relegated to the sole domain of planners or policy researchers. Illuminating the unintended and undesirable effects of governance arrangements can be a first step in helping to configure them otherwise; a point which highlights the important role that Valverde's thought and research in socio-legal studies brings to urban scholarship.

Secondary sources and references

Blomley, N. (2011) *Rights of Passage: Sidewalks and the Regulation of Public Flow*. New York: Routledge.

Scott, J. (1998) *Seeing Like a State: How Certain Regimes to Improve the Human Condition Have Failed*. New Haven, CT: Yale University Press.

Valverde, M. (1985) *Sex, Power and Pleasure*. Toronto: The Women's Press.

Valverde, M. (1991) *The Age of Light, Soap, and Water: Moral Reform in English Canada, 1885–1925*. Toronto: University of Toronto Press.

Valverde, M. (1998) *Diseases of the Will: Alcohol and the Dilemmas of Freedom*. Cambridge: Cambridge University Press.

Valverde, M. (2003b) 'Police science, British style: Pub licensing and knowledges of urban disorder', *Economy and Society*, 43(2): 234–253.

Valverde, M. (2005) 'Authorizing the production of urban moral order: Appellate courts and their knowledge games', *Law and Society Review*, 39(2): 415–455.

Valverde, M. (2006a) *Law and Order: Signs, Meanings, Myths*. New Brunswick, NJ: Rutgers University Press.

Valverde, M. (2006b) *The Force of Law*. Toronto: Groundwood Books.

Valverde, M. (2015) *Chronotopes of Law: Jurisdiction, Scale and Governance*. London: Routledge.

38 Loïc Wacquant

Tom Slater, University of Edinburgh

Key urban writings

Wacquant, L. (2002) 'Scrutinizing the street: Poverty, morality and the pitfalls of urban ethnography', *American Journal of Sociology*, 107(6): 1468–1532.

Wacquant, L. (2004) *Body and Soul: Notebooks of an Apprentice Boxer*. New York and Oxford: Oxford University Press.

Wacquant, L. (2008) *Urban Outcasts: A Comparative Sociology of Advanced Marginality*. Cambridge: Polity Press.

Wacquant, L. (2009a) *Punishing the Poor: The Neoliberal Government of Social Insecurity*. Durham, NC and London: Duke University Press.

Wacquant, L. (2016a) *The Two Faces of the Ghetto*. New York: Oxford University Press.

Introduction

The prolific student of two giants of social science, Pierre Bourdieu and William Julius Wilson, Loïc Wacquant is an interdisciplinary sociologist who has made varied and original contributions to urban studies, although his influence extends well beyond cities. His foundational writings on carnal sociology, the penal state, ethnoracial domination and social theory have been translated into two dozen languages and have triggered debates in multiple disciplines. He is best known among urbanists for his comparative analyses and conceptualization of advanced marginality and territorial stigmatization. He is also widely read for his thesis on the penalization of poverty, and his rethinking of the vexed question of the ghetto. His work is rooted in his insistence upon intensive fieldwork as an instrument of epistemological rupture and theoretical construction. Wacquant's emphasis on the role of the state as producer of marginality, the weight of symbolic structures in the production of dispossession in cities and the need to fuse theory, ethnography and comparison has proven especially instructive and provocative.

Wacquant is Professor of Sociology at the University of California, Berkeley and a Researcher at the Centre Européen de Sociologie et de Science Politique in Paris.

Academic biography and research focus

Wacquant was born and raised in the south of France and moved to Paris in 1979 to study at France's top management school, the École des Hautes Études Commerciales. In January of 1981 his intellectual trajectory was altered by an exhilarating public lecture given by Pierre Bourdieu, who soon became his mentor and intellectual inspiration as Wacquant switched from economics to sociology at the University of Paris in Nanterre, and then at the University of North Carolina at Chapel Hill. In 1985 Wacquant then moved to the University of Chicago to pursue a doctorate in sociology. There, he worked with the celebrated sociologist William Julius Wilson, author of *The Truly Disadvantaged* (1987) a seminal study of racial segregation in American cities (see Wacquant and Wilson, 1989). Wacquant was troubled by the lack of reflexivity and the gaze from afar that dominated scholarship on the ghetto, and especially by the presumption of social disorganization and what he characterized as the scholarly myth of the urban underclass. Departing from Wilson's approach, Wacquant brought Bourdieu's approach to theory and social research into the American ghetto. He joined a boxing gym and began conducting an ethnography, interpreting the post-1960s transformation of the historic 'Black Metropolis' depicted by Drake and Cayton (1993 [1945]). He subsequently expanded his research focus to a transatlantic comparison of urban marginality in response to the moral panic that swept through France and much of Western Europe in the 1990s about the alleged 'ghettoization' of peripheral urban districts undermined by deindustrialization.

The comparison between Chicago and Paris, mixing fieldwork, survey data and institutional comparison, yielded two urban monographs: a carnal ethnography of boxing *in* the ghetto seen from inside and below, *Body and Soul* (2004), and a macro-analytic dissection *of* the ghetto seen from above, *Urban Outcasts* (2008). Wacquant has also produced a raft of influential articles that shed light on the revamping of symbolic, social and physical space in the city, and entailed conceptual innovation regarding the ghetto, territorial stigmatization, the precariat, ethnographic methodology, the tangled nexus of social and penal policy in the city, and neoliberal statecraft (see Wacquant, 2002, 2009b, 2012, 2014).

Key ideas

Often read as a strictly Bourdieusian sociologist, numerous influences melt in Wacquant's writings on cities. Bourdieu's teachings do provide the epistemological underpinnings and analytic frame, but in order to map and diagnose the fate of the urban 'precariat' (the precarious fractions of the post-industrial working class destabilized by the fragmentation of wage labour and the spread of a dishonour of place) Wacquant draws on a wide range of intellectual sources, notably Engels, Durkheim, Weber, Mauss, Wittgenstein, Elias and Goffman. Frustrated by the depoliticized portraits of poverty and place crafted by scholars from the Chicago School of sociology and by the economic determinism of research spawned by Marxist or Weberian variants of political economy, Wacquant's approach is characterized by: (1) an insistence on the role of state structure and policy in determining the forms, distribution and intensity of urban marginality; (2) the importance of symbolic systems – of which cities are major centres of production and diffusion – that do not simply mirror social relations but help constitute them; (3) the effort to track down the mutual conversion and mapping of symbolic, social and physical space at multiple scales and to spotlight the role of space in social domination. This triple focus is characterized by a combination of abstract theory and concrete ethnography, and has advanced conceptual formulations around the nexus of marginality, ethnicity and penality (Wacquant, 2014). In particular, two key ideas stand out for the further enquiries they have spawned across national and disciplinary boundaries.

First, Wacquant's comparative investigations reconceptualize the ghetto as an instrument of ethnoracial closure based on the double reciprocal assignation of a stigmatized category and a reserved territory (Wacquant, 2016a). Based on a comparison of three canonical cases – the socio-spatial seclusion of Jews in Renaissance Europe, black Americans in the Fordist industrial metropolis and Burakumin in Tokugawa-era Japan – Wacquant argues that the ghetto is an institutional form, a social-organizational device that employs space to fulfil the two conflictive functions of economic extraction and social ostracization. He shows that the ghetto was created by city rulers to maximize the material value extracted out of a disparaged ethnic category, while minimizing intimate contact with its members. As a consequence, a ghetto exhibits distinctive sociological properties, chief among them the development of a set of parallel institutions (places of worship, press, schools, medical clinics, businesses, civic associations) that duplicate those of the city from which its residents are banished. Those institutions act as at once a sword, effecting closure to the benefit of the dominant, and a shield, offering a protected space wherein the dominated can experience reciprocity and dignity, hence Wacquant's characterization of the ghetto as Janus-faced. Contra portrayals of the ghetto as a space of material destitution and social disintegration – which are hegemonic in journalism, politics and large segments of urban research – Wacquant shows that ghettoization typically translates into the economic improvement, social strengthening and symbolic unification of the target population. Wacquant (2016a) uses this articulation of the second face of the ghetto to advocate for what he calls 'a diagonal sociology' capable of capturing the dynamic meshing of verticality (exploitation and inequality) and horizontality (reciprocity and equality) in urban life and in institutions more generally. It was the elaboration of the historical meaning and sociological contents of the ghetto that allowed Wacquant to account for the collapse of the communal ghetto in the United States and its mutation into a hyperghetto (devoid of economic function due to macroeconomic transformation and state retrenchment). It anchored his critique of the loose or opportunistic use of the term ghetto to describe working-class territories or immigrant districts in the European urban periphery, which in fact sport considerable ethnic diversity, fail to produce a shared identity, and are deeply penetrated by the state (leading Wacquant to call these zones 'anti-ghettos' as they move away from the pattern of the ghetto as conceptualized above).

Second, Wacquant developed the concept of territorial stigmatization after analysing the crystallization of what he termed a 'blemish of place' (2007: 67): the profound sense of neighbourhood taint emerging on both sides of the Atlantic. Having heard

French urban policy officials speak of lower-class districts with disgust in their voices, and then hearing residents of La Courneuve outside of Paris (and Woodlawn inside of Chicago) internalizing and/or reassigning onto their neighbours those degraded images, Wacquant set about conceptualizing spatial disgrace and its effects by drawing on the theories of Goffman and Bourdieu. He combines Goffman's relational view of stigma at the micro level, whereby an individual is assigned 'an undesired differentness' from 'normals' (1963: 18), with Bourdieu's (1991) more macro theory of symbolic power: the performative capacity to make reality (by making representations of reality stick and come true). Bourdieu was centrally interested in symbolic struggles between different classes, and particularly the ways that authoritative agents and institutions strive to impose a definition of the social world suited to their interests (cf. **Teresa Caldeira**). Wacquant extends this insight to struggles over and in space as a marker of identity. This blend of theory helps him diagnose territorial stigma as 'arguably the single most protrusive feature of the lived experience of those trapped in these sulphurous zones' (Wacquant, 2008: 169). This is a distinctive feature of advanced marginality in the 21st century due the autonomization of spatial taint from other bases of stigmatization. Wacquant highlights how certain areas of disrepute in advanced societies become renowned across class levels, racialized and portrayed as emblems and vectors of disintegration, unlike the disreputable wards of the metropolis in the industrial era which were perceived as an organized counter-society. He maps out how spatial stigma impacts social strategy and identity at multiple scales in ways that entrench marginality (Wacquant, 2014). He also warns that scholars who deploy the trope of the ghetto for rhetorical dramatization in hopes of inciting progressive policy intervention actually contribute to the further symbolic degradation of dispossessed districts, and thus to the very phenomenon they should be dissecting.

Viewed through Wacquant's urban sociological lenses, the state is not a bureaucratic monolith delivering uniform goods, nor an ambulance that comes to the rescue in response to 'market failure', but rather a potent 'stratifying and classifying agency' (2014: 1699) that continually moulds social and physical space, and particularly the shape, recruitment, structure and texture of lower-class districts. The marginal spaces of the metropolis are construed as a product of the material and symbolic powers of the state as they percolate down through the class and spatial structure. Advanced marginality is characterized by Wacquant (2008) as an ascendant poverty regime in post-industrial cities typified by the fragmentation of wage labour, the recoiling of the social state and the buckling of the social economy of reciprocity based on kinship and place that was a feature of working-class districts in the Fordist-Keynesian era.

Contributions to urban studies

Wacquant lectures regularly around the world, and his work circulates widely beyond academic circles to inform and influence public debate in Europe and Latin America in particular. His writings have proved especially useful to scholars studying the impact of neoliberal restructuring at the bottom of the urban order, and his characterization of neoliberalism as 'market-conforming state-crafting' (via the organizational triad of economic deregulation, 'restrictive workfare' and 'expansive prisonfare') (2012: 71) has influenced urban research across several disciplines from sociology and anthropology to criminology and planning, to geography, law and social work. By emphasizing the value of ethnography as an 'instrument of rupture' to pierce the screen of common sense and policy categories, Wacquant's work has stimulated scholars conducting fieldwork to uncover views of the fractured neoliberal city from below. His theoretically guided ethnography – as opposed to an inductive 'get-your-ideas-in-the-field' approach favoured by practitioners of the Chicago School (see **Elijah Anderson**) – has sparked vigorous debate. In 'Scrutinizing the street', Wacquant (2002) anatomizes three canonical ethnographies of race and poverty in the contemporary US as exemplars of 'a certain epistemological posture of unreflective surrender to folk apperceptions, to ordinary moralism, to the seductions of official thought and to the rules of academic decorum' (2009b: 122). For Wacquant, this posture causes scientific errors and policy misdiagnoses of urban problems, and fosters the subordination of scholarship to the categories and concerns of state elites smitten with neoliberal nostrums. Unsurprisingly, this epistemic critique was not welcomed by broad factions of the American sociological establishment who dismissed it as polemic. Another recurrent criticism of Wacquant's work has been his insistence that class, not ethnicity or religion, is the primary principle of division of urban space and determinant of life chances in the lower-class districts of the French and European metropolis. Schneider (2014) argues that he does not pay sufficient attention to the concentration of black and Arab youth in these districts, and asks what leads them to set their neighbourhoods aflame if they live in a society devoid of racial discrimination, racial profiling and police violence. Wacquant's (2016b) response is that the primacy of class is an empirical fact shown by the rise of a small but spatially mobile postcolonial petty-bourgeoisie and by the growing similarity in the demographic profile of foreign and national populations everywhere.

Wacquant's most important contribution to urban studies is his demonstration that ignorance of the role of symbolic structures in the production of marginality in the city means that neighbourhoods are made into the *cause* of poverty rather than the expression of underlying problems to be addressed. The vast literature on neighbourhood effects, sustained by the postulate that where one lives affects one's life chances, ignores the mechanisms and consequences of the stigmatization of place. Indeed, in many instances this literature contributes to that very stigmatization via a disparaging gaze trained upon marginalized neighbourhoods. Wacquant's work demonstrates that social science has a role to play in casting free of that gaze and 'break[ing] through the screen of often absurd, sometimes odious projections, that mask the malaise or suffering as much as they express it' (Bourdieu, 1999: 629).

Secondary sources and references

Bourdieu, P. (1991) *Language and Symbolic Power*. Cambridge: Polity Press.
Bourdieu, P. (1999) *The Weight of the World: Social Suffering in Contemporary Society*. Cambridge: Polity Press.
Drake, S. and Cayton, H. (1993 [1945]) *Black Metropolis: A Study of Negro Life in a Northern City*. Chicago: University of Chicago Press.

Goffman, E. (1963) *Stigma: Notes on the Management of Spoiled Identity*. London: Penguin.

Schneider, C.L. (2014) *Police Power and Race Riots: Urban Unrest in Paris and New York*. Philadelphia: University of Pennsylvania Press.

Wacquant, L. (2007) 'Territorial stigmatization in the age at advanced marginality', *Thesis Eleven*, 9(1): 66–77.

Wacquant, L. (2009b) 'The body, the ghetto and the penal state', *Qualitative Sociology*, 32(1): 101–129.

Wacquant, L. (2012) 'Three steps to a historical anthropology of actually existing neoliberalism', *Social Anthropology*, 20(1): 66–79.

Wacquant, L. (2014) 'Marginality, ethnicity and penality in the neoliberal city: An analytic cartography', *Ethnic and Racial Studies*, 37(10): 1687–1711.

Wacquant, L. (2016b) 'Revisiting territories of relegation: Class, ethnicity and the state in the making of marginality', *Urban Studies*, 53(6): 1077–1088.

Wacquant, L. and Wilson, W.J. (1989) 'The cost of racial and class exclusion in the inner city', *Annals of the American Academy of Political and Social Science*, 501: 8–25.

Wilson, W.J. (1987) *The Truly Disadvantaged: The Inner City, the Underclass, and Public Policy*. Chicago, IL: University of Chicago Press.

39 Fulong Wu

I-Chun Catherine Chang, Macalester College

Key urban writings

Wu, F. and Yeh, A.G. (1999) 'Urban spatial structure in a transitional economy: The case of Guangzhou, China', *Journal of the American Planning Association*, 65(4): 377–394.

Wu, F. (2002) 'China's changing urban governance in the transition towards a more market-oriented economy', *Urban Studies*, 37(9): 1071–1093.

Wu, F. (2004) 'Urban poverty and marginalization under market transition: The case of Chinese cities', *International Journal of Urban and Regional Research*, 28(2): 401–423.

Wu, F. (ed.) (2007a) *China's Emerging Cities: The Making of New Urbanism*. London: Routledge.

Wu, F. (2015a) *Planning for Growth: Urban and Regional Planning in China*. London: Routledge.

Introduction

Among the most extraordinary urban transformations of the late 20th century has been China's transition from a central planning regime to a market-oriented economy. Fulong Wu is a scholar of urban planning and urban geography who has been a leading documenter of these changes. Wu is perhaps most renowned for his work describing the transformations of urban governance in China at local and national scales. His early case studies on southeastern coastal cities (mainly Shanghai, Guangzhou, Nanjing) reveal how globalization and foreign investment during the post-economic-reform era drove entrepreneurial, place-promotion policies that transformed Chinese cities from production units to sites of capital accumulation, fueling China's rapid process of urbanization. Wu further examines changes in China's urban planning, and offers a regulatory explanation for the 'growth first' development approach embraced by many cities. In addition to his focus on urban governance, Wu also writes extensively about China's urban issues such as land commodification, gated communities, housing stratification, residential relocation, urban poverty, rural to urban migration, and suburbanization. He is one of the most important chroniclers of China's transformation from a largely rural to an urbanized society.

Fulong Wu is the Bartlett Professor of Planning at University College London and the Siyuan Professor in the Department of Urban and Regional Planning at Nanjing University of China.

Academic biography and research focus

Fulong Wu was born in Shanghai and educated in both Mainland China and Hong Kong. He earned Bachelor and Master's degrees in Geography from Nanjing University (China) in 1986 and 1989, respectively. He then served as a lecturer in the department between 1989 and 1992. Working with Professor Anthony Gar-On Yeh, Wu subsequently completed his PhD study in the Center of Urban Planning and Environmental Management at the University of Hong Kong in 1995. His doctoral thesis, *Changes in the Urban Spatial Structure of a Chinese City in the Midst of Economic Reforms: A Case Study of Guangzhou*, was a pioneering work exploring the linkage between urban spatial structure, land use, and economic reform in China. Based on this research, Wu published 'Urban spatial structure in transitional economy' in the *Journal of the American Planning Association* in collaboration with Yeh in 1999.

After a year at the University of Hong Kong on a postdoctoral fellowship, Wu moved to the UK where he took a faculty position in the School of Geography at the University of Southampton in 1998, and was promoted to Reader in 2004. Wu moved to Cardiff University in 2005 as Professor of East Asian Planning and Development in the Department of City and Regional Planning, and also became the Director of the Urban China Research Centre. In 2011, he moved to University College London as the Bartlett Professor of Planning.

Wu's initial research interests focused on land use and spatial structure by analyzing GIS data, using cellular automata stimulations to understand rural–urban land conversion in Guangzhou (cf. **Karen C. Seto**). Over time he has developed a mixed-methods research strategy and expanded his view to various urban issues in relation to China's transitional economy. One notable line of research among Wu's ever-expanding scholarship is his work on China's changing residential patterns. Through historical lenses, Wu depicts the transition from the socialist system of work-based housing units to the rise of commercial gated communities, and discusses the social implications of the transition. His writing advances the understanding of the rapidly transforming housing market in urban China since the late 1990s. In particular, it reveals the underlying structural factors in urban governance that led to the continuous accumulation of disadvantages among marginal populations. Wu's broad scholarly engagement in various issues on Chinese urbanization can be further read in his two edited books, *Globalization and the Chinese City* (2006) and *China's Emerging Cities: The Making of New Urbanism* (2007a).

Although his most celebrated work concerns urban issues at the local scale, Wu is also a regulatory political economist who has addressed the role of the nation-state and broader neoliberal processes in the making of contemporary Chinese urbanism. Wu maintains that China's nation-state re-solicited its territorial power in spite of the parallel development of fragmented localism at the urban level since the market reform (Wu, 2010). Incorporating this argument, Wu revisited his earlier works to present a theoretical synthesis in *Planning for Growth: Urban and Regional Planning in China* (2015a).

This book traces how China's planning regime serves as a strategic tool to promote continuous development-oriented urbanization and economic growth, and intermediates dynamic interactions between local governments and nation-state.

Key ideas

While keenly attentive to local particularities, Wu strives to bring nation-state and regulatory structures into the understanding of Chinese patterns of urbanization, and to build a generalizable explanation for contemporary developments. For Wu, many Chinese urban phenomena reflect broader strategic and institutional changes during China's transition from state socialism to socialist market economy. In the state social-ism era, cities were where most state-enterprises resided and therefore served as geographic centers in the socialist regime's central-planning economic platform. To prioritize production, the state maintained tight control over capital flows, and limited domestic consumption and investment in the local built environment. Later under the socialist market economy, China underwent a series of reforms that restruc-tured state-owned enterprises, the tax-sharing system between local and central governments, and the markets for land, housing, and labor. These reforms offered local governments more autonomy, and also opened Chinese cities up to foreign and domes-tic investment. A considerable portion of Wu's scholarship both theorizes and details how these changes – and the massive transformations that have accompanied them – have reconfigured Chinese cities from production hubs into sites of capital accumulation.

Wu further explains how the strategic regime shift from state socialism to socialist capitalism brought about the creation of new urban administrative institutions as well as entrepreneurial competition between Chinese cities. The former change is the prod-uct of a market economy that dismantles the old governance structure based on work-units and fosters new activities beyond the jurisdiction of pre-existing state insti-tutions. New layers in the state apparatus, such as new municipalities, towns and counties, street offices, and residents' and villagers' committees, were created to govern these new activities. Wu refers to these government bodies as new 'territorial organ-izations' that extend national state power into different scales and social spheres (Wu, 2002). Meanwhile, rising inter-city competition has driven local governments toward greater fiscal flexibility and responsibility. As most Chinese cities by design had few reliable internal revenue streams other than those levied upon sales of previously state-owned land and agricultural land, cities turned to property-based, growth-ori-ented development to attract extramural investment (He and Wu, 2005; Wu, 2000). Aside from fiscal reasons, this property-based development approach is highly favored as the individual promotion of local political leaders depends on the cities' GDP per-formance (Wu, 2002). The place-promotion strategies adopted by Chinese cities to compete for investment include promoting entrepreneurial visual images and narra-tives, designation of special development zones, preferential treatment to investors, new land-leasing instruments, close coordination between the mayor's office and devel-opment industries, and increasing investment in infrastructure (Wu, 2003: 66–69).

With the proliferation of place-promotion strategies in Chinese cities, Wu also offers an important account of how the Chinese urban planning system has evolved to serve new regulatory functions. Before the economic reform, Wu summarizes that the major role of urban planning in China was to provide technical support and physical designs strictly based on commands passed on from its supervisory government departments and the national planning standards. The job of urban planners at this time was merely about producing blueprints of master plans and detailed construction plans according to predetermined, inflexible industrial production and workers' basic living standards, and to coordinate between competing demands among different government sectors. After the economic reform, Wu finds that urban planners have taken on a more active role in helping craft local economic and development goals in order to enhance urban competitiveness and attract external investment. Their work has gradually moved away from meeting the development goals set in national five-year plans, and toward project-based planning. Chinese urban planners nowadays, in addition to producing blueprints, write policy statements and recommendations, and even design catchy slogans; planners are expected to envision urban futures, initiate economic restructuring, and promote strategic infrastructure construction (Wu, 2007b: 382). These expanded roles for planners have brought about new dynamics into China's urban planning system, particularly the increasing involvement of international consultancy in designing urban master plans and strategic plans. In this process, international consultancy helps diversify the previously bureaucratic and inflexible protocols by enlisting private sector actors and other stakeholders in the planning process. Still, Wu identifies the limits of this seemingly more democratic planning process: ultimately, international consultancy works to serve its clients, which in most cases are the local political leaders. When international consultancy's primary objective is to materialize the personal visions of the mayors or other party leaders, urban designs become less accountable to the local residents as many would expect (Wu, 2007b, 2015a).

Wu argues that the changing functions of urban planning in China reflect the dominance of the state during market transition and the making of socialist capitalism. Chinese cities use urban planning to 'justify their expansionist approach to the central government, to circumvent the regulatory constraints imposed by the central government, and even to capture opportunities such as special entitlements when up-scaling governance' (Wu, 2015a: 191). Meanwhile, the central government often uses urban planning to control territorial development, arrange capital investment, reduce urban–rural contention, and to balance regional differences. Urban planning in China adapted to the new challenges and reinvented itself as an indispensable tool for cities to survive during the state's regime transition. For Wu, urban planning in China is therefore significantly different from urban planning in the West. He observes that, while urban planning in the UK and the US has been considerably 'streamlined' because it is regarded as a bureaucratic constraint to economic growth (Wu, 2015a: 116, 190), urban planning both as a governmental apparatus and as a profession has grown rapidly in China because it is regarded as an indispensible tool for growth. While capitalist globalization results in the 'hollowing out' of state functions in Western Europe and North America, the change of the urban planning regime in China reflects the solicitation of state power to leverage for strategic development goals.

But parallel to the experience in Western Europe and North America, globalization and market reform also increases the socio-geographical disparity in China. Although 'planning for growth' reasoning is often legitimized through the widespread belief that economic growth from property development will eventually trickle down to all citizens, Wu finds that the trickle-down effect is relatively small. Rather, signs of deepening social inequality abound. Several of his more recent studies examine inequality issues by analyzing unequal urban landscapes, including spatial concentration of urban poverty (2004), gated communities (2005), suburbanization (Feng et al., 2008), urban villages (2009), market-oriented new town development (Shen and Wu, 2012), and housing markets (2015b). In these works, Wu reveals how growth-oriented urban development reinforces social and spatial inequalities that have roots in the socialist era, while simultaneously also producing new ones. Many people who were disadvantaged in the uneven industrialization and the urban–rural dichotomous *hukou* system are still in a precarious situation even decades after market reform. Wu's findings provide a critical lens on the otherwise seemingly glamorous urban developments currently transforming contemporary China.

Contributions to urban studies

Wu is a pioneer in studying the transformation of Chinese cities since the socialist market reforms. He has provided a series of sociologically nuanced accounts of the dynamics of China's urban development and its urban planning regimes. With his practical experience in urban planning in Nanjing, Wu has strong professional connections with many of China's leading urban planners (for example, Baojun Yang, the chief planner at the China Academy of Planning and Design). Likely because of these experiences and professional connections, Wu's scholarship manages to attend to the intricate specifics of the case studies while also to properly contextualize these cases in China's broader political economic transitions. His work has demonstrated the evolving relationships between urbanization patterns and the regime of urban planning. In particular, he has provided unique insights into how urban planning serves as a state apparatus that intermediates between local development ambitions and national territorial development goals. This is the perspective that most distinguishes Wu's intellectual engagement from other scholars on contemporary Chinese cities.

Wu has published over 100 articles and books on various aspects of China's urban development. While his early research shaped understandings of urban governance transformation in China, Wu's recent work has increasingly focused on issues of social and institutional justice. In addition, Wu has begun connecting his work to the rising paradigm of provincializing urbanism. He strives to provide a 'comparative gesture,' as **Jennifer Robinson** advocates for, to better understand the complexity inherited in cities in the Global South that cannot be captured by theories presuming 'Northern' urbanization as the norm (Wu, 2015a: 207; cf. **Ananya Roy**). This undertaking is spearheading a welcoming paradigmatic shift in the research of urban China. For decades, studies on urban China have too often resorted to what may be summarized as the Chinese exceptionalism approach in explaining results that deviate from existing theories, which includes Wu's regulatory accounts for explaining China's urban development. This Chinese exceptionalist stance has since undermined the room for intellectual dialogue and theoretical generalizability. Fortunately, the endeavor taken up by Wu and other scholars offers a promising alternative by resituating Chinese cities in the research of Southern urbanism.

Secondary sources and references

Feng, J., Zhou, Y. and Wu, F. (2008) 'New trends of suburbanization in Beijing since 1990: From government-led to market-oriented', *Regional Studies*, 42(1): 83–99.

He, S. and Wu, F. (2005) 'Property-led redevelopment in post-reform China: A case study of Xintiandi redevelopment project in Shanghai', *Journal of Urban Affairs*, 27(1): 1–23.

Shen, J. and Wu, F. (2012) 'The development of master-planned communities in Chinese suburbs: A case study of Shanghai's Thames town', *Urban Geography*, 33(2): 183–203.

Wu, F. (2000) 'Place promotion in Shanghai, PRC', *Cities*, 17(5): 349–361.

Wu, F. (2003) 'Globalization, place promotion and urban development in Shanghai', *Journal of Urban Affairs*, 25(1): 55–78.

Wu, F. (2005) 'Rediscovering the "gate" under market transition: From work-unit compounds to commodity housing enclaves', *Housing Studies*, 20(2): 235–254.

Wu, F. (ed.) (2006) *Globalization and the Chinese City*. London: Routledge.

Wu, F. (2007b) 'Re-orientation of the city plan: Strategic planning and design competition in China', *Geoforum*, 38(2): 379–392.

Wu, F. (2008) 'China's great transformation: Neoliberalization as establishing a market society', *Geoforum*, 39(3): 1093–1096.

Wu, F. (2009) 'Land development, inequality and urban villages in China', *International Journal of Urban and Regional Research*, 33(4): 885–889.

Wu, F. (2010) 'How neoliberal is China's reform? The origins of change during transition', *Eurasian Geography and Economics*, 51(5): 619–631.

Wu, F. (2015b) 'Commodification and housing market cycles in Chinese cities', *International Journal of Housing Policy*, 15(1): 6–26.

40 Sharon Zukin

Mark Jayne, Cardiff University

Key urban writings

Zukin, S. (1988) *Loft Living: Culture and Capital in Urban Change*. London: Radius.
Zukin, S. (1991) *Landscapes of Power: From Detroit to Disney World*. Berkeley: University of California Press.
Zukin, S. (1995) *The Culture of Cities*. Cambridge, MA: Blackwell.
Zukin, S. (2004) *Point of Purchase: How Shopping Changed American Culture*. London: Routledge.
Zukin, S. (2010) *Naked City: The Death and Life of Authentic Urban Places*. Oxford: Oxford University Press.

Introduction

Sharon Zukin is a sociologist who over the past 20 years has become one of a handful of the more-often-than-not cited theorists who dominate critical understandings of the city. Zukin has helped to blur disciplinary boundaries across urban studies, and her work is founded on rich and detailed observations of the relationships between structural political and economic change and everyday life. Put simply, Zukin is interested in capital and culture and her writing unpacks the complex relationships between everyday practices and the political and economic forces that shape built environments and cultural landscapes. Key writings pursue this research agenda with regard to urbanism in the USA, and more specifically through a fascination with, knowledge of and clear love for one city in particular – New York City.

Sharon Zukin is Professor of Sociology at Brooklyn College and at the City University of New York Graduate Center. She lives in a Manhattan loft apartment.

Academic biography and research focus

Sharon Zukin grew up in Philadelphia, completed a Bachelor of Arts at Barnard College in 1967, and graduated with a PhD in Political Science from Columbia

University in 1972. Zukin is the author of five single authored books, co-editor of four books, has published around 30 journal articles and book chapters and has been the subject of numerous newspaper stories, interviews and media features. Zukin was Broeklundian Professor at Brooklyn College from 1996 to 2008, received the Lynd Award for Career Achievement in urban sociology from the American Sociological Association and secured the prestigious C. Wright Mills Book Award for her book *Landscapes of Power* (1991).

In her first major publication in 1975, Zukin drew on classical Marxist theory to understand the changing dynamics of politics in Yugoslavia. In *Beyond Marx and Tito*, Zukin pondered a decline of revolutionary activism and a rise of disillusionment and cynicism by unpacking structures of political participation, decision-making and the ways in which socialism was discursively constructed through cultural models and norms. The book highlights the roots of Zukin's interest in structural political and economic change and everyday cultural forms and practices. It took, however, 13 years, from Zukin's early studies in Yugoslavia via an edited collection a decade later on *Industrial Policy: Business and Politics in the United States and France* (1985), for the key touchstones in Zukin's intellectual career to be embedded in what is still arguably her most influential piece of writing: *Loft Living: Culture and Capital in Urban Change* published in 1988.

In *Loft Living*, Zukin outlined for the first time in academic literature the importance of elements which are now a recognizable 'script' of urban gentrification that has been serially reproduced and re-enacted in cities throughout the world. Zukin's next major book, *Landscapes of Power*, investigated the transformation of cities in the USA from the 1980s onwards, and charts how political, economic and cultural power shifted to post-industrial production and consumption cultures. This narrative continues in her subsequent book, *The Culture of Cities* (1995), where Zukin theorizes the reshaping of urban politics via conflicts over gentrification and public space by focusing on 'urban culture' such as the emergence of 'trendy' coffee houses, restaurants, fashion boutiques and bars. In her 2004 book, entitled *Point of Purchase: How Shopping Changed American Culture*, Zukin advances her work on these topics by focusing in a more detailed way on how consumption has come to dominate American life; driving individual aspiration and defining social and cultural identities. To a large degree tying together all of the key ideas of her previous work is Zukin's most recent book, entitled *Naked City: The Death and Life of Authentic Urban Places* (2010), which investigates notions of urban symbolic economy, consumption and authenticity.

Alongside her most well-known texts are numerous other publications that to differing degrees intertwine with Zukin's research interests. A co-edited collection considers the attacks of 11 September 2001 in light of New York's urban history (Sorkin and Zukin, 2002). The book examines how the World Trade Center's 'twin towers' came to be built, highlighting the numerous neighbourhoods that had to be destroyed to make way for their construction and what it was that the initial plans for construction of a 'freedom tower' in the footprint of the twin towers had to say about democracy in NYC. A further co-edited book on consumption practices in 'local shopping streets' around the world from Amsterdam to Shanghai (Zukin et al., 2015) has also taken Zukin's arguments from the streets of New York for scrutiny in diverse urban settings.

Key ideas

There are three key ideas that underpin Sharon Zukin's contribution to urban studies: first is her work that advances our understanding of the importance of an urban symbolic economy. For example, in a foreword to *Loft Living*, **David Harvey** signals Zukin's landmark investigation of urban capital and culture. Harvey described *Loft Living* as a sophisticated understanding of the emergence of the 'new' service economy, its key protagonists and the spaces and places where economic power and everyday practices intertwined. With her focus on the cultural symbol of the 'loft' – new 'design-led' residential living in empty industrial workspaces in Soho, New York City – Zukin highlighted how forgotten urban spaces (and real estate) were reimagined and re-used, arguing that 'loft living' told us something about broader global political and economic restructuring. Zukin described how artists were the (un)witting avant-garde of a 'coalition' of property speculators and finance houses which capitalized on empty or derelict property in 'unfashionable' and 'undesirable' neighbourhoods in US cities in the 1980s. Attracted by low rent, space, light and 'original' residential and industrial design features, 'edgy' living alongside the urban 'other' attracted young middle-class artists into neighbourhoods previously dominated by working-class residents, diverse ethnic groups, squatters and homeless people. Artists were the first to (re)colonize urban spaces that had become abandoned and unpopular since 'the urban crisis' which followed the Wall Street Crash of the 1930s and subsequent decades of economic depression, social unrest and urban restructuring associated with 'white flight' and suburbanization. Zukin explained that artists were followed into – and along with the existing residents, ultimately priced out of – these newly 'cool' neighbourhoods by 'yuppies' (young upwardly mobile professionals) as 'waves' of capital accumulation led to restructuring of real estate markets. The theoretical and empirical focus on spaces and places of 'home' and 'play' where money and lifestyle collide were also an enduring feature of Zukin's insightful and groundbreaking work which, of course, still remain pertinent today.

Zukin's interest in how an urban symbolic economy was emerging through new formations of capital and culture was further investigated in both *Landscapes of Power* and *The Culture of Cities*. For example, in *Landscapes of Power*, Zukin investigated urban community, public accountability and moral values bound up with the transformation of US cities from the 1980s onwards – expanding her interest from New York City to a diverse range of cities from Detroit to Disneyland. Exploring the ways in which contemporary capitalism led to the 'creative destruction' of America's once prosperous industrial heartlands, Zukin charted how political, economic and cultural power shifted through the increasing dominance of post-industrial production and consumption cultures. This interest continues in her subsequent book, *The Culture of Cities*, where Zukin theorizes the reshaping of urban politics and a newly emerging urban symbolic economy that was underpinned by identities, lifestyles and forms of sociability relating to 'a new middle class' constituted through the emergence of financial, service, tourism, media, retail and entertainment industries and articulated, negotiated and contested in streets, parks, shops, museums, restaurants and so on.

Second, Sharon Zukin has contributed to our understanding of urban life through her focus on consumption (see Jayne, 2005). In *Point of Purchase* Zukin argues that shopping is definitive of a 'fading' American dream, where low prices are seen as 'democratic', and brand names are key indicators of self-identity, family life, gender, selfhood, community and belonging. Zukin invites us to think about a diverse range of consumption spaces and to consider eating at expensive restaurants or enjoying street food, shopping at expensive boutiques, at street-stalls and online, taking us to museums, and letting us sit for a while in 'Disneyfied' public spaces and, by contrast, in community gardens located on abandoned urban space. In translating such everyday urban experiences for the reader Zukin traces changing fault lines of how, where and when wealth, power and capital, social divisions and mixing are constructed and played out in 'spectacular' and 'mundane' urban spaces and places alike (cf. **García Canclini**). For example, Zukin details the fascinating history of Woolworths, 'five and dimes', department stores and mail order catalogues of the mid-19th century. Zukin also considers the early days of online shopping through platforms such as eBay and Amazon, the emergence of shopping in 'themed environments' such as Banana Republic and Super Stop & Shop; and argues that 'ghettos' are interesting, rich and diverse spaces of consumption deserving of just as much theoretical and empirical attention as designer shops and high-end shopping streets. In a similar vein, Zukin critiques the development of out-of-town 'retail boxes' and the supremacy of chains such as Walmart and usefully draws links between families purchasing jeans in US stores and their production in the factories of China and Bangladesh.

Third is Zukin's most recent substantive contribution to urban studies through her discussion of authenticity. In *Naked City: The Death and Life of Authentic Urban Places* Zukin argues that rapid and pervasive demand for authenticity has underpinned ever-increasing house prices and led to an 'overheated' property market in parallel with a proliferation of consumption-led gentrification, which together have been responsible for driving the working class, the artistic middle classes and immigrants from their homes, indeed a displacement of the very people who had helped make the urban neighbourhoods in cities in the USA 'interesting' in the first place. In doing so, Zukin (2010) looked in detail at the economic, social and cultural development of six areas of New York City – Williamsburg, Harlem, The East Village, Union Square, Red Hook and East New York. Zukin also studied the proliferation of community gardens, flea markets and 'ethnic quarters' as a material and symbolic response by some local residents to creeping gentrification of their neighbourhoods. To a large degree *Naked City* aims to be a 'sobering update' of **Jane Jacobs**' 1961 book *The Death and Life of Great American Cities* and following on from the narratives tested in *Loft Living*, Zukin is interested to explore how people give neighbourhoods their 'sense of place', but that an emphasis on 'distinctiveness' is increasingly used as a tool of elites to enable the privatization and commercialization of public space.

To summarize, the work of Sharon Zukin has made a definitive contribution to urban studies by establishing the theoretical and empirical importance of symbolic economy, consumption and authenticity as key ways in which an ever-increasing interpenetration of culture and capital since the birth of the modern city in the late 18th century has now come to dominate the contemporary city. While to a large degree the nature of this relationship is now unquestioned as a key tool with which to interrogate urban change around the world, such an acknowledgement is testimony to Zukin's contribution to advancing work in this area of urban research. Zukin thus introduces us to a diverse range of people and places in the city in order to explain how capital accumulation (especially real estate) and popular cultural forms and practices (such as shopping) offer insights into conflicts and tensions between elite visions of city development and more democratic or everyday experiences of urban life. By challenging us to understand the lives of immigrants, artists, street peddlers, security guards, yuppies, artistic gentrifiers, discount shoppers and those who love haut-couture in cities in the USA, Zukin makes us think about who, and what, defines, dominates, resists and challenges visions of public urban cultures.

Contributions to urban studies

Sharon Zukin's most important contribution to urban studies has been to foreground 'culture' as a topic that is *as important* as 'political' and 'economic' practices and processes in advancing our understanding of 'the city'. In doing so, Zukin's writing has engaged with a diverse range of key debates that have dominated voluminous amounts of writing by urban studies scholars over generations (class, real estate, planning, policy, everyday life, gentrification, identity, purification of public space, consumption).

Zukin's ideas and arguments have developed in parallel with other oft-cited peers of her 'generation' who have sought to explain globalizing urbanism (**David Harvey**, Ed Soja, **Mike Davis, Saskia Sassen**, etc.) and more specifically with theorists who have historically dwelt on the politics and economics of urban everyday social and cultural life (Walter Benjamin, Pierre Bourdieu, **Henri Lefebvre**, Michel de Certeau, **Jane Jacobs, Richard Sennett**, etc.). Recent writing has nonetheless critiqued such 'globalizing' theory as establishing and sustaining urban studies dominated by research into political, economic, social and cultural practices and processes unfolding in a handful of large cities in Europe and North America (see Bell and Jayne, 2006; Edensor and Jayne, 2012; Robinson, 2006). These arguments suggest that such broad-brush approaches to understanding the city have worked to restrict our understanding and imaginaries of urbanity throughout the world and can indeed hide as much as they illuminate.

Such comments notwithstanding, Sharon Zukin has made a significant contribution to the understanding of how cities change and why, by focusing on the relationship between capital and culture, in the US context and consistently through detailed studies of diverse spaces and places in New York City. Her publications trace how cities have been reshaped through deindustrialization, gentrification, immigration, the emergence of 'new' middle classes and have become, and undoubtedly will remain, key touchstones in academic understanding of the city.

Secondary sources and references

Bell, D. and Jayne, M. (2006) *Small Cities: Urban Experience Beyond the Metropolis*. London: Routledge.

Edensor, T. and Jayne, M. (2012) *Urban Theory Beyond the West: A World of Cities*. London: Routledge.

Jacobs, J. (1961) *The Death and Life of Great American Cities*. New York: Random House.

Jayne, M. (2005) *Cities and Consumption*. London: Routledge.

Robinson, J. (2006) *The Ordinary City: Between Modernity and Development*. London: Routledge.

Sorkin, M. and Zukin, S. (2002) *After the World Trade Center: Rethinking New York City*. London: Routledge.

Zukin, S. (1975) *Beyond Marx and Tito: Theory and Practice in Yugoslav Socialism*. Cambridge: Cambridge University Press.

Zukin, S. (1985) *Industrial Policy: Business and Politics in the United States and France*. New York: Praeger.

Zukin, S. (1989) 'Urban lifestyles: Diversity and standardization in spaces of consumption', *Urban Studies*, 35(5–6): 825–839.

Zukin, S. and DiMaggio, P. (1990) *Structures of Capital: The Social Organisation of the Economy*. Cambridge: Cambridge University Press.

Zukin, S., Kasinitz, P. and Xiangming, C. (eds) (2015) *Global Cities, Local Streets: Social Spaces and Everyday Diversity*. New York: Routledge.

Index